Created and Directed by Hans Höfer

INSIGHT GUIDES
New Zealand

Edited by Gordon McLauchlan
Principal photography by Max Lawrence
Managing Editor: Andrew Eames

Editorial Director: Brian Bell

HOUGHTON MIFFLIN COMPANY

APA PUBLICATIONS

ABOUT THIS BOOK

Höfer

McLauchlan

McGill

King

Leggett

This is a new edition of a guidebook to a country which is really beginning to make its mark. New Zealand, the last nation in the world to be settled, has come bursting on to the travel map of top destinations. This is the nation where eco-tourism comes naturally, where the air tastes like chardonnay, and a popular form of recreaction is dangling in chasms on a bouncy rope. This is also the nation of the largest Polynesian city in the world, of possums (80 million), of sheep (56 million) and the occasional human being (3 million). In New Zealand, pioneers are still at work – particularly in tourism. The choice is immense, the possibilities huge.

Such a destination lends itself especially well to the approach taken by the 190-title *Insight Guides* series, created in 1970 by **Hans Höfer**, founder of Apa Publications and still the company's driving force. Each book encourages readers to celebrate the essence of a place rather than try to tailor it to their expectations and is edited in the belief that, without insight into people's character and culture, travel can narrow the mind rather than broaden it.

Insight Guide: New Zealand is carefully structured: the first section covers the country's whirlwind history, and then analyzes its culture in a series of magazine-style essays. The main Places section, which begins on page 149, provides a comprehensive run-down on the things worth seeing and doing. Finally, a listings section contains useful addresses, telephone numbers and opening times.

Led by one of the best known writers and broadcasters in the land, **Gordon McLauchlan**, a team of top local writers and photographers produced, and subsequently revised for this latest edition, *Insight Guide: New Zealand*. McLauchlan was born in Dunedin and worked in radio and print journalism before going freelance in the early 1970s. He published the controversial and acclaimed social commentary *The Passionless People* in 1976. His other books include *The Big Con* (1992), a range of historical and biographical works, and the *New Zealand Encyclopedia*, a bestseller now available on CD-Rom. McLauchlan has hosted a number of television magazine shows and writes a weekly column in the *New Zealand Herald*.

The geological origins chapter was written by palaeontologist **Graeme Stevens**, who has twice won New Zealand's premier literature award, the Montana, with his books *Rugged Landscape* and *New Zealand Adrift*.

Michael King, (pre-European history and Modern Maori), has been a journalist, teacher and broadcaster. His books include *Te Puea*, *New Zealanders at War*, *Maori*, *Moriori*, *Being Pakeha* and *A Land Apart*.

David McGill was ideal for both the Melting Pot and Wellington chapters because of his book on minorities, *The Other New Zealanders*. Besides national journalism, McGill has written histories of Lower Hutt City, the Customs Department, the police and trade unions. Other books include *A Dictionary of Kiwi Slang* and *Ghost Towns of New Zealand*.

The Waikato/Taranaki chapter was by **Janet Leggett**, a freelance in Hamilton, the main city of the Waikato, where the grass grows so fast for the dairy cattle that you can almost see it move. Leggett's own book *Hamilton* is an historical, descriptive and pictorial book on her home city.

Harvey

John Harvey, editor of Palmerston North's *Evening Standard*, has also worked as a journalist in Britain, and was the 1994 David Low Fellow at Oxford. The Poverty Bay and Hawke's Bay chapter was originally by former editor of the *Napier Daily Telegraph*, the late **Geoff Conly**, and has been revised by the newspaper's chief reporter, **Geoff Collett**, who has been working in Napier for five years.

Charteris

The Christchurch, Chatham Islands and farming chapters were written by **John Goulter**. After a spell in Wellington as chief parliamentary reporter on the *Evening Post*, Goulter recently moved back to his native Christchurch as a freelancer.

Several South Island stories are by two of New Zealand's top tourism writers, **Les Bloxham** and **Robin Charteris**. Bloxham, a Cantabrian who covers Canterbury, Westland and Central Otago, reckons he has travelled about 7 million kilometres on story assignments. Bloxham now operates his own syndication agency. Robin Charteris was the Cathay Pacific New Zealand Travel Writer in 1993. He is deputy editor of the *Otago Daily Times*, Dunedin's daily, and has served as London correspondent for New Zealand Associated Press.

Lind

Southland and Fiordland, and also Stewart Island, have been covered by editor of the *Southland Times*, **Clive Lind**, author of a number of books on the history of Southland. **William Hobbs** compiled the Nelson/Marlborough story. He was once radio New Zealand's Nelson reporter and is now a freelance writer and broadcaster.

Phil Gifford, writing about sport in this book, has a well-known national newspaper column in the rugby season under the byline "Loosehead Len". A gifted raconteur, Gifford has proved a prolific sports commentator on radio, television and in print.

Findlay

Katherine Findlay (The Cultural Scene) was a reporter and director of *Kaleidoscope*, perhaps the best known New Zealand television arts programme. **Terence Barrow** (Maori art) is a former ethnologist at the Dominion Museum, Wellington, who now lives in the United States. He is the author of *An Illustrated Guide to Maori Art*.

Costello

John Costello (Horse Racing) wrote the definitive history of New Zealand horse racing. **Jim Wilson**, (Outdoor Adventures) is an academic, top mountaineer and friend and fellow adventurer of Sir Edmund Hillary's.

Photographer **Max Lawrence** criss-crossed the country chasing the superb images in this book. Lawrence offers his thanks to Kodak New Zealand, Mount Cook Line, Fiordland Travel Ltd, the Royal Akarana Yacht Club (Auckland), Air New Zealand and Documentary Photographs. Additional photographs were provided by **David Lowe** of Lodestone Press and Photobank (NZ) Ltd.

Now Sydney-based, **Wendy Canning** did a wide range of background work for the book, especially the photo research, and contributed in many ways to the final product with her broad publishing expertise. Revision of the Travel Tips section was done by **Ross McLauchlan**, who has been involved in the tourism industry for nearly 20 years.

Production in the London office of Apa Publications was supervised by **Andrew Eames** and **Roger Williams**. Proof-reading and indexing were completed by **Carole Mansur**.

Eames

CONTENTS

History

Genesis 19

Geological Origins
by Graeme Stevens 23

Arrival of the Maori
by Michael King 33

Voyages of Discovery
by Gordon McLauchlan 39

Settlement and Colonisation
*by Gordon McLauchlan and
Peter Hutton* 47

**Social Progress and
Dominion**
by Gordon McLauchlan 58

A Country is Born
by Gordon McLauchlan 63

Features

Meet the People
by David McGill 77

The Melting Pot
by David McGill 79

Modern Maori
by Michael King 87

Maori Art
by Terence Barrow 93

The Cultural Scene
by Katherine Findlay 103

Outdoor Adventures
by Jim Wilson 113

Farming Life
by John Goulter 119

Good Sports
by Phil Gifford 125

Horse Racing
by John Costello 131

**Antarctica: A Land for
Heroes**
by David McGill 136

Places

Introduction 149

Auckland: City of Sails
by Gordon McLauchlan .. 155

Historic Northland
by Jack Adlington 171

**Coromandel and
Bay of Plenty**
by Joseph Frahm 180

Waikato and Taranaki
by Janet Leggett 187

CONTENTS

Rotorua and the Volcanic Plateau
by Colin Taylor 195

Poverty Bay and Hawke's Bay
by Geoff Conly 207

Manawatu and Wanganui
by John Harvey 212

Wellington and the Wairarapa
by David McGill 219

Nelson and Marlborough
by William Hobbs 234

Christchurch
by John Goulter 245

Canterbury's High Country
by Les Bloxham 259

The West Coast
by Les Bloxham 268

Queenstown and Central Otago
by Les Bloxham 277

Dunedin: Otago's Confident Capital
by Robin Charteris 288

Southland and Remote Fiordland
by Clive Lind 298

Stewart Island
by Clive Lind 308

Chatham Islands: Where Day Begins
by John Goulter 310

Cook Islands and the Pacific
by Terence Barrow and Gordon McLauchlan 315

Maps

North Island 150
South Island 151
Auckland & Vicinity 156
Auckland 158
Bay of Islands 173
Rotorua Lakes 197
Wellington 220
Wellington & Vicinity ... 227
Christchurch 246
Christchurch & Vicinity 252
Otago High Lakes 277
Dunedin & the Otago Peninsula 289
Stewart Island 308
New Zealand's Pacific Family 316

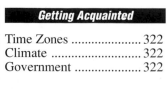

Getting Acquainted

Time Zones 322
Climate 322
Government 322

Planning The Trip

What to Bring/Wear 322
Health 322
Currency 322
Public Holidays 323
Getting There 323

Practical Tips

Emergencies 323
Business Hours 323
Tipping 323
Media 323

Getting Around

Domestic Travel.............. 324

Where To Stay

Hotels and Motels 324
Motor Camps 329
Farm and Homestay 329

Eating Out

What To Eat 330
Where To Eat 330

Attractions

Culture 331
Shopping 333

Further Reading

Collections &
Anthologies 334
Other Insight Guides 335

Art/Photo Credits 336
Index 337

GENESIS

This is New Zealand. *Haere mai*. Welcome. This is a land of majestic snow-capped peaks and unexplored rain forests, of pristine lakes swarming with trout and turquoise ocean bays speckled with wooded isles, of glaciers and fiords, geysers and volcanoes. It is a land of kauri forests and kiwifruit plantations, of modern cosmopolitan cities and backcountry sheep stations, of the flightless kiwi, the prehistoric tuatara, Phar Lap, paradise ducks and Sir Edmund Hillary. Perhaps most important of all, it is the land of the Maori, the indigenous Polynesian inhabitants who have made these islands their home for at least 12 centuries.

Pacific anthropologists say the Maori came to these islands by outrigger canoe in about the 8th century AD. Maori legend tells a much different story, about the birth of all life in the stillness of a long dark night, Te Po, from the primordial parents – Rangi, the sky father, and Papa, the earth mother.

Tane, the god of the forests and their eldest son, pulled himself free of his parents in the darkness and with great effort, over a long period of time, pushed them apart. He decorated Rangi with the sun, moon and stars, and Papa with plant and animal life, thereby flooding this new universe with light and colour. But Rangi's sorrow at the parting from his mate caused tears to flood from his eyes, filling her surface with oceans and lakes.

Today, it is not hard to understand why New Zealanders have such a strong attachment to their native land. The waters of Rangi's tears have contributed to a recreational wonderland perhaps unrivalled on Mother Earth. The unique flora and fauna are only part of a staggering variety of attractions. Enter these pages and discover them.

Preceding pages: various Kiwi transports of delight – by bungee into the river; by boat into Fiordland; by jeep on to Northland's Ninety Mile Beach; on foot into the Southern Alps; and by Shotover Jet around the very ragged rocks. **Left,** Pohutu Geyser at Rotorua.

New Zealand is surrounded on all sides by a vast undersea panorama of submerged ridges and troughs, rises, swells and plateaus, together providing dramatic evidence of the way the earth's crust in this part of the world has been crumpled into huge folds, rather like a gigantic rumpled tablecloth. These features are in turn often cleft by deep submarine trenches and peppered by submarine volcanoes, all providing a measure of the stresses and strains accompanying such movements. Although much of this great system of folds is submerged, a small part of it has been shaped into a group of mountainous islands known as New Zealand.

Movements similar to those that have shaped the sea floor have also affected the New Zealand land mass. The evidence for these upheavals is recorded in the rocks exposed in mountains, rivers and streams and in sea cliffs around the coasts. The intense folding and cracking often seen in these rocks suggests that New Zealand has long been part of one of the earth's "mobile belts" – zones of weakness in the earth's crust along which breaking occurs.

The rocks are cut by innumerable great fractures called faults, along which up, down and sideways movements have occurred. Many of the faults have broken the present land surface, showing that they have been moving during the past few thousand years. Some faults have moved in the last century (producing major earthquakes) and these movements, together with almost continuous smaller-scale earthquake and volcanic activity, indicate that New Zealand is very much "on the move" today.

Earth movements in the region have tended to be concentrated into "bursts", of which the recent activity is an example, but geological record indicates that change has nevertheless been continuous for at least the past 500 million years. The change has involved geographic position (latitude and longitude) as well as size, shape and degree of insularity. New Zealand has not always been a sea-girt island country and up to some 130 million

Preceding pages: Rotorua mineral lakes. **Left,** Maori hunted the moa to extinction.

years ago shared a common coastline with New Caledonia, eastern Australia, Tasmania and Antarctica. The modern shape of the country is a product of the last 10,000 years.

Great Gondwana: New Zealand's long voyage through time commenced in the Cambrian period, 570 to 500 million years ago, when it was part of a super-continent called Gondwana, made up of the land masses now comprising Australia, New Guinea, New Caledonia, New Zealand, Antarctica, South America, Africa, Arabia, Malagasy and India. New Zealand lay on the eastern edge of the super-continent, wedged between Australia, Tasmania and Antarctica, and facing an ancestral ocean called the Tethys, separating Gondwana from another super-continent called Laurasia which was then a number of separate lands that were later to coalesce. The Laurasian lands included North America, Kazakhstan, southern and central Europe, Baltica (Scandinavia and European Russia), Mongolia, Siberia, China and Southeast Asia.

In the early part of New Zealand's history, during the Cambrian and succeeding Ordovician and Silurian periods (500 to 410 million years ago), the edge of Gondwana occupied by New Zealand, New Caledonia and Australia projected northwards into the Northern Hemisphere, lying in latitudes 45 degrees north in the Cambrian, and 20 degrees north in the Ordovician and the Silurian. The northward orientation of Gondwana brought New Zealand and Australia into contact with China, Southeast Asia and Kazakhstan so that both shared with these countries a number of coastal marine animals and their close relatives.

Such coastal links gradually faded, however, as Gondwana began to swing to the south, bringing Australia and New Zealand into the Southern Hemisphere. Southeast Asia, China and Kazakhstan moved in a northwards direction towards their present geographic position. Thus by the Devonian period, 410 to 350 million years ago, New Zealand, while still retaining strong coastal links with Australia, also developed marine links to southern South America, via Antarctica – reflecting the gradual southward shift of this part of Gondwana.

Southerly drift continued throughout the succeeding Carboniferous and Permian periods (350 to 235 million years ago) and many areas of Gondwana, including Australia and New Zealand, were carried into close proximity to the South Pole and felt the effects of glaciation.

About this time most of the area that now forms parts of New Zealand and New Caledonia became a section of a huge, slowly sinking, broad depression in the sea floor, called a geosyncline. Mud, sand and gravel eroded from the surrounding areas of Gondwana accumulated in this depression. Erupting volcanoes on both land and sea also contributed deposits of lava and ash. The

and squeezed up areas of old sediment to form small archipelagos of land. Much of this land had links to the adjacent continental areas and it is likely that the ancestors of some New Zealand's distinctive native forest trees came at this time – including the New Zealand kauri (*Agathis australis*), some of the distinctive New Zealand native pines, called podocarps (rimu, totara, kahikatea) and many ferns.

Rotation of Gondwana away from the South Pole continued into the succeeding period of geological time, the Jurassic (192 to 135 million years ago). The rotating movements were such that by middle and late Jurassic times southern South America,

geosyncline extended northwards to New Caledonia, eastwards to beyond the Chatham Islands, westwards to the Lord Howe Rise and southwards to beyond Auckland and Campbell Islands.

In the Triassic period (235 to 192 million years ago), continuing rotation of Gondwana moved much of the continental areas away from the South Pole, leading to retreat and eventual disappearance of the ice sheets. None the less, rivers and the sea continued to erode the land, thus maintaining the flow of sediments into the geosyncline. By middle and late Triassic times, however, earth movements within the geosyncline had compressed

southern Africa, Antarctica, New Zealand, New Caledonia and Australia were all situated in middle and low latitudes and had tropical, subtropical and warm temperate climates. The equable nature of the climate, together with the close grouping of the continents – so that a variety of routes were available across land and around shorelines – provided numerous opportunities for both terrestrial and marine organisms to spread across Gondwana.

It is highly probable, therefore, that during this period New Zealand received the ancestors of many of its native plants and animals. Probable middle Jurassic migrants include the ancestors of animals such as the tuatara (*Sphenodon*) and native frog (*Leiopelma*). Other animal groups that reached New Zealand at this time included the ancestors of the native earthworms, native snails, and slugs, some insects (notably wetas and some spiders), freshwater crayfish, freshwater mussels and some freshwater fish. More native pines and varieties of ferns probably also arrived at this time. These animals and plants are today often called "living fossils".

The reptiles gave rise to the first birds in the late Jurassic period. Early birds, with their superior means of dispersal, soon spread to many parts of the world. It is thought that one group of distinctive primitive birds, called

the ratites, appeared in South America about this time and, using Antarctica as a stepping stone, gained access to New Zealand, Australia, New Guinea, Malagasy and southern Africa – to develop into the moas and kiwis in New Zealand, emus (Australia), cassowaries (New Guinea, Australia), elephant birds (Malagasy), ostriches (southern Africa) and rheas (South America).

Birth of the Tasman Sea: The first substantial land mass to exist in the present New Zealand region extended southward to the edge

Left, the tuatara is a prehistoric relic. Above, the nation was created and divided by volcanoes.

of the Campbell Plateau, eastward to beyond Chatham Island and westward to the Lord Howe Rise. Long fingers of newly created land also stretched northward towards New Caledonia, Lord Howe Island and Norfolk Island. Almost as soon as it was created this "Greater New Zealand" was eaten into by rivers and streams while the sea nibbled away at its edges. By the end of early Cretaceous time (110 million years ago) some areas, especially those around the edges of the land mass, had been worn down to such an extent that the sea was beginning to flood in across the eroded remains of the folded and contorted rocks.

About this time the first cracks and splits in the earth's crust appeared along the site of the modern Tasman Sea and also in the area lying between the edge of the Campbell Plateau and the coast of Antarctica's Marie Byrd Land. These huge rifts, into which the sea soon flooded, heralded the opening of the oceans now separating New Zealand from Australia and Antarctica. Marine incursions along the rift valleys then soon began to disrupt the overland migration routes to the north and west of New Zealand. Southern land routes still remained, however, and New Zealand continued to be linked with western region of Antarctica.

The splitting movements along the embryonic Tasman Sea and Southern Ocean were accompanied by similar movements signalling the start of the opening of the South Atlantic and Indian Oceans. The days of the old super-continent Gondwana were drawing to a close. Such splitting movements on a global scale had the effect of swinging the eastern edge of Gondwana – comprising New Zealand, New Caledonia, Australia, Antarctica and southern South America – closer to the South Pole, so that in early Cretaceous times New Zealand was at 70 to 80 degrees South Latitude, and in the middle Cretaceous it was within a few degrees of the South Pole.

Although land links to the north and west of New Zealand had been lost early in the Cretaceous period, southern links were still evident, allowing ancestors of the Protea family to enter New Zealand in the early Cretaceous and southern beech (*Nothofagus*) in the middle Cretaceous – both using Antarctica as a stepping stone. However, 80 million years ago a new sea floor began to form both in the Tasman Sea and in that part of the Southern Ocean lying between New Zealand and Antarctica. New Zealand became surrounded by continuous coastlines and seas of oceanic depths. At about this time the first marsupials (kangaroos, koalas, and so on) appeared in South America and probably migrated into Australia via Antarctica; however, their way into New Zealand was barred by stretches of open ocean.

The Tasman Sea opened up to its full width over the period between 80 and 60 million years ago. It is likely, though, that at some time before attaining its full width the Tasman was crossed by ancestral bats, using their powers of flight (and perhaps with some

and then ceased altogether in the Tasman 60 millions years ago, opening of the Southern Ocean continued inexorably, progressively weakening New Zealand's marine connections to South America via Antarctica. Thus, although many "southern" coastal marine animals were still shared by New Zealand, western Antarctica and southern South America in Paleocene and early Eocene times (65 to 49 million years ago), such forms had been drastically reduced by late Eocene times and disappeared completely at the end of the Eocene (37 million years ago).

Meantime, about 55 million years ago, sea began to open up between Australia and Antarctica. The new area of sea floor thus

assistance from westerly winds) to cross the new ocean before it became too wide and too stormy. The bats that came at this time gave rise to a distinctive New Zealand bat of a primitive type – the only mammals in the country's original fauna. The early Polynesians later introduced dogs and rats.

It is also likely that the ancestors of some of New Zealand's distinctive native birds such as the wattlebirds (huia, saddleback and kokako), native thrushes (piopio) and native wrens (rifleman, bush wren and rock wren) also arrived at the same time after winging their way across the infant Tasman.

Although creation of new sea floor waned

created linked with that already forming between New Zealand and Antarctica, so that Australia and New Zealand together began their long journey northwards, and Antarctica its journey southwards.

As Antarctica had moved into higher latitudes it lost its role as a stepping stone for southern migrants. Initially in Paleocene, Eocene and Oligocene times (65 to 24 million years ago), many parts of Antarctica, especially the coastal areas of western Antarctica, were covered by beech forests similar to those in New Zealand and southern South America today. However, as Antarctica moved southwards, and as cold marine currents began to flow around the now-ocean-encircled continent, ice fields formed on the mountaintops and glaciers began to reach down the valleys towards the sea.

At the same time as ice was building up on Antarctica, the oceanic gaps between this southernmost continent and its neighbours were widening. This allowed free oceanic circulation; combined with the onset of cyclonic conditions developing around the Antarctic ice cap, it set the scene for establishment of the circum-Antarctica system of winds and ocean currents that today dominates the meteorology and oceanology of the Southern Hemisphere.

The Circum-Antarctic Current, the world's around New Zealand, the huge ancestral land mass formed in late Jurassic and early Cretaceous times had been slowly shrinking in size and shape. The originally rugged mountainous terrain had been progressively lowered by eroding rivers and streams. The open Pacific to the east and the newly created oceans to north, west and south established eroding coastlines around the entire perimeter of the land mass. The scene was set then, for the gradual wearing-away of "Greater New Zealand" and its submergence by the sea. By 37 to 24 million years ago, the remnants of land consisted of an elongated, narrow-gutted archipelago and a few scattered islands.

Tropical immigrants: The steady northwards

largest ocean current, circulates clockwise around the entire Antarctic continent, and is associated with systems of prevailing westerly winds that encircle the globe at latitudes between 40 and 60 degrees south, giving rise to the "Roaring Forties", "Furious Fifties" and "Screaming Sixties". These winds are so powerful and constant that floating material, animals and plants can be readily transported between the southern continents.

While all these changes were going on

Left, land still in the making at White Island in the Bay of Plenty. **Above**, geothermal power at Wairakei near Rotorua.

drift of New Zealand and Australia gradually brought them into the mid-latitude regions of the Southern Hemisphere. At the same time, southward movement of the Southeast Asia-Indonesia region, resulting from opening and expansion of the South China Sea, progressively closed the gap between the Indonesian islands and Papua New Guinea. Thus an increasing number of oceanic currents of tropical origin were able to reach the Australian and New Zealand coasts, bringing with them a variety of warm-water organisms (but only those capable of crossing open ocean, either as eggs, larvae or adults).

Although migrants from tropical sources

first appeared in New Zealand waters in late Eocene times, their numbers declined in the uppermost Eocene and lowermost Oligocene as the sea cooled in response to the build up of ice fields on Antarctica. Climate improved, however, in the early and middle Miocene period (24 to 12 million years ago). At this time tropical seas lapped around New Zealand and reef-building corals lived around the northern and central parts of the North Island. Temperatures of these seas were 7 to 10 degrees (centigrade) warmer than today. On the land, palms were widespread at this time and coconut groves existed in parts of the northern North Island.

Meanwhile, continued expansion of the

South China Sea rotated Malaysia, Indonesia and the Philippines closer to Papua New Guinea. The intervening oceanic gap was gradually closed until in the Miocene period it had been narrowed to such an extent, and had probably been at least partially bridged by volcanic archipelagos, that land snakes were able to move into Papua New Guinea and eventually into Australia.

By this time, however, the Tasman Sea had opened up its full width and ancestral New Zealand and New Caledonia had lost their land links to the remainder of eastern Gondwana. Snakes therefore were unable to reach either New Zealand or New Caledonia

– and they became two of the few snake-free countries in the world, much to the relief of the present inhabitants.

Throughout this entire period the ancestral New Zealand land mass was essentially stable; this stability allowed it to be gradually worn away and to be eventually submerged by the sea. The comparative tranquillity ended, however, in the Miocene period, and from this time onwards the New Zealand islands were the scene of restless activity. Patterns of folds, welts and troughs developed under the influence of deep-seated earth movements. Changes in geography occurred frequently as troughs sank rapidly and welts rose in complementary fashion. Segments of land moved up and down under the influence of interfingering and branching folds. Large areas of New Zealand had the form of an ever-changing archipelago.

One of the most obvious consequences of the establishment of the westerly pattern of winds and oceanic currents was substantial strengthening of trans-Tasman migration. Although New Zealand has always received animals and plants from Australia and Tasmania, the sheer numbers involved increased dramatically from Miocene times onwards. Many of the sea creatures that populate New Zealand's shores today came originally from the west, having been transported by the west wind drift – either from Australia and Tasmania, or from even farther westwards around the globe from as far as South Africa or South America.

Birds are also notable riders of the west wind and from Miocene times onwards New Zealand gained a number of groups of land birds of Australian origin. Some bird groups have been in New Zealand longer than others and therefore have had sufficient time to diverge genetically from the parent Australian stock. The takahe, for example, represents an older migration; whereas the pukeko is from a younger migration and is indistinguishable from Australian forms.

Trans-Tasman migration of Australian land birds continues today: colonists in the past century include the spur-wing plover, black-fronted dotterel, white-faced heron, Australian coot, royal spoonbill, grey teal, welcome swallow and wax eye. Other would-be colonists have lingered but not survived – the avocet, little bittern and white-eyed duck. Many Australian insects also arrive in the aftermath of westerly gales, but few survive to colonise, although the monarch butterfly is a notable survivor.

The Ice Age Cometh: Although steady deterioration of climate in the late Miocene and Pliocene times had progressively thinned out many of the warmth-loving immigrants New Zealand had received earlier, the *coup de grâce* was delivered by the severe climates of the Pleistocene glacial occurring between 2 million and 10,000 years ago. During a number of these glacials, temperate organisms were restricted to northernmost New Zealand and to a few coastal refuges where the influence of the sea moderated the glacial climate. As there was no escape northwards beyond 35 degrees south latitude, many of the warmth-loving organisms disappeared completely, never to return.

The northern retreat of warm and temperate organisms was matched by advance of those with cold-temperate requirements. Thus fur seals and subantarctic shellfish and crabs moved northwards into the central part of the North Island in the early Pleistocene. During the last glacial phase, extending from about 65,000 to 10,000 years ago, native pine (podocarp) forests were pushed into the area north of Hamilton.

Then, as the climate warmed 10,000 years ago, some of the gaps in the New Zealand flora and fauna resulting from Pleistocene extinctions were filled by temperate organisms riding the west wind drift. Forest gradually became re-established throughout New Zealand but its recovery from the repeated disruptions during the successive glacials was a long and slow process; it is believed that even within the span of man's occupation of New Zealand, vegetation changes have occurred which are related to this long-term recovery process. Coupled with this, however, has been the effect of climatic changes – notably the Climatic Optimum (a warm period 7,000 to 4,000 years ago) and the Little Ice Age (a cold period between AD1550 and 1800).

Without a doubt, the arrival of Polynesian people about 1,000 years ago initiated a long train of biological events that continued even more rapidly after the visits of Tasman and Cook and the arrival of European settlers.

Left, landslip at Abbotsford, near Dunedin. **Right**, kowhai blossom, unique to New Zealand.

The early Polynesians (the "Moa Hunters") used the easily hunted birds as protein sources, and so deprived the New Zealand fauna of many of its older distinctive elements – including moas, and native New Zealand geese, swans, eagles and crows. The fire brought by humans, and used by them in hunting and agriculture, destroyed large areas of forest in coastal and central North Island and eastern South Island and also reactivated many areas of hitherto stable sandy country so that sand dunes invaded fertile land in many coastal regions and valuable land was lost.

The Polynesian rat and dog added to the effects of hunting and use of the fire. Euro-

pean settlers introduced, by accident or design, a wide variety of animals and plants from other parts of the world that competed, often successfully, with native species. In particular, New Zealand's formerly abundant bird life was decimated. Many birds disappeared altogether, while others became restricted to Fiordland and various islands off the New Zealand coast.

Thus the arrival of the human race, with fire, rats and dogs, coming on top of the effects of the Ice Age, sounded the death-knell for many of New Zealand's unique primeval organisms, some dating as far back as tens of millions of years.

London Published by Alex.r Hogg at the King's Arms N.°16 Paternoster Row.

A curiously ARCHED ROCK on the Coast of New Zealand.

A New Zealand Chief whose head is ingeniously TATAWED and a Subaltern Warrior of the same Country.

Apart from Antarctica, New Zealand was the last major land mass to be explored by people. These earliest Pacific navigators preceded those from Europe by some 800 years. They were "Vikings of the sunrise" and their descendants came to be called Maori.

Few subjects have been the source of more controversy than the origins of the Maori. Nineteenth-century scholars devised bizarre theories. Some asserted Maori were wandering Aryans, others believed that they were originally Hindu, and still others that they were indisputably a lost tribe of Israel. Interpretations of evidence in the 20th century have been more cautious. The current consensus among scholars is that Maori were descendants of Austronesian people who originated in Southeast Asia. A few authorities dispute this. Minority opinions have suggested they came from Egypt, from Mesopotamia and from South America.

Linguistic and archaeological evidence establishes, however, that New Zealand Maori are Polynesian people; and that the ancestors of the Polynesians sailed into the South China Sea from the Asian mainland some 2,000 to 3,000 years ago. Some went southwest, ultimately to Madagascar; others southeast along the Malaysian, Indonesian and Philippine chains of islands.

What appears to have inspired these vast journeys was the introduction of the sail to Southeast Asia and the invention of the outrigger. Among the Austronesian languages shared by the people of the Pacific and the Southeast Asian archipelagos, the words for sail, mast, outrigger float and outrigger boom are among the most widespread and therefore among the oldest.

The Pacific Austronesians who made their way along the Melanesian chain of islands, reaching Fiji by about 1300 BC and Tonga before 1100 BC, left behind fragments of pottery with distinctive decorations. It has been called Lapita, and the same name has been given by archaeologists to the people who made it. With their pottery they also

carried pigs, dogs, rats, fowls and cultivated plants. All of these originated on the mainland of Southeast Asia, except the kumara, a sweet potato from South America.

Polynesian culture as recognised today evolved among the Lapita people in Tonga and Samoa. It was from East Polynesia, possibly from the Society or Marquesas Islands, that a migration was eventually launched to New Zealand. The East Polynesian characteristics of early Maori remains, the earliest carbon dates and the

rate of growth and spread of the Maori population, all indicate that a landfall was made in New Zealand around AD 800.

The first New Zealanders: The land was unlike anything that Polynesians had encountered elsewhere in the Pacific. It was far larger – more than 1,500 km (over 800 miles) from north to south – and more varied than islands they had colonised previously. It was temperate rather than tropical and sufficiently cold in much of the South Island to prevent the growing of crops. Other than bats, there were no mammals ashore until the ancestors of the Maori released the rats (kiore) and dogs (kuri) they had brought with them. It is

Preceding pages and **left**, images of the Maori by an artist on one of Cook's expeditions. **Right**, tattooed chief wearing a feather headdress.

probable that they also brought pigs and fowls, but these did not survive.

The lack of meat was compensated for by a proliferation of seafood: fish, shellfish, crayfish, crab, seaweed, sea-egg and the sea mammals, whales, dolphins and seals. The land provided fern root that offered a staple food (though it had to be heavily pounded), and there were nearly 200 species of bird, many of them edible. Inland waterways contained additional resources: waterfowl, eel, fish and more shellfish.

To all these the immigrants added the cultivated vegetables they had carried with them: taro, kumara, yam, gourds and the paper mulberry. For meat, in addition to

these artefacts and crafts the New Zealand Polynesians developed one of the world's most sophisticated neolithic cultures.

Perhaps the most spectacular of the new country's resources was the huge flightless bird, the moa. There were several species, ranging from the turkey-sized anomalopteryx to the gigantic dinornis maximus. They offered a food supply on a scale never before encountered in Polynesia, other than when whales were cast ashore. Some early groups of Maori based their economy around moas in areas where the birds were relatively plentiful, until extensive exploitation eventually led to their extinction.

The history of the first colonists, from the

Representation of A WAR CANOE of NEW ZEALAND, with a View of Gable End Foreland.

birds, fish and sea mammals, there were limited supplies of dog and rat.

The New Zealand forests offered larger trees than Polynesians had seen previously. With these they built bigger dugout canoes and evolved a tradition of carving. Later, they used wooden beams in the construction of dwellings. Materials such as raupo and nikau made excellent house walls and roofs. Flax plaited well into cords and baskets and provided fine fibre for garments. There was an ample sufficiency of suitable stone for adzes, chisels and drill points, varieties of bone for fish-hooks, spear-heads and ornaments, and obsidian for flake knives. Through

time of their arrival until the advent of Europeans, is a history of their adaptation to the environment just described – the matching of their skills and cultural resources to it, and the evolution of new features in their culture in response to the conditions that the environment imposed.

Competitive tribalism: Ethnologists now recognise two distinguishable but related phases in that culture. The first is New Zealand East Polynesian, or Archaic Maori, displayed by the archaeological remains of the earliest settlers and their immediate descendants. The second is Classic Maori, the culture encountered and recorded by the earliest

European navigators to reach the country. The process by which the first phase evolved into the second is complex, and one on which scholars have not yet reached agreement.

What can be said with confidence, however, is that by the time James Cook and his men observed New Zealand in 1769, New Zealand Polynesians had settled the land from the far north to Foveaux Strait in the south. The language these inhabitants shared was similar enough for a speaker to be understood anywhere in the country, although dialectal differences were pronounced, particularly between the North and South Islands. While regional variations were apparent in the details and traditions of the culture, of living was related to every other. And the universal acceptance of concepts such as tapu (sacredness), mana (spiritual authority), mauri (life force), utu (satisfaction) and a belief in makutu (sorcery) regulated all these aspects of life.

Maori hierarchy: Maori society was stratified. People were born into rangatira or chiefly families, or they were tutua (commoners). They became slaves if they were captured as a consequence of warfare. Immediate authority was exercised by kaumatua, the elders who were family heads. Whole communities, sharing as they did descent from a common ancestor, were under the jurisdiction of the rangatira families whose authority was in

the most important features were practised throughout the country.

Competitive tribalism, for example, was the basis of Maori life. The family and hapu (sub-tribe) were the unit of society that determined who married whom, where people lived, where and when they fought other people and why. Tribal ancestors were venerated, as were gods representing the natural elements (the earth, the sky, the wind, the sea, and so on). The whole of life was bound up in a unified vision in which every aspect

Left, Maori war canoe and, **above**, Maori fort (known as a pa), reminders of a warlike race.

part hereditary and in part based on past achievement. Occasionally federations of hapu and tribes would come together and join forces under an ariki (paramount chief) for joint ventures such as waging war against foreign elements, trading or foraging for resources. The most common relationship among hapu, however, even closely related hapu, was fierce competition.

Communities ranging from a handful of households to more than 500 lived in kainga or villages. These were usually based on membership of a single hapu. The kainga would be close to water, food sources and crops. Sometimes the settlements were fortified (in which case they were called pa), although fortifications were by no means universal. More often the kainga were adjacent to hilltop pa, to which communities could retreat when they were under threat.

Maori pa were elaborately constructed with an interior stronghold, ditches, banks and palisades. Some proved impregnable; others were taken and lost several times in the course of a lifetime. Such defences were one of the features of Polynesian life that evolved in a more extensive and more complex manner in New Zealand than elsewhere in the Pacific. Some scholars speculate that the need for hilltop pa originated out of the need to protect kumara tubers from marauders.

obtain satisfaction from hapu whose members had allegedly transgressed the social code; and sometimes as a result of serious disagreements over control or authority.

Such reasons were often flimsy and could be nurtured from generation to generation. The more important factor, perhaps, was that war or rumours of war kept successful communities and individuals alert, strong and resilient. It also brought about the annihilation of some hapu who did not display these qualities. For the most part, however, warfare was not totally destructive prior to the introduction of the musket. It often involved only individuals or small raiding parties, and ambush or sporadic attacks of short duration.

Communal patterns of life in Maori settlements were organised around food gathering, food growing and (in areas where fighting was common) warfare. Cultivation and foraging were carried out by large parties of workers, seasonally. When items of food became scarce, they had a rahui or prohibition laid on them to conserve supplies.

The spoils of war: Warfare evolved as an important competitive feature of Maori life in most parts of the country. It was sometimes conducted to obtain territory with food or other natural resources (stone for toolmaking, for example); sometimes to avenge insults, either real or imagined; sometimes to

Even when larger groups met in head-on confrontation or siege, the dead rarely amounted to more than a few score. Most battles occurred in the summer months only and, except when a migration was under way, fighting was rarely carried on far from a tribe's home territory.

For individual males, as for tribes, the concept of mana was paramount. It was intensified and enlarged by the status of victor, and diminished by that of vanquished. Courage and proficiency in combat were also essential ingredients in initiation, and in acceptance by male peers, especially in the case of chiefs, who had to establish their authority over others. The weapons most favoured in this combat were taiaha (long wooden-bladed swords) and short clubs known as patu and mere.

Artistic refinement: Non-combatants were able to achieve high standing in the arts, or in the exercise of esoteric powers as tohunga (priests or experts). An ability to carve was prized highly and the working of wood, bone and stone reached heights of intricacy and delicacy in New Zealand seldom seen elsewhere. The best of the woodcarving was seen on door lintels, house gables and canoe prows; and in stone and bone in personal ornaments such as tikis, pendants and necklace units. New Zealand jade or greenstone

was especially valued for this latter purpose. Like the other Polynesians, the Maori had no access to metals.

Personal decoration in the form of moko or tattooing was also a feature of Maori art. Men were marked primarily on the face or buttocks, women largely on the face and breasts. Only in the Marquesas Islands did such decoration achieve comparable intricacy, with patterns apparent both in the original and mirror image. The Maori practice of the art usually involved a straight rather than

Left, early depiction of the traditional greeting, the hongi. **Above**, Maori chief in dogskin cloak.

a serrated blade. This served not only to inject pigment under the skin; it left a grooved scar which was more like carving in appearance than tattooing.

In spite of competition, warfare and regional and tribal demarcations among Maori, trading was also extensive. South Islanders exported greenstone to other parts of the country for use in patu, adzes, chisels and ornaments. Bay of Plenty settlers distributed high-quality obsidian from Mayor Island. Nelson and D'Urville Island inhabitants quarried and distributed argillite. Food that was readily available in some districts but not in others, such as mutton birds, was also preserved and bartered. People were prepared to travel long distances for materials and food delicacies. Although ocean-going vessels seem to have disappeared from New Zealand by the 18th century, canoes were still widely used for river, lake and coastal transport.

A short, brutish life: The gauze of romance that early fictional and ethnological accounts threw over pre-European Maori life was misleading. In many of its aspects, that life was brutish and short. There was always the danger of being tortured or killed as a result of warfare. There was ritual cannibalism. There was the possibility of disinheritance and enslavement in defeat.

Further, medical examination of pre-European remains reveals that the span of life was unlikely to exceed 30 years. From their late twenties, most people would have been suffering considerably as a consequence of arthritis, and from infected gums and loss of teeth brought about by the staple fern-root diet. Many of the healthy-looking "elderly" men, on whose condition James Cook commented favourably in 1770, may have been, at the most, around 40 years of age.

Such were the contours of Maori life that Cook and other navigators encountered towards the end of the 18th century. The population was probably some 100,000 to 120,000. The Maori people had no concept of nationhood or race, having been so long separated from other races and cultures. They were tribal beings who were fiercely assertive of the identity that they took from their ancestry and hapu membership. Most felt as far removed from Maori to whom they were not related as they did from the European invaders, but they all belonged to Aotearoa – "the land of the long white cloud".

The southern Pacific was the last habitable part of the world to be reached by Europeans. It was then inaccessible by sea except at the end of long-haul routes down the coast of South America on one side and Africa on the other. And once inside the rim of the world's largest ocean, seafarers faced vast areas to be crossed, always hundreds or thousands of miles away from any familiar territory.

So it required not only steady, enduring courage to venture into this unknown region but a high degree of navigational skill.

The countries of the South Pacific – tucked down near the bottom of the globe – were left to the Polynesians undisturbed for nearly 150 years after the Europeans first burst into the Western Pacific. And then New Zealand was left alone for another 130 years after the Dutchman Abel Janszoon Tasman first sighted the coast and paid a brief visit.

It was the Englishman James Cook who put all the Pacific in the context of the world.

A famous New Zealand historian and biographer of Cook, Dr J.C. Beaglehole, wrote of the three great Cook voyages: "... his career is one of which the justification lies not so much in the underlining of its detail as in the comparison of the map of the Pacific before his first voyage with that at the end of the century. For his was a life consistent and integrated; to a passion for scientific precision he added the inexhaustible effort of the dedicated discoverer; and his own devotion was matched, as nearly as any leader could hope, by the allegiance which was rendered him by his men."

The Dutch traders: European knowledge of the Pacific Ocean had gradually expanded during the 16th and 17th centuries following the first view of it by Vasco Nuñez de Balboa from the Isthmus of Panama in 1513. Intrepid Spanish and Portuguese seafarers such as Magellan, Mendana and Quiros, and England's Francis Drake, made their epic expeditions. The Spanish were motivated by their evangelising for the Catholic Church and the search for rare and precious metals and spices.

But towards the end of the 16th century,

the Dutch emerged as the great seafaring and trading nation of the central and western Pacific, setting up a major administrative and trading centre at Batavia (now Jakarta) in Java early in the 17th century, an operation dominated by the Dutch East India Company. For 200 years the Dutch were a power in the region. For most of that period, voyages of exploration were incidental to the activities of trade. The Dutch sailors seemed by temperament and training to be concerned almost exclusively with the business of sailing their ships along proven routes safely and methodically in the interests of commerce. On the few occasions when they did divert, it was generally in response to rumours of other lands with commodities of potential value for trade.

The Dutch ships eventually found that by staying south after rounding the Cape of Good Hope and catching the consistent westerlies almost as far as the western coast of Australia, they could make the journey to Java more quickly than by adopting the traditional route – sailing north close to the east coast of Africa and then catching seasonal winds for the journey eastwards. And so islands off the west coast of Australia and stretches of the coast itself began to be noted on charts but were not recognised at the time as the western side of a huge continent.

Then an ambitious and highly competent governor of Batavia, Anthony van Diemen, showed a more imaginative interest in discovering new lands for trade than most of his predecessors, during the second quarter of the 17th century. Tasman, then in his thirties, was the captain of one of two ships in an expedition dispatched by van Diemen to explore Japan and the northern Pacific.

Tasman's visit: Tasman was next chosen to lead a new expedition, to be accompanied by a highly competent specialist navigator, Frans Visscher. This was in 1642. The proposed voyage had been planned in detail, mainly by Visscher, and would take them first to Mauritius, then southwest to between 50 and 55 degrees south in search of the great southern continent, Terra Australis Incognita. The expedition, aboard the vessels *Heemskerck* and *Zeehaen*, was then to come eastwards if

Left, Captain Cook in wax. Cook's chart of New Zealand was relied upon for 150 years.

no land had been found to impede their progress and to sail across to investigate a shorter route to Chile, a rich trading area and the monopoly of the Spanish. The expedition went only as far as 49 degrees south before turning eastwards, whereupon it made two great South Pacific discoveries – Tasmania (or van Diemen's Land, as he named it) and New Zealand (or Staten Landt).

On 13 December 1642, they saw what was described as "land uplifted high", the Southern Alps of the South Island, and in strong winds and heavy seas sailed northwards up the coast of Westland, and rounded Cape Farewell into what is now Golden Bay.

Tasman's first and only encounter with the major success immediately but ultimately he was given his due for a gallant and well-recorded journey of exploration. Later he charted a large segment of the northern and western coast of Australia and retired, a wealthy man, in Batavia.

Cook's oyster: Within a year or two, other navigators had discovered that New Zealand could not be attached to a huge continent which ran across to South America. The name was therefore changed from Staten Landt (the Dutch name for South America) to New Zealand.

James Cook opened up the South Pacific like a huge oyster and revealed its contents. The son of a Yorkshire labourer, Cook was

Maori was disastrous. When a canoe rammed a small boat travelling from the *Zeehaen* to the *Heemskerck*, fighting broke out and there was loss of life on both sides. Tasman called the place Murderers' Bay and headed north again, not realising that he was inside the western entrance to Cook Strait. A voyage eastwards of only a few miles would have shown him that he was not on the edge of a continent but in the centre of two islands.

He did not land again and had much better luck with the Polynesians on Tongatapu, which he put on European maps on the way home. He also sailed through the Fiji group.

Tasman's voyage was not regarded as a born in 1728. He served as an apprentice seaman on a collier, and then volunteered as an able seaman with the Royal Navy during the Seven Years' War. He helped survey Canada's St Lawrence River, an essential preliminary to the capture of Quebec by General James Wolfe, and he enhanced an already growing reputation as a marine surveyor by charting the St Lawrence and parts of the Newfoundland and Nova Scotian coasts. In 1766, he observed an eclipse of the sun and the Royal Society and the Admiralty were both impressed with his report.

It was primarily to observe the transit of the planet Venus over the disc of the sun in

June 1769 that he was dispatched in 1768 to the South Seas in the 368-ton *Endeavour*, a bark built in Whitby, similar to the colliers he had sailed in as a young seaman. He was instructed to sail to Otaheite (Tahiti) for the transit and then to sail southwards as far as 50 degrees south latitude on another search for the great southern continent, fixing on the map the positions of any islands he may incidentally discover.

Cook rounded Cape Horn and entered the Pacific Ocean for the first time on 27 January 1769. After observing the transit of Venus and investigating other islands in the group which he named the Society Islands, he sailed south and then westwards. On 6 October, a

ship's boy, Nicholas Young, sighted the east coast of the North Island where it is today called Young Nick's Head.

Two days after this first sighting of what he knew to be the east coast of New Zealand, the land reported by Tasman, the *Endeavour* sailed into a bay where smoke made it obvious there were inhabitants. As New Zealand historian Keith Sinclair has pointed out, the arrival of the Englishmen must have been to the Maori what a Martian invasion would be

Left, based on Dutch explorations, a chart published in 1690 by Vincenzo Coronelli shows Cape Maria van Diemen (North Island). **Above**, Tasman.

to the modern New Zealander. Their first visit ashore ended with violence when a band of Maori attacked four boys left guarding the ship's boat and one of the attackers was shot dead.

It was discovered that a Tahitian chief on board the *Endeavour*, Tupaea, could converse with the Maori in his own tongue. He was taken back ashore with Cook the next morning. But the Maori were in a threatening mood and Cook was forced to order one of them shot to make them retreat. That afternoon, the firing of a musket over a canoe (to attract the attention of its occupants) brought an attack on the ship's boat from which the shot had been fired; to repel the canoe, three or more Maori were shot. Cook was saddened by the violence but he had learnt quickly that the inhabitants of this country were powerful, aggressive and brave. He called the place Poverty Bay because he could not find the supplies he wanted.

The *Endeavour* sailed south into Hawke's Bay, and then north again around the top of East Cape. It spent 10 days in what is now called Mercury Bay because an observation of the transit of the planet Mercury was made there. In Mercury Bay, for the first time, the explorers made friends with the local Maori and traded trinkets for supplies of fish, birds and clean water. They were shown over the Maori settlement and inspected a nearby fortified pa which greatly impressed Cook.

The expedition circumnavigated New Zealand and with brilliant accuracy made a chart of the coastline which proved basically reliable for more than 150 years. Cook's two celebrated errors were attaching Stewart Island to the mainland as a peninsular, and mapping Banks Peninsula as an island.

Cook and his crew spent weeks in Ship Cove, in a long inlet which he called Queen Charlotte's Sound, on the northern coast of the South Island, refurbishing the ship and gathering supplies. The stay gave the two botanists aboard, Joseph Banks and Daniel Solander, a wonderful opportunity to study closely the flora and fauna of the area, and while the ship was being cleaned, the boats did detailed survey work.

The *Endeavour* left for home at the end of March 1770, sailing up the east coast of Australia, through the Dutch East Indies and then rounding the Cape of Good Hope to complete a circumnavigation of the world.

The expedition was an extraordinary feat of seamanship putting New Zealand firmly on the map and gathering a huge amount of data.

Antarctic R & R: Cook twice again led expeditions into the Pacific – from 1772 to 1775 and from 1776 to 1780. During the second of these, he twice took his ship south into the Antarctic Circle where no vessel was known to have gone before; he was unlucky not to become the first person ever to see the Antarctic continent.

It was to Dusky Sound in New Zealand that he repaired for rest and recovery after the extreme hardships faced by crew in the southern ocean. During the 7 weeks his expedition was there, the crews set up a workshop, an

On his third voyage, Cook sailed into the Arctic Circle through the Bering Strait in search of a northwest passage from the Atlantic into the Pacific. He again came to New Zealand, especially to his home from home at Ship Cove. By now he had a friendship with some of the local Maori that had lasted nearly 10 years. And he was impressed with them despite his loathing for the cannibalism. In his journals, he referred to the Maori as "manly and mild", less given to stealing than other Polynesians in the Pacific and "they have some arts among them which they execute with great judgement and unwearied patience."

Cook seemed to personify the Great Dis-

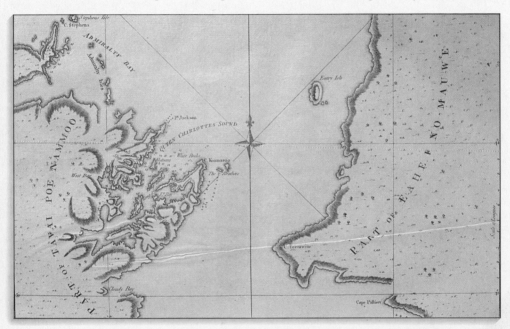

observatory, and restored their health with spruce beer (to defeat scurvy) and the plenitude of fish and birds. They made contact with a single family of Maori in an area which has never been thickly populated, then or now. They planted seeds on the shore of the sound, and then sailed for their favourite anchorage in Ship Cove at the other end of the South Island.

On his later return to New Zealand during his second voyage, on his way home, he gave pigs, fowls and vegetable seeds to Maori near Hawke's Bay before he again sailed for Ship Cove to a rendezvous with another vessel of the expedition, *Adventure*.

coverer as defined by his biographer, Beaglehole: "In every great discoverer there is a dual passion – the passion to see, the passion to report; and in the greatest this duality is fused into one – a passion to see and to report truly." Cook's first voyage was one of the most expert and detailed expeditions of exploration in all history.

In January 1778, Cook and his men became the first Europeans ever to set eyes on Hawaii. And then after his drive up into the Bering Sea, he returned to where the people seemed awed by the Europeans to the point almost of worship. He was to meet his death later at the hands of the natives of Hawaii.

After their departure, the ship suffered damage in a storm and although Cook felt he might have outworn his welcome, he was virtually forced to return to the same community in Kealakekua Bay. After a series of thefts from the expedition, a ship's cutter was stolen and Cook went ashore to seize a hostage in order to have the boat returned. It was during the confused outcome of this stratagem that Cook was struck, pushed into the water and stabbed to death.

Cook had done such a thorough job of charting the coasts of New Zealand that there was little else for explorers to discover without going inland. But a number of navigators followed during the remaining years of the

To begin with there were the sealers, with the first gang put ashore on the southwest coast of the South Island in 1792. There was a brief boom in the early years of the 19th century but it wasn't long before the seals became in short supply and the ships had to go farther south to the sub-Antarctic islands.

Next came the whalers at the turn of the century, some of them driven from the Pacific coast of South America because of the dangers there brought about by the war between Spain and Britain. These ships from Britain, Australia and the United States sought the sperm whale in this region and visits brought their crew-members into frequent contact with the Maori of Northland at

18th century – Frenchmen de Surville (only two months after Cook arrived the first time), du Fresne and d'Entrecasteaux; an Italian, Malaspina, who commanded a Spanish expedition; and George Vancouver.

In 10 years, within the decade of the 1770s, Cook and his contemporaries had opened up the Pacific entirely and, in 1788, Sydney was established as a British convict settlement. Traders were soon based there ready to extract whatever valuable goods they could find in the region.

Left, a map of Cook Strait from Cook's expeditions. **Above**, Maori entertain early European visitors.

Kororareka (later renamed as Russell).

At first, relations between Europeans and Maori were peaceful and friendly. But visits were infrequent for a few years after the burning of a vessel called the *Boyd* in 1809, and the massacre of its crew as a reprisal against previous punishment of high-born Maori seamen by Pakeha skippers.

The inland exploration of New Zealand took place mostly during the second quarter of the 19th century, mainly in those parts which were fairly accessible from the coast. But vast areas of the interior of the South Island were not successfully explored until this century.

HARRIETT
HEKE'S WIFE
HEKI
KAWITI

THE WARRIOR CHIEFTAINS
of
NEW ZEALAND

Drawn by Jos.ʰ J. Merrett

Drawn on Stone by W. Nicholas

Published by Mr.ˢ R.ᵗ Ford
George S.ᵗ Sydney

SETTLEMENT AND COLONISATION

The bleak experiences of Abel Tasman along New Zealand's west coast and the much more successful endeavours of James Cook 127 years later had no immediate impact on the future of the two main islands. The Dutch were preoccupied with getting all they could out of the Indonesian archipelago; the British (as the Honourable East India Company) were concerned with consolidating and expanding their trading territories in India.

New Zealand, it seemed, had little to offer a colonial power. "Botany Bay", not so far across the Tasman Sea, was established as a penal settlement in 1788 as a direct result of American victory in the War of Independence (and as a by-product of Cook's voyages), but the Land of the Long White Cloud remained ignored – or almost so.

As the 19th century opened, Europe was engulfed in war. Although international trade suffered through a series of blockades and battles, demand increased for so-called "essential" commodities, and such commodities included sealskins and whale oil. Seals and whales were plentiful in New Zealand waters, and enterprising skippers from Port Jackson (Sydney's harbour) and the newer settlement of Hobart, in Van Diemen's Land, Tasmania, were soon complying with the economic law of supply and demand.

Many of them found a convenient watering-hole at Kororareka (now Russell) in the Bay of Islands. The anchorage there was calm and well-protected; there was a ready supply of kauri wood for spars and masts; and they were not too worried by occasional visits by French ships. The Napoleonic wars were reaching their crescendo, and Anglo-French rivalry – back home in Europe – was at its peak. Who cared? Most of the sealers and whalers were renegades of one sort or another, escaped convicts or remittance men who had broken a bond; their captains weren't much better; and the French hadn't been in touch with France for a year or more.

Kororareka, with its new European arrivals, rapidly became a lusty, brawling town.

Preceding pages: forest rangers engage the Maori. Left, Honi Heke with his wife, Harriet, on his right and Chief Kawiti on his left.

Whatever its size in the early 1800s, the missionaries who followed swiftly on the heels of the Pakeha intruders were equally swift in damning it as the "hell-hole of the Southwest Pacific". This was hardly surprising: the newcomers, few of whom ever settled ashore or established permanent ties with the Bay of Islands, managed to introduce a destructive influence which in time completely eradicated some of the Maori tribes and hapu, and seriously affected others. The influence arrived in the form of muskets, hard liquor or "grog", prostitution, and a host of infectious diseases – many of which could prove fatal – to which the Maori had never previously been exposed.

Nevertheless, relations between Maori and Pakeha were tranquil in the early decades of the 19th century. Isolated hostilities, such as the burning of the brig *Boyd* and the killing and eating of its crew in Whangaroa Harbour in 1809, certainly occurred, and "the *Boyd* incident" discouraged Europeans from attempting to settle in the Whangaroa area for another 10 years.

"The *Boyd* massacre", as it was also known, was bitterly revenged some months later by whaling crews in the Bay of Islands. Some 60 Maori were killed, among them a chieftain whom the Pakehas wrongly believed to have been responsible for the *Boyd* tragedy.

That tragedy was a classic example of "culture shock". A Whangaroa chief, sailing as a crew-member on the *Boyd* from the North Island to Sydney, had been flogged for some misdemeanour on the return voyage. The flogging insulted his mana, and tribal loyalty demanded utu (or vengeance) for the insult. The crew of the *Boyd*, and their fellow-whalers and shipmates in Kororareka, had no understanding of either mana or utu; equally, the Maori themselves would not have understood the discipline demanded by the commander of a 600-ton brig in 1809.

Despite such ugly episodes, contacts between Maori and Pakeha remained essentially peaceful. A barter trade flourished, the Maori trading vegetables and flax for a variety of European trinkets and tools and weapons (including, of course, the musket, which they employed in their inter-tribal forays).

The Maori helped cut down giant kauri trees and drag the trunks from bush to beach; they crewed on European sealing and whaling vessels; they were physically strong and vigorous; and they were also proud – a fact overlooked by most Europeans.

Marsden's missionaries: The Reverend Samuel Marsden is still reviled in Australia as the "flogging parson", a result of his tenure as a magistrate at Port Jackson. Kiwis see him in a different light, as the man who introduced Christianity to New Zealand.

James Cook had claimed New Zealand for the British Crown in 1769. The Dutch had done much the same thing more than a century previously, and the French were playing with the same idea towards the end of the 18th century. But Cook's claim on behalf of Great Britain was never disputed.

Nor, in the 1780s, did anyone in Britain suggest that New Zealand be developed as a repository for convicted felons – that dubious honour being granted to what is now Sydney, the capital of New South Wales, to which many Maori sailed in the early 1800s.

The sealers and whalers who penetrated the Bay of Islands and areas farther south in the early years were, in a sense, accidents: they were not part of any grand British plan to colonise, and they themselves certainly did not see their role as that of colonists.

British colonisation of Australia had begun in 1788. Even though the first 30 years of New South Wales's existence had been full of problems, there was some semblance of law and order. In 1817 the legislation of the Colony of New South Wales was extended to include New Zealand; six years later, in 1823, the local juridical implementation of such legislation was introduced.

Amid this turbulence, Samuel Marsden arrived from New South Wales in 1814. His decision to go to New Zealand in a missionary role had been influenced by the Maori he had met in Sydney, including Ruatara, a nephew of the renowned fighting chief Hongi Hika. Marsden had been planning to establish a Christian mission in New Zealand as early as 1808, a plan frustrated by the reverberations of the *Boyd* incident in 1809.

Marsden was a dedicated evangelist. He sincerely believed that missionary tradesmen, "imported" from England under the auspices of the Church Missionary Society, would not only encourage the conversion of Maori to Christianity but also develop their expertise in carpentry, farming and the use of European technology. The Maori had been an agricultural people, with their staple crop being the sweet potato (or kumara), but with no experience in animal husbandry or graingrowing. (It is said that when Maori first grew wheat, they pulled the crop from the ground and looked for food at the roots.)

Marsden was also responsible for introducing the country's first horses and cattle. The excitement of the Maori on seeing these animals for the first time, according to one account, "was soon turned into alarm and confusion, for one of the cows, impatient of restraint and unmanageable, rushed in among

them and caused a serious panic. They thought the animal was some preternatural monster which had been let loose to destroy them and took to their heels in fright. Later, when Marsden mounted a horse and rode up and down the beach, he was at once given a status of more than mortal."

Six years later, in 1820, the first plough was demonstrated by John Butler, another Bay of Islands missionary. Butler wrote: "On the morning of Wednesday the 3rd of May, 1820, the agricultural plough was for the first time put into the land of New Zealand at Kiddie Kiddie (now Kerikeri) and I felt much pleasure in holding it after a team of six bullocks brought down by the 'Dromedary'. I trust that this auspicious day will be remembered with gratitude and its anniversary kept by ages yet unborn." Such pomposity was typical of Butler. He was also an irascible man, and quite soon left the country following bitter arguments with fellow missionaries.

The missionary-tradesmen-teachers in whom Marsden had placed his faith were in fact an ill-assorted bunch, most of whom fairly quickly fell before the onslaught of temptations. They bickered quite violently, and could hardly be regarded as a civilising, evangelising force by the people they had come to convert when so many of them

language, and in 1820 accompanied two famous chiefs, Hongi and Waikato, to Britain. Then there was William Colenso, who arrived at Paihia in 1834 and set up a printing press that played a major role in the development of Maori literacy.

By 1830, Maori were involved in export trading. In that year 28 ships (averaging 110 tonnes) made 56 cross-Tasman voyages, carrying substantial cargos, including tonnes of Maori-grown potatoes, mainly to Sydney. In 1835, the famous naturalist Charles Darwin visited the mission station at Waimate North and wrote: "On an adjoining slope fine crops of barley and wheat were standing in full ear; and in another fields of potatoes and

Kororarika Bay of Islands N.Z. 1836

became involved in gun-running, adultery, drunkenness, and even sorties into pagan rites. It is not surprising that 10 years passed before the first Maori baptism, and another 10 before the second. Not until the third decade of the century did the Maori begin to find Christianity an attractive proposition.

Some achievements were registered. Thomas Kendall, who succumbed to the Maori's different attitude towards sex, was none the less instrumental in compiling the first grammar and dictionary of the Maori

Left, Samuel Marsden, the 'flogging parson".
Above, early settlement in the Bay of Islands.

clover...There were large gardens with every fruit and vegetable which England produces."

The inclusion of New Zealand within the framework of the laws of New South Wales in 1817 and 1823 had not made New Zealand a British colony. The extension of legislation across the Tasman Sea from Sydney had been prompted by the desire of the early governors of New South Wales to control the lawlessness prevailing in the Bay of Islands. The sentiment was admirable enough. The main problem was that the legislation was directed principally against the crews of British ships, and the governors had no way of proving charges nor of enforcing their authority while a ship was in New Zealand waters; and they had no authority whatsoever over American vessels and their crews.

Additionally, the missionaries who found their way to New Zealand in the two or three decades after 1814 were, for once, united in a common aim: they did not want to see New Zealand colonised. This was a view shared by virtually all British Christian humanitarians and evangelists of the period, who felt that New Zealand should be left to the missionaries who (it was hoped) would spread what they saw as the benefits of Christian civilisation among the Maori, leaving the latter uncorrupted by depravity introduced to earlier colonies by European settlers and the settlement of New Zealand, South Australia and parts of Canada; his view was also shared by some of the early missionaries in New Zealand.

On a less idealistic level, there was also pressure among Britons for new colonies with land for settlement, and it was becoming known that the New Zealand climate was just about perfect for Europeans. It was also becoming obvious (or so it seemed at the time) that if Britain did not take sovereignty over New Zealand and populate it with European immigrants, some other colonial power – most probably France – would do so. In retrospect, it seems doubtful that the French in the opening decades of the 19th century

adventurers. But, inevitably, there was dissension "back home". The powerful Church Missionary Society ideally wanted British protection for New Zealand, and perhaps even some formal inclusion of the country within the Empire.

On the other hand, there was a substantial body of opinion which believed that settlement arranged in an organised and responsible manner by "good men" would be able to avoid the disasters inflicted by Europeans upon indigenous peoples of other countries. The leading proselytiser of this view in Britain was Edward Gibbon Wakefield whose theories on colonisation strongly influenced had any specific designs upon New Zealand, but their explorers and seamen had been to New Zealand waters since the time of Cook.

Predictably, the "home government" remained steadfastly irresolute, and the issue of colonisation was allowed to drift. By the 1830s, the scramble for land was in full swing – a scramble that was to produce tragic results within 20 years.

Man-of-war without guns: The Maori had no concept of permanent, private ownership of land. Their land was held by tribes traditionally inheriting it. A chief's authority was generally strong enough to have a sale accepted by most members of the tribe – but even this could be complicated by conflicting claims of ownership among tribes or sub-tribes, and such claims could involve very large areas. Many deals in land transfer between Pakeha and Maori led to conflicts in the 1860s; some of them are still being legally contested today.

There was also the problem of what was being bought. The settlers, and the rapacious speculators in Britain, thought they were buying outright freehold land; in many cases, the Maori believed they were merely leasing their lands for a fee.

The missionaries (with the possible exception of Marsden, whose idea of justice was to strip the flesh off a man's back) were not

skilled in matters of British law, and certainly not in the area of land conveyancing. Nor were they renowned as administrators and they did not want to become involved because of their professed anti-settlement beliefs. The time had finally come for government intervention, however reluctant.

In 1833, with the arrival in the Bay of Islands of James Busby as British Resident, the move was made.

The notion of "resident" was vague in

Left, Nelson Haven in Tasman Bay, by Charles Heaphy in 1841. **Above**, Edward Gibbon Wakefield, who founded the Colonisation Society.

1833 and became no clearer in the next century of British colonial rule in many parts of the world. A resident, in most cases, had the full backing of Her or His Majesty's Government as a diplomat representing British interests in a territory that had not yet been annexed by the Crown. He could advise local chieftains, he could cajole, he could woo – but he had no real power.

Poor Busby! Lacking any means of enforcing his authority, such as it was, he became known among the Maori as "the man-of-war without guns".

Busby did what he could. He attempted to create some unity and overall sovereignty among the disparate Maori by formally establishing a confederation of Maori chiefs, and then in 1835 he proposed that Britain and the United Tribes of New Zealand should agree to an arrangement under which the confederation would represent the Maori people and gradually expand their influence as a government while the British government, in the meantime, administered the country in trust.

Despite his nickname, Busby won personal respect from the Maori. Even so, he keenly felt his own impotence and knew he could never achieve law and order without the backing of some adequate force.

The missionaries, divided as they were, could not prevent the eventual large-scale colonisation of New Zealand, and in 1840 their anti-settlement policy was rebuffed with the signing of Treaty of Waitangi.

Men who came to stay: While most of the British and American whalers and sealers were not the type of men to settle down on terra firma in a remote corner of the globe, there were, from the early 19th century, a number of men of European stock who were willing to put down roots in the new land and to face the risks and hardships involved. By the 1830s a few thousand Pakehas had settled, almost all of them in the Bay of Islands.

The Weller brothers – Edward, George and Joseph – were among the pioneer settlers in Otago. As whalers, they became so well established that in 1833 they sent a trial export shipment of merchandise to London. Unhappily for them, what could have proved a bonanza was thwarted by British Customs: New Zealand was a "foreign country", and the Wellers faced duties of £26 per ton on their whale oil. They abandoned the whole enterprise and, later, they left Otago as well.

John Jones, another whaler, established a base a few miles north of Dunedin, and in the late 1830s had a chain of seven whaling stations operating in the south of the South Island and employed 280 people. Born in Sydney, and believed to have been the son of a transported convict, he later operated a shipping line and owned large land-holdings at Waikouaiti on the coast north of Dunedin.

Richard Barrett, widely known as "Dickie", arrived in New Zealand as an adventurer in 1828. He married Rawinia Waikaiua of the Taranaki Ngati-te-Whiti tribe and fought for his wife's people in tribal wars. He later became a whaler in the Cook Strait region, and a notable translator and mediator in land-sale deals around Wellington; he also took part in negotiations for the Wellington land purchase by the New Zealand Company for the initial settlement there in 1840.

Others of the original settlers also threw in their lot with the Maori. Phillip Tapsel was a Dane who served with the British merchant marine and first arrived in New Zealand in 1803. In the late 1820s he set up a trading post on behalf of a Sydney merchant at Maketu in the Bay of Plenty. He married three Maori women, had a number of children, and his name is now a common one among the Arawa people of the area. Frederick Maning emigrated to Tasmania with his father and brothers in 1824, and decided to settle in Hokianga, North Auckland, in 1833. He married Moengaroa, the sister of a powerful Maori chief, Hauraki, and they had four children before she died in 1847. Maning took part in inter-tribal warfare, supporting his wife's people, and was later appointed a judge of the Native Land Court. He wrote two books about his experiences, both under the pseudonym "A Pakeha-Maori". They were *War in the North* and the more famous *Old New Zealand*, both of which give vivid accounts of tribal life.

"Pakeha-Maori" was a common term used to describe those Europeans who joined the tribal life. Even during the debauchery and violence amongst the Bay of Islands' Pakehas, there were a number of men treating the Maori with respect and actually adopting their way of life.

There were also farcical interludes. A character calling himself Baron Charles Philip Hippolytus de Thierry, Sovereign Chief of New Zealand, King of Nukuheva, decided to establish himself at Hokianga. He had arranged the purchase of a large estate from Hongi Hika through the agency of Thomas Kendall when they visited Britain.

De Thierry arrived in New Zealand in 1837, was quickly deserted by his followers, soon ran out of money, and fairly quickly faded into a bizarre chapter of history. His life was the basis for a novel, *Check to Your King*, by Robin Hyde.

De Thierry's background was mostly English, but there was one other genuine if half-hearted French interest in the country. A colonising organisation, the Nanto-Bordelaise Company, established a settle-

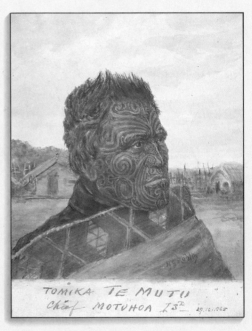

TOMIKA TE MUTU
Chief MOTUHOA Isᴰ 29.12.1865

ment at Akaroa on Banks Peninsula, with some support from the French government, on the eve of the British decision to annexe New Zealand. The French operation, however, was a small one, and any influence it might have had on the British move has been overstated in the past.

The Wakefield Scheme: In the course of the 1830s it had become obvious in New South Wales, which provided what little British administrative control there was, that land buying was going to cause serious trouble. Speculators were gambling on Britain taking over and settling the country; while Busby, the British Resident, was powerless to prevent such "deals" from taking place. Colonisation, in fact, was developing a kind of inevitability. In 1836, Edward Gibbon Wakefield told a committee of the House of Commons that Britain was colonising New Zealand already, but "in a most slovenly and scrambling and disgraceful manner".

In 1837, at the behest of the government of New South Wales, Captain William Hobson, commanding *HMS Rattlesnake*, sailed from Sydney to the Bay of Islands to report on the situation. Hobson suggested a treaty with the Maori chiefs (which Busby thought he had already achieved) and the placing of all British subjects in New Zealand under British rule. Hobson's report provoked a response,

heiress, Ellen Turner. This time his plan misfired. He was apprehended, tried, and sentenced to three years in prison.

While in prison Wakefield wrote two books. One, *A Letter from Sydney*, outlined his philosophy of colonisation and attracted the attention of some influential people. Following his release, he founded the Colonisation Society to spread his theories.

Disliking what he perceived as the bad results of colonisation in the United States, Canada, New South Wales and Tasmania, he believed that if land was sold at what he called "a sufficient price" to "capitalist" settlers, labourers among the immigrants would not disperse thinly but would stay in the new

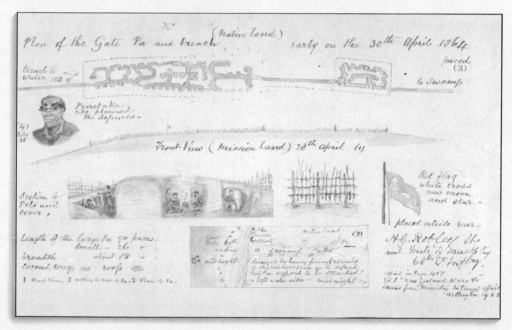

but without Wakefield's influence there might not have been such an outcome.

Wakefield was born in London in 1796, the eldest of a large family. In 1816 he persuaded a wealthy young woman, Eliza Susan Pattle, to elope with him. She died soon afterwards, but had borne a son, Edward Jerningham Wakefield, who was to become significant in New Zealand's history.

Ten years later, in 1826, Wakefield made a second runaway marriage with a schoolgirl

Left, Tomika Te Mutu, chief of Motuhoa Island. **Above**, a plan of the Gate pa, which was taken during the New Zealand Wars.

communities working for landowners – at least for a few years until they could save enough to buy land for themselves at the "sufficient price" and employ more recently arrived immigrant labour.

Land prices were crucial to Wakefield's system. Unfortunately he underestimated the aspirations of immigrant labourers who were prepared to suffer extreme isolation in order to farm their own land; and he did not foresee the readiness with which "capitalists" would move out of the centralised settlements to areas they considered more profitable.

During the late 1830s and early 1840s Wakefield was ostensibly involved in Canadian colonisation matters, but much of his time and energy were in fact absorbed by the organisation of the New Zealand Company. The Company, originally formed as the New Zealand Association in 1837, was revamped in the following year as a joint stock company at the behest of the British Secretary of State for the Colonies, who (not unreasonably) wanted to ensure that the people involved would bear the costs of establishing the settlements they planned.

The Treaty of Waitangi: At the same time as Wakefield's hopeful "capitalists" and "labourers" were starting to pack their sea-trunks, the British government was at last responding to the anti-colonial feelings of

the missionary groups. Britain decided that the Maori should be consulted on their own future, and that their consent should be given to the annexation of their country. The result was the Treaty of Waitangi, signed at the Bay of Islands on 6 February 1840, by Lieutenant-Governor William Hobson on behalf of the British government. The treaty was later taken to other parts of the country for signing by most of the Maori chiefs.

Ironically, the treaty was never ratified. Within a decade the Chief Justice, Sir William Martin, ruled that it had no legal validity because it was not incorporated in New Zealand's statutory law. The second irony is that

the date of the original signing of the treaty is now said to be the "founding day" of New Zealand as a British colony, the reverse of what the missionaries had hoped to achieve.

The treaty itself remains a bone of contention. The text of the document was written in English, apparently amended by Hobson after it was first explained to the assembled Maori leaders, with a rather loosely translated version in Maori (that version being the one signed by most of the Maori leaders). The Maori had put much faith in advice from the missionaries, being told that they were signing a solemn pact, under which New Zealand sovereignty was being vested in the British Crown in return for guarantees of certain Maori rights. Many Europeans (and also Maori) genuinely believed this, and for some years the British government upheld the agreement.

It is almost impossible now to regard the treaty objectively. In the context of its time it was an example of enlightened and humane respect for the rights of an indigenous population. But because it was never ratified, and never truly honoured by the white settlers hungry for land, it is easily construed these days as an expedient fraud.

Organised immigration: The formal British annexation of New Zealand implicit in the 1840 Treaty of Waitangi was quickly followed by the arrival of the first ships carrying immigrants organised by Wakefield's New Zealand Company. *Tory*, despatched from English before the treaty had been signed and arriving early in 1840, long before the treaty could have been received in London, carried Colonel William Wakefield (who had earlier assisted his brother Edward in the abduction of Ellen Turner, and had been gaoled for it) and a batch of immigrants who were to settle in Wellington. The Wanganui district received its first settlers shortly afterwards, and in 1841 a subsidiary of the Company, based in Plymouth, England, and drawing emigrants from Devon and Cornwall, established New Plymouth.

The South Island was not ignored. Captain Arthur Wakefield, another of Edward's many brothers, arrived at Nelson in 1841 and was followed by 3,000 settlers in 1842.

Despite (or perhaps because of) the Treaty of Waitangi, land claims soon became a matter of dispute. Arthur Wakefield, in 1843, led a party of 21 other Nelson settlers into the fertile Wairau Valley, near Nelson, which he contended had been bought by the Company. The local chief Te Rauparaha and his nephew Rangihaeata thought otherwise: they assembled their warriors and killed all 22 of the Pakehas.

Nor was the Wellington settlement in the bloom of health. The first site in the Hutt Valley had been flooded; there had been serious clashes with the local tribes; potentially arable land was scarce, and even when available such land was proving difficult and expensive to develop.

In the Bay of Islands, the events in the south were having their repercussions. Hone Heke, a signatory to the Treaty of Waitangi,

declined, and Hone Heke got fractious. He and his warriors demolished the flagpole (symbol of royal authority) on three occasions, and once sacked the entire town as Pakehas scampered off into the woods or took to boats.

George Grey, who arrived as Governor in 1845, called in the army to suppress Hone Heke. With the help of Maori dissidents who refused to support Heke, Grey won the day.

Pragmatic pastoralism: Such open conflict did not encourage emigration. The New Zealand Company, Wakefield's idealistic dream, went into a decline. It eventually became almost bankrupt in the late 1840s, surrendered its charter, and handed over to the

had become more than disenchanted with the treaty's implications. Although Kororareka (Russell) had been the *de facto* "capital" of New Zealand before the signing of the treaty, Lieutenant-Governor Hobson – in his wisdom – decided that Auckland should be the site of the new country's capital. The protective sweep of Auckland's harbour quickly proved his point, but left a lot of noses out of joint in Russell. Well-established Yankee skippers felt badly done by, the town's trade

Left, reverse side of the New Zealand Cross, awarded during the New Zealand Wars. **Above**, stagecoach fording a North Island stream.

government some 400,000 hectares (about 1 million acres) of land for which about $500,000 were due; it was dissolved in 1858.

Even with the writing on the wall in its last decade of operation, the New Zealand Company remained active, lending its organisational support to members of the Scottish Free Church who established Dunedin in 1848, and to the Anglicans who founded Christchurch in 1850 and quickly opened up the excellent pasturelands of the Canterbury Plains. Although Governor Grey was less than enthusiastic about pastoralism – indeed, he does not seem to have understood what it was all about – more and more new settlers imported sheep, mostly merinos, from Australia. What became New Zealand's principal economic asset was soon under way: sheep-farming on a large scale, at first purely for wool, later for lamb and mutton.

Edward Wakefield, architect-in-absence of planned settlement, eventually arrived in New Zealand for the first time in 1852, the year in which the colony was granted self-government by Britain. He was elected to the Wellington Provincial Council and the House of Representatives in 1853, but retired shortly afterwards because of ill health.

Wakefield achieved much. At the same time, he lived long enough (he died in 1862) to see that his ideal of cohesive but expanding communities, complete with "capitalists" and "labourers", was not viable. The immigrants didn't necessarily make the choice for "town life", and many left the infant settlements to establish – or, at least, attempt to establish – agricultural or pastoral properties well beyond the confines of the towns. But, thanks largely to his efforts, the settlement and colonisation of New Zealand were achieved in a more orderly manner than had been the case, several decades earlier, in Canada and Australia.

The new settlers were not the only people interested in taking advantage of the fertile land. The Maori themselves had quickly learned the agricultural lessons taught by the early missionaries (even if they had responded less quickly to the lure of Christianity), and by the end of the 1850s huge areas of Maori land in Waikato and the Bay of Plenty were under cultivation or carrying livestock. One commentator reported that a Maori population of about 8,000 in the Taupo-Rotorua region "had upwards of 3,000 acres of land in wheat, 3,000 acres in potatoes, nearly 2,000 acres in maize and upwards of 1,000 acres planted with kumara". On the surface, the new colony appeared peaceful.

The New Zealand Wars: In fact, the new colony was anything but peaceful. There had been a great deal of speculation in land sales, and many Maori were beginning to realise this: land was being sold for as much as 20 times what they had been paid for it.

A direct result of this injustice was the election in 1858 of a Maori "king" by tribes in the centre of the North Island. There had never been such a title among the Maori, who owed their allegiance to a tribe or sub-tribe, but it was hoped that the mana of a king, uniting many tribes, would help protect their land against purchase by the Pakehas. It didn't work out that way.

To the west, the Taranaki, another group of tribes, rose up against the government in June 1860 following a blatantly fraudulent land purchase by the colonial administration, the Waitara Land Deal. British regular troops, hastily assembled, were virtually annihilated south of Waitara.

For the next few days, the North Island was ablaze with clashes between Maori and Pakeha. The "Second Maori War", as military historians term it (remembering the outbreaks in 1840), was marked by extraordinary courage on both sides. The conflicts were frequently indecisive, but bloody. On the Pakeha side, the brunt of the early fighting, until 1865, was borne by British regular troops, 14 of whom received Britain's highest battle honour, the Victoria Cross.

Between 1865 and 1872 (which was the "official" end of the war, though there was sporadic fighting until the formal surrender of the Maori king in 1881), locally raised militia and constabulary forces played an important role – assisted, surprisingly, by a large number of Maori tribes that had decided not to join the king's confederation.

A little-known sidelight of the New Zealand Wars was the institution of the New Zealand Cross, a unique and extremely rare medal awarded for gallantry. A 15th Victoria Cross had been awarded to a member of the Auckland Militia who took part in an action at Waikato in 1864, but because the VC could be won only by a man serving with the Imperial Forces, or under imperial command, the NZC was created as an honour for outstanding gallantry shown by a member of a locally raised non-imperial unit. Only 23 medals were ever awarded – three of them going to Maori.

Despite war, the prospects of the country continued to improve. The discovery of gold in the South Island led to a fresh influx of migrants in the early 1860s; the capital was moved from Auckland to Wellington in 1865; and the pursuit of pasture was opening up vast tracts of the country. Wakefield might not have liked it, but the individualistic "cow-cockie" was on his way.

Right, gold brought many settlers to New Zealand.

Progress towards full independence from Britain began almost as soon as the Maori-Pakeha land wars began to settle down.

An economic boom in the 1870s was sparked by Sir Julius Vogel, who as colonial treasurer borrowed heavily overseas for public works construction, notably railways. A flood of immigrants, mainly from Britain but also from Scandinavia and Germany, followed. But Vogel – an ebullient, imaginative and impatient man who remained in the forefront of New Zealand politics from 1873

to 1887, and was twice premier during that time – miscalculated the negative impact of his borrow-to-boom credo.

By the end of the 1870s, British banks had begun to contract their credit. In 1880, New Zealand only narrowly averted bankruptcy. Within a few years, the prices of first wool, then grain, dropped so hard that depression set in and unemployment spread rapidly. In 1888, more than 9,000 hungry settlers left the colony, most of them for Australia, which had remained relatively prosperous.

These years of hardship may have had something to do with the emergence of New Zealand as one of the most socially progressive communities in the world. Free, compulsory and secular public-school education was created by law in 1877, and another piece of legislation two years later gave every adult man – Maori as well as Pakeha – the right to vote.

In the 1880s, Sir Harry Atkinson, a cautious man who had reacted against Vogel's borrowing and "profligacy", advocated a national social security scheme to protect New Zealanders against illness and pauperism. Although he was elected premier five times between 1876 and 1891, Atkinson's scheme was ridiculed by his Parliamentary colleagues. "It's unChristian," they told him. Unrepentant in defeat, Atkinson responded: "Our successors in office will take up and pass every one of these measures."

He was right. In the waning years of the 19th century, a barrage of social reforms was fired by a new Liberal Party government headed by John Ballance. Sweeping land reforms were introduced, breaking down the large inland estates and providing first mortgage money to put people on the land. Industrial legislation provided improved conditions for workers, as well as a compulsory system of industrial arbitration, which was the first of its kind in the world. The aged poor were awarded a pension. And for the first time anywhere (with the exceptions of tiny Pitcairn Island and the American state of Wyoming), women were granted the right to vote on an equal basis with men, to the delight of the women's suffrage movement throughout the world.

Powerful leadership: The principal minds behind these great social reforms were William Pember Reeves, a New Zealand-born socialist, the political theorist of the Liberal Party and a man determined to test the intellectually exciting new Fabian ideas then in vogue in Britain; and Richard John Seddon, who succeeded to the office of Prime Minister when Ballance died in 1893 and was perhaps the most admired leader in New Zealand history. Seddon's legendary toughness and political judgement gave him enormous power within the party and in the country. He died in offiece in 1906.

Even in the depths of the depression of the

1880s, a new industry was being created. In 1882, the refrigerated vessel Dunedin was loaded with sheep's carcasses at Port Chalmers, the deepwater port for the South Island city of Dunedin. It sailed on 13 February and arrived in England 3½ months later, on 24 May.

The voyage was an anxious one: sparks from the refrigeration machinery several times set fire to the sails, and the captain was nearly frozen to death as he attended to a malfunction in the freezing chamber's main air duct. But the meat arrived safely and, despite the transport costs, profits in England were much higher than they would have been for the same meat back in New Zealand.

MacKenzie. Assisted only by a remarkable sheepdog named Friday who took its orders in Gaelic, he is said to have stolen 1,000 sheep from a Canterbury run and led them across vast distances of open land. He was arrested and brought to trial, but was subsequently pardoned. Today the vast Mackenzie Country west of Christchurch bears his (misspelled) name.

The new and burgeoning frozen meat industry and the expansion of dairy exports during the early years of the 20th century saw the rise of the small farmer in both the North and South Island – especially the "cowcockie", as the dairy farmer came to be known. While Seddon became more con-

This was a blessing from the gods for the isolated colony. The timing was perfect for Britain, too. Population was increasing with urbanisation, and people had more money to spend on food. As farmers began breeding sheep for meat as well as wool, the frozen meat industry became an economic staple.

Wealth wrought by sheep-breeding naturally attracted a handful of men who sought to get rich quick, most notably New Zealand's best known scallywag, one James

Left, Richard John Seddon, prime minister from 1893 to 1906. **Above**, Labour Day procession down Auckland's Queen Street in 1899.

servative in the latter years of his Liberal administration, the farmers' affluence and influence grew, until in 1911 – a few years after New Zealand had politely refused an invitation to become a part of the new Commonwealth of Australia, and was subsequently upgraded by the Empire from "colony" to "dominion" – the new Reform Party squeezed into power. New prime minister William Massey was himself a dairy farmer, and while his government had the backing of conservative businessmen, his election helped consolidate New Zealand's position as an offshore farm for Britain.

World War I: War brought a new sense of

nationalism to New Zealand while at the same time reinforcing the country's ties to England. Under Seddon in 1899, 6,500 Kiwis had volunteered for service in the Boer War in South Africa; now, between 1914 and 1918, 100,000 joined the Australia-New Zealand Army Corps (ANZAC) forces and sailed for North Africa and Europe.

By the time the war had ended, almost 17,000 New Zealanders had lost their lives, and many thousands more returned home with crippling wounds. Indeed, the casualties were out of all proportion to the country's population, then about a million. The futility was underscored by the debacle on Turkey's Gallipoli Peninsula, from 25 April

1915 (a day now marked in memoriam as "Anzac Day") until British naval evacuation some eight months later; the affair cost dearly the lives of 8,587 Anzacs, and there were another 25,000 casualties. Somehow this heroic tragedy gave New Zealand a new identity within the British Empire.

The Great Depression of the 1930s gripped hard on New Zealand. Curtailed British demand for meat, wool and dairy products led to severe unemployment and several bloody riots, notably on Queen Street, Auckland, in April 1932. The new Labour Party swept into power in 1935 to take advantage of the resurgent world economy and quickly pull

the nation out of the doldrums. Under prime minister Michael Savage, the nation again moved to the forefront of world social change, establishing a full social security system.

Savage died soon after the outbreak of World War II, into which he threw his country with vigour on 2 September 1939, only an hour or so after Britain declared war on Hitler's Germany. He was succeeded as prime minister by Peter Fraser, whose administration financed the war effort almost entirely from taxation and internal borrowing. This time, nearly 200,000 Kiwis were called to battle, many of them under General Douglas MacArthur in the nearby Pacific campaign, others in North Africa, Italy and Crete. More than 10,000 died.

Enhanced self-respect: Back home, a successful economic stabilisation policy and full employment made the 1940s a decade of relative prosperity. The country emerged from the war with a developed sense of nationhood. It was an appropriate time, in 1947, for the government to adopt the Statute of Westminster and formally achieve full independence from Britain. (In fact, the statute had been approved by commonwealth legislatures before it was passed by British Parliament in 1931, granting complete independence to self-governing member countries. But it did not, however, apply automatically to New Zealand or Australia, both of which had to adopt it by legislation.)

The Labour Party had lost its vigour. The young men who had steered it to victory in the mid-1930s, and who had transformed the nation into a modern welfare state, could not meet the challenge of the new era. They were dilatory in decontrolling the economy after the war and were in effect suppressing the desire of the community to enjoy a freer economic environment.

They were defeated in 1949 by the National Party, a political movement which had first fought a general election in 1938 and been soundly beaten by Labour. National had in the meantime attracted many young businessmen who wanted greater private-enterprise influence in the economy. Their victory ended an era and paved the way for the shaping of modern New Zealand.

Left, "modern girls" in New Zealand of the 1920s. **Right**, the tallest and the shortest members of the regiment sent to aid Britain in the Boer War.

A COUNTRY IS BORN

In the years since World War II, New Zealand has been profoundly remade as a nation, both economically and socially.

In 1950, the country was still a small, isolated, relatively wealthy welfare state with powerful trade unions, few wealthy people, no poor, and an economy built around pastoral farming exports to Britain.

Over the following 30 years, isolation broke down as long-haul commercial jets began to criss-cross the world and television's global eye opened up in every home.

Then Britain joined Europe and dislocated the tidy trading arrangement that had lasted since refrigerated shipping first made New Zealand meat and dairy produce available in Britain in the 1880s. Successive administrations from the late 1960s tried to ride out the storm by tying the economy up in more and more regulations.

And then, suddenly in the 1980s, one of the most regulated economies anywhere was deregulated. The traditional government intervention in economic affairs, which had become unrelenting and dire, ceased virtually overnight. Kiwis had to cope with the pell-mell pace of change.

A political tremor: The 1950s began with a political tremor as a new National Party government abolished the Legislative Council, the upper house of the national Parliament. This appointive body, like almost every other constitutional device, had been built on a British model, in this case the House of Lords. The Legislative Council gave New Zealand a bicameral Parliament but to a pragmatic House of Representatives it seemed simply an obstruction. When the council was done away, the government, led by Sir Sidney Holland, said it would be replaced by an elective body and, in the meantime, no legislation would be passed within a month of its introduction to Parliament. Neither undertaking was honoured.

So New Zealand has been one of few democratic nations with a unicameral legislature. This has given inordinate power to the executive – a Cabinet made up from members of the party with a majority in the House of Representatives. This power to change the law dramatically and within hours enabled the Labour Party for six years after 1984 to transform the nation's economy and, thus, its whole social structure.

One of the first actions taken by the unicameral House was the ratification of the Anzus (Australia-New Zealand-United States) mutual security pact in 1951. In World War II, the United States had played the major role in protecting both South Pacific

nations from the Japanese advance (ironically, the ANZAC forces were in Europe at the time); and the signing of this Anzus pact was a clear indication on the part of New Zealand and Australia that they had to look away from Britain to meet their defence requirements.

But the first post-war revolution came with the end of isolation. As in 1900 in South Africa and during the 1914-18 world conflict, young New Zealand men flocked to join the armed forces again in the 1940s to fight Britain's enemies. As a percentage of population, the contribution was huge. While there was a great sentimental attachment to

Left, visits from the royals are still well received. **Right**, Sir Keith Holyoake, governor general.

the "Old Country" or "Home", as it was often called, part of the attraction to enlist was a once-in-a-lifetime chance to see the world.

For a century, New Zealanders – whether they were born here or arrived as migrants – were confined to their country because of its extreme geographical isolation. Some few went to Australia but the yearning was to go to Europe. Almost no one did unless to fight someone else's wars or because they were among the few rich. Before mass travel became a possibility, hotels shut at 6pm, restaurants were forbidden to sell liquor and a rigid 40-hour, five-day working week meant shops' hours were strictly controlled and most families spent weekends at home.

World's greatest travellers: The result was the radical change during the 1960s and 1970s of a narrow, closed, highly controlled society. Kiwis quickly became among the greatest travellers of any people in the world. Air New Zealand nows calls itself "the airline of the world's greatest travellers".

By the 1980s, shops were staying open to offer extended services into the evenings and weekends, most restrictions were lifted from hotels and taverns, the best New Zealand wines were considered as good as any anywhere, and restaurants and cafés made eating out part of the national culture, offering a wide range of local and international cuisine. On the back of such sophistication,

SHOULD AULD ACQUAINTANCE BE FORGOT?

Society remained in that time warp until, in the 1950s, passenger ships began their trade again and thousands of young Kiwis travelled away for their "OE" (overseas experience), almost always to London, and for the first time they had grounds for comparison between their society and the old world.

In 1965, the first commercial jet began service to New Zealand and a few years later the wide-bodied aircraft made mass international travel available to everyone. At the same time, the small nation with a developed infrastructure and an educated population was also released from the fetters of isolation by rapidly expanding telecommunications.

tourism has boomed and forecasts are that by the turn of the century this country with fewer than four million inhabitants will host more than two million visitors a year.

In the early 1970s, New Zealand began grappling with the problem of diversifying both its production away from bulk commodities and its markets away from Britain. Also at that time, oil prices soared, and debt began to pile up as both Labour and National administrations borrowed and hoped primary production prices would pick up and that countries other than Britain would start buying. It was a matter of marketing. But marketing was something New Zealanders had never needed to do. They had lived well, high on the sheep's back, for so long, by the relatively simple process of farming well, that the British jump into the EEC in 1973 left them in confusion and bewilderment.

Under Prime Minister Keith Holyoake (1957 and 1960–72), the country had continued its socially progressive tradition, becoming the first nation outside Scandinavia to create within the government the appointive position of "ombudsman". In effect a parliamentary commissioner, the ombudsman's role is to investigate and expedite the claims of private citizens against bureaucracy and officialdom. Where the claims are justified, the ombudsman assures that

accident compensation scheme. Anyone injured in an accident, no matter who was at fault, was entitled to free medical treatment and income replacement. The right to sue for negligence causing an accident was forfeited.

So despite the first signs of significant unemployment and growing international debt, governments were still gradually expanding the welfare system and were financially promoting primary production. During the 1970s, sheep numbers rose past 70 million for the first time as farmers received state payments to boost stock numbers. Primary industry was widely subsidised and manufacturing tightly protected during a National Party government between 1975

action is taken – restoring lost pensions, moving boundary markers, and the like. Where the claims are not justified, he explains the government's position to the complainant. This idea has proven to be successful since it was first enacted in 1962.

A Labour prime minister, Norman Kirk, was elected to power in 1972 and before he died in office less than two years later he had given drive and intellectual support to the anti-nuclear movement and introduced an

Left, Britain's entry to the European Community was a serious blow to the economy. **Above**, New Zealand has adopted a nuclear-free policy.

and 1984. The party which had traditionally espoused private enterprise had become almost as economically interventionist as some eastern Europe regimes.

The trade barriers imposed on Britain by EEC membership, combined with rocketing oil prices, sent the cost of industrial goods sky high. So New Zealand on the one hand was producing goods whose prices dawdled behind, held back by artificially underpriced competition from subsidised, over-protected production in the EEC and the United States; and on the other hand, it was paying more and more for industrial goods because it had to import most of them.

Led by Sir Robert Muldoon – who had served as finance minister in the Holyoake ministry – National doubled the tight measures imposed by Labour on immigration, imports and the dollar. Muldoon, pugnacious and controversial but never dull, provoked the anger of trade unionists throughout the country by imposing a wage freeze, but held his line in the face of numerous retaliatory strikes and demonstrations. The Muldoon government also had to deal with some racial problems, and with a brain drain of young New Zealanders to Australia and other foreign countries. In the 1980s, more than 30,000 Kiwis were leaving annually to seek better opportunities elsewhere. Muldoon

Zealand farmers through supplementary minimum prices (SMPs) and other economic devices. A wages-price freeze from 1982 cut inflation to around 4 percent, but all the regulation and readjustment caused an agony of doubt about the short-term future of the economy. By 1984, unemployment had reached 130,000 and the national overseas debt stood at NZ$14.3 billion.

But when a new Labour government came to power towards the end of 1984, farm and other production subsidies were withdrawn overnight, import licences abandoned, wage structures dismantled and a broad policy of economic *laissez-faire* put in place.

During the 1960s, as France began step-

shrugged – the average intelligence quotient of departing New Zealanders, he said, compared to the average IQ of Australians, meant the migration was "raising the collective IQ of both countries".

A country remade: By 1975, Britain was taking only 22 percent of New Zealand's exports and most of the rest was going to Australia, Japan and the United States as the country cast around for new markets. By the end of the Seventies and the beginning of the Eighties, internal inflation was raging so strongly (up to 17 percent) that farm costs skyrocketed and the Muldoon ministry humiliatingly had to bolster subsidies to New

ping up a campaign of nuclear testing in its Polynesian possessions, New Zealand scientists began to monitor radioactivity in the region. Protest ships travelled to French Polynesia intentionally to block tests; back home, there were several mass demonstrations.

This strong anti-nuclear feeling reached its peak when the Labour government refused nuclear-armed or nuclear-powered United States naval vessels entry to New Zealand ports. The Americans insisted on their right as allies under the ANZUS Pact and promptly broke off all defence arrangements with New Zealand.

Led by David Lange – a former lawyer for

the poor who at 41 became New Zealand's youngest prime minister of the 20th century – Labour pledged to set up a 320-km (200-mile) nuclear-free zone around the shores of New Zealand, and to re-negotiate the 33-year-old ANZUS security pact to force the United States to keep nuclear armaments out of New Zealand ports.

Division within the Labour government on other issues had grown so wide, however, by 1989 that Lange resigned and his deputy, Geoffrey Palmer, took over as prime minister. Palmer resigned in early September 1990, almost two months before the national elections, and was succeeded by foreign affairs and Trade Minister Mike Moore.

But opposition to nuclear weapons had become so widespread that the National government, which won office in 1990 and which had castigated the government on the issue while in opposition, was forced by public opinion to maintain the anti-nuclear stance – so the rift was never truly healed.

The Labour administration began to self-destruct after four years as one faction moved for more rapid change of policy towards less government, lower taxes and almost total deregulation, and another wanted some in-

Past prime ministers: Sir Robert Muldoon (left) and David Lange (above).

tervention as productivity declined and unemployment soared. By the end of the decade, Labour was in disarray with three prime ministers in quick succession; so, in 1990, National was returned to power. However, the new prime minister Jim Bolger quickly made it clear his government would stay with economic deregulation. In the mid-1990s New Zealand began to recover and the government eased up slightly on its expenditure and its tight monetary policy.

Free trade with Australia: Early in the postwar period, New Zealand had realised its best economic hope for the future was some sort of pact with its nearest neighbour, Australia. In 1965, the New Zealand Australia Free Trade Agreement, known then as NAFTA, was signed. The plan was gradually to dismantle trade barriers between the two countries over a 10-year period. The two governments were to add to a list of products that would move across the Tasman free of tariffs and licences.

The principle seemed to enthuse politicians and business people in both countries much more than the actuality. Almost every move towards expanding the list of goods met with heavy counter-pressure from any industrial interests that might feel they would be disadvantaged in some way. A second 10-year period was agreed to in 1975 but by the early 1980s it was apparent that some more dramatic pact was needed if real progress was to be made towards free trade.

In 1983, the two governments signed what has come to be known as CER, an acronym for Closer Economic Relations. The difference was that CER had a time-frame built in with steady progress inevitable. By the beginning of the 1990s, free trade was virtually in place across the Tasman Sea, with only some services still not completely liberated. Some progress had been made also towards making the commercial laws and conventions of the two countries compatible.

Both New Zealand and Australia have now turned their economic attention northwards to Asia. Prime Minister Jim Bolger has said New Zealand is part of Asia and his government has put its weight behind a number of campaigns to push trade with the burgeoning Asian economies.

Japan is New Zealand's second biggest market (behind Australia). More than one-third of exports go to Asian markets – more than to North America and Europe combined, and almost one-third of imports come from that source as well. Japan and Singapore have long been trading partners but business is building up with Korea, Thailand, Malaysia, Indonesia, Taiwan, China and the Philippines.

Transport gives a clue to how the pace of orientation is accelerating. In the mid 1980s, Air New Zealand had one flight a week to Japan. Ten years later there were 14. In 1993, one flight a week linked New Zealand and Korea. Less than a year later, there were six, Korea had supplanted Britain as the fourth biggest trading partner, and ranked among the top nations of immigrants.

against the plunder of native trees in many other countries.

Waitangi tribunal: During the 30 years of social and economic turbulence since the 1960s, New Zealand proved to be one of the most stable democracies in the world. Among the most persistent issues was a racial time-bomb which in many other countries had exploded into serious violence.

The 1984-1990 Labour government acknowledged the validity of resurging Maori claims for land, fishing grounds and other assets they insist were taken from them over the years since European settlement. Their claims are based on the Treaty of Waitangi, signed in 1840 by the Queen's representa-

One campaign called "Asia 2000" had multi-million-dollar support from the government and money from private industry to send Kiwi students, business people and journalists to Asia to learn languages and cultural and business practices.

As if to sign off their approval of New Zealand becoming a member of the Asian community, tourists from Singapore, Korea, Taiwan and other nations in the region began flooding in. And trade with Asia, especially in exotic timber products from man-made forests, boomed. This renewable resource was helping to replace timber from native forest as environmentalists won their fight

tives and Maori chiefs, which both Maori and Pakeha agree gave certain guarantees.

The Labour government set up the Waitangi Tribunal to consider specific Maori claims and the tribunal received the same sort of support from the subsequent National government. Many land claims were conceded, particularly where the land was held by the government, and a major fishing concession has been awarded to Maori. An attempt was made to settle all claims with a one-off payment of a billion dollars.

Although there is a consensus among New Zealanders that redress is due, a great deal of tension has prevailed over particular Waitangi claims. Maori make up around 13 percent of the population (about the same as blacks in the US) and they have been vociferous. But both sides have shown common sense and tolerance and no outbreaks of political violence have occurred.

Although every country in the Western world has been affected by the pace of modern change, the transmutation from laid-back weekender to round-the-clock urbanite, from colonial farmer to sharp-edged hustler in the global economy has been extraordinary; and it's important to look at the immediate past to understand it.

New Zealand has had one of the least diverse population mixes of any country colonised during the great expansion of European colonialism in the 18th and 19th centuries. Settlement was predominantly organised and achieved by English and Scots, with some Irish sneaking in through the South Island's West Coast mostly from Australia during the gold rush period, and through Auckland which has always been the most commercial and cosmopolitan of the cities.

The Maori, of course, were here first and they have lately become a more potent political force because they have come to live in the cities. At the end of the 19th century, they were deemed a dying race, and until the end of World War II, they mostly lived in the rural areas. Pakeha New Zealanders were proud to fight alongside them in the last war during which they distinguished themselves with toughness and courage. As fewer workers have been needed in rural industries, Maori have moved into urban areas, adopting other ways of earning a living.

A large immigration of Samoans, Tongans, Cook Islanders and Niueans and Indians from Fiji over the past 30 years has diversified the population mix, and more recently ethnic Chinese have arrived in numbers.

The British connection: But while the population mix is predominantly Maori, English, Scottish and Pacific Island, since the middle of the last century the ambience has been British. Historian Keith Sinclair wrote:

"Ever since the late 19th century New Zealand has commonly been considered the most dutiful of Britain's daughters. It is a reputation which many New Zealanders,

Left, Maori welcomes Asian in the traditional way. **Right**, reminder of the "mother" country.

especially prime ministers intent on making an impression in London, or on securing commercial concessions, have fostered on every oratorical opportunity. Few Canadians, Australians or South Africans have cared to contest the claim ..."

The journalist and novelist David Ballantyne wrote a few years ago: "New Zealand immigration policies through the years have been pretty shrewdly geared to ensuring that the country keeps its low-key image. God's Own country has no need of stirrers. The preference has always been for folk of British stock, meaning working-class and middle-class types from the Old Country – dependable, more likely to fit in than Italians

and suchlike flighty foreigners. Next preference has been for the Dutch, maybe because it was a Dutchman, Abel Tasman, who first sighted New Zealand (in 1642), more likely because the phlegmatic Dutch don't play up..."

In the lazy summer of New Zealand culture (about the middle of the century when the country moved without the slightest lurch into adulthood with the adoption of the Statute of Westminster 1947, which ended its status as a Dominion of Britain) there was more than a touch of xenophobia about Kiwis, who had formulated a set of aspirations and a fair measure of contempt for those of other peoples. One of of the most perceptive essays written about the country and its people, at about that time, came from James A. Michener in the preface of his New Zealand story in the *Return to Paradise* collection. The story, later made into a major Hollywood feature film, was *Until They Sail*, but the essay transfixed the New Zealand of the time with unerring skill and accuracy:

"The typical New Zealander wears grey flannel trousers, an expensive sleeveless sweater, and a trim sports coat. When he dresses up it's in a stiff, high-breasted dark suit with vest, which he never discards, even on sweltering days. He is quiet, modest, eager to defend his honour, and addicted to

Bravest soldiers: Michener said it could be claimed that the bravest soldier in each of the world wars was a New Zealander – Bernard Freyberg in the first, and in the second "a stumpy square-jawed chap" whose "behaviour under fire seems incredible", the only fighting man ever to win the Victoria Cross twice, Charles Upham.

All these factors – the end of extreme isolation, the rupture of trade with Britain and the turn towards Asia, the economic deregulation at a faster rate than in any other Western country – have led to an explosion of modernity. Whereas, in the 1960s, it was difficult to find a restaurant outside a hotel (and only hotel restaurants served wine then),

dreadful jokes. Along with the Spaniard, he is probably the most conservative white man still living. He is most unsentimental, which probably explains why there has been no first-rate art of any kind produced in New Zealand to date. Yet he can become maudlin if you mention the gallant All Blacks, (their) famous Rugby team (all-black jerseys with silver badges). Few Americans appreciate the tremendous sacrifices made by New Zealand in the last two wars. Among the Allies she had the highest percentage of men in arms – much higher than the United States – the greatest percentage overseas, and the largest percentage killed."

there are now hundreds of ethnic restaurants in Auckland, Wellington, Christchurch and many in some of the smaller provincial cities. Wine, once regarded as "plonk" and never drunk regularly with meals, is today a thriving industry. In fact, New Zealand white wines now rank with the world's best and the quality of the reds is improving too.

Social attitudes: Cosmopolitan influences, and the economic infrastructure which has broadened business opportunities, have dramatically re-oriented New Zealanders' social attitudes – not in ways most would consider an improvement. Whereas for 150 years there was a national sense of egalitarianism, a levelling out of income and opportunity in a bid to gain widespread security, there has been a new belief spreading – that to hold its place in the world the country and its people must work harder and compete more fiercely, both on the domestic market and overseas, in a bid to achieve greater economic efficiency. This has changed the society from one in which everyone was considered entitled to a job and a share of the national cake into one in which unemployment is high and in which there is a growing division between the rich and the poor.

With more Maori unemployed, proportionately speaking, than Pakehas, social unrest, which sometimes assumes racial over-

tones, is greater than at any time since the land wars between the two races in the third quarter of the last century. This in turn has brought a new volatility to national politics. The old and narrow division between the two political groupings, neither of them far from the centre, doesn't seem wide enough to contain the national aspirations any more. New parties, however, blooming briefly in the discontent with the two main parties (National and Labour), give way when it

Left, even the Cook Islands – here marking ANZAC day – sent soldiers to war in Europe. **Above**, a more traditional style of warrior.

seems they cannot articulate the confused aspirations of the dissidents.

The dissatisfaction of Kiwis with the rapid change and with the performance of both the recent Labour and present National governments was expressed in a referendum on electoral reform. The country voted in favour of a complicated preferential voting system to replace the first-past-the-post British-style elections that go back to the beginnings of the nation. This new system comes into effect at the next general election in 1996 and is expected to further fragment the structure of political parties.

More like Americans: The cutting of the umbilical cord to Britain, the subsequent broadening of national contacts and the turning towards America despite the anti-nuclear issue have accelerated these cultural changes. New Zealand does seem to sit more comfortably in the Pacific these days, acknowledging its presence among the Polynesian islands, the peoples of Southeast Asia and those with the same roots in European culture, namely Australia and the United States. Both New Zealanders and Australians are becoming perceptibly more like Americans than people of the old Western world in their dress, manner and in a full range of social mores.

If the indications are fulfilled, New Zealanders should make a strong contribution to this Pacific region. Since before the end of last century, when New Zealand-born Ernest Rutherford, a great scientist in the field of nuclear physics, left for Britain, a consistent trickle of people from this small country has gone to Europe and done gifted work for science, medicine and in many other forms of endeavour. They are now tending to stay. New Zealand entertainers and film-makers are attracting attention around the Pacific rim, and in Australia expatriate Kiwis have been steadily emerging as leaders in the media and in business.

Change is always relative and there is much about Kiwi life at home that is still enviable. New Zealand and New Zealanders have been remade but the country remains relatively clean, green and uncluttered and by far the majority still enjoy the outdoor life of beach and barbecue, or tramping and camping, or in that flower and vegetable garden most still have surrounding their suburban homes.

The idea persists that the archetypal Kiwi is a country person – a farmer: dogs at heel, sandpaper hand holding a stick, face burnished by the nor'wester, eyes creased against the hard light of the afternoon as he peers into the hills for sheep to muster. Perhaps this is because of New Zealand's traditional image as a producer of meat, wool, dairy and horticultural commodities for the international market.

In reality, the New Zealander is an urbanite. More than 2 million of the 3.6 million New Zealanders live in or on the perimeter of major cities; there are more people living in the Greater Auckland urban area than in the whole of the South Island. About 90 percent of New Zealanders live in towns of more than 1,000 people; in some rural areas hundreds of families living on their farms may be less than a half-hour away from a city of 50,000.

The majority of the Europeans (given the name Pakehas by the Maori) who began to populate New Zealand, less than 200 years ago, were of British origin. Today, close to 80 percent of New Zealanders are of European origin, overwhelmingly from Britain but also from Holland, Yugoslavia and Germany. Maori make up 13 percent and Pacific Islanders five percent.

Beginning with the Chinese in the last century and followed by Scandinavians, Germans, Dalmatians, Greeks, Italians, Lebanese, refugees from Nazi-occupied Europe and from more recent tragedies in Indo-China, there has been a steady flow of immigrants into New Zealand. Since the beginning of the 1990s, immigration from Hong Kong, Taiwan and Korea has more than doubled and people of Asian origin have become common in the larger cities.

Together, Maori, Pacific Islanders and Pakehas are evolving in New Zealand a culture that is neither wholly Polynesian nor wholly Western, but an exciting amalgam of both – something that is distinctively New Zealand in character.

Preceding pages: an interesting mix at the helm of a nation; Haka party put on a show. Left, southern South Island still has strong Scottish links.

Several years ago in the inner capital city suburb of Newtown a multiracial group of nine-year-olds was showing how much they had learned about Maori culture. Assimo, Irene, Sealli, Sharmily, everybody had a try at talking about such Maori foods as puha, kumara and pipi. Maori action songs were performed, a Samoan boy was elected class chief, an Indian boy gave the best version of an ancient Maori dance. Then two newly arrived Russian girls, knowing nothing of Maori, told Russian fairy stories instead.

Inner-city suburbs such as Newtown and Grey Lynn in Auckland have been cheap places handy for work where immigrants first congregated and gave shape to the society to come. Later some spread around the country and new immigrants took their place. Today there would still not be a more international roll-call than the one in Newtown: Samoan, Niuean, Cook Islander, Greek, Indian, Chinese, Russian, Chilean, Hungarian, Italian, Romanian, Tongan, Dutch, Turkish, Lithuanian, Lebanese, Danish, Malay, as well as Maori and the descendants of the majority British referred to by the Maori as Pakeha.

It was only in the 1980s that New Zealand moved officially from a virtually "white only" immigration policy to one of positive discrimination towards Asian and Pacific migrants. Already this is having an impact on a country that has been more than four-fifths British stock since its inception 150 years years ago. The original inhabitants, the Maori, make up one eighth of the population in the latest census, but such is the impact of the melting pot immigration policy that Maori have expressed concern about the balance between them and new settlers, and have sought more consultation on this policy. The changed policy means that New Zealand will enter the next century with a wide range of different ethnic and cultural values.

Migrations: Pacific Islanders represent the next biggest ethnic grouping in New Zealand, with 4 percent of the population in the recent census. Although there was a dip during the economic downturn of the late 1970s, most of the immigrants have arrived since the 1960s, their numbers jumping from 14,000 in 1961 to 153,000 in 1991. This is surely appropriate when most Pacific Islanders belong to the same Polynesian ethnicity as the Maori and share the same mythical homeland of Hawaiki.

The first great Polynesian migration to this country took place over 1,000 years ago, when Maori began arriving after epic canoe journeys across the Pacific. The second wave of migration is Polynesians from homelands scattered across the Pacific from Tonga in the west to the Cook Islands in the east.

This second migration had its small beginnings when Pacific Islanders were brought to New Zealand for training by missionaries. After World War II the islanders came in to fill labour shortages in New Zealand's industrial expansion. Once settled, they brought in their families, forming links that extend into virtually every village in the Cook Islands, Western Samoa, Niue, the Tokelaus and Tonga.

A special quota arrangement has allowed Western Samoans into New Zealand, and they make up almost half the numbers of Pacific Islanders here. The Cook Islanders, who have New Zealand citizenship, make up a fifth. In the case of Niue and the Tokelaus, more live in New Zealand than on their home islands. Two-thirds of the Pacific Islanders live in Auckland, many congregated in the southern suburb of Otara. Together with its Maori numbers, this makes Auckland the biggest Polynesian settlement in the world. Most of the other Pacific Islanders have settled in the Wellington area, particularly in the Porirua basin.

The Ministry of Pacific Island Affairs is charged with encouraging Pacific Islanders to contribute fully to New Zealand life, and works to close the gap in the areas of education, employment, health and housing. The ministry also helps to transmit cultural values important to the identity of the different island groups. While most Aucklanders would be familiar with the site of huge numbers of Islanders dressed in colourful lavalava skirts playing their version of cricket in local

Left, traditional dances and ethnic costumes survive in local celebrations.

parks, a less obvious growth in the last seven years has been the explosion of Pacific Island language groups. In 1987 there were 14, now there are more than 200. There is a religious emphasis to these language nests, reflecting the Christian intensity of Pacific Island life.

The Samoans: According to a sociology study, as well as being the largest Island group here at almost 70,000, the Samoans have maintained a stronger church and extended family system than the Cook Island Maori. All of Sunday is given over to church attendances, whether Catholic, Presbyterian, Methodist, Congregationalist, Assembly of God, Seventh Day Adventist or Mormon.

with half of Samoa's foreign exchange coming from cash payments from relatives. This led to children not always being supervised and not learning their language, and social problems of young men brawling.

These problems have eased with the improved conditions Samoans have earned for themselves here by the sweat of their brow, and the institution of language schools. An advisory group to the minister of Pacific Island affairs and an employment development trust have also promoted a variety of economic opportunities.

The perceived brawling has been channelled into sporting success. The current Samoan assistant coach and former assistant

Full-throat singing and the language are the emphasis of the church activity.

The matai or chief system has not fared so well, its role tending to be taken over by the churches. One problem of adjustment in New Zealand has been the workplace, which has reversed the traditional Island role by promoting young people and rejecting the older, respected matai. The problem has been compounded by a vigorous work ethic, the man of the house during the day and on any shift work available, the woman at night, often in cleaning jobs. This pays much more than the rent, with tithes to the church and money remitted to the extended family back home,

Auckland coach Bryan Williams was an All Black trailblazer several decades ago. Now it is difficult to find a non-Samoan in the All Black back line, not forgetting the impact New Zealand-based Samoans have had on the explosion of Western Samoa on to the international rugby stage. Now, too, Tongan and Fijian players are regulars in provincial New Zealand teams and some have stepped up to the All Blacks.

Cooks, Tongans and others: Cook Islanders of course come and go between the two countries so frequently, most New Zealanders would not distinguish them from Maori. To see the distinctive language, culture and dance of the 27,000 resident here, you would have to attend Cook Island church services, social gatherings or branch meetings of the Cook Island political party in such places as Otara, Porirua, Napier and Hastings, or Rotorua and Tokoroa, where they work in the forest industry. Of course, the Cook Islanders might well remind you that several of the great migrating canoes came from the Cooks to New Zealand and that Maori is but a dialect of the parent Cooks language.

The distinctiveness of the Tongan community in New Zealand was defined back in the 1950s when Queen Salote founded the Tongan Society in Auckland, to bring people together and organise social functions.

that their island is too small to support them. The almost 10,000 Niueans here retain their language and identity largely within their church congregations.

The situation is even more parlous for the low-lying Tokelaus, which have been almost wiped out by hurricanes several times, and New Zealand has been their sanctuary. The Tokelauans are among the most celebrated storytellers in the Pacific, stories being an excellent means of sustaining morale amidst fragile atoll life. They have brought the storytelling with them. An Auckland anthropologist went to the end of Petone wharf in Wellington to locate Alohio Kave. He took time out from the other outstanding

Tongans have since spread around the country, some even working in Christchurch and Dunedin. The church has been the major meeting point in the dispersal, particularly the Wesleyan, Free Tongan and United churches. Here Tongans have divided where possible into the same village groups as those back home.

Although the United Nations helped nudge New Zealand into giving Niue independence in 1974, the majority of Niueans choose to live in New Zealand. The simple reason is

Left, Cook Island couple. **Above**, Polynesians tend to do the heavy manual work.

Tokelau skill, fishing, to help her record his islands' famous tales, available in the National Library's Turnbull Library.

The largely Melanesian Fijians have been more recent arrivals to New Zealand, initially as seasonal workers without peers for tobacco picking and scrub cutting. Small communities have become established in Auckland and Wellington, doubling to almost 3,000 in the last five years. Fiji Day is when their celebrated dancing is on display.

The positive immigration bias towards Pacific Islanders can also be seen in the doubling of Tongan numbers here in the last five years to more than 18,000. Government projections expect a doubling of the Pacific Islands population in the next 30 years.

The Celtic question: The negative policy of the white Anglo-Saxon society last century even extended to a mostly successful attempt to exclude the very white Catholic Irish for the first generation of settlement — some Irish convicts escaped out of Australia and into Auckland. The policy was swept away by the gold flood, which saw just about every nationality on earth pour into the goldfields of New Zealand for the few years of the great rush in the 1860s. The Irish were prominent, accounting for a quarter of the West Coast in the gold fever years. They brought with them the divisions of Ireland, the 10 percent Orange Protestants clashing with the Catholic majority. A Catholic priest and a New York Irish editor whipped up rebellious West Coast goldfield feelings to such a degree that the state stepped in and convicted them of sedition, jailing them for a month. It was the only such jailing last century in New Zealand, and it took the sting out of the rebels.

Although there have been occasional violent protests centring on Orange and Catholic politics and religion, generally the Irish have been absorbed into the Pakeha mainstream. Their gift of the gab has found its outlet in their traditional occupations as policemen, publicans, bar patrons and politicians. Richard John Seddon first made his voice heard on the West Coast, where the Irish still have a strong presence. He went on late last century to become the country's most pugnacious prime minister. The only serious challenger was Robert Muldoon, of Irish-Liverpudlian extraction, who emerged out of another significantly Irish settlement, Auckland, to become prime minister in the mid-1970s and early 1980s. Pubs became the focus for a strong interest in Irish music.

In the 1990s almost one-quarter of the country of Scottish Presbyterian descent have begun to emerge out of the quiet 100 or so Scottish and Caledonian piping and Highland dancing societies to identify their own Celtic contribution to the New Zealand melting pot. Wellington recently hosted the first Scottish Festival, where pipes and dancers were joined by poets and pontificators upon this wee corner of the Scottish diaspora.

Asian increase: In 1992 the government set up an Ethnic Affairs Service to provide contacts, information and legislative advice for the more than 50 ethnic groups of 155,000 adopted New Zealanders of non-British and non-Pacific Islands origin. This was aimed to cope with the changed positive discrimination policy that sees 20 percent Asian among migrants in recent years compared to 29 percent Pacific Island and a European decline of 10 percent.

Hong Kong contributed the greatest number of new permanent residents, 5,322. These were not refugees as some other Asians have been. Each had to bring in half a million or more dollars, depending on where it was invested. They were the culmination of a decade in which New Zealand saw its largest ever Asian migration. Chinese, including

many from Taiwan, doubled in just five years to almost 38,000. Indians more than doubled in the same period to 27,000, almost the same for the total of other Asian races such as Vietnamese, Cambodians, Japanese, Thais, Malayans and Filipinos.

The Chinese have experienced the biggest swing in policy, from when the first Chinese came in the goldrushes. Those Chinese who did not strike gold and were marooned here were characterised by prime minister Seddon as "undesirable" and legislatively excluded from the old age pension. These single male Chinese lived miserable lives as laundry workers, their gambling and opium dens vigorously raided by the Irish-dominated police force. Those who survived worked their way into market gardening, and in recent times have succeeded in the professions. Their cuisine was always good, and can now be appreciated by *gwailo* (foreigners) on the open days at the spectacular red and gold Chinese Anglican community centre, a stone's throw from the Embassy of China in inner Wellington.

The Indians in recent times have fled from Fiji's political discrimination, although Fiji was always a conduit into this country. Indians began coming from Gujarat province around Bombay from the 1920s, joining the Chinese in similar occupations as market

dred families of mostly Buddhist Sri Lankans who have settled here recently are educational refugees, most of the breadwinners are doctors who could not get work back home.

Jews and other Europeans: The Jews encountered no offical discrimination and Jewish merchants have been among the leading citizens in the main centres. It is probably only in their places of worship that people such as two early and two recent mayors of Auckland would be identified as other than British. In the 1870s Jewish treasurer and later prime minister Sir Julius Vogel borrowed money from London contacts such as the Rothschilds to finance this country's great leap forward, bringing in 100,000 im-

gardeners and fruiterers. The Indians, however, did not maintain the same silence, vigorously objecting to prejudice and shaming the authorities out of thumb-printing proposals. Most are of merchant origins, reflected in their high ownership of small shops in the suburbs. However, the first Indian here was a Sikh, and the Sikh numbers are enough for a small temple outside Hamilton. Many of the majority are Muslim rather than Hindu, and this is reflected in the Islamic Centre built in Auckland. Several hun-

Left, a Thai vendor of rattan. **Above**, celebrating Eastern European origins.

migrants from Europe to develop the country's road and rail. Last century Jews tended to come from Britain, this century from Europe, many simply identified by their country of origin. This led to problems with Jews incarcerated among Nazis here in World War II. Since then synagogues and gravestones have been subject to defacing, but this is sporadic and unrepresentative.

Perhaps the most successful of Vogel's immigrants were the 5,000 mainly Danish but also Norwegians who cut down the forests of the lower North Island and settled such places as Norsewood and Dannevirke. Eventually double that number arrived, settling as quietly into the monoculture as the 1,000 Swiss dairy farmers who were persuaded by Swiss wanderer Felix Hunger to settle the other side of the North Island in the latter half of last century.

The most popular immigrants, however, were the 5,000 Germans who came at the same time as the British and have been coming ever since, except during the two world wars. Once war ended in 1945, New Zealand was recruiting migrants in Austria and Germany. The spick and spartan little white wooden Lutheran churches around New Zealand testify to the tidy presence of these industrious settlers.

The biggest postwar surge was 30,000

instead of 50 fishing boats in the bay. The smells of fresh pasta, tomato, cheese and oregano are no longer restricted to the foreshore homes with backyards piled with nets and crayfish pots.

Also at the end of the 19th century, about 1,000 Dalmatians fled the Austro-Hungarian army and joined British digging for kauri gum in the north. Such was their success, they attracted the resentment of the British and Seddon's condemnation as locusts ravaging British lands. The best gumfields were reserved for the British, but the Dalmatians made up for this with hard work.

When the gum ran out they turned to making wine. Ironically they were lumped in

Dutch, who left the limited opportunities of their crowded country and fitted easily into the boom times here. Not surprisingly perhaps, they favoured the construction industry, many building their own homes soon after arrival. Overnight they introduced a taste among Kiwis for coffee and pastries.

The 3,000 Italians who made their own way here from the end of last century, mostly from the Sorrento and Stromboli areas, took longer to see their cuisine catch on. Many took up their familiar work as fishermen and tomato growers, and the Wellington suburb of Island Bay is still known as Little Italy, although the priest now only gets to bless 10

with the Germans when the World War I broke out and suffered local bully-boy behaviour and prejudice. They persisted, establishing New Zealand's wine industry, initially in the Auckland area. Their names continue to dominate the industry.

The other significant wine label in New Zealand is also an Auckland one, Corbans, but the family is Lebanese, and typical of 5,000 prominent in New Zealand business. A Corban has been a recent local Auckland mayor, though in this an exception to the quiet achievements of the Lebanese.

Greeks, Serbs and Croatians: The Greeks have trickled here in the same chain migrations as the Italians, and mostly stayed where they arrived, in inner Wellington. However, their presence is flamboyantly apparent around the magnificent Greek Orthodox church. Considerations of community have triumphed over those of climate, and Wellington has benefited over the years from some of the more extrovert eating experiences. There may be only several thousand here, but they have made their mark, none more so than Masterton takeaway proprietor George Pantelis, who had the inside of a local church converted into the glories of Greek Orthodox iconography.

The only thing to compare with it is the iconostasis or great carved altar of the Roma-

nian Orthodox church in the Wellington suburb of Berhampore, focus for a small Romanian congregation. A few hundred metres away is one of two Serbian churches in Wellington, while several hills away the Croatian community is gathered around its priest, who himself moved across town to join these political refugees from the former Yugoslavia. Two different Yugoslav clubs once opposed each other across an Auckland street, reflecting different waves of migrants. The older Dalmatians have been here long enough to inspire the local ethnic stories of

Left to right, a rich variety of Pakehas.

Amelia Batistich. Likewise, Yvonne du Fresne has written her Huguenot/Danish stories in the Manawatu, and Renato Amato was a promising Italian Kiwi writer.

Post-war arrivals: A one-off group of 733 war-orphaned Polish children were given sanctuary here in 1944 following the efforts of prime minister Peter Fraser's wife Janet. They settled mostly in Wellington, and more than 5,000 Polish refugees followed. Now a third generation of Polish New Zealanders is taken to the clubrooms where so much of their Catholic Polish culture is expressed, where one visitor was the cardinal who is now Pope. There had been a trickle of refugees from Europe in the 1930s, but these children were the first of successive small waves of refugees.

Post-war refugees included Czechs and Slovaks, and in 1968 several hundred more political refugees followed the crushing of the Prague Spring. The other Soviet satellite invasion, of Hungary in 1956, resulted in 1,000 Hungarians coming here. At least as many Russians have found their way here as piecemeal post-war political refugees, many also Jews. The theatre, restaurant and night-life contributions of these European migrants to the capital in particular is out of all proportion to their numbers.

More than 7,000 Indo-Chinese "boat people", fleeing conflict there from the mid-1970s, have accounted for more than 90 percent of refugees in recent times. Small numbers of Russian Jews, Chileans, East Europeans and Assyrians make up the remainder. The Cambodians, Vietnamese and Laotians have been processed through the Mangere immigration centre and helped into jobs around the country, but the majority have settled in Auckland, suggesting that the capital has ended its days as the migrant clearing house.

Migration has transformed New Zealand's urban areas in the last two decades into places with a fair cosmopolitan diversity of restaurants and delicatessens. Earlier migrants have ensured we have wine to drink with our ethnic meals, while beer hangs on to the declining stakes of the rugby and racing and roast leg of lamb Kiwi tradition. Pavlova is largely a thing of the past, but dragon races are increasingly popular events in Auckland and Wellington. New Zealand is officially bi-cultural, but effectively multicultural.

Forty years ago visitors could have mistaken New Zealand for a European country with native reservations. The cities and towns were overwhelmingly Pakeha in appearance and orientation. The Maori population was confined largely to remote rural settlements and the only contact tourists were likely to have with the indigenous people was in the resort centre Rotorua, where Maori culture was on display.

By the 1990s, all that had changed; Maori had surged into urban areas. Maori faces were as likely to be seen on busy city streets and in the work place as Pakeha ones. Maori were going into business and the professions in small but increasing numbers. Meeting houses were springing up where previously there had been only European dwellings and community facilities.

The features of 20th-century Maori culture are a fusion of both Polynesian and Western ingredients. Maori wear European clothes, the vast majority speak English and many are active members of Christian churches. But those who identify with their Maori background do all these things in a distinctively Maori way. Maori weddings, twenty-first birthday parties, christenings or funeral ceremonies are quite different in character from that of the Pakeha counterpart. They will include speeches in Maori, Maori songs, Maori proverbs, and an openness about expressing feelings – joy, sorrow, anger – that one does not see among New Zealanders of Anglo-Saxon origin.

Maori values, too, pulsate beneath the cloak of Western appearances. Concepts such as tapu (sacredness), its opposite, noa, wairua (things of the spirit) and mana (authority), all persist in modern Maori life. The fact that the country's two major races now live shoulder to shoulder means that non-Maori are having to show more respect than they displayed previously for Maori ritual, and for places that are tapu (sites of sacred objects, historic events or burials) according to Maori beliefs. Maori ceremonials – especially the hui (gathering), the tangi (mourning), and karakia

Left, the late Sir James Henare, noted Maori leader. **Right**, a welcoming smile.

(prayer) – are increasingly honoured by Pakehas. Governments no longer try to impose Western values and institutions on them. Maori are no longer punished in schools for speaking their own language.

The hui offers the most revealing and most moving glimpse of the Maori being Maori. It will usually be held on a marae (a courtyard in front of a meeting house) under the supervision of the tangata whenua or host tribe. Visitors are called on to the marae with a karanga – a long, wailing call that beckons

the living and commemorates the dead. This is performed by women only. Answering the call, the visitors enter the marae led by their own women, who are usually dressed in black. Then follows a pause and a tangi (ritual weeping) for the dead. This is succeeded by the mihi (speeches) of welcome and reply, which will be made by male elders. At the end of each speech the orator's companions get to their feet and join him for a waiata (song), usually a lament. These formalities over, the visitors come forward and hongi (press noses) with the locals and are absorbed into the ranks of tangata whenua for the remainder of the function.

The hui will then be taken up with public and private discussion of matters of local, tribal and national Maori interest, especially land issues (many earlier instances of European seizure of Maori land are currently under official investigation). It will also include community eating, singing and religious services. The participants sleep together in the large meeting house or hall, where further discussion is likely to go on until the early hours of the morning.

Even the food served on such occasions is likely to be different from that which Europeans would serve: meat and vegetables are steamed and cooked in a hangi or earth oven. There will be a preponderance of seafood,

Ngata (1874-1950). The extent and variety of his contributions to Maoridom make him a figure of enormous significance. By the late 1920s, knighted and made Minister of Native Affairs, Ngata had devised legislation to develop Maori land, established a caring school at Rotorua and initiated a work programme for the building of meeting houses and other Maori community facilities.

Working closely with Ngata to implement national policy at a local level was a group of community leaders such as Princess Te Puea Herangi of Waikato (1883–1952). Te Puea was for 40 years the effective force behind the Maori King Movement, which had grown out of the Maori-Pakeha wars of the 1860s.

with delicacies such as shellfish, kina (sea egg), eel and dried shark. Fermented corn is a speciality, as is titi (mutton bird). The bread offered is likely to be rewena (a scone-like loaf) or another variety similar to fried doughnuts. Far more than in Pakeha society, eating together is a ritual means of sharing common concerns and communicating goodwill. Acceptance of such hospitality is as important as being prepared to offer it.

A knight and a princess: If there has been one person more responsible than any other for the survival of Maori culture into modern times, it was the great parliamentarian from the east coast of the North Island, Sir Apirana

She raised the morale of her people, revived their cultural activities, built a model village at Ngaruawahia which became the nerve centre of the King Movement, and established thousands of Waikato Maori back on farm land. She also won a wide degree of Maori and Pakeha acceptance for the institution of the Maori kingship, which had previously been regarded with suspicion outside Waikato. Turangawaewae Marae at Ngaruawahia became and remains a focal point for national Maori gatherings.

Today Te Puea's great-niece, Queen Te Atairangikaahu, keeps the movement alive and commands the direct allegiance of about

100,000 Maori and the respect of the rest.

Further consolidation for the Maori people came with the election of a Labour government towards the end of the Great Depression in the 1930s. Labour's welfare programme did more to lift Maori standards of living than any previous measures and ensured the physical survival of the Maori race. The Maori electorate acknowledged this fact by returning only Labour Members of Parliament from that time.

Maori-Pakeha relations: Following World War II, however, there was a major shift. Previously the majority of Pakehas did not know any Maori personally and had never seen them in indigenous environments. The migrants to the city had had no preparation for the life and many initially floundered. Some youngsters born in the new environment, feeling neither truly Maori nor Pakeha, reacted in a strongly anti-social manner and the Maori crime rate increased.

Over a generation, however, these problems have been dealt with patiently by members of both races. Citizens' advice bureaux and social workers have helped adults with matters such as budgeting and legal difficulties. Legal aid and translation facilities are now available through the courts. The education system has made a concerted effort to promote Maori language and aspects of Maori culture while a Race Relations Office has

decline in rural employment coinciding with a rapid expansion of secondary industry in urban areas brought Maori into the cities in increasing numbers. In 1945, for example, more than 80 percent of Maori still lived in rural settlements. By the 1980s the figure was less than 10 percent. For the first time, Maori and Pakeha New Zealanders had to live alongside one another.

This new relationship brought difficulties. There was a degree of anti-Maori discrimination in some areas of employment. Most

Left, the hongi, formal Maori greeting. **Above**, the war canoe, still in ceremonial use.

been established under the Justice Department to monitor and correct instances of racial discrimination.

The major institution devised to help Maori recover lost ground is the Waitangi Tribunal, established in 1975. This allows Maori to claim compensation – in the form of land, cash or fishing quota – for resources unfairly taken as a consequence of the European colonisation of New Zealand. Based on the 1840 Treaty of Waitangi, the tribunal has done more than any other measure to dissolve lingering Maori grievances over injustices resulting from the British annexation of their country. And it continues to do so.

Names of Tatus

V Shape centre f

Bands on foreh
and temples

Where these
in inside o
the eyelids

ornament on
of Tiwhana,
corner of eye
Pu

ornament ove
between the
Ko

double spiral
upper part f

notching do
nose. Wha

double spirals
nostrils
Pong

pattern over
lip H

Both lips ta
Ngutu pu
Pattern on th
Kau

8 Bands from
to chin patte
RER

stab on the outer
centre of the O

SPIRAL on the upper cheeks
KOWIRI —

lines of above, just under the eyes
KUMEKUME —

lines between Kowiri and f

note 1/8 inch

The classic art of New Zealand Maori is an unsurpassed Pacific tribal art. Many creative styles and much skilled craftsmanship yielded objects of great beauty. To appreciate the achievements of Maori arts and crafts an understanding of the materials used, the techniques of crafts, design and symbolism, and the economic, social and religious requirements that inspired the making of art objects, is invaluable.

Maori visual arts, the arts and crafts, involved the artistic working of wood, stone, bone, fibre, feathers, clay pigments, and other natural materials by skilled craftsmen. Woodcarving was the most important of the crafts. Canoes, storehouses, dwellings, village fortifications, weapons, domestic bowls, and working equipment were made of wood; Maori culture was basically a wood culture.

Maori craft productions were of three distinctive categories: 1) those of communal ownership, such as war canoes made for tribal welfare; 2) intimate things for personal use, such as garments, greenstone ornaments, combs, musical instruments, and indelible skin tattoos. The things used in daily toil, the tools of the carver, lines and fishhooks of the fisherman, gardening tools of the field worker, the snares and spears of a fowler, were possessions usually made by the users and should be included in this category; and 3) the artefacts of ritual magic kept under the guardianship of priests (tohunga) — godsticks, crop gods, and anything else used in ceremonial communication with gods and ancestral spirits. Such things were often elaborate versions of utilitarian objects; an ordinary digging stick in its ritual form was ornately carved.

Periods of Maori art merge, yet there are four distinctive eras with characteristic features: Archaic, Classic, Historic, and Modern. The first is that of the Archaic Maori or moa hunters, the immediate descendants of the Polynesian canoe navigators who first settled New Zealand. For centuries they survived by hunting, fishing, and foraging land

Preceding pages: inside a Waitangi meeting house. **Left**, sketch of a Maori facial tattoo in Hawke's Bay Museum. **Right**, making up.

and sea and are best known from archaeological evidence. Their art work, including carvings and bone and stone work, is characterised by austere forms that, as pure sculpture, can surpass much of the later work.

Craft specialists: In time, the cultivation of the sweet potato (kumara) and other crops, along with an advanced ability to exploit all natural resources of forest and ocean, allowed a settled way of village life. With it there came food surpluses, a tightly organised tribal system, and territorial boundaries.

Craft specialists supported by the community also became established. These people have been called the Classic Maori. They were well described by Captain (then Lieutenant) James Cook, some of whom he met when he landed on New Zealand soil from H.M. barque the ship *Endeavour*, on 9 October 1769. Classic Maori culture was, in the 18th century, in full flower. Life and art seem to have reached their limits of development in the prevailing stone-age conditions. Great war canoes were then the focal point of tribal pride and warfare was an accepted way of life. The making of various weapons of wood, bone and stone with the glorification of fighting men by their tattoos, garments, and ornaments, was considered a matter of prime importance.

The Historic period of Maori art underwent rapid changes due to the adoption of metal tools, Christianity, Western fabrics, newly introduced crop plants, muskets and cannon. After 1800 warfare became particularly horrible as the first tribes to possess muskets descended on traditional enemies still armed with clubs and spears. Palisaded villages (pa) were no longer defendable so they were duly abandoned. The great war canoes also became useless as the gunpowder weapons changed the strategy of battle. Large storehouses were built as the new

The fourth period of Maori art, the Modern, was under way before 1900, and remains with us. The great rise in interest in Maori culture (Maoritanga) in recent decades is in step with a general renaissance of Maori culture inspired by the new social identity and new aspirations of the race. The roots of this Maori art resurgence reach well back into the 19th century, yet it was the early 20th-century leaders, notably Sir Apirana Ngata and Sir Peter Buck (Te Rangi Hiroa) ,who advocated in a practical way the study and renewal of Maori art. The meeting house proved an ideal, practical medium.

Well-dressed warriors: Maori society and the arts have always been intimately associ-

 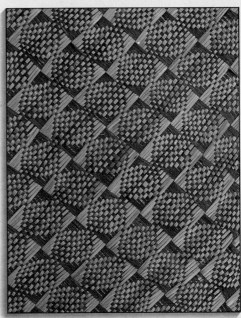

potato crops and the acquisition of foreign goods ushered in a new type of economy. These structures became obsolete as Western-style sheds and barns proved more practical in meeting the needs of changing times.

Fine storehouses (pataka) of this era have been preserved in museums. One, named Puawai-o-te-Arawa (Flower of the Arawa), first erected at Maketu, Bay of Plenty, in 1868, is in the Auckland Museum. The great days of the pataka ended, yet communal meeting houses became increasingly useful during the Historic period. Indeed, they became the focal point of Maori social life and of a Maori art revolution.

ated with aristocratic fighting chiefs who exercised their hereditary rights in controlling tribal affairs. There were always the best dressed, ornamented, and accoutred in the community; tribal prestige (mana) depended on these leaders.

Society as a whole was an autocratic hierarchy. Individuals belonged to extended families (whanau) which in turn clustered to form subtribes (hapu) which were allied as tribes through blood ties. Genealogical trees led back to ancestral canoes (waka), the names

Left, Maori handiwork in close-up: the underside of a treasure box and (**right**) detail of a basket.

of which provided tribal names.

Society was divided into two classes that to a degree overlapped. The upper class was composed of the nobles (ariki) and the generals or chiefs (rangatira). The majority lower class was made up of the commoners (tutua). Outside these classes were the slaves (taurekareka) who held no rights. These unfortunates did menial work and often died as sacrificial victims or to provide food when special events required human flesh.

People dressed according to rank, yet when engaged in daily routine work both high and low classes used any old garments. Men and women wore a waist wrap, plus a shoulder cloak when weather or ceremony required. Everyday dress was simply a waist garment. Pre-pubescent children usually went about naked. On attaining adulthood, it was an indecency to uncover the sexual organs.

The special indication of rank was facial tattoo. Tattooists were well paid in goods and hospitality according to their skill. Men were tattooed over the whole face in painful, deep-grooved cuts made by birdbone chisels dipped in a sooty pigment, which looked blue under the skin. Northern warriors often had additional tattoos over buttocks and thighs. Women were deeply tattooed about lips and chin, but the lips were made blue by the use of comb-type "needles". The remarkable art of the tattooist is best seen on Maori mummified heads in museum collections. Traditionally, the heads of enemies were taken home to be reviled but those of kinsfolk were preserved to be mourned over. Mummification was by a process involving steaming, smoking and oiling, and heads so treated remained intact and retained hair, skin and teeth. Out of respect for Maori feelings such heads are rarely shown as exhibits in museums.

Tattooists and other craft specialists were generally drawn from the higher ranks and were respected priests. Skill in craft work was honoured by chiefs and commoners alike, and even the nobles turned their hands to creative art work. High ranking women enjoyed making fine garments and chiefs often filled in leisure hours with carving chisel in hand, working on a box or some other small item.

Wooden treasure boxes (wakahuia) were made to contain precious items such as greenstone ornaments or feathers. They were portable and were often collected by early visitors to New Zealand. These lidded boxes, designed to be hung from house rafters and possessing a variety of carving styles from many tribal districts, were ornately carved on all sides, especially on the underside as they were very often looked at from below.

The personal possessions of the Maori demonstrate their most exquisite art work. Combs, feathered garments, treasure boxes, cloak pins, greenstone ornaments of several types, including hei-tiki ancestral pendants, and weapons have the "personal touch". A well-appointed warrior was not fully dressed without his weapons: a short club thrust into his belt and a long club held in hand. Weapons were always near, mostly for the practical purpose of defence, as a stealthy, sudden attack on an unsuspecting foe was admired. Weapons were essential in the practice of oratory as they were flourished to stress the points of a speech.

Art for the gods: Religious inspiration in Maori art was based on the prevailing beliefs about gods and ancestral spirits. In pre-Christian times supernatural beings were believed to inhabit natural objects. Rituals and chants were thus necessary to the successful pursuit of any task.

People, hand-made things and natural objects were thought to have an inner psychic force called mana. This key idea is essential to the understanding of Maori art and behaviour. Mana had many shades of meaning, such as prestige, influence, authority, and most significant, psychic power. Mana's presence was manifested in efficiency or effectiveness, such as a warrior's success in a battle or a fishhook's fish-catching ability and increased with success or decreased through improper contact or pollution. If a chief or his possessions were touched by a person of lower rank, then there was pollution and mana was diminished.

The sexes were kept apart in all craft activities. While men worked the hard materials of wood, bone and stone, women followed crafts using soft materials such as flax strips (as in mat and basket plaiting) or they prepared flax fibres used in making garments and decorative taniko borders. It was believed women were created from the earth by Tane. The first man was a direct spiritual creation of the god Tu. Thus it was that women were "noa" – non-sacred – and the male, conversely, a sacred "tapu" being. This attitude put females in a position of subservience which precluded them from the high religious practices and those crafts and activities in which high gods and ancestral spirits were directly involved. Women were not allowed to approach men working at their crafts. This was the law and severe punishment followed any infringement .

The workers with the highest status were the chiefs and the priests; their positions were arrived at only after long apprenticeship with training in religious rites.

Art also had peaceful ends. Wooden stickgods (tiki wananga), bound with sacred cords and dressed in red feathers, were used

into the sea, en route to the ancient homeland of Hawaiki. Burial chests often have a canoe-like form, some even possess a central keel ridge. These magnificent chests, concealed in caves or hidden places, were found in the Auckland districts and many have been preserved in museums.

Monuments and cenotaphs of various forms were erected in memory of the dead. Some were posts with carved tiki while others took the form of canoes buried in the earth deeply enough to stand vertically. Posts were also erected to mark tribal boundaries and to commemorate momentous events.

Maori motifs: Maori art can appear as a disordered jumble. However, an under-

by priests when communicating with gods and ancestral spirits to protect the welfare of the tribe. Stone crop gods (taumata atua) were placed in or near gardens to promote fertility in growing crops.

Remarkable wooden burial chests of tiki form, hollowed out and backed with a slab door, were used to contain the bones of the deceased. Maori burial practice, at least for persons of rank, required an initial burial, then a recovery of the bones a year or two later when final ceremonial burial would take place. The spirit of the deceased was thought to journey to Cape Reinga, at the North Island's northern tip, where it plunged

standing of the small number of symbols and motifs used reveals orderliness. The human form, dominant in most compositions, is generally referred to as a tiki and was first created man of Maori mythology. Tiki represents ancestors and gods in the sculptural arts, and may be carved in wood, bone, or stone. The nephrite (greenstone) hei-tiki is the best known of ornaments. In ceremonial meeting-house architecture, ancestral tiki were carved on panels supporting the rafters or on other parts of the structure. They were highly stylised with large heads to fill in areas of posts or panels. This design arrangement also served to stress the importance of the head in Maori belief. The head was, along with sexual organs, the highly sacred part of the body.

Sexual organs were often carved large in both male and female figures and both penis and vulva were regarded as centres of potent magic in promoting fertility and protection. Small birth figures were placed between the legs or on the bodies of tiki representing descending generations. The bodies of panel figures were often placed in the contorted postures of the war dance. The out-thrust tongue was an expression of defiance and of protective magic.

Local styles of carving differ in many respects. The figures of the east coast Bay of

These bird motifs were superimposed on the basic human form to create a hybrid — a bird-man — and probably came from the belief that the souls of the dead and the gods used birds as spirit vehicles.

The manaia, another major symbol, is a beaked figure rendered in profile with a body that has arms and legs. When it is placed near tiki it appears to bite at them about the head and bodies. Sometimes manaia form part of the tiki themselves and often alternate with tiki on many door lintels. There is a possibility they represent the psychic power of the tiki. In form, it is a bird-man or lizard-man. Lizards made rare appearances in Maori woodcarving and other sculptural arts.

Plenty region are square while those of Taranaki and Auckland districts are sinuous.

The general purpose of the Maori tiki carver was to provide material objects to serve as the vehicles of gods and ancestral spirits. Some post figures are portraits depicting an individual's tattoo, though most are stylisations of beings not of the mortal world. Tiki figures often have slanted, staring eyes, clawed hands with a spur thumb, beaked mouth, and other bird-like features.

Left, the house of Te Rangihaeata on Mana Island, Cook Strait. Above, portrait with gourd and (right) a Maori king (both Lindauer paintings).

Whales (pakake) and whale-like creatures appeared on the slanting facades of storehouses. The head part terminates at the lower end in large interlocking spirals representing the mouth. Some fish, dogs, and other creatures occurred in carvings, but on the whole they are rare; there was no attempt to depict nature in a naturalistic way.

Marakihau, fascinating mermen monsters of the taniwha class, those mythical creatures that lurked in river pools and caves, appeared on panels and as greenstone ornaments. Marakihau were probably ancestral spirits that took to the sea and are depicted on the 19th-century house panels with sinuous bodies terminating in curled tails. Their heads have horns, large round eyes, and tube tongues, and were occasionally depicted sucking in a fish. Marakihau were supposedly able to swallow canoes with their crews.

Painted patterns can be seen on rafter paintings and are based on a curved stalk and bulb motif called a koru. Combinations of koru have infinite possibilities: Air New Zealand uses one as the company logo.

Stone and bone: The tools and materials of the Maori craft work were limited to woods, stone, fibres and shells; metal tools did not exist. The principal tools of woodcarvers, adzes, were made of stone blades lashed to wooden helves. Adzing art was basic to all

older carvings. The later practice of overpainting old carvings with European red paint was unfortunate in that it obliterated much patination and often the older ochres resulting in the loss of much polychrome-painted work of the Historic period.

New Zealand offered a remarkable range of fine-grained rocks for tools, weapons, and ornamental use. The relatively soft yet durable totara and kauri trees, the latter available only in the warm northern parts of the North Islands, were favoured by the carvers. Hardwoods were also abundant. The nephritic jade (pounamu), known today as greenstone, was valued as a sacred material. Found only in the river beds of the Arahura

traditional Maori wood sculpture. Forms were first adzed, then chisels were used to give surface decoration. Greenstone was the most valued blade material. Chisels had either a straight-edged or gourge-type blade which was lashed to a short wooden handle. Stone-pointed rotary drills and various wooden wedges and mallets completed the Maori stone-age tool kit. When Europeans introduced metals, the old tools were cast aside in favour of iron blades with subsequent effects on carving techniques.

The introduction of oil-based paints quickly ousted the old red ochre pigment (kokowai), which can be seen today only in traces on

and Taramakau on the West Coast of South Island, this rare commodity was widely traded. Greenstone is of such a hard texture it cannot be scratched by a steel point. To work it in the days before the diamond cutters of the lapidary was laborious. The worker rubbed away with sandstone cutters to abraid a greenstone piece into the form of a pendant, hei-tiki, weapon or some other object.

Bone was put to use in many ways. Whalebone was especially favoured for weapons while sperm whale teeth made fine ornaments and dog hair decorated weapons and cloaks. The brilliant feathers of New Zealand birds were placed on cloaks in varied patterns. The iridescent paua shell was used as inlay in woodcarving and textile dyes were made from barks. A deep black dye was obtained by soaking fibres in swamp mud.

Flax plants were used by Maori in many ways. Green leaf strips, which served in the quick manufacture of field baskets or platters, could, when scutched, water-soaked, pounded and bleached, produce a strong fibre for making warm garments, cords and ropes. Maori war canoes, houses, and foodstores were assembled using flax cord. Metal nails did not exist and the idea of using pegs as wooden nails, the technique so widely used by Asian craftsmen, was either unknown or unwanted by the Maori artisan.

Most of the actual gatherings were in the large open area (marae) in front of the principal houses.

These large meeting houses were constructed with the aid of steel tools and milled timbers. In due time, corrugated iron roofing was added and Western architectural ideas, combined with Maori concepts of building, proceeded into the 20th century, culminating in the modern community halls. Sometimes the house of a chief would serve as a meeting house though carvings were small and lightly decorated. War canoes and storehouses were of more importance. In the 1900s, highly ornamented meeting houses continued to be the focus of Maori social activities.

Communal meeting houses: Ornate meeting houses (whare whakairo) played a vital role in the 19th century in providing the Maori people places to congregate for social purposes and where the common problems of the tribe could be resolved. The ravages of foreign diseases, destruction and loss of lands, wars with traditional enemies, and the fighting with settlers and the British had placed most of the Maori people in a desperate situation. Meeting houses were built in large numbers and were of an ever-growing size.

Left, Maori carver Keri Wilson working on wood. **Above**, close-up of a woodcarving.

Often, important Maori houses were named after an ancestor and symbolised the actual person; the ridge pole represented the spine, the rafters were his ribs, and the facade boards, which at times terminated in fingers, were his arms. At the gable peak was the face mask. This notion still lives on such that when a tribe member enters a particular house he or she is entering the protective body of the ancestor.

Many communal houses can be visited, a fine example is Tama-te-Kapua at Ohinemutu, Rotorua, built in 1878. While Maori meeting houses are often on private property visitors are welcome with prior permission.

Some of New Zealand's greatest exports have been its artists. Two of the most famous, writer Katherine Mansfield and painter Frances Hodgkins were prophets without honour in their own country. With increased speed of travel and the sophisticated communications of the "information super-highway", local artists have been able to make an international impact while staying at home. Over the past decade New Zealand arts and crafts have begun to carve out their own identity – one with its roots in the South Pacific. A tradition of artistic mimicry has given way to a new Kiwi self-confidence expressed perhaps most strongly in literature, films and theatre. Opera megastar Kiri Te Kanawa, once a more familiar sight in Milan than Masterton, now makes regular trips back to New Zealand to perform. Writers such as Witi Ihimaera, Albert Wendt, Patricia Grace and Keri Hulme are all international figures and "ours".

Geographical isolation has become a "plus" as more artists and musicians feel they can live and work here, yet extend the audience for their work beyond New Zealand shores.

Fine arts: The "Buttocks of a Dead Cow": Some years ago a cynic might have said that light, landscape and sheep have preoccupied New Zealand painters. The same cynic might have placed the visual arts into three categories – representational, abstract and chocolate box.

The locals have not always been receptive to art. In 1963 the Auckland City Gallery director proposed to spend 950 guineas on a Barbara Hepworth sculpture. Several councillors were outraged. "It looks like the buttocks of a dead cow," said councillor Tom Pearce, the most vociferous critic. "I wouldn't give five bob for it," added the mayor. "Art or a cow's hambone?" questioned the newspapers. Letters raged back and forth and there was standing room only at a public meeting to discuss the use of ratepayers' money for this purpose. The piece was eventually bought by an anonymous donor. When

it was unveiled, a record 1,700 people filed past it in four hours. "It needs Brasso on it," was one verdict.

In 1982, the McDougall Gallery in Christchurch planned to spend $10,000 on a painting by Colin McCahon, arguably the country's most significant and contentious painter. Again there was outrage: "It looks like a school somewhere has lost its blackboard," was one comment.

But McCahon (1919–87) has been reified in the last decade. His paintings fetch high

prices and are held in many international collections. He painted in virtual seclusion, used to a high level of incomprehension of his work which embraced the pre- and postmodern, the religious, the abstract and a love of the land. McCahon was never part of any art "ism", but his work and teaching continues to influence generations.

A contemporary of McCahon is Gordon Walters, an artist who investigates the relationship between a deliberately narrow range of forms, mostly the "koru" or fern bud. The interpretation of this local Maori symbol in a European abstract style which has much in common with Klee or Mondrian gives

Preceding pages: a potter's workshop. Left, short-story writer Katherine Mansfield. Right, sculptor Joan Morrell with bust of poet James K. Baxter.

Walters's work a distinctively New Zealand flavour. The visionary, romantic work of Tony Fomison (1939-1990) has a unique power, much of it reflecting his awareness of an identity rooted in the South Pacific. One of New Zealand's enduring and financially successful popular painters is Peter McIntyre. His landscapes are unashamedly representational and cause no irate letters to editors.

With the stock market boom in the 1980s New Zealand fine arts became increasingly seen for their investment potential. Auckland's Aotea Centre has a permanent collection of modern New Zealand art on display and numbers of dealer galleries exhibit the work of upcoming as well as established

women such as Robyn Kahukiwa, Kura te Waru Rewiri and Shona Rapira Davies demonstrate a concern for the land, whanau (family), anti-racism and anti-sexism, and reflect the resurgence of Maori pride and values.

Len Lye (1901–80) may yet be the greatest expatriate new Zealand artist. He won an international reputation as a pioneer of direct film techniques (scratching images directly on to celluloid) and as a kinetic sculptor. His "steel motion" compositions were first exhibited in the auditorium of the Museum of Modern Art in New York; they were small versions of work which he planned to build on a grand scale. Before his death he gave permission for these works to be built post-

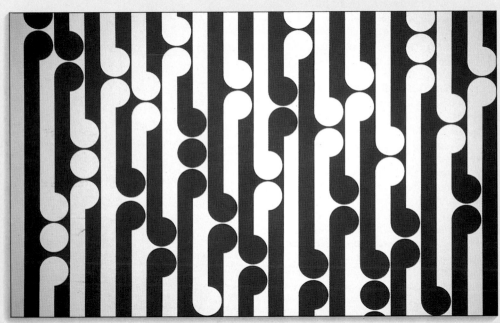

international New Zealand artists such as Sir Toss Woollaston, Gretchen Albrecht, Pat Hanly and Ralph Hotere.

Increasingly, New Zealand visual artists have allied themselves with political causes or movements. During the 1980s artists protested against the worldwide proliferation of nuclear arms. Many used their art to protest the controversial 1981 Springbok rugby tour. The response to events is probably strongest from women artists who paint from a feminist perspective. They include Juliet Batten, Di Ffrench, Carole Shepheard, Jacqueline Fahey, Julia Morrison, Jacqueline Fraser and Fiona Pardington. The works of Maori

humously and several are to be found at the Govett Brewster Gallery in New Plymouth, which specialises in collecting the work of New Zealand sculptors.

Photography has emerged strongly as an artistic medium, nurtured by Photoforum, an organisation which has promoted serious photography for the past 20 years. Brian Brake (died 1988) inspired many younger photographers and published some of his work in National Geographic magazine. Ans Westra's and John Miller's depiction of Maori subjects and events have provided a lasting legacy for historians, as have Robin Morrison's (died 1993) affectionate portrayals of characteristically New Zealand people and places. Glen Jowitt's photography reaches into the South Pacific for its subject matter. More fine arts photographers include Fiona Pardington, Christine Webster and Peter Peryer whose work is popular in the United States and Germany where he has been the subject of a major retrospective.

Prose and poetry: "I made my first story on the banks of the Mataura River after a meal of trout and billy tea: 'Once upon a time there was a bird. One day a hawk came out of the sky and ate the bird. The next day a big bogie came out from behind the hill and ate up the hawk for eating up the bird.' The story's not unusual told by a child of three. As I still

The Piano) brought Frame's autobiography to the screen with her highly successful adaptation, *An Angel at My Table*. Frame, who has led a reclusive life, charts mental and physical landscapes with agility and perception in her books.

Apart from the Frame phenomenon, Maori and Pacific Island post-colonial novelists have arguably had the biggest impact on the New Zealand literary scene over the past decade. Witi Ihimaera, Patricia Grace and Albert Wendt have produced novels and short stories which create new ideas of what it means to be a New Zealander. Keri Hulme achieved worldwide literary status with her Booker Prize-winning novel, *The Bone Peo-*

write stories I'm entitled to study this and judge it the best I've written."

So said novelist Janet Frame in the New Zealand literary magazine, *Landfall*. Her love of writing was nurtured as a child living in a poor South Island family. Born in 1924, Frame has published over 20 novels, four collections of stories, poetry and children's books and three volumes of autobiography – *To the Island*, *An Angel at My Table*, and *The Envoy From Mirror City*. New Zealand-born film director Jane Campion (director of

Left, *Maheno* **by Gordon Walters. Above, poet James K. Baxter. Right, Janet Frame.**

ple in 1985 and continues to write from her Okarito home in the South Island.

New Zealand poets on the whole have been a colourful lot. Perhaps most colourful of all was James K. Baxter, who wrote in his school notebook, "Born June 29th, 1926, will die when he and Nature see fit." Nature saw fit rather prematurely in 1972. Baxter, a fanatical convert to Catholicism, expressed social and religious concerns in his poems. In the latter years of his life he left his family to set up a commune at Jerusalem, a small Maori settlement on the Whanganui River. Here he lived as a self-appointed guru, spurning materialism and churning out verse. He communicated sometimes in doggerel like this to contemporary poet Sam Hunt:

Dear Sam I thank you for your letter
And for the poem too, much better
To look at than the dreary words
I day by day excrete like turds.

Music: "We got through that New Zealand thing – if it's local it must be scungy – we believed that what we had was good and we could take it to the world." Erstwhile Split Enz singer Tim Finn's words, recorded in an interview in the mid-1980s have proved prophetic for many musicians. The remnants of Split Enz became Crowded House and took their music to the world, while still recording here and deliberately seeking a "New Zea-

the New Zealand Symphony Orchestra and regional orchestras in the four main centres and there is a flourishing chamber music and jazz scene. Opera has made a real comeback in New Zealand. World-class productions are regularly staged in the main centres, each of which has its own opera company. Performances by Dame Kiri Te Kanawa, Dame Malvina Major and Sir Donald McIntyre guarantee packed houses.

Experimental music has come from the universities where composers such as Douglas Lilburn, Jack Body, and John Rimmer taught. Avant-garde percussion group From Scratch cross boundaries between music, movement, sculpture and philosophy.

land" sound. The "Dunedin sound" epitomised by bands such as The Chills has become increasingly popular in the US and Europe. Rock bands no longer have to go to Australia, or be considered Australian to make it. New Zealand has the largest number of radio stations per head of population in the world and though many still pump out American pop music, local musicians' chances of air time have increased. Dead Flowers, Headless Chickens, Annie Crummer, Moana and the Moa Hunters, and young "black" rappers such as Upper Hutt Posse produce a distinctly local sound.

Classical music-lovers are well served by

Theatre: Professional theatre is just over 30 years old but you need only to tune into Parliament on radio to discover what an acute sense of drama the New Zealander possesses. Perhaps that is why, despite financial problems, new and ever more innovative theatre groups arise from the ashes.

The playwright to whom New Zealand actors and writers owe a great debt is the late Bruce Mason. He was a one-man theatrical band whose source material was purely local. Mason performed his classic works, *The End of the Golden Weather* (now a feature film) and *The Pohutukawa Tree*, many times in theatres, country halls and schools up and down the land, thus becoming part of the theatrical experience of thousands of young schoolchildren.

Before Mason's death in 1982, fellow-playwright Roger Hall wrote to him: "It has never ceased to amaze me that in a profession so ego-ridden as the theatre is, yours remained not only normal but you had the generosity continually to be supporting, encouraging and stimulating others..."

Hall himself has enjoyed enormous success with his plays *Glide Time*, *Middle Age Spread* (which was performed in London's West End) and *By Degrees* among others. *His Conjugal Rites* has been made into a British television series. Other contempo-

and The Depot in Wellington has become a vehicle for Maori works. Training schools, such as the New Zealand Drama School in Wellington, the Performing Arts School and the university drama course in Auckland, offer courses for "wannabes".

Film: In recent years New Zealand directors have certainly made their mark. Although based in Australia, New Zealanders claim Jane Campion, director of the hugely successful film *The Piano* as their own. *Once Were Warriors* by Maori director Lee Tamahori, featuring an all-Maori cast, enjoyed box office success and several awards.

The feature film industry has enjoyed considerable success since the late 1970s, start-

rary New Zealand classics include Greg McGee's *Foreskin's Lament*, Stuart Hoar's *Squatter* and Renee's *Wednesday to Come*.

Because it is hard for actors and writers to sustain a full-time living in the theatre, many move between plays, films and television work. Some of the most vibrant theatre happens outside the mainstream as young actors take their works into the local streets and schools. The Watershed Theatre in Auckland is known for innovative productions

Left, rock singer and fomer leader of the group *Split Enz*, now *Crowded House*, Tim Finn. Above, scene from one of Roger Hall's plays.

ing with Roger Donaldson's *Sleeping Dogs*, which starred international film and television actor, Sam Neill. The industry received a considerable boost from the New Zealand Film Commission and many local smash hits have followed. They include Geoff Murphy's *Goodbye Pork Pie*, Roger Donaldson's *Smash Palace*, the animated feature *Footrot Flats – The Dog's Tale* (from Murray Ball's popular cartoon strip) and Vincent Ward's *Vigil*, *The Navigator* and *Map of the Human Heart*. New Zealand films are now regular award-winners at international festivals such as Cannes. The last decade has also seen the rise of a new generation of female film makers such as Merata Mita, Gaylene Preston, Alison McLean and of course Jane Campion. Another film phenomenon is Peter Jackson with his comic "splatter" films *Bad Taste* and *Brain Dead*.

A corps of highly skilled technical crews has grown up, particularly based around Auckland. Many international co-productions are shot in New Zealand these days, taking advantage of expertise, cheap costs and beautiful locations.

Dance: With the popularity of music videos and aerobics, dancing in New Zealand has definitely become "uncissy". The backbone of dance, however, is still ballet and each week thousands of little girls and boys duti-

world and continually tour their companies in New Zealand.

Pottery: An outsider might conclude that half the nation was up to its elbows in clay. Pottery began after World War II with a stream of immigrants from Britain and Europe who brought old-world craft traditions with them. With its rich clays and do-it-yourself ethic, New Zealand was ripe for potting. During the 1950s and 1960s potteries sprang up in town and country. The beauty and relative isolation of areas like Nelson and the Coromandel Peninsula suited the alternative lifestyle that pottery offered. Barry Brickell in Coromandel, Harry and May Davis of Crewenna and the Lairds of Waimea

fully plod through their pirouettes and pliés and dream of a place at the New Zealand School of Dance or the Royal New Zealand Ballet both based in Wellington.

The Royal New Zealand Ballet Company faces the dilemma of maintaining the delicate balance between commercial survival and artistic relevance. The survival of contemporary dance is precarious too. For many years Mary-Jane O'Reilly's Limbs dance company showed New Zealanders a different way of dance. Limbs has been succeeded by Douglas Wright and Michael Parminter, two local contemporary dancers and choreographers who work in many parts of the

Potteries (both in Nelson) were responsible for training and galvanising many contemporary potters. Helen Mason on the east coast inspired a generation of young Maoris. Len Castle of Auckland, with his emphasis on simple forms and "clay for clay's sake", was one of the first full-time potters. Queen Elizabeth II owns a Len Castle pot.

By the late 1970s pottery began to shrug off its solid, earthy image. Potters began to experiment with colour, form and firing methods such as raku, saggar and pit firing. Names such as Jeanne and Andrew Van der Putten and Warren Tippett have since moved into finer clays and more delicate and decorative shapes more reflective of the post-modern 1990s.

Weaving and glass: In a nation of so many sheep, it's hardly surprising that spinning, weaving and the fibre arts are very high on the craft profile. Many weavers are moving into spectacular "art" tapestries, some of them multi-dimensional. There has also been a revival of the traditional Maori art of flax weaving led by weavers such as Rangimarie Hetet and Diggeress Te Kanawa and Emily Schuster. Others have created Maori-inspired works which are highly contemporary.

A number of craftspeople, both Maori and Pakeha, now carve wood, bone and the traditional greenstone (pounamu) to create their

panels into buildings. They also realise the designs of established artists such as Nigel Brown, Pat Hanly and Ralph Hotere.

Architecture: New Zealand is a laboratory for the student of architecture who, with care, can observe every style from Renaissance, Gothic, Victorian and Bauhaus to "*nouveau* concrete".

While the glass towers of Auckland, the Aotea Centre and the new casino site are rather dubious tributes to the work of late 20th-century architects, Wellington's cityscape is probably the best example of the work of contemporary architects. Architect Ian Athfield, whose distinctive style amounts to a one-man revolution, has been instru-

own uniquely Pacific designs or imitate traditional Maori ones. The Te Taumata Gallery and Fingers jewellery co-operative, both located in Auckland, display examples of this distinctive style of jewellery.

Glass-blowing and stained-glass work have reached high levels of sophistication. The works of individual glass artists such as Ann Robinson and Gary Nash fetch high prices and are in much demand world-wide. Stained-glass artists Ben Hanly and Suzanne Johnson work directly with architects to incorporate

Left, potter Len Castle. **Above**, one of Lindauer's paintings in the Auckland City Art Gallery.

mental in erecting or rebuilding some of the capital's more spectacular buildings. His new public library adjoins the Michael Fowler Centre (designed by Miles Warren) and the new Wellington City Art Gallery to provide a unified and flowing cultural "heart" to the city. The new Museum of New Zealand – Te Papa Tongarewa – reflects the influence of design which has its roots in Pacific culture.

Local manufacturers are finally recognising the importance in competitive global markets of good design and packaging, and the "Made in New Zealand" label is rapidly becoming the signal of unique and high-quality products.

The climbers clambered over a huge boulder and plunged into dense scrub again. Just as it was getting dark, buried in bushes on a high moraine, they found a rock bivvy – a dank cave with sloping bumpy floor. For two hours a wet-wood fire was coaxed to cook a meagre meal, then sleep came slowly. As they retreated next morning a brief clearing cruelly revealed their abandoned goal – high above cloud the col's snow crescent curved into the unclimbed ridge of the mountain.

Mountaineering is perhaps this country's most famous outdoor sport and with memories of Edmund Hillary's achievement in being the first to climb the world's highest mountain, this is not surprising. A New Zealander could equal the toughness of a Sherpa because of the sort of trip evoked above. New Zealand mountaineers have few huts and have become accustomed to living high up in rock and snow caves and in tents. Since their weather comes from a wild western sea, sun changing to savage storm with fearsome speed, they are often thwarted in their goals but are swift to succeed on fine days. The rock is mainly loose and treacherous, and fast-moving glaciers and icefalls are split by crevasses and swept by avalanches. Such tough training has been a foundation for success on Himalayan heights.

Among the highest peaks there are some climbing huts, and a guiding service, but here too the ice is active, the rock loose, and the weather fickle. The story is told of two climbers who were nearing the summit of Mount Cook, New Zealand's highest, when a storm broke out without warning. For two weeks they had to huddle in a hole hollowed in the wall of a crevasse, unable to descend safely in the winds which howled outside.

In winter, the mountains are a playground for skiers as well as climbers. At commercial and club fields, in North Island and South, there are facilities familiar to skiers in Europe and North America, with restaurants etc on site. Some club fields, however, have a distinctive New Zealand style. Long ropes on pulleys, driven by converted tractor engines, pull people up ungroomed slopes. Club huts are lively social centres for members ranging in age from seven to 70. Some fields can be reached only by walking an hour or more, with skis and food on one's back or shoulder. Devotees declare these fields are friendlier, and break fewer bones, than those where you can step from car to ski.

Ski-mountaineering can be more rugged still. Even in areas with huts, food, fuel and sleeping gear have to be taken in, and elsewhere tents are also necessary. This is hard work on foot on skis, but the rewards are considerable – scintillating descents through criss-crossed crevasses and eerie ice cliffs, with high peaks crowding the sky. And in the central alps, and from some commercial ski fields, helicopters and ski planes provide easier access to mountain skiing. Mountain winters also service skaters as small lakes freeze to form natural rinks.

Tramping: Winter and summer mountain valleys and passes are the domain of trampers and bushwalkers and trips vary greatly in difficulty. All European walkers, however, should be aware that, while there are no poisonous snakes or spiders, the distances, facilities and rescue resources are all rather different to what they might be used to back home. A proposed national walkway from one end of the country to the other, with comfortable huts easy distances apart, is in an early stage of development, concentrating on areas close to urban centres. National and Forest Parks provide tracks and huts spanning a middle range. Wilderness areas are being preserved, with neither huts nor tracks, and humans venture into untamed nature dependent on their own wits and resources.

A trans-alpine crossing in the South Island is the most dramatic tramp. From the east, in the rain shadow of the ranges, the mountains are approached through wide and spacious shingle and tussock valleys. Once over the Main Divide, however, the track drops suddenly into deep-cut gorges and dense forests. Sombre and mysterious in the rain, in sunlight these forests dance with shifting shades of green and yellow, and are always alive with the songs and swift movements of birds. The trekker is immersed in the realm of

Preceding pages: Outward Bound in the Marlborough Sounds. **Left**, Kiwis like a challenge.

Outdoor Adventures 113

beneficent Tane, the Maori god of forests.

Having evolved in isolation, many of Tane's plants and birds are unique to New Zealand and are the central attraction for other groups of forest visitors. Patient birdwatchers drift silently through, sensitive to complex interactions of species, and active, along with many others, in attempts to preserve native forests from further felling for timber. Prior to European settlement there were no browsing animals, but now thar, chamois, wild pigs and goats can all be found in New Zealand's forests and mountains.

Dangling in chasms: From New Zealand's mountains swift rivers race down rapids and carve deep gorges – ideal for river running.

Queenstown, which is also the main centre for New Zealand's own invention, now gone worldwide: bungee-jumping, usually done from river gorge suspension bridges. These days you can bungee-jump from a helicopter if you so wish.

Fishing is the other major river and lake activity. In past days eels and native fish were an important source of Maori food, harvested with a variety of nets and traps. Europeans brought brown and rainbow trout in the 19th century, stocking rivers and lakes. They acclimatised well, and frequently trout of 3 kg (7 lbs) or more are caught with rod and fly. During the season salmon run in many rivers too. Fishermen on Lake Taupo

Expert canoeists shoot arrow-like through wild water, and rubber-dinghy enthusiasts crash down a turmoil of rocks and white waves. Commercial rafting companies are now making some of these thrills available to a wider range of people.

Another sort of craft, a New Zealand invention, carries people up these rivers. The jet-boat is driven by a pump which sucks water in and shoots it astern in a deflectable plume. It is highly manoeuvrable and needs only a few centimetres of water when planning at speed, making it ideal for shallow or rocky rivers, and rapids. White-water rafting and jet-boating is most developed around

enjoy a 90 percent chance of catching a fish.

Sailing is the premier sea sport. Every weekend, and in the leisurely evening light of summer, thousands waft out with the wind particularly in the Hauraki Gulf off Auckland (one in four Auckland households supposedly own a boat). Some sail small centreboard boats on estuaries or harbours; the keels of others cleave deeper waters out from the coast. Some sail for fun, others compete in fierce-fought races which have thrown up an astonishing number of international winners. The island climate's wayward weather, changing rapidly from calm to chaos, adds a distinctive and dangerous New Zealand note.

Power-boats are also popular for family recreation and picnics, and for racing. Water-skiers and wind-surfers have multiplied in recent years and some of the more popular stretches of water are close to becoming overcrowded. Board-surfing is also gaining in popularity.

As the prevailing weather is westerly, the Tasman Sea has the biggest swells. East-coast waves are generally smaller, but the funnelling effect of bays and points gives good breaks at select spots. The surf doesn't match that of the world's main surfing centres; New Zealanders can only envy Bali's perfect tubes or Hawaii's walls of water.

In earlier times the sea was more than a

recreation area. For traditional Maori society it was the realm of Tangoroa, god of the sea, and the vital source of *kai moana* (seafood). To this day it retains much of its cultural and spiritual significance for Maori, and some of its economic importance too – Maori predominate amongst those who fish and gather shellfish for food in a non-commercial way. For them and for others, however, sea-fishing is also recreational. From wharves and sea walls and boats young and old hopefully hang hooks, others drag nets through rich

<u>Left</u>, yacht race in Auckland Harbour. <u>Above</u>, big ones that didn't get away in the Bay of Islands.

waters of estuaries, or fare out to sea to battle with deep-water fish.

Some go further. Snorkelling and scuba-diving are popular. Though much coastal water is murky there are some superb diving areas. At the Poor Knights Islands, north of Auckland, cliffs plunge sheer beneath the sea for hundreds of metres. And in the fiords of south Westland the water is opaque on the surface but very clear below. A rewarding sight is a black coral, normally only found far down, but growing here at moderate depths.

Sky High: Going up rather than under, New Zealanders take to the air for recreation as well. The most dramatic powered flights lift people from airstrip to mountain in moments – rock cliffs and teetering ice outcrops seemingly at the wingtip. Gliders, and even hang-gliders, fly among mountains too, whispering by valley walls and along ridges. Indeed, gliding is another New Zealand speciality. Many ranges rear at right-angles to strong northwest winds, creating towering wind waves which have lifted New Zealand glider pilots to world records.

New Zealanders enjoy outdoor living in more relaxed ways. Camping is almost a national way of life during summer holidays. The densest concentration are in well-appointed camping grounds at popular beaches, rivers and lakes. Often groups of families return again and again to the same place, creating for two weeks each year a canvas community possibly more stable and significant to them than that of their shifting urban lives. Others seek more secluded spots, assisted by New Zealand law which retains river beds and lake and sea-shores in public ownership. On occasions storms and floods assail these tent dwellers though most people endure this cheerfully as an inevitable part of the contrast they seek to their normal lifestyle. In good weather they revel in freedom and informality.

Family camping holidays and tramping trips introduce many New Zealanders to outdoor life at an impressionable age, allowing them to grow up with the ability to gain deep pleasure from simple and relatively inexpensive pursuits. They take for granted, perhaps, the ease with which they can do so. Sometimes it takes an overseas visitor, who is used to dense populations, crowded beaches and polluted rivers, to remind them of their good fortune.

New Zealand grew to prosperity on the sheep's back, exporting its meat and wool. Lately, farmers have fallen off the animal's back. They've had to find new ways to trade in the world's markets. It's been a hard ride.

The old visitor's observation that there are far more sheep in New Zealand than people is still true. But it is less true than it used to be. At last count, New Zealand's sheep population was 52.5 million, down from a high of 75 million. The reason for the decline is simple – the world does not want sheep-meat as much as it used to, and the old market in Britain has long since ceased to regard New Zealand as its farmyard.

The changes in New Zealand farming have been dramatic. On one side, the country has seen a toll of declining land values, farmers selling up when they can't make bank loan repayments and workers being made redundant as their meat-processing plants close down, in a seemingly endless toll.

On the positive side, there have been success stories as farmers explore new products and markets, "discoveries" that crops or animals once thought hopelessly exotic for New Zealand can prosper here, and strange shifts such as the slaughtering of most New Zealand sheep in accord with Muslim techniques to meet the demands of new markets.

Since the refrigerated vessel *Dunedin* sailed for Britain in 1882 loaded with 4,908 frozen sheep carcasses, meat exports have been New Zealand's mainstay, along with wool.

Through shaky times since then, meat and wool have been the country's prime international commodities. Sheep farms are spread throughout the country; in the North Island in the Waikato, Poverty Bay, Hawke's Bay and Manawatu; and in the South Island in Marlborough, Canterbury and Southland. They are the best areas – with help from the tonnes of fertilisers farmers apply.

Sheep-farming is essentially a simple business. It's all about converting grass into meat and wool, via a docile and easily managed animal. But the quest for improved effi-

ciency and productivity has made it a sophisticated game. Breeds have been developed to suit different climates, topography and markets. New Zealand farmers are unsurpassed in their ability to farm on a scale seen in few other countries, using techniques sometimes more akin to the assembly line than the tranquil image of the shepherd and his flock. Flocks of 2,000 are common. Many farmers have geared themselves with computers to keep stock of everything from fertiliser rates to cycles for artificial insemination of cattle.

Gentlemen's business: Large-scale wool-growing got off the ground in the 1850s. It was in the hands of gentlemen from England who became the closest race to the country's aristocracy. They moved in, claimed their massive chunks of land, cleared them and set out the sheep. The first centre was in the Wairarapa, a fertile valley in gentle hill country north of Wellington, the capital. Land could be bought or leased for peppercorn prices, and wool prices, errant though they were through booms and busts, could amass tidy family fortunes.

Sheep-farming soon spread to Marborough in the South Island and south to the plains

Preceding pages, a few of the 50 million sheep. **Left**, logging skills in competition. **Right**, the fastest shearers complete 300–350 sheep a day.

and hill country of Canterbury. The "runs" were vast, many covering thousands of acres. The most famous run-holder was Samuel Butler, author of *Erewhon*. In 1860 he came to New Zealand and took up a sheep run called Mesopotamia in the foothills of Canterbury's Southern Alps.

Rough and ready Australians soon got in on the South Island's sheep boom. The sheep themselves had come from Australia. Many were merinos, a tough breed with fine wool and stringy meat, perfectly suited for grazing the rocky, tussock-covered slopes of the high country runs. To help them out, run-holders regularly set fire to the hillsides, encouraging new growth of tender and edible young

outnumbered all other breeds combined. Its wool was strong and coarse. And so, from an innovation brought about for better meat, developed another of New Zealand's industries – the growing of coarse wool for carpet-making. It became a major export.

Hard times: Visitors to New Zealand often wonder why their aircraft is sprayed with aerosols when they arrive. The reason is simple. New Zealand relies so heavily on its farming for export dollars that disease is guarded against with near-neurotic urgency. A disease which threatened the country's farm stocks or horticulture could debilitate exports. The perils are as diverse as foot-and-mouth disease to the Californian fruit

tussock. Hence was born a still huge problem in New Zealand's hill country – erosion.

The coming of the frozen meat export industry changed everything and solved a big problem. On one side of the world, New Zealand's sheep grew wool in abundance but their meat was next to worthless. There was no market for it. On the other side of the world, a city-living industrial population was hungry for protein. Refrigerated shipping was an idea whose time had come.

New breeds of sheep were developed, with better meat than the merino. The classic breed was the Romney – solid, hardy and a great producer of fat lambs. By the 1920s it

fly. Quarantine regulations are among the strictest in the world.

But even the best quarantine standards can't keep more insidious international developments at bay. And two of them have hit farming harder than anything else in its history in the last generation. They were Britain's entry into the European Community and the trend away from red meats in many Western markets. Both hit New Zealand in the early 1970s, and the effects are still being dealt with. The industry has hard a hard time coming to grips with them.

Britain, in a traditional agreement between the "Home Country" and its erstwhile colony, had always been the prime market for New Zealand's lamb and mutton. When it threw in its lot with Europe, access to the market became limited and trade became subject to quotas and tougher regulations. Politically, the problem was a much tougher one than the feat, a century before, of working out how to ship meat around the world. New Zealand had to find new markets. It has, in places such as Japan, Iran, Korea and – before there were payment problems – Russia.

The Middle East demands lambs slaughtered according to Muslim religious practices, so most meat plants have set up halal killing chains which face towards Mecca. Muslim slaughtermen recite a prayer over

each lamb before the killing. The companies' attitude is: "If it gets a sale, we'll do it."

Then there's what the economists call the downturn in the world red meat market. The traditional roast is not so popular in these cholesterol-conscious days. Chicken, pork and fast foods are what the world wants.

More aggressive marketing of New Zealand's meat has tried to counter the trend since the 1970s. The aim now is not so much to get carcases across the world but prime

Left, prize stock at the Hereford Conference. **Above**, young farmer in the making at the Arrowtown Autumn Festival.

cuts on to supermarket shelves and restaurant menus. The industry has tried to give the consumers what they want: oriental-style slices for Japan and Korea, kebabs for Greece, tidy boneless packages for North America.

At the same time, totally new products have arisen to fill new markets. Where once farmland was a seamless web, now smaller but more intensive horticultural blocks have sprouted. Flowers are flown fresh each day to Tokyo. Deer antler are harvested for "velvet", regarded as an aphrodisiac in Taiwan and Korea. Kiwifruit, that furry vine fruit once know as the Chinese gooseberry, was a short-lived boom, until world markets became flooded with competing "kiwis" from countries such as Chile and Italy.

Increasingly politics not products determine the fate of New Zealand's farmers. In the mid-1980s New Zealand's government deregulated farming along with all other sectors of the economy. All subsidies were removed, as were tariffs that protected New Zealand producers from competition from abroad. Provisions that protected the privileged place of New Zealand farmers, such as cut-rate interest loans, went by the board.

The response was abrupt and critical. Farmers' returns dropped, land values plummeted and many faced a debt crisis. Farmers understandably complained that while they had had their props removed, they were still competing with subsidised producers in Europe and North America.

To level the playing field, New Zealand put enormous diplomatic effort in the latest round of talks on GATT, the General Agreement on Trade and Tariffs. The aim was to secure free world trade for agriculture, a dismantling of the quotas and other trade barriers faced by farmers when they export to other countries. The result was an almost unqualified success. The benefits could add millions to the country's export receipts. But they will be a long time coming.

New Zealand's farmers, with generations of free-enterprise individualism behind them, are now working in an environment where that is the reality, not the myth. Some have decided that the business of turning grass into wool just isn't worth the effort any more. They have either sold up, or moved into distinctly new product lines. So today, perhaps there is a boutique winery where once the woolshed stood.

When it comes to sport, there's nothing that appeals to New Zealanders more than the volatile mixture of skill, running, and occasional violence involved in rugby union and rugby league.

The rugbies: Union has been the game of choice for New Zealanders for more than 100 years. It began at public schools in England, evolving from the brutal bullying described in *Tom Brown's Schooldays* to the blood and thunder of modern internationals.

Just why it took such a hold in New Zealand is hard to pinpoint, although the mateships of the game probably appealed, while men hacking a living from the bush might have found the physical rough and tumble of rugby light relief from their day-to-day work.

Rugby also offers a place for all shapes and sizes, from minute halfbacks built like soccer star Diego Maradona, to giant forwards, who would not be out of place as linebackers in American football.

The rules are complicated, and get more so every year, but at its best even the uninitiated can find the game thrilling. Because the players do not wear padding they move faster, and hit each other harder, than American football players. The best runners are almost balletic in their grace; the toughest players are as fierce as prize-fighters.

For atmosphere the best rugby matches are internationals, usually played in New Zealand at any time between June and September. Club and provincial rugby starts earlier, in April, and does not finish until the middle of October.

Worth checking out too are Ranfurly Shield matches, provincial games on a challenge basis at the holder's home ground, played late in the season. The games between the leading teams see normally stolid New Zealanders painting their faces, waving team flags, wearing team scarves, and screaming team chants and names. But don't fear for your safety. New Zealand has never seen the sort of crowd violence that blights British

Preceding pages: the New Zealand All Blacks and the French lock heads. **Left**, a winning combination in the making, perhaps.

soccer, even on jammed terraces where up to 15,000 people stand shoulder to shoulder.

New Zealand's best ground is Eden Park, in Auckland, where 47,000 people can be guaranteed of a numbered, reserved, seat. There is a catch. For test matches they could probably sell 100,000 seats, so there is always a huge shortfall in tickets for sale.

There are no large-scale ticket touts or scalpers in New Zealand, but scan the small ads section of the local newspapers, try last minute buying outside the ground on the afternoon of the test, or, at a last resort, try the hotel of the visiting international team and ask any large man in a tracksuit if he has tickets to sell. Touring sides are always allocated tickets, and usually sell them at the team hotel to add to team funds.

At the other end of the country, in Dunedin, is the second-best ground for rugby, Carisbrook. For a start there is a free view from the railway track that runs above the ground, and the terraces in Dunedin, a student city, contain the liveliest spectators in the country. If your taste runs to beer with your football, next door to Carisbrook is a huge tent city, where beer and lumps of smoked and barbecued meat are for sale. It's not subtle, vegans would faint, but it'll sustain you through the coldest southern day.

Lancaster Park in Christchurch is relatively charmless, although the spectators are famous for being noisily one-eyed, to a level that's almost an entertainment in itself. Athletic Park in Wellington is a dump, but plans for a new stadium near the railway yards have been approved, and by the end of the 1990s there should be a sparkling new stadium ready to go.

If there are no test matches on during a winter visit to New Zealand, consider watching a club match. On most club grounds there are clubrooms, and a newcomer showing mild interest will usually be welcomed in for a drink. League's headquarters used to be at Carlaw Park, a ramshackle, downtown ground in Auckland. But from 1995 New Zealand has a team in the Australian club competition, which is run from Sydney. The Auckland Warriors will play every second game at home. Their games will be at Mt

Smart stadium, a large natural amphitheatre that could hold almost 40,000 people. That's the good news. The bad news is that it's in southern Auckland, and probably the most difficult to find of all the major sports grounds in the entire country. But don't be put off. The level of skills will be extremely high, so grab a taxi.

Cricket: The ambience of a football game can also be found at one-day cricket internationals, played, mainly, at the same grounds that they play test rugby.

Unless you're a cricket buff, test matches, played over five days, often without a result, are a mystery. Both teams wear a white strip, the players aren't numbered or named, and

and runs to 6pm, grows less genteel as more beer is swilled, and the sun beats on open terraces. Sometimes the commentators are witty, more often they're just scatologicial, and naked streakers, both male and female, are hauled away by police from most of the games. A Munich beer hall in a Southern Hemisphere summer is the best way to explain what to expect.

Golf: This is a huge sport in New Zealand, with an estimated 200,000 members of clubs, plus half as many again who enjoy a hack round the public courses, which offer golf at a price unheard of in most of the world. It has been suggested, not in jest, that it would be cheaper for a golfer to fly from Tokyo to

just why the fanatics politely clap when a ball is blocked is something anyone who doesn't love the game could never understand.

But one-day cricket, perfected for Australian television, strips away the subtleties. What is left is a contest in which men like New Zealand's Danny Morrison, or Pakistan's Wasim Akram, hurl down a hard, leather-coated ball at speeds approaching 160 kmp (100 mph) at batsmen, who must hit it as hard as possible as often as possible. The teams play in coloured uniforms, with the players' names across their backs.

There is nothing genteel about the spectacle, and the day, which begins at about 11am,

Auckland or Christchurch, and play golf there, than to stay in Japan and join a club.

The main tournaments for spectators are in early summer, usually in December, and while even the biggest events don't usually drag in the superstars of the world circuit, occasionally a Hale Irwin will pause between US Open triumphs for a tournament at Auckland's Titirangi course, and just before his career sky-rocketed on the American PGA tour, Nick Price was winning in New Zealand. The true golf buff can play spot-the- emerging-star, and do it at close range. Compared with most major American tournaments, New Zealand crowds are relatively small, and you can check out a new hero's backswing at close range.

On the waterfront: Two of the best chances to see New Zealanders at play en masse both occur in Auckland. On the last Monday of every January the Auckland Anniversary regatta for yachts is held, with more than 1,000 entries making it the biggest one-day yachting event in the world. Auckland harbour is an attractive, safe, yachting nursery, and has been the training ground for Olympic gold-medal winners, round the world Whitbread race winners, and some determined challengers for the America's Cup.

On Auckland Anniversary day the harbour is almost covered in yachts, from little

Bays run, the biggest fun-run in the world. It started in a modest way in 1974 with a couple of thousand people running from the Town Hall to St Heliers, and has now become one of the biggest gatherings of New Zealanders, only matched on the occasion of visits from the Pope and David Bowie.

Walk the course, or jog it, and nobody will object if you have no official entry form. If you do make it round the waterfront to St Heliers, take the time to wander among the dozens of tents set up near the finish line. The people around you will be in a fiesta mood, cooking food and sharing ice-cold drinks. They will be sweaty, but you will never see New Zealanders looking happier in a crowd.

boys and girls in one-person P-class yachts to the majestic A-class keelers, many of them previously raced in deep water classics. The whole magnificent sight can probably best be viewed from Mt Victoria on North Head in the suburb of Devonport, or from ferry boats that cruise from the terminal in downtown Auckland.

On a Saturday in early March the waterfront drive in Auckland is covered for 11 km (7 miles) by more than 70,000 runners, joggers and shufflers in the annual Round-the-

Once marathons drew huge entries as well, but their appeal has dwindled with the onset of triathlons, where contestants swim, bike and then run. The triathlon was invented in Hawaii, where the water section is comfortable, but the biking and running near enough to a glimpse of Hell on earth. In most triathlons the swimming is bone-chilling, but the rest much easier to handle. The biggest triathlon of the year, an iron-man event where the winners take over seven hours, covers some of the Round-the-Bays course, and can be viewed in later summer, usually in March.

Left, parapenting, a new challenge for the daring. **Above**, skiers going up at Mount Hutt.

Team sports: Along with rugby, league and one-day cricket, the most exciting team spec tator sport in New Zealand is netball, the major sport for women.

Netball is similar to basketball, but players cannot bounce the ball on the court, and there are no backboards for the nets. Most netball is played outside, but for the best games, test matches (usually in June and July) and the club and provincial championships (in September), indoor courts are used. The skill level is high, and tests against New Zealand's greatest traditional rivals, Australia, thrill to the bone, with high speed, see-saw scoring.

Basketball here revolves around a national league, played through the winter. American imports, the men just below the standard

needed for NBA play, have raised the level of local players, and in some venues, most notably Christchurch, Nelson and New Plymouth, capacity crowds are common, with the sort of raucous, homemade support and cheering sections you'd find at smaller American high-school games.

The other winter sports involving major international competition are soccer and field hockey. Hockey had a moment of true glory in 1976 when the national men's team won a gold medal at the Montreal Olympics. But the sport has never really captured the imagination of the New Zealand public. Even for tests involving sides as highly rated interna-

tionally as the Australians, the Germans or the Indians, there will always be plenty of room for spectators.

Soccer jumped in public esteem in 1982, when the national sides, the All Whites, went to the World Cup in Spain. At that time almost 40,000 people were cheering New Zealand on at Mt Smart during their qualifying matches. But the sport was never able to build on those golden moments, and today languishes in the huge shadows cast by rugby and league.

Olympic champions: Rowing has enjoyed its share of international success over the years, with Olympic and world champions from New Zealand. The national championships are held late in February, with Lake Karapiro, near Hamilton, and Lake Ruataniwha, in the South Island's Mackenzie Basin, offering the best spectacle.

Motorsport in New Zealand roughly divides into track racing, in summer, and rallying, in winter. In recent years a leg of the world rally championship has been held in New Zealand, starting and finishing from Auckland, with special sections in the city, where the crowds can get near enough to sniff the exhaust fumes. The biggest track racing is in January, including the New Zealand Grand Prix, which, it should be pointed out, is not part of the world championship, or even raced to Formula One regulations.

Boxing has a small following, with New Zealand's limited population making it difficult to offer purses large enough for the world's best to fight here. If there is a noteworthy bout it is rare enough to earn huge media attention. You won't miss it.

At the time of writing legal gambling in New Zealand on sporting events was being fiercely debated. In the meantime the alternatives are private wagers, credit card bets with Australian bookies, or betting on horses.

There are no legal bookmakers in New Zealand, but government betting shops, known as the TAB (Totaliser Agency Board) are located in even the smallest towns. Horse racing, both gallops and trotting, goes right through the year, and all daily papers carry a special racing section. You should never have to go to the races uninformed.

Left, **Maori competitor in the Commonwealth Games**. **Right**, **Hawkeye, the world's largest rugby mascot**.

In retrospect, the 1950s in New Zealand were halcyon years. Dreamy years of gentle growth, full employment and no inflation. Times when the "Godzone" tag seemed appropriate and the less spiritual description of the national religion as being "rugby, racing and beer" seemed pretty accurate too.

There *were* occasional worries. Would the All Black tourists in the United Kingdom avenge that infamous disallowed try against Wales? Should Rising Fast be disqualified from racing? Would the budget see the price of beer go up again? Would this new-fangled rock 'n' roll music corrupt our children? Overall we coped well with such problems.

Four decades down the track, after Vietnam, oil shocks, the rise and fall of the Soviet Empire, unemployment, deflation, recession and yet another All Black coaching drama, the Unholy Trinity of rugby, racing and beer (RR&B) have weathered otherwise dramatic changes remarkably well.

Horse racing is the middle member of the Unholy Trinity; a sport which should have begun to dwindle and wither when cars drove the horse from the roads; a cash-intensive sport (and industry) which, though it survived the Great Depression, has to fend off intensifying competition for those leisure dollars, of the stay-at-home television syndrome and, most tellingly, of its loss of the country's gambling monopoly.

Betting problems: Racing *has* felt the shock waves of all those changes. The establishment and entrenchment of the huge gambling game Lotto and the legalisation of gaming machines have bitten deeply into betting (the chief source of the industry's income). From a peak of $1,040 million in 1989 (with Lotto still a fledgling rival), total on-and off-course bets on horse racing (including a modest share for greyhound racing) bottomed out at $902 million four years later before beginning a gradual rise again.

The economic effects were felt in the breeding industry too. Foal crop numbers actually (for the first time since the Great Depression of the 1930s) fell each year from 1989 until again appearing to bottom out in 1993–94.

Left, someone who knows the form.

This was parallelled by sales figures at the breeding industry's annual showcase, the National Thoroughbred Yearling Sales at Karaka, just south of Auckland.

New Zealand racing is a resilient beast. And New Zealand near the end of the 20th century remains, as it was in the 19th century, a remarkably racing-mad country.

Courses for horses: Despite centralisation and retrenchment, this remote little nation of three and a half million people still has more race-courses per capita than any other country excluding its huge neighbour Australia. Fifty-seven to be precise (hosting 82 clubs), compared with 59 in the United Kingdom, birthplace of thoroughbred racing and a country with some 15 times the population.

Again on a per capita basis, New Zealand's foal crop remains the biggest in the world: 5,163 in the 1994 trough against 5,319 in Britain, 3,756 in France and 17,000 (remember we're talking per capita) in neighbouring Australia.

In New Zealand, harness racing (trotting) thrives alongside the thoroughbred sport, with 60-plus clubs racing on 34 tracks. The annual crop of standard-bred foals (the light-harness breed) is not much smaller than its thoroughbred counterpart.

The horses: Australia has known the value and merit of horses bred in its small neighbouring dominion for well over a century. Carbine, perhaps the first universally acknowledged Australian turf champion, was bred and did his early racing in New Zealand before sweeping all before him in Australia, climaxed by his wonderful victory under the still record weight of 10 stone 5 pounds in the 1890 Melbourne Cup.

New Zealand-bred too were Phar Lap, 40 years later, and Tulloch, in the 1950s; the other two whom most Australians would have agreed were true champions. Unsurprisingly, Australians have always been prominent on the buyer's bench at New Zealand yearling sales.

Difficulties of travel, and of acclimatisation, made it harder to establish the relative merits of the southern-bred in the Northern Hemisphere. Over many years very few bothered to try, though Carbine, after a brief but outstanding stud career in Australia, went to England and founded a triple Derby-winning dynasty there; and Phar Lap made that one ill-fated foray to North American to win the Agua Caliente Handicap in Mexico before his tragic death.

Americans sporadically bought New Zealand yearlings, and sometimes our already proven racehorses, in the two decades following World War II. Cadiz and Daryl's Joy were two to show the flag in the United States with notable success.

But it wasn't until the mid-1970s that a tough and classy "colonial-bred" named Balmerino set off on a remarkable world odyssey. Europe's richest and most prestig-

with considerable success. But flat racing is the Grand Prix circuit of the thoroughbred world and the Japan Cup became a target for New Zealand and Australian trainers from the early 1980s.

Success came in 1989 when the grey New Zealand mare Horlicks beat the high-class international field in world-record time. There was no longer doubt that New Zealand-breds – and Australian-breds, as Better Loosen Up showed in the same race a year or two later – were competitive in the world arena.

Reasons for success: The gambling dollar has always been essential to racing's survival, but gambling fervour alone does not provide a satisfactory explanation.

ious race race for three-year-olds and upwards, the Prix de l'Arc de Triomphe in France, was *Balmerino*'s target. He finished an unlucky second to the high-class European three-year-old Alleged, meeting him at an age and weight disadvantage, but his campaign was a resounding success.

Between April and October that year, 1977, Balmerino raced and won in New Zealand, Australia, the United States, England and Italy – and almost won the most important race in France!

The tougher and more rugged New Zealand-breds have continued to infiltrate the European (and American) jumping scene

Kiwis do love to bet, but their per-head betting figures are four times lower than, for example, neighbouring New South Wales. And Asian gamblers in Hong Kong, Singapore-Malaysia, Japan and tiny Macau make even the free-spending Australians seem penny-pinching punters by comparison.

New Zealand's soil and climate, so ideal for intensive stock-raising, goes some way to explaining the quality of New Zealand-bred thoroughbreds. The country's temperate climate, large tracts of limestone country and plentiful pasture have provided an ideal thoroughbred nursery.

The home-bred racehorse tends to be

sound-legged, strong of bone and constitution and virtually free, through isolation, of the more devastating equine diseases.

The relatively huge prize money available for juveniles has led to a concentration of precocity and early speed, giving breeders in New Zealand (where the racing of two-year-olds is pursued less vigorously) an advantage when it comes to the distance races for older horses.

Nevertheless, the disproportionately high success rate of New Zealand-bred horses in Australia's Group (top-tier) races across the board suggests that it is really their early advantage in their place of birth and rearing which counts.

All of which might explain the strength of New Zealand's thoroughbred breeding industry (it would survive if it was only a nursery for Australian racing) but does little to explain why little New Zealand can itself sustain so many race-courses. Here the reasons probably lie in the history and character of the country itself.

When the last wave of British Empire expansionism washed immigrants on to the shores of distant New Zealand, both new settlers and the indigenous Maori people

Left, every major town has its own race-course. **Above**, trotting is particularly popular.

took to the sport of racing with enthusiasm.

Virtually every new settlement soon had a race-course pegged out on the outskirts; by the end of the 19th century, when the first official New Zealand Stud Book was produced, most courses were properly levelled and railed, with grandstands of varying size. Some clubs and courses had already vanished, through economic reasons, before that century's end.

In 1884, for example, during the Otago goldrush days, there were 46 clubs racing "south of the Aitaki River", the recognised boundary between North Otago and South Canterbury. A century later there were 14.

More clubs, though only a relative handful, went out of existence in the 1930s Depression and some race-courses were closed, or became training tracks only, in moves toward centralisation from the 1960s on. Yet to the visitor the impression remains that every township of any size boasts a neatly railed race-course on its outskirts.

In pioneering days, the local race-course was an important community facility. Not only did it host one of the highlights of the community's year, the race meeting; the catering and liquor-dispensing facilities in the stands were often the venue for weddings, dances and other events. Not infrequently, the green sward also provided sports facilities such as rugby and soccer grounds.

Therefore, when the centralisers wanted to close down courses, local communities were losing more than just a race meeting and were prepared to resist to the last ditch.

As the social and economic impacts of the late 1980s began to affect the racing industry, it was the city tracks (at Ellerslie and Avondale in Auckland, Te Rapa in Hamilton, Trentham in Wellington and Riccarton in Christchurch) which most felt the steady dwindling of on-course attendances.

At country and provincial courses, overall, race-days seem as brisk as ever, and as eagerly attended by the local community. The same applies for representative rugby matches. And at both recreations, the consumption of a few ales continues to be part of the fun.

So overseas visitors today, as they would have 40 or 50 years ago, will still gain the impression that New Zealanders have a curious love affair, bordering at times on the obsessive, with rugby, racing and beer.

Antarctica is the coldest, windiest and most remote continent on Planet Earth, an environment utterly inimical to people. It has teased our curiosity for centuries and its short history is peopled by heroes. It was the last challenge explorers overcame before they turned their attention to the stars.

Those who have been there report awesome encounters with the raw forces of the weather, but also times of ineffable, luminous peace and beauty. Technological advances have made Antarctic visits for tourists possible and many have gone there in the summer months, but every now and then the southern continent extracts its revenge for the invasion.

"Nelson would be able to step off his column into a boat..."

But there are oases in Antarctica: the "dry valleys" – opposite Ross Island near McMurdo Sound – as well as other ice-free areas, and some "hot-lakes" beneath the ice-cap. These oases are under intense study by scientists.

In search of a continent: The exploration of Antarctica has close associations with New Zealand. The existence of a great southern continent had been mooted for hundreds of

Antarctica, which is generally accessed from Christchurch, is the last great wilderness, with close to 90 percent of the world's ice sprawling over an area larger than the United States, and packed up to an average height of 2,000 metres (6,550 feet). If the ice melted the continent would be about three-quarters of its present size and much less mountainous than now. In addition, the rest of the world would have a problem – sea level would rise. As one writer has put it:

years before the Dutch explorer, Abel Tasman, was sent from Java in the Dutch East Indies to find if there was a sea passage eastwards across the southern ocean to South America. When Tasman arrived off the west coast of New Zealand in 1643 he believed it might be the western edge of a continent that stretched across to South America. Accordingly he called it Staten Landt, the then name for South America. A year later, when it was decided there was no huge nation across the South Pacific, the name was changed to Zeelandia Nova.

The next European visitor to New Zealand, Captain James Cook, also showed an interest in a possible southern land mass. In one of the most daring voyages ever made, Cook sailed along 60 degrees latitude and then penetrated as far as 71 degrees 10 minutes south without sighting the legendary continent. He stayed south so long, his crew was on the verge of mutiny.

The first known sighting came 50 years later when the Russian navigator von Bellinghausen sailed completely round the world between 60 and 65 degrees south, dipping to 69 degrees on two occasions, thus becoming the first man to see land inside the Antarctic Circle.

In 1840 James Clark Ross discovered that area of Antarctica south of New Zealand

New Zealanders took part in the explorations by Englishmen Robert Falcon Scott and Ernest Shackleton between 1900 and 1917, and Australian Sir Douglas Mawson during the years before World War I. Scott and all the men in his party which drove overland for the South Pole, died on their return journey, having learned on their arrival at the Pole that the Norwegians under Amundsen had beaten them to it.

In 1923, the unwelcoming territory south of latitude 60 degrees south and between longitudes 160 degrees east and 150 degrees west was claimed by the British government and placed under the administration of the Governor-General of New Zealand and

which has been within the country's sphere of interest throughout this century. In fact, it is believed that the first person to step ashore on Antarctica was New Zealander Alexander von Tunzelmann, the 17-year-old nephew of a pioneer settler and explorer of Central Otago, at Cape Adare, in January 1895. Exploration on the land began soon afterwards and, although New Zealand showed no enthusiasm for mounting its own expeditions,

Preceding pages: Another time, another place in Antarctica, the southern continent. Left, Scott's expedition began from the *Discovery*. Above, unchanging polar transport.

named as the "Ross Dependency".

Between 1929 and 1931 a British-Australian-New Zealand Antarctic-Research Expedition focused interest on the continent, as did the exploration from the air by the United States Navy under Admiral Byrd. In 1933 the New Zealand Antarctic Society was formed, but it was not for another 15 years that the first New Zealand onshore base was established, near Cape Adare.

The New Zealand base was first set up during the International Geophysical Year in 1957 when Everest conqueror Sir Edmund Hillary led a group of five fellow countrymen on an overland dash by tractor to the

South Pole. He was to have acted solely as a support for Britain's transpolar expedition led by Sir Vyvian Fuchs, laying down supply bases on the New Zealand side of Antarctica for Fuchs to use as he made the journey from the Pole across to the side below New Zealand. Hillary and his small group made such progress and got so far ahead of schedule that they decided to push for the Pole themselves, becoming the first to make it overland since Scott 45 years before.

Since 1958, parties from New Zealand have wintered over, exploring and trapping huge areas, intensively researching the geology of the region. New Zealand has always operated in close association in the Antarctic

with the United States Navy which has its own base at McMurdo Sound. In 1964, when a fire destroyed most of the equipment at the combined NZ–US base at Cape Hallett, New Zealand erected a new base of her own (named Scott Base after Captain Scott), at McMurdo Sound.

Care of resources: Five years earlier, the Antarctic Treaty designed to "ensure the use of Antarctica for peaceful purposes only and the continuance of international harmony" had been signed by 12 nations – New Zealand, the United States, Australia, Britain, Belgium, Chile, France, Japan, Norway, South Africa, Russia and Argentina. Poland

also became a signatory in 1977. All these Antarctic Treaty signatories have signed a convention since 1980 for the protection and proper exploitation of Antarctic marine living resources. This culminated in a Convention on the Regulation of Antarctic Mineral Resource Activities (CRAMRA) in Wellington in 1988. But the final fate of this Convention was placed in doubt the following year when France and Australia – both claimant nations to Antarctica – announced they would not ratify it. They want the area to become a wilderness park instead.

The economic exploitation of Antarctica began with the hunting of whales and seals in the sub-Antarctic islands and surrounding seas south of the Pacific Ocean at the close of the 18th century. The stocks were so depleted that there is little prospect of them ever recovering. However, Russian and Japanese scientists are investigating the krill, which are plentiful in the Antarctic waters and could become a major protein resource.

There has been much discussion also about mineral resources on the Antarctic mainland and it is thought probable that mineral-bearing rocks of the sort prevalent in Australia and South Africa are common. It is known that there are huge deposits of sub-bituminous coal and large deposits of low-grade iron ore. The CRAMRA agreement was an attempt to impose the strictest rules on any possible exploitation activities. This response has now combined with growing environmental awareness to put pressure on the Treaty partners to consider some total protection regime.

Tourism interest in Antarctica remains strong with visitors attracted by the eerie majesty of the scenery. For many years, the Mount Erebus aviation disaster at the end of the 1970s discouraged commercial airlines from making sightseeing flights, especially when a subsequent inquiry revealed some distinctive dangers if pilots were not used to the Antarctic environment.

However, there is renewed enthusiasm for flights over the great ice cap. Access is still extremely difficult and likely to stay that way for many years. If it becomes easier, protection of this special place may have to include stringent controls on tourism.

Left, the icy wastelands of central Antarctica. **Right**, tell-tale signs of the Antarctic experience.

People aside – albeit friendly people worth knowing – it's places in New Zealand that nudge your sense of wonder, that make you take a quick breath with a sense that "Here and only here can I experience this." Milford Track with the Sound at its end, the pristine silver dazzle of the Southern Lakes, the bush-wrapped solitude of Lake Waikaremoana, the boiling surprises of the thermal regions... they all have pulled superlatives from the mouths of even the most-travelled visitors.

Authors Rudyard Kipling, Anthony Trollope and Robert Louis Stevenson paid tribute to the loveliness of the landscape. James A. Michener wrote in *Return to Paradise* in 1951 that "New Zealand is probably the most beautiful place on earth" with "natural beauty difficult to believe". Thirty years later, in a magazine article entitled "The Memoirs of a Pacific Traveller", he listed Milford Sound as "The Most Stirring Sight" in the world.

The Maori story of the creation reveals that land and human being are one, flesh and clay from the same source material. Maori emotional attachment to place is profound.

The first Europeans, 20,000 km from the tailored communities of Europe they still called home, tried at first to remake the face of the countryside into a Britain look-alike. They cut and burned the forest and sowed grass. But when they had the leisure to look around, they realised that packed into their small new country was a whole world of diverse and dramatic scenery.

The first place to attract world attention was Lake Rotomahana, with what were known as the Pink and White Terraces along her shore. The terraces were formed from silica deposits as water from boiling pools washed down the steep shore of the lake. Tourists could bathe in the cooler pools: "It is a spot," wrote Trollope, "for intense sensual enjoyment." The terraces were all brutally destroyed one night in 1886 when nearby Mount Tawawera exploded.

The spas and hot pools of the North Island earned an early reputation for their curative powers. In 1901, the government hired an official balneologist and formed a tourist department, the first government-sponsored tourism promotion organisation in the world.

The thermal regions today still draw enormous attention from travellers. But nowadays – in a world packed with ever-increasing numbers of people in dense and clogged cities – it is mainly the unsullied, uncluttered landscape, the sense of space and timelessness, that attracts thousands of visitors who just like to ogle the scenery, and an ever increasing number who want to walk in the wilderness. For them a tramp through New Zealand's outposts of scenic beauty becomes a sort of purification rite.

Preceding pages: skiplanes take tourists on to the glacier at Mount Cook; pastures and peaks in perspective; a sea of sheep in the hills; the South Island's memorable Milford Sound. Left, on the road near Queenstown.

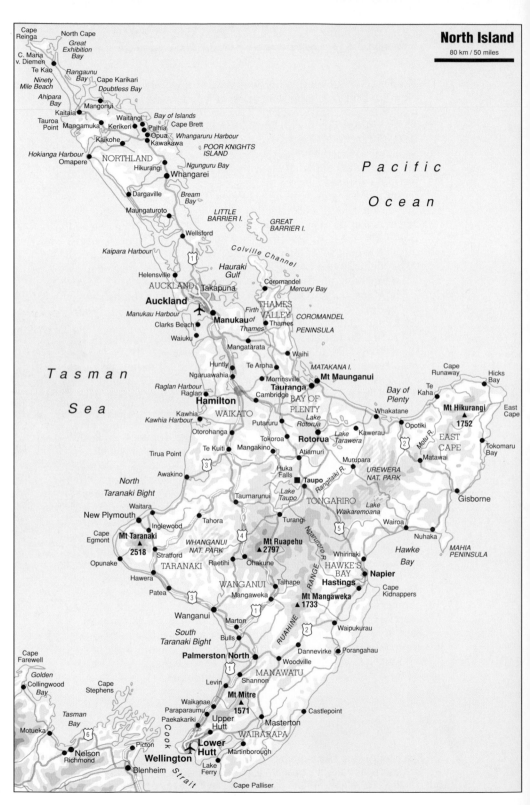

North Island

80 km / 50 miles

Cape Reinga
North Cape
Great Exhibition Bay
C. Maria v. Diemen
Te Kao
Rangaunu Bay
Cape Karikari
Ninety Mile Beach
Doubtless Bay
Ahipara Bay
Mangonui
Kaitaia
Waitangi
Bay of Islands
Tauroa Point
Mangamuka
Kerikeri
Paihia
Cape Brett
Opua
Kaikohe
Kawakawa
Whangaruru Harbour
Hokianga Harbour
Omapere
NORTHLAND
POOR KNIGHTS ISLAND
Hikurangi
Ngunguru Bay
Whangarei

Pacific

Ocean

Dargaville
Bream Bay
Maungaturoto
LITTLE BARRIER I.
GREAT BARRIER I.
Wellsford
Kaipara Harbour
Colville Channel
Helensville
Hauraki Gulf
Coromandel
Mercury Bay
AUCKLAND
Takapuna
Auckland
THAMES VALLEY
Manukau Harbour
Firth of Thames
COROMANDEL
Clarks Beach
Manukau
Thames
PENINSULA
Waiuku
Mangatarata
Waihi
Huntly
Te Aroha
MATAKANA I.
Cape Runaway
Ngaruawahia
Morrinsville
Tauranga
Hicks Bay
Raglan Harbour
Mt Maunganui
Te Kaha
Raglan
Cambridge
BAY OF PLENTY
Bay of Plenty
Hamilton
WAIKATO
Mt Hikurangi
Kawhia
Whakatane
1752
Kawhia Harbour
Putaruru
Lake Rotorua
Kawerau
Opotiki
EAST CAPE
Otorohanga
Tokoroa
Rotorua
Lake Tarawera
East Cape
Te Kuiti
Mangakino
Atiamuri
Matawai
Tokomaru Bay
Tirua Point
Murupara
UREWERA NAT. PARK
Awakino
Huka Falls
Taupo
Gisborne
North Taranaki Bight
Taumarunui
Lake Taupo
TONGARIRO
Lake Waikaremoana
Waitara
Turangi
Wairoa
New Plymouth
Inglewood
Tahora
Nuhaka
Cape Egmont
Mt Taranaki
Whirinaki
Hawke Bay
MAHIA PENINSULA
2518
Stratford
WHANGANUI NAT. PARK
Mt Ruapehu
RANGE
Opunake
TARANAKI
Raetihi
Ohakune
2797
HAWKE'S BAY
Napier
Hawera
WANGANUI
Taihape
Hastings
Patea
Mangaweka
RUAHINE
Mt Mangaweka
Cape Kidnappers
1733
Wanganui
Marton
Waipukurau
South Taranaki Bight
Bulls
MANAWATU
Dannevirke
Porangahau
Cape Farewell
Palmerston North
Woodville
Golden Bay
Collingwood
Cape Stephens
Levin
Shannon
WAIRARAPA
Tasman Bay
Waikanae
Mt Mitre
Castlepoint
Motueka
Paraparaumu
1571
Paekakariki
Masterton
Upper Hutt
Nelson
Picton
Cook Strait
Lower Hutt
Richmond
Wellington
Martinborough
Blenheim
Lake Ferry
Strait
Cape Palliser

Tasman

Sea

South Island

80 km / 50 miles

Cook Strait

FAREWELL SPIT

D'URVILLE ISLAND

Cape Farewell

Golden Bay

Collingwood

Tasman Bay

Picton

Motueka

Blenheim

Nelson

Richmond

Ward

TASMAN MTS

Karamea

Matupika

Karamea Bight

Kawatiri Junction

NELSON BAYS

Owen River

St Arnaud

MARLBOROUGH

Awatere River

KAIKOURA RANGES

Kaikoura

Westport

Mt Travers
▲
2338

Reefton

Springs Junction

Hanmer Springs

Waiau R.

Cheviot

PAPAROA NATIONAL PARK

Barrytown

Runanga

Ngahere

Culverden

Greymouth

Mt Longfellow
▲
1898

Waipara

Kumara Junction

Hokitika

Otira

Rangiora

Kaiapoi

Pegasus Bay

Ross

WEST COAST

Mt Murchison
▲
2400

Oxford

Christchurch

BANKS PEN.

Mt Whitcombe
2644 ▲

Springfield

CANTERBURY

Little River

Akaroa

Harihari

Mt Hutt

Leeston

Lake Ellesmere

Franz Josef Glacier

Rangitata

Ashburton

Cantorbury Bight

Fox Glacier

Mt Cook
▲
3754

Mayfield

Bruce Bay

Mt Cook (Hermitage)

Tasman Glacier

Lake Tekapo

Fairlie

Temuka

Lake Pukaki

Timaru

Haast

Twizel

Lake Benmore

Waimate

Wainono Lagoon

Jackson Bay

Makaroa

Omarama

Waitaki R.

Mt Aspiring
3027 ▲

Lake Wanaka

Kurow

Oamaru

Awarua Point

MT. ASPIRING NATIONAL PARK

3265
▲

Wanaka

Tarras

Ranfurly

Milford Sound

CLUTHA CENTRAL

Cromwell

Hyde

Milford Sound

Arrowtown

Queenstown

Alexandra

OTAGO

Palmerston

George Sound

Lake Wakatipu

Blueskin Bay

Caswell Sound

Kingston

Roxburgh

Clarks Junction

Mosgiel

Lake Te Anau

Mt Lyall
1905 ▲

1968
▲

Mataura R.

Clutha R.

Taieri R.

Dunedin

Pacific Ocean

SECRETARY ISLAND

Te Anau

Moss-burn

Edievale

Doubtful Sound

FIORDLAND

Manapouri

Lumsden

Oreti R.

Balclutha

Molyneux Bay

RESOLUTION ISLAND

FIORDLAND NATIONAL PARK

Gore

Clinton

Dusky Sound

Winton

SOUTHLAND

Edendale

Owaka

Tuatapere

Te Waewae Bay

Riverton

Invercargill

Tokanui

Chalky Inlet

Bluff

Foveaux Strait

T a s m a n

S e a

Halfmoon Bay

Paterson Inlet

Mason Bay

STEWART ISLAND

Southwest Cape

AUCKLAND: CITY OF SAILS

To Aucklanders it is the "City of Sails" or the "Queen City", the biggest and brightest metropolis in New Zealand; and in the summer evenings and at weekends throughout the year, the sails are there, bobbing along the waterways on which the city is built.

Some immodest residents may claim "New Zealand ends at the Bombay Hills", about 40 km (25 miles) south of the city. While this statement is made tongue-in-cheek, it effectively summarises the sentiments of many of the million inhabitants – more people than in the whole of the South Island – that everything they need can be found within the boundaries of the Auckland region. For such smug souls, the rest of the country does not exist.

To underprivileged Kiwis living in New Zealand's wop-wops (provincial backcountry), and especially those in the capital city of Wellington, Auckland is "The Big Smoke" and "Sin City", where people are preoccupied with the three b's: beaches, boats and barbecues. The allegation contains more than an element of truth, but who can blame Aucklanders? They happen to be blessed with two beautiful harbours, scores of safe swimming beaches, a coastline dotted with secluded offshore islands, sophisticated city living and a summer climate that insists on outdoor life.

Water, water everywhere: This agreeable, aquatic lifestyle has largely been decreed by the city's geographical situation within the Hauraki Gulf. Apart from slender necks of land to the west and south, Auckland is surrounded by water and the natives love it. They paddle in it, swim in it, surf on it, sail on it, ski on it, dive in it and fish in it.

The city is bounded by the Waitemata Harbour in the north and east, by the Manukau Harbour to the south and west. Just outside Waitemata Harbour, Hauraki Gulf is one of the most favoured sailing playgrounds anywhere.

Within one hour's drive of the city centre there are 102 mainland beaches and, while these beaches may appear to be sparsely populated to most overseas visitors, Auckland's "boat people" can seek solitude in the hundreds of sandy bays nestled in 23 offshore islands in the gulf. To celebrate this natural, marine playground, Auckland has the greatest number of pleasure boats per capita of any coastal city in the world. A conservative estimate puts the total number of yachts, launches and power-boats at around 70,000; one for every four homes in the Greater Auckland area.

Fittingly, the sporting highlight of the year is the Auckland Anniversary Day Regatta, held annually towards the end of January, in which up to 1,000 sailboats ranging from two-metre yachts to 30-metre keelers compete on the Waitemata Harbour.

Equally spectacular is the "Round-the-Bays" run held annually in March in which up to 80,000 joggers (one in 12 Aucklanders) have "run for fun" over a 10.5-km (6.5-mile) course from Victoria Park along the waterfront to St Heliers Bay. The *Guinness Book of Records*

Preceding pages: yacht race, Auckland Harbour. **Left,** downtown Auckland from Devonport. **Right,** Round-the-Bays run.

once listed the race as having more participants than any other single athletic event in the world.

Origins: The Auckland isthmus itself was formed dynamically through the geologically recent eruption of 60 volcanoes, the oldest 50,000 years ago and the youngest – the bush-clad offshore island of Rangitoto – blasted from the sea about 800 years ago. Just two centuries ago, Rangitoto's last blast buried a Maori settlement on the adjoining island of Motutapu.

Some speculate that Rangitoto, only 8 km (5 miles) from downtown Auckland, is only slumbering and will one day again burst into life. But experts believe Auckland's volcanoes were gentle members of their breed; if Rangitoto did erupt it would probably make a brilliant tourist attraction rather than a fiery holocaust.

Human habitation of Auckland has a no less turbulent history. Ancestors of the Maori are believed to have arrived around AD 800 and settled on the offshore islands of the Hauraki Gulf after journeying from eastern Polynesia. Traditions of the Maori tribes tell the visitor of incessant warfare and bloodshed over the possession of such a salubrious region as the population expanded.

Auckland's waterways assumed strategic importance as "canoe highways". At one time or another, every volcanic cone in Auckland was the site of a fortified pa or Maori village. Some vantage points like One Tree Hill and Mount Eden still bear the evidence of a system of terraces along which wooden palisades were erected; the pa on these hills may have boasted hundreds of warriors 200 years ago.

"Tamaki of 100 lovers": It was the bloody inter-tribal conflicts that gave Auckland its early Maori name, Tamaki, the word for "battle". The isthmus was also called, rather charmingly, Tamaki makau rau or the "Battle of 100 lovers". This poetic description had absolutely nothing to do with love and romance but accurately portrayed Tamaki as a highly desirable region which was longed for and fought over by many tribes.

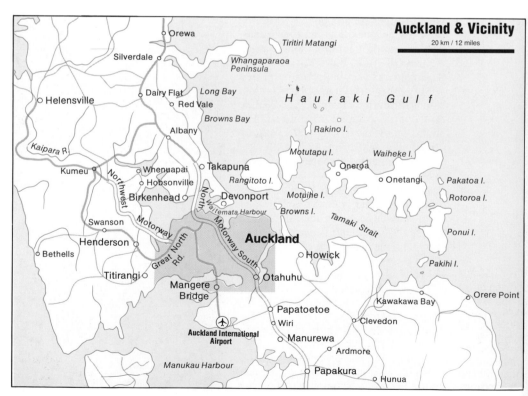

The British settlement of Auckland began with the visit of the adventurous missionary, Samuel Marsden, in 1820. Marsden, based in Sydney, Australia, was aboard the sailing ship *Coromandel*, which ventured into the Hauraki Gulf seeking masts and spars. While timber was being felled, the intrepid preacher covered about 900 km (550 miles) along rough tracks, by whaleboat and in canoes offered by the friendly Maori of Mokoia village, near the site of the present Auckland suburb of Panmure. Marsden is credited with being the first European to cross the Auckland isthmus (9 and 10 November 1820).

The last recorded tribal battle in Auckland was in 1827, then the Ngati Whatua Maori attacked the Ngapuhi tribe and seized control of the territory. The fighting had reduced the Maori population such that 13 years later, on 20 October 1840, the British found it much easier to win Auckland from the fierce Ngati Whatua. They purchased the area now comprising the heart of Auckland city for a shopping list of groceries and hardware: 50 blankets, 20 trousers, 20 shirts, 20 waistcoats, 10 caps, four casks of tobacco, one box of pipes, 100 yards of gown material, 10 iron pots, one bag of sugar, one sack of flour, 20 hatchets and a cash sum of £50 sterling, with another £6 paid the following year. Their prize: 1,200 hectares (3,000 acres) covering three bays from Freemans Bay to Parnell and inland to Mount Eden. Today just one acre of downtown land is worth at least NZ$12 million.

Plonked ignominiously on a traffic island in downtown Auckland, at the entrance to King's Wharf, is a piece of rock and a greening metal inscription marking Auckland's birth on 18 September 1840. The shabby memorial is hardly a tourist attraction, but none the less, it marks the spot where Auckland's founder and New Zealand's first governor, Captain William Hobson, declared the settlement to be the capital.

On a point about 30 metres (100 feet) above the plaque, but long since demolished during harbour reclamation, the Union Jack was hoisted up a flagpole.

Queen Street as it was.

Those assembled drank toasts and cheered while two naval ships in the harbour saluted with cannons. The first Auckland Regatta then took place, comprising a race for Maori canoes and two for rowing boats.

Urban sprawl: A pioneer of the time described the settlement as consisting of "a few tents and huts and a sea of fern stretching as far as the eye could see". Today the eye ranges over a sea of suburbs. It's no accident that Auckland and Los Angeles have sister city status – both are gateways to their respective nations and both sprawl over huge areas.

Auckland and its urban area occupy 1,016 sq km (378 sq miles) and are spread 80 km (50 miles) along the coast from Whangaparaoa and Torbay in the north, to Papakura and Drury in the south. This is partially due to the Kiwi's penchant for a house and garden on a "quarter-acre section" (lot) and the abundance of easy building land. On the positive side, this has created a decentralised city with plenty of open spaces.

But rapid change has seen the development of hundreds of apartment blocks and townhouse complexes in the inner city and inner suburbs during the 1990s. After the commercial slump of 1987, a number of city office blocks were redeveloped as apartment buildings, and new buildings are under construction, some of them prompted by money from Asian immigrants. And along the low hills that curve cosily around the central city area, many old wooden homes have been replaced by clusters of townhouses.

The liveliness of city and suburbs has been enhanced by a revolution which has opened up shopping hours from the severe restrictions that prevailed for 50 years until the late 1980s. It was once commonly joked that visitors arrived in Auckland and found it closed. But now most shops, and all tourist retail outlets, stay open from early to late on weekdays and through the weekends.

Although the city centre is now a more bustling place, Auckland's suburban sprawl has not made it the easiest place for tourists to get around. Taxis are not cheap but bus services are available to take visitors almost anywhere in the region – to Waiwera in the north, Helensville in the west, Panmure and Howick in the east and Manukau in the south. Daily coach tours leave the city on sightseeing excursions ranging from three to eight hour's long, with commentaries along the various routes.

Information on bus tours and on the location of attractions such as museums, art galleries, historic buildings, beaches and parks is readily available from the Auckland Visitor Centre in Aotea Square or down by the waterfront in Queen Elizabeth Square.

Key areas: Auckland's "Golden Mile" is **Lower Queen Street**, offering the best assortment of shopping in New Zealand. Souvenir and sheepskin shops sell hand-made woollen garments. Maori carvings, greenstone (jade) ornaments, paua (abalone) shell jewellery, opossum fur coats and woolly car-seat covers. Queen Street is complemented by arcades and side-streets containing traders in antiques, rare books, stamps, second-hand jewellery, paintings, pottery, crafts and various knick-knacks.

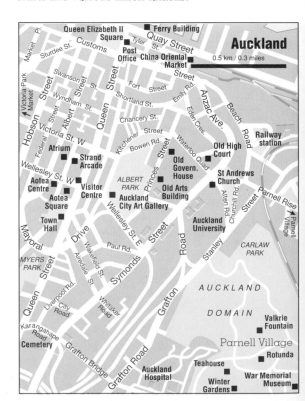

Pausing at the intersection of Queen and Fort streets, it's hard to imagine waves once lapped the shore at this spot. Little more than a century ago, Fort Street was the beach front, and Shortland Street in the next block was the main street of early Auckland. Queen Street in the 1840s was a bush-covered gully.

At the bottom of Queen Street, on the edge of the harbour, is **Queen Elizabeth Square**, a favourite place for lunchtime office workers, and occasionally for soapbox orators and protest groups. A Visitor Information Centre, a decorated fruit barrow, an ice-cream parlour and other snack stalls attract business in the square, where many people meet before crossing the street to the ferry building and embarking on cruises of the harbour and the Hauraki Gulf. The yacht, *Pride of Auckland*, makes regular cruises and visitors are encouraged to take part in the sailing of the boat.

A hundred metres or so from the square is the new **National Maritime Museum** with a number of historic vessels berthed alongside. The museum and the adjacent Viaduct Basin are surrounded by taverns and restaurants. Thousands of locals and tourists gather in the area on summer evenings. The Viaduct Basin was redeveloped for the stopover of the 1994 Whitbread round-the-world yacht race.

Historic shops: Sitting majestically opposite the Downtown Complex on the corner of Customs and Albert streets, is the **Old Customhouse** which was the financial heart of Auckland for more than 80 years. Designed in French Renaissance style, the building was completed in 1889 and is one of the last remaining examples of monumental Victorian architecture to be found in the central business district. Turn-of-the century liberal Prime Minister Richard Seddon, better known as "King Dick", preferred to sleep in the cramped, topmost turret of the Customhouse where he could watch the ships coming and going, shunning repeated requests to stay in the best hotels.

The Customhouse cost $30,732 to erect but more than $3 million has been

Waterfront, with the Old Customhouse.

spent on its restoration. Open every day, it houses gift shops and restaurants. Between the Customhouse and the plush Regent Hotel, in Albert Street, is a block of the most luxurious visitor apartments in Auckland.

Ten minutes' walk to the west are the **Victoria Park Markets**, located on the disused site of the city's former rubbish destructor. Completed in 1905, the yellow brick buildings were opened by Mayor Arthur Myers, who was hauled to the top of the 40-metre (131-foot) chimney in a ship's bo'sun chair to lay the final brick. In a pioneer conservation move, heat from the old destructor was used to generate electricity in 1908 and 94 horses were stabled to haul 10,000 tonnes of garbage from around the city to the furnaces. The historic site now offers seven-day buying at fruit, vegetable and craft shops or hawkers' barrows and food stalls.

Movies and museums: Halfway up Queen Street is **Aotea Square,** dominated by the monolithic Auckland City Council administration building and with the old Town Hall, built in 1911, forming the eastern boundary. On the western side of the square is the city's new cultural complex, the **Aotea Centre**, which was built amid much controversy for a total of $120 million. It has a 2,300 seat multi-purpose theatre, a convention centre, exhibition foyers, meeting rooms and a restaurant.

Central Queen Street is the city's cinema centre, housing a dozen movie theatres. Recently cinema complexes have been opened in suburban Newmarket and on the North Shore.

A block away, in Lorne Street, is the **public library**'s reading room – popular with homesick travellers and immigrants devouring newspaper pages from the foreign press. Not far away, in Wellesley Street East, is the city **Art Gallery**, occupying a French Renaissance-style building opened in 1887 and containing the biggest collection of New Zealand paintings in the country. They date back to works by John Webber and William Hodges, who accompanied Captain Cook on his South Pacific voyages in the late 18th century.

Griffins and muskets: Above the Art Gallery is picturesque **Albert Park**, once the site of Albert Barracks, built in the 1840s against attacks by warring Maori tribes. Remains of the barrack walls containing musket holes can be seen in the **Auckland University** grounds behind the main library on the eastern side of the park.

The intricate clock tower of the university's Old Arts Building, completed in 1926 in "New Zealand Gothic" style, was dubbed "The Wedding Cake" by locals because of its decorative pinnacles and original white-stone construction. Grinning griffins and gargoyles, created by German engraver Anton Teutenberg, adorn the exterior walls of the castle-like Supreme Court in nearby Water Quadrant, built in 1868.

Also within the university confines, a stone's throw from the gargoyles and directly opposite the Hyatt Hotel, is the Old Government House, erected in 1856 and now used as a common room.

A few steps away is **Parliament Street**, another vestige of Auckland's former glory as New Zealand's capital. The first meeting of an elected General Assembly was held in 1854 in a parliament building constructed with great haste at the corner of Parliament and Eden streets on a site later destroyed in the formation of Anzac Avenue. Pressure from the gold-rich South Island and vigorous new settlements further south in the North Island resulted in the movement of the capital from Auckland to Wellington, 660 km (410 miles) to the south on the grounds that it is geographically more central.

Founding father: South along Symonds Street, opposite the Sheraton Hotel, lies the body of Captain Hobson who selected Auckland as the site of the nation's capital.

Hobson chose Auckland because it was strategically placed between two main areas of Maori population (Northland and Waikato) and was central for the main European settlements (Russell and Wellington). He named the fledgling capital after the Earl of Auckland, George Eden, Viceroy of India – a personal gesture on Hobson's

Downtown architectural contrasts.

part because it was Lord Auckland who, as First Lord of the Admiralty, gave Hobson captaincy of the naval frigate *HMS Rattlesnake*. Hobson's patron is also remembered by his family name "Eden" in Mount Eden, Eden Park and other place names.

Hobson did not live long to see his newly-founded capital develop for he collapsed and died in Auckland two years later. Each year a wreath-laying ceremony attended by Auckland's mayor and the naval commodore is held at his graveside.

Hobson is also remembered in landmarks like Mount Hobson, Hobson Bay and Hobsonville (15 km/9 miles northwest of the city). Hobsonville was the site Hobson first selected for the capital but he rejected it in favour of the city's present location on the advice of his surveyor-general, Felton Mathew.

K-Road: Up at the top end of Queen Street, opposite Grafton Bridge – the biggest ferro-concrete span in the world on its completion in 1910 – is **Karangahape Road**, known to locals as "K-Road". Home to Polynesian Airlines, Air Nauru and Pacific consulates, it is the shopping place of the Pacific Island community of Samoans, Fijians, Tongans, Nuie and Cook Islanders. Shops display brilliantly coloured cloth, taro, yams, papaya, mangoes, green bananas, coconut products and other tropical foods.

Auckland is the biggest Polynesian city in the world with more than one-quarter of the 440,000 people nationally who claim Maori ancestry and approaching 90,000 Pacific Islanders in the urban area. And both these ethnic groups have greater natural growth than any other in the city. The ethnic Chinese population is growing proportionately faster than others because of immigration, particularly from Hong Kong and Taiwan. Most of the Asians settle in Auckland.

Thanks to immigration, Auckland's restaurant cuisine now ranks for quality and variety with the most cosmopolitan in the world. For inner-city visitors, the most restaurants are in Ponsonby Road, K-Road and along Tamaki Drive from

Across the water, Auckland Harbour.

162

Okahu Bay to St Heliers. For the latest restaurant ratings, cuisine standards and dollar value, seek the advice of a local or consult a popular entertainment guide.

Touring the suburbs: On wheels by either car or coach, there is much more to see in Auckland. A little east of the centre is historic **Parnell**, the city's first suburb, where pioneer homes like Ewelme Cottage (1864) and Kinder House (1858), both in Ayr Street, are open to the public. In Judge Street is tiny St Stephen's Chapel (1857) with a pioneer cemetery, and the wooden Gothic Church of St Mary's (1888) is in Parnell Road. Farther south in Gillies Avenue is the 15-room Highwic dated 1862.

Parnell Village on Parnell Road is a favourite shopping area with quaint Victorian-style shops, restaurants and boutiques. The Village is one of the successes of millionaire property developer Les Harvey, bane of town planners, who was awarded an MBE for protecting Auckland's remaining historical buildings from so-called "bulldozer vandals".

Historic One Tree Hill.

For years, Harvey bought up single- and double-storeyed buildings, restored and leased them for enterprises in keeping with their character, thus foiling "hideous, high-rise development", much to the chagrin of modern architects. He usually made his purchases on the northern side to preserve low-level structures and allow Aucklanders to "keep walking in the sun".

Four hundred metres (249 miles) to the south from the top of Parnell Rise is the bustling shopping centre of **Newmarket**. Once the smallest borough in New Zealand, it was absorbed by Auckland at the end of the 1980s. A number of major retail chains opened stores in the shopping strip and triggered a boom that has run unabated since. Recently a housing subdivision with more than 400 homes and apartments has been developed, starting just behind the main shopping street, ensuring continued retail development and an expansion of the restaurant and fast-food business, which is already considerable.

Big boat, big bird: To the south of Parnell, overlooking the city and har-

bour, is the **War Memorial Museum** located in the rambling grounds of the **Auckland Domain**. With the appearance of a Greek temple, it houses one of the finest displays of Maori and Polynesian culture in the world with exhibits of artefacts dating back to AD 1200. A highlight is the 30-metre (98-foot) war canoe, *Te-Toki-A-Tapiri* ("The Axe of Tapiri"), carved in 1836 from a single giant totara tree and used to carry 80 Maori warriors on their patrols in the Gisborne area.

The hall of New Zealand birds is another unique feature of the museum incorporating skeletons and a reconstruction of "Big Bird", the now-extinct, 4-metre, flightless moa.

East from Parnell, along the Tamaki Drive seafront, are Judges Bay, Okahu Bay, Mission Bay, Kohimarama and St Heliers – luring weekend hotdog vendors and family fun-seekers with soft sands, saltwater baths, mini-golf and bicycle, yacht and windsurfer hires. **Kelly Tarlton's Underwater World** is on the waterfront between Okahu Bay and Mission Bay. Visitors enter a huge Perspex tunnel to be entranced by dozens of varieties of fish swimming around and above them in the first aquarium. In the second are sharks and stingrays.

At Mission Bay stands the **Melanesian Mission** building which was constructed in 1859 as a mission school. It now houses a restaurant and museum of Melanesian artefacts.

A half-hour east of Auckland, the coast road arrives at Howick and **Colonial Village** with 19 restored buildings. A feature is an 1847 "fencible" cottage – a survivor of four military village outposts built outside Auckland by the Royal New Zealand Fencibles to buffer the city against Maori attack.

High points: Just south of the city centre, via Symonds Street or the Gillies Avenue motorway off-ramp, is the 196-metre (643-feet) extinct volcanic cone of **Mount Eden**, Auckland's highest point, affording a dramatic 360-degree panorama of the entire region. In an old lava pit, on the eastern side, Eden Gardens provides a dazzling display of more than 500 camelias, rhododendrons and azalias amidst 1,000 trees and shrubs.

A short distance south again arises the landmark cone of **One Tree Hill**, carrying a lone pine tree and the tomb of the "Father of Auckland", Sir John Logan Campbell. Sir John set up a tent as Auckland's first store at the bottom of Shortland Street on 21 December 1840, and was the city's most prominent businessman until his death in 1912 at the age of 95, by which time the city had swelled to 115,750 inhabitants. With his partner, William Brown, he built a house called Acacia Cottage in 1841. Now Auckland's oldest building, it is preserved in **Cornwall Park** at the base of One Tree Hill.

A philanthropist, Sir John presented his 135-hectare (335-acre) farm, encompassing One Tree Hill, as a park for the use of the people of Auckland, in 1901. The event was timed to coincide with the visit of the Duke and Duchess of Cornwall. The obelisk beside his grave was erected at his request to record his admiration for the Maori people.

Off the Western Motorway at West-

Stained glass in the War Memorial Museum.

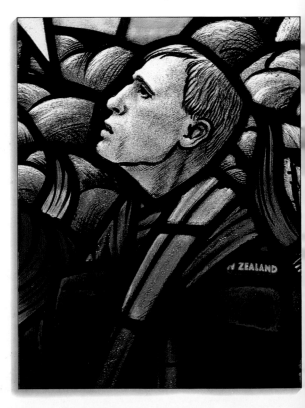

ern Springs is **MOTAT** – the Museum of Transport and Technology – containing working displays of vintage vehicles, aircraft and machinery. Volunteer enthusiasts operate many exhibits on the weekends and the static displays include an aircraft built by New Zealander Richard Pearse which may have flown in March 1903, months before the Wright Brothers. Also at MOTAT is the Science and Technology Hall where visitors of all ages enjoy "hands-on" experience of a wide range of scientific equipment and phenomena.

A brief ride in an old tram or a pleasant walk around Western Springs lake leads to **Auckland Zoo**, starring New Zealand's unique, flightless kiwi bird and the tuatara lizard, a "living fossil".

Westwards: A popular drive out west climbs over the forested Waitakere Ranges via Titirangi, home of ardent conservationists and woodland-dwelling "bush freaks". Tall kauri trees, giant ferns and nikau palms line the road to the rugged black-sand, surfing beach of Piha and the kauri park at Swanson.

Forest Hill Road provides an escape route from the trees, down into the grape-growing district of Henderson where visitors can choose from among 30 vineyard wine-tasting bars.

Just before Helensville, about 50 km (30 miles) from Auckland through the wine-growing centres of Kumeu, Huapai and Waimauku, is the thermal resort of Parakai. In this haven tired limbs can be soothed in hot mineral waters which bubble out of the earth into tiled pools where they are then pumped down exhilarating water chutes.

Over the bridge: Offering dramatic harbour views is the **Auckland Harbour Bridge**, the city's best-known landmark. Built in 1959 as a four-lane span, its capacity was doubled 10 years later when Japanese engineers built two more lanes ("The Nippon Clip-ons") on each side. A bridge to connect the city with the **North Shore** was suggested as far back as 1859 when it was estimated a pontoon structure would be "be crossed daily by 110 people, 10 wagons, 20 horses, 10 cows, 12 sheep and 5 pigs".

Auckland's landmark Harbour Bridge.

Today the Harbour Bridge carries an average of 125,000 vehicles a day.

Ferries, with snacks and alcoholic beverages, give comfortable, high-speed service regularly through the day between downtown Auckland and **Devonport** just across the harbour. Devonport has a charming, stylish shopping centre that attracts commuters who like to enjoy the quiet lifestyle, and tourists looking for a pleasant day in the sun. The North Shore can also be reached by ferry from the downtown waterfront. The *Kestrel*, launched in 1905, travels between the city and Devonport on Friday and Saturday nights, to the accompaniment of live music. At other times, the *Kea*, a modern seabus, does the 10-minute journey.

At Devonport, the volcanic promontories of **Mount Victoria** and **North Head** give unobstructed views into downtown Auckland and across the harbour to the Eastern Bays. The two hills were honeycombed with fortified tunnels during a Russian invasion scare in the 1870s and were inhabited by Maori communities over a 700-year period through to 1863. A monument and plaques in English and Maori on the foreshore between the two hills commemorate the landing of the Tainui Maori canoe around the 14th century.

North from Devonport the coastline is an endless procession of sheltered coves and white-sand beaches stretching to the tip of the North Island.

Hot pools: Less than one hour's drive north of Auckland are the popular holiday resorts of **Orewa** and **Waiwera**. Waiwera means "hot water" and refers to thermal springs percolating up from volcanic layers onto a sandy beach in which the Maori dug holes and lay in pools of hot mineral waters.

The Waiwera Hot Pools are a good deal more sophisticated today with a number of public and private pools of varying temperatures, barbecue facilities, picnic grounds and devastating steel water chutes called The Choobs.

A few kilometres north of Orewa is the **Puhoi pub**, whose interior is a veritable museum of the pioneers of that

Greeting in the Puhoi pub.

area. The entertaining antics of the pub's proprietor and owner, Ron Seymour, provide an added attraction.

In the Gulf: On a sparkling, calm day there is no substitute for a leisurely cruise to the offshore islands in the **Hauraki Gulf**. Cruise launches and ferries leave the wharves daily at the bottom of Queen Street to Rangitoto, Motuihe, Motutapu, Rakino and the holiday resort island of Pakatoa.

A speedy catamaran service also links Auckland with **Waiheke Island**, only an hour away in the Hauraki Gulf but a thousand miles away in terms of pace and lifestyle. Waiheke is home for some 6,000 residents, of whom about 1,000 commute to Auckland, but in the summer its population swells to 30,000. Hardly surprisingly, it is billed as Auckland's holiday island.

A more in-depth look at the islands can be gained by a weekend cruise to **Great Barrier Island**, 90 km (56 miles) northwest. The *Gulf Explorer*, a 48-metre (157-foot) cruise ship which offers a variety of cabin accommodation for 80 passengers, leaves Marsden Wharf on Friday evenings and returns on Sunday afternoons. High-speed catamarans provide a daily service.

For a quick look at the harbour the restored vintage steam tug *William C. Daldy* takes day-trippers on one-hour voyages from Marsden Wharf on Sundays and public holidays.

Leaving Auckland: Setting off for Northland, a diversion to Sandspit (at Warkworth) allows for a four-hour launch excursion to historic **Kawau Island** – site of the restored Mansion House built by controversial New Zealand Governor Sir George Grey, in 1862. Kawau is still the home of the parma wallaby, thought to be extinct in its Australian homeland.

Departing from Auckland in the south, train buffs can leave the motorway at Drury and follow the signs from Waiuku Road to the **Glenbrook Vintage Steam Railway** which operates on weekends and public holidays.

Beyond lies the rest of New Zealand. Beyond the Bombay Hills.

Mansion House, Kawau Island.

HISTORIC NORTHLAND

Tribal warfare, bloody clashes between Maori and Pakeha, debauchery, insurrection, missionary zeal, a treaty of peace and promises – all are part of Northland's historical backdrop.

This is the birthplace of the New Zealand nation. Here, Maori Aotearoa succumbed to British New Zealand.

But Northland has more to offer than the past. It is a place to relax, to enjoy the sun, food, sights and distinctive way of life. It is famed for its scenery – its pastoral, productive south and the wilder, remoter and legendary far north. It is noted for its game fishing, unspoiled beaches, pleasant climate, thermal pools, kauri forests – and friendliness.

The winterless Northland: This irregular peninsula juts upwards some 450 km (280 miles) north from Auckland to the rocky headlands of North Cape and Cape Reinga, the topmost tips of the land. Its "winterless north" label means mild, damp winters; warm and rather humid summers. A feature are the pohutukawa trees, which in early summer rim the coast and decorate the hinterland with their dark red blossoms.

For those waiting to explore the region freely, it is best to work from a base at Paihia, a Bay of Islands township on the far northeast coast. Both Air New Zealand Link and Ansett New Zealand offer daily flights to Whangarei, and Air New Zealand Link flies daily to both Kerikeri, on the northern coast of the Bay of Islands, and to Kaitai, further north again. Alternatively, it's a pleasant three-and a half-hour drive up Highway One from Auckland.

Bay of Islands: The route from Auckland begins across the Harbour Bridge, proceeds along the Hibiscus Coast with its beachfront resorts, then continues through the small farming towns of Warkworth and Wellsford and around Whangarei city, gateway to the north. Drivers leave the main highway at Kawakawa (where the railway still runs down the main street) and snake down the harbourside resort of **Paihia**.

This is the Bay of Islands, the cradle of New Zealand. The bay's irregular 800-km (500-mile) coastline embraces 150 islands and is steeped in historical association with the country's early settlement. Looking across the harbour from Paihia towards Russell, the first capital of New Zealand, and to the islands shimmering beyond, it is hard to believe this lovely, tranquil spot was once a sin centre of the South Pacific.

Polynesian explorer Kupe is said to have visited here in the 10th century followed by another canoe voyager, Toi, 200 years later. Captain Cook discovered the harbour for Europeans in 1769. Impressed, he gave the sheltered waters of the bay their name.

In the scattered group are eight larger islands and numerous islets. The biggest measures 22 hectares (54 acres). Many are uninhabited; two are privately owned; some are Maori reserves. About 4,000 people live permanently in the region, but in the summer holiday, from Christmas to late January, up to 50,000 people head north to camp, boat, swim,

fish, relax and enjoy themselves. As most Northland visitors go to the bay, this period requires accommodation reservations well in advance.

Since the 1950s, the small, sleepy township of Paihia has been revamped to meet the challenge of tourism. Modern motels have sprung up alongside a neat, expanded shopping centre. A variety of eating places and modest nightlife make it a worthy hub of Northland. The wharf, its focal point, caters for island cruises and fishing trips.

Paihia has marked its places of historical note with bronze plaques along the red-sand seafront. It has many firsts: New Zealand's oldest Norfolk pine stands here. A mission station was created on the town site in 1823. Missionaries built and launched the country's first ship, the *Herald*, here in 1826.

From the first printing press, brought from England in 1834 by William Colenso, came the first Bible in Maori. The William Memorial Church, a tribute to pioneer-missionary the Rev. Henry Williams, has a barrel organ in the vestry which played 11 tunes. Colonial history is etched in the graveyard.

Kelly Tarlton's Shipwreck Museum is like a visit to Davy Jones's Locker. The beached bark houses an intriguing array of relics salvaged from wrecks around the New Zealand coast – coins, gold, silver, bronze, precious stones and other souvenirs. Below decks, swinging lanterns, realistic sailing-ship sound effects, and the smell of ropes and tar create a seagoing illusion. The ship's owner was a diver, photographer and journalist. Kelly Tarlton died several years ago after completing his impressive "Underwater World" in Auckland – a vision he offered Paihia but which the local council declined.

The Waitangi treatment: The most significant act in New Zealand's early history took place on the lawn of the **Waitangi Treaty House**, located about 2 km (1 miles) north of Paihia, across a one-way bridge which also leads to the Waitangi Reserve and a golf course.

In 1840, with Governor William Hobson signing on behalf of Queen

Waitangi Treaty House.

Victoria, Maori chiefs and English gentlemen inked a pact to end Maori-Pakeha conflict, guarantee the Maori land rights, give them and the colonists Crown protection, and admit New Zealand to the British Empire.

At the time the Treaty of Waitangi was signed, the house was the home of James Busby, British Resident in New Zealand from 1832 to 1840. Later, the gracious colonial dwelling, with its commanding views of the bay, fell into disrepair. When put up for sale in 1931, it was bought by the governor-general of the time, Lord Bledisloe. He gave it to the nation on the condition it be fully restored to its 1840 glory.

That condition was met and today the Treaty House is a national museum and a prime visitor attraction. Inside, with its artefacts and copy of the famous treaty itself, it is cool, quiet and full of atmosphere. Visitors are usually impressed by the splendour of an adjacent Maori meeting house and awed by a massive war canoe. Access is through a information-reception centre, which provides ample background plus an audiovisual on the treaty signing.

Gone fishing: Deep-sea fishing for some of the world's biggest gamefish is a major lure at the Bay of Islands. American Western author Zane Grey, a noted angler, was a regular visitor in the 1920s. His base camp was at Otehei Bay on Urupukapuka Island; it was popularised by his 1926 book, *Tales of Angler's Eldorado, New Zealand*. This single volume has reeled in thrill-seeking fishermen ever since.

The main fishing season is December through June when the huge marlin are running. Many world records for marlin, shark and tuna were set here. Yellowtail kingfish, running on till September, provide good sport on light rods. Snapper, one of New Zealand's favourite table fish, is plentiful.

Fighting fish up to 400 kg (880 pounds) are caught in the bay, and weigh-ins attract appreciative crowds. Competitions for line-fishing and surf-casting are frequently held, with prizes for the winners; the foremost are in January.

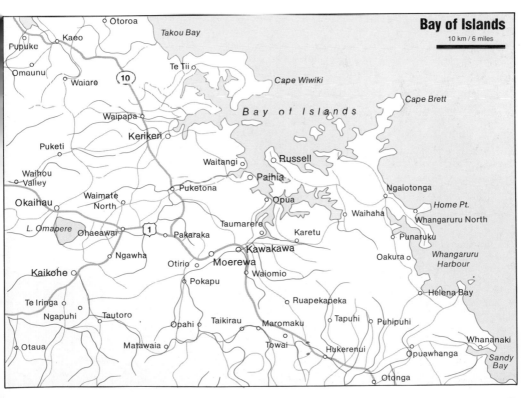

Bay of Islands
10 km / 6 miles

Despite the "seasons", fishing is a year-round sport here. Charter boats are available at Paihia or Russell for half- or full-day hire, and on a share basis.

Sin city: Runaway sailors, escaped convicts from Australia, lusty whalers, promiscuous women, brawling and drunkenness: **Russell**, formerly Kororareka, has known them all.

Colonists first arrived in 1809, making it New Zealand's first white settlement. Today it's small, quiet and peaceful. There's an aura of stored history, of romance, of skeletons jangling in those Victorian cupboards. But things liven up at Christmas and New Year when celebrating boaties and other visitors get the place rocking again. This former (but short-lived) capital of New Zealand is linked by a regular launch service to Paihia and Waitangi. A vehicular ferry also serves the small peninsula from the deep-sea port of Opua south of the harbour.

Today's Russell services the needs of national and international yachts, as well as game fisherfolk and those visitors of historical bent. Strong efforts are made to retain the township's 19th-century Victorian appearance.

In the early 1830s, the port was always full of whaling and trading ships and adventurers. Lust and lawlessness prevailed. Up to 30 grog shops operated on the tiny waterfront. Friction developed between Maori and European. Guns were traded, Maori shanghaied and badly treated. Shocked early settlers responded by building Christ Church in 1835, New Zealand's oldest church. Its bullet-holed walls are grim reminders of its siege in 1845.

Charismatic Maori chief Hone Heke reluctantly signed the Treaty of Waitangi in 1840, then grew discontented over government land dealings. In 1845, he defiantly chopped down the British flagstaff, symbol of the new regime, on Maiki Hill behind Russell. Meanwhile, chief Kawiti burned and sacked the town, sparing church property. Heke chopped down three more flagpoles that year. Two bitter battles for rebel strongholds resulted in defeats for British troops.

Kerikeri Old Stone Store.

The showdown came in 1846 near Kawakawa, at Kawiti's pa Ruapekapeka. A strong Redcoat force captured this formidable fortress somewhat unfairly on a Sunday when the converted Maori were busy worshipping their new Christian god. Heke was eventually pardoned and his men freed.

Pompallier House, a Catholic mission house, was spared in the fighting. It is now an elegant, refurbished tourist attraction. Russell's **museum** has a quarter-sized seagoing model of Cook's *Endeavour*. Its Duke of Marlborough Hotel is a pub of character.

Trips: The true beauty of islands in the bay can best be appreciated from a position of comfort on the foredeck of one of the daily Cream Trips. These water tours out of Paihia and Russell retrace the voyages of bygone days when cream was regularly collected from island farms. Mail and provisions are still handled this way.

The Fullers launch cruise covers 96 km (60 miles). Passengers see the island where Captain Cook first anchored on his 1769 voyage of discovery; the cove where French explorer Marion du Fresne, along with his 25 crew members, were slain by Maori in 1772; and bays where the earliest missionaries landed. A luncheon stop is made at Zane Grey's favourite Otehei Bay.

The catamaran *Tiger Lily III* offers a four-hour cruise and a three-hour scenic trip to the Cape Brett lighthouse and Piercy Island and, weather permitting, passes through the Hole in the Rock.

Sweet township: The "sweetest" place in Northland is **Kerikeri**. Twenty-three km (14 miles) north of Paihia by a pretty inlet, it is a township of unusual interest and character with a rich backdrop of early Maori and European history.

Today, Kerikeri's fertile land grows much of the country's finest citrus and subtropical fruits, including kiwifruit.

The township and its immediate environs – with a population of more than 1,600 – has become a thriving centre for handicrafts and cottage industries. The climate and relaxed lifestyle have attracted many creative residents, along with wealthy retirees from other New Zealand centres and from the world's political trouble-spots.

Samuel Marsden established his second mission station at Kerikeri in 1819. The first plough in New Zealand dug into Kerikeri soil that year.

Down at the inlet are two of New Zealand's oldest buildings in a fine state of preservation. **Kemp House** is the oldest, built in 1822 of pit-sawn kauri and totara. It has been fully restored. Four generations of the Kemp family have lived in it, through turbulent times when pioneer womenfolk had to endure the grisly sight of decapitated heads stuck drying on the stake fence separating the property from the adjoining Maori pa. Tribal raids by fierce chief Hongi Hika meant souvenired heads to be dried and shrunken, and they then became part of Maori war games early last century.

Next door is the **Old Stone Store**, constructed by missionaries in 1833 of thick stone to protect their wares from marauding tribesmen. It is still serves as a shop, with a museum upstairs.

Digging for kauri gum.

Kororipa Pa should not be overlooked. This was Hongi Hika's forward army base between 1780 and 1828. Warriors were assembled here before launching raids on southern tribes (as far south as Cook Strait), whose primitive weapons were no match for muskets, bartered from the Europeans.

Not far from Kerikeri is **Waimate North**, the first inland settlement for white people and earlier inland mission station. Built in 1831-1832, the two-storeyed kauri mission house was the home of Bishop George Augustus Selwyn, New Zealand's first bishop, in 1842. He regularly walked the 16 km (10 miles) to his library in the Kerikeri Stone Store, and back. The house was built by Maori labour except for the English hearthstone and blown pane glass. It has been fully restored and is full of antiques.

Final shore: In Maori mythology, Cape Reinga is where the spirits of the dead depart on their homeward journey back to the ancestral land of Hawaiki.

Coach tours now make their way up this legendary flight path, along the Aupori Peninsula to its northernmost point, and splash back down Ninety Mile Beach. Coaches leave Paihia daily at 7.30-8am, returning about 6pm. It's a tiring trip, but worthwhile, especially since the road north of Te Kao is too rough for an ordinary car.

The east-coast route traverses the worked-out gum fields north of Kerikeri, a relic of the huge kauri forests that covered this region eons ago. The dead trees left pockets of gum in the soil which early settlers found to be a valuable export for fine varnish. In fact, it triggered off a "gum rush". By the 1880s, more than 2,000 men were digging away. Most of them were immigrants from Dalmatia ; some made their fortunes. When the gum fields were exhausted, they turned to farming or came south to Auckland to found the city's vineyards (near Henderson).

In **Whangaroa Harbour**, a deep-sea fishing base, lies the wreck of the *Boyd*. The ship called in for kauri spars in 1809 and sent a party ashore. The party

Lonely sandy strand of Northland.

was murdered by Maori, who donned the victims' clothes and rowed back to the vessel to massacre the rest of the crew and set fire to the ship. This episode is said to have delayed Christian settlement in New Zealand for years.

Further on is **Doubtless Bay**, named by Cook, with a string of superb, gently sloping sandy beaches. **Coopers Beach**, lined with pohutukawa trees, is likewise attractive. So is **Cable Bay** with its golden sand and colourful shells. Both have camping, motels and restaurants.

At Awanui, the coach heads north through **Te Kao**, the largest Maori settlement in the far north, to **Cape Reinga** with its much-pictured lighthouse. At nearby Spirits Bay is the gnarled old pohutukawa from where Maori souls, homeward bound to Hawaiki, were said to take off. The whole district is rich in Maori lore.

Views from the cape are impressive. You can see the turbulent meeting line of the Pacific Ocean and Tasman Sea; the Three Kings Islands discovered by Abel Tasman in 1643; neighbouring capes and secluded, lonely beaches. It is a desolate place with only gulls screeching and waves crashing against jagged, foam wreathed rocks far below.

Ninety Mile Beach is actually 60 miles (96 km) long. Its firm, sandy length is lined with dunes and hillocks of shell, the reminders of bygone feasts. It is noted for its shellfish, particularly the succulent, protected, toheroa.

The route back to Paihia is via Kaitaia, New Zealand's northernmost town, and the Mangamuka Scenic Reserve with its native bush.

The West Coast: Travellers can return to Auckland via a west-coast route where sleepy harbourside hamlets cling close to their pioneer past, and where forest giants live. A prime destination is **Hokianga Harbour**, 80 km (50 miles) across country. This long harbour, with its score of ragged inlets, is quiet, serene, rural. The scattered residents don't tout much for tourists: the harbour's perilous sandbar has already claimed 15 ships. Kupe is said to have left from here in AD 900 to return to Hawaiki.

Kaikohe, the midway town, has a hilltop monument to chief Hone Heke (a descendant of the old renegade chief) who became a Member of Parliament. It has spectacular views of both coasts. Nearby, Ngawha Hot Mineral Springs offer a tempting soak in mercury-and-sulphur waters, claimed to be curative for rheumatism and skin troubles.

The tiny seaside resort of **Opononi** at the harbour mouth briefly became famous around the world in the southern summer of 1955-56, when a young dolphin began frolicking with swimmers at the beach. Opo, as she was called, played games with bottles and balls, let children ride on her back, and won her way into a nation's heart. Opononi had a three-month tourist boom. When Opo was found dead, stuck between tidal rocks, the nation mourned. She is remembered in a song and a monument.

Fathers of the Forest: The road heads south through the **Waipoua Kauri Sanctuary** with its 2,500 hectares (about 6,100 acres) of huge, mature kauri trees, the largest pocket of kauri forest left in the land. Two giants (close to the unsealed road) tower above them all: Te Matua Ngahere ("Father of the Forest"), about 2,000 years old, and brother Tanemahuta ("Lord of the Forest"), 1,200 years old with a girth of 13.6 metres (44.6 feet). Further south at Trounson Park are more fine kauris, including one with four stems.

Dargaville, 184 km (114 miles) from Auckland, was founded on the timber and kauri gum trade. The town museum has many fine gum samples and is a museum-piece itself – built of clay bricks brought in from China as ship's ballast.

The highway turns east to **Whangarei**. This lightly industrialised city of some 40,180 is a deep-sea port and boasts a harbour, glassworks, cement plant and a oil refinery. There is plenty of quality accommodation. Mount Parahaki gives panoramic views of city and harbour. Major attractions are the Clapham Clock Collection (400 timepieces dating from the 17th century), safe swimming beaches, the deep-sea fishing base of Tutukaka, and the city's handsome parks, reserves, picnic grounds and bushwalks.

Auckland is two hours' drive away.

COROMANDEL AND BAY OF PLENTY

"Coromandel: Mine Today, Gone Tomorrow!" The slogan reflects the strong feelings of its inhabitants that the Coromandel Peninsula's greatest asset is not mineral wealth but its natural attractions. Save the area for its recreational potential; "treasure from tourism".

The stand-off is between mining companies and the hundreds of alternative lifestylers who call Coromandel home. The companies have continued prospecting but have made no move to mine yet on the peninsula itself. In Waihi, to the south, however, miners are expanding the old diggings and pulling out quantities of gold.

The Coromandel region once yielded treasures of gold, kauri timber and gum. Reminders of these bonanzas abound, with colonial buildings, old gold-mine shafts and kauri relics.

Seen from Auckland, the Coromandel Peninsula is a lumpy, irregular profile, almost a caricature of a theatre backdrop for some vast outdoor scene. "Outdoor" is the area's lodestone, whether visitors engage in driving, diving, fishing, boating, swimming, camping, tramping, or fossicking for gemstones. The earlier thousands who flocked here were gold-seekers, gumdiggers and bushmen.

Gold fever territory: At the base of the peninsula, **Thames** was officially declared a goldfield in August 1867. The ensuing gold rush swelled the town's population to 18,000 at its peak. In its heyday, Thames was busy with more than 100 hotels. Today there are just four, the oldest (1868) being the **Brian Boru** on the corner of Pollen and Richmond streets, which is now gaining fame for its Agatha Christie-style "murder weekends".

To appreciate the town's past, one should visit the Mineralogical Museum and adjacent School of Mines. Nearby, at the old gold mine and gold-stamper battery (well-signposted at the northern end of Thames), members of the Hauraki

Preceding pages: ancient forest. Below, Thames.

Prospectors' Association demonstrate the technology used to retrieve gold.

Kauaeranga Valley, also signposted in Thames, is the site of the Conservation Department's visitor and information centre, 10 km (6 miles) from Thames. The first kauri spars from here were taken in 1795, mainly for the Royal Navy; by 1830, kauri trees were being cut in greater numbers. The logging and milling lasted for a century.

Late in the 1800s, huge kauri timber dams were built across creeks and streams on the peninsula in order to bank up water and then float the logs to the sea. About 300 such dams were built throughout the peninsula, more than 60 of them in the Kauaeranga Valley. Many are still there, slowly disintegrating. A working model of a kauri dam (made of pine, not of kauri) has been built near the information centre. In summer tours are organised to show visitors how the dams worked.

oday the Kauaeranga Valley is a favourite spot for camping and tramping. Along more than 50 km (31 miles) of

tracks, visitors have plenty of access to the wilderness with basic overnight hut accommodation available.

The Thames area owes its name to James Cook, who charted the Coromandel coast in 1769. What is now the Waihou River, he called the Thames; and while the river reverted to its Maori name, the tongue of sea lapping the coast remains the Firth of Thames.

"Square" trees and potters: North of Thames, heading for the town of Coromandel, up the west coast of the peninsula, with the Hauraki Gulf on the left, one soon experiences a winding road and spectacularly changing views. The road hugs the coast for much of the way, passing bays where holiday homes huddle on the shore.

Tapu, 18.5 km (11½ miles) north of Thames, is the junction for the Tapu-Coroglen road, a scenic route climbing to 448 metres (1,470 feet) above sea level. The road goes over the peninsula to the west coast but is rough and, in winter, dangerous. Most travellers to the west coast make the journey across at Kopu, just south of Thames.

Coromandel township, near the northern end of the peninsula, offers a quiet, alternative life for painters who farm, potters who garden, weavers who rear their own sheep for wool. The town and peninsula were named after the Royal Navy ship the *HMS Coromandel*, which called into the harbour there for spars early in the 19th century. The township was the site of New Zealand's first gold find by Charles Ring in 1852. More than 2,000 people dashed across the gulf from Auckland at the news, but they found that the gold was deeply embedded in quartz rock and expensive to extract. It wasn't until 15 years later that a gold-bearing reef rich enough to warrant expensive extraction machinery was discovered. It brought wealth to those who worked it.

Coromandel has an air of the past about it and, even at the height of the summer holiday season, the pace is slow and the lifestyle relaxed. It remembers its past with such institutions as the School of Mines with its collection of rock samples, mostly from the peninsula itself but some accumulated from around the world.

Mythical Turehu: Beyond Coromandel, 28 km (17 miles) north, is Colville, the last store before Cape Colville and the northernmost tip of the peninsula. Enthusiasts insist that visitors cannot experience the full spirit of the peninsula unless they travel to the end of this road. En route, the road skirts the Moehau Range, whose 891-metre (2,923-foot) peak is the highest point on the peninsula. According to Maori legend, it is home of Turehu or Patupaiarehe, a short, fair-skinned people. But unlike the Himalayas' yeti or America's bigfoot, not so much as a footprint of the Turehu has ever been found. Today's visitors might, however, manage to see the small, rare, native frog (*Leiopeima archeyi*). A refugee from the remote past, it lives only on the Coromandel Peninsula and is sometimes seen in this vicinity.

The unspoilt beauty and isolation of Port Jackson and Fletcher Bay draw people to enjoy some solitude. **Fletcher Bay**, at the end of the road, is also the starting point for the **Coromandel Walkway**, a three-hour walk to Stony Bay. The more sedentary can visit Stony Bay by taking the road just north of Colville, across the peninsula to Port Charles, then returning via Kennedy Bay on the east coast to Coromandel.

Two roads lead from Coromandel to Whitianga on the opposite coast of the peninsula. The first, longer and less developed, leads east to Whangapoua Harbour and Kuaotuna Beach. (Here, make a point of travelling the Black Jack Road, renowned as the most hair-raising route in the region.) Another 17 km (10.5 miles) southwest of Kuaotuna, just beyond the sheltered expanse of Buffalo Beach (named for a British warship wrecked there in 1840), is Whitianga. The second route, 15 km (9.5 miles) shorter, climbs to 300 metres (984 feet) before descending to approach the town from the south, along the Whitianga Harbour edge.

Whitianga, opposite the present town, is said to have been occupied for more than 1,000 years by the descendants of the Polynesian explorer, Kupe. Kauri gum was shipped from Whitianga from 1844, peaking in 1899 with the shipment of 1,100 tons. From 1864, kauri timber was also shipped from the harbour and around 500 million feet left the region in the next 60 years.

Today's visitors enjoy fishing, swimming or rock-hunting. The latter draws those in search of the area's semi-precious gemstones, jasper, amethyst, quartz, chalcedony, agate and carnelian.

South of Whitianga lies **Coroglen** (formerly Gumtown). Eight km (5 miles) east is the access road to two areas which are essential stops – **Cooks Bay** and **Hot Water Beach**. It was at the former location (also known as Mercury Bay) that Captain Cook first hoisted the British flag in New Zealand in November 1769 to claim the territory in the name of King George III. While here, he also observed the transit of Mercury; the occasion is marked by a cairn and plaque at the top of Shakespeare Cliffs.

Hot water: An absolute must on the peninsula is the unique Hot Water Beach, where thermal activity causes steam to

Bovine runaway.

rise from the sand in places and the visitor can dig a thermal hot pool on the beach, using "sand-castle" walls to keep the sea out or let it in to regulate the temperature. It is a great way to relax travel-weary bodies from the bumps and bends of the roads.

The new centre southward is **Tairua**, on the harbour of the same name. The area is dominated by 178-metre (584-foot) Mount Paku, whose summit offers views of nearby Shoe and Slipper islands. Across the harbour is the resort of **Pauanui**, billed as a "Park by the Sea" but described by some as almost "too tidy to be true". It provides a marked contrast to the haphazard development of many New Zealand beach areas.

Whangamata Beach, 40 km (25 miles) farther south, is well-known both as a popular family holiday spot and the prime surfing beach of the peninsula.

The road winds inland from here. Thirty km (19 miles) south is **Waihi**, where a rich gold-and silver-bearing lode was discovered in 1878. Martha Hill mine was the greatest source of these minerals. Shafts were sunk to a depth of more than 500 metres (over 1,600 feet); in 60-plus years, more than NZ$50 million worth of gold and silver was retrieved. Further gold is being won by an opencast mining venture which has laid bare the original mineshafts on Martha Hill.

The bullion trail led through the Karangahake Gorge to Paeroa, from where the ore was shipped to Auckland. A walkway through part of the gorge between Waikino and Karangahake, where the relics of the Victoria stamper battery, has been developed.

The Bay of Plenty was named by Cook; his description proved to be prophetic. Perhaps the greatest current evidence of plenitude is the phenomenal growth of the "furry" kiwifruit, which has made the township of Te Puke the "Kiwifruit Capital of the World". Just beyond Te Puke is **Kiwifruit Country**, an orchard park, information centre and restaurant, with a "kiwifruit train" to take visitors for trips around the park.

Waihi Beach, just north of Tauranga

Cooks Bay.

Harbour, is considered the boundary point between Coromandel Peninsula and the **Bay of Plenty**. By road through the Athenree Gorge south of Waihi, one reaches Katikati — promoted as "The Gateway to the Bay of Plenty".

The coastal city of **Tauranga** is both a tourist focal point and an important commercial centre, served by a busy port at nearby **Mount Maunganui**.

Flax-trading began here 150 years ago; missionaries arrived in 1838; and in 1864, during the New Zealand Wars, Tauranga was the site of fierce fighting during the battle of Gate Pa. That battlefield was also the scene of heroic compassion when Heni Te Kirikamu heard mortally wounded British offices calling for water, and risked death during the battle to take water to his enemies.

The site of the original military camp, the Monmouth Redoubt and the mission cemetery holds not only the remains of the British troops killed at Gate Pa, but also the body of the defender of Gate Pa, Rawhiri Puhirake, killed during the subsequent battle of Tc Ranga.

Among the leading attractions in Tauranga are Tauranga Historic Village (on 17th Avenue), which explains the pioneer history of the area, and The Elms mission house in Mission Street, dating from 1847.

Across the harbour from Tauranga is the Mount Maunganui holiday resort. It is built around the 231-metre (758-foot) "Mount", affording views of Tauranga and the surrounding area. Visitors who are reluctant or lack the energy to climb the "Mount" can simply laze on the beach or swim in the hot saltwater pools near the foot of the hill.

Te Puke is 28 km (17 miles) southeast of Tauranga. Its subtropical horticulture has brought prosperity. The kiwifruit, originally known as the Chinese gooseberry, was introduced to New Zealand from China in 1906, and thrived best in the Bay of Plenty. In 1937, Te Puke farmer Jim MacLoughlin planted an acre of the vines. He is regarded as the father of the industry although it was close to 40 years before demand burgeoned internationally. In the 1970s and

Mount Maunganui.

early 1980s, many farmers became millionaires from a harvest off only two or three hectares. High demand and high prices made Te Puke the wealthiest small town in the country. Acreage expanded swiftly through other New Zealand regions and gradually to other countries, until nowadays kiwifruit is just another orchard crop. The industry's biggest regret is that it didn't register the kiwifruit name.

Acting as a man: About 100 km (62 miles) from Tauranga and 85 km (53 miles) from the thermal centre of Rotorua is **Whakatane**, at the mouth of the Whakatane River and at the edge of the fertile Rangitaiki Plains. Until it was drained 70 years ago, the area was a 40,000-hectare (about 100,000-acre) tract of swampland.

Whakatane takes its name from the arrival of the Mataatua Canoe from Hawaiki at the local river mouth. Legend records that the men went ashore, leaving the women in the canoe, which then began to drift away on the incoming tide. Though women were forbidden to touch paddles, the captain's daughter, Wairaka, seized one and shouted: "Kia whakatane au i ahau!" ("I will act as a man!"). Others followed her lead and the canoe was saved. A bronze statue of Wairaka now stands on a rock in the river-mouth. Above the area, known as The Heads, is Kapu–te Rangi ("Ridge of the Heavens"), reputedly the oldest Maori pa site in New Zealand, established by the Polynesian explorer Toi.

Clearly visible from Whakatane and adjacent coasts is **White Island**, a privately owned active volcano 50 km (31 miles) from Whakatane. Scenic flights pass over the steaming island, which was mined for sulphur ore between 1885 and the mid-1930s. In 1914, 11 men lost their lives on the island during a violent eruption; the camp cat was the only survivor. Cardboard has been produced at the **Whakatane Board Mills** since 1939. Visitors may tour this plant and that of the Tasman Pulp and Paper Company mill at **Kawerau**, 32 km (20 miles) from Whakatane towards Rotorua.

Just over the hill, 7 km (4½ miles) from Whakatane, is the popular **Ohope Beach**, described by former New Zealand Governor-General Lord Cobham as "the most beautiful beach in New Zealand". A visit to the beach on a sunny day might convince many travellers Whakatane is the sunniest location in the North Island.

The last centre of note between Whakatane and the eastern boundary of the Bay of Plenty at Cape Runaway is the rural centre of **Opotiki**. Here in 1865, missionary Rev. Carl Volkner was murdered by a Maori rebel leader, Kereopa, in a gruesome episode which saw Volkner's head cut off and placed on the church pulpit, and the communion chalice used to catch his blood.

Beyond Opotiki, the road to East Cape winds along the coast for 115 km (71 miles) to Cape Runaway. En route, it passes through the small settlements of Te Kaha and Waihau Bay, a popular camping area. Like the tip of the Coromandel Peninsula, this is the Bay of Plenty's own remote area, and it has a unique charm.

Kiwifruit.

WAIKATO AND TARANAKI

Dawn birdsong in the central and western region of the North Island has an unusual accompaniment – the chugalug-chugalug of electric milking machines. Grass grows quicker here through the year than anywhere else in the world and the cows that crop it daily have brought prosperity to generations.

Twice a day for about nine months of the year, the "cow cockies" or dairy farmers drive their docile stock to the milking sheds. There they relieve the beasts of their butterfat-rich milk from which New Zealand's famous yellow, mild cheddar cheese, butter and milk powder are made.

Carefully bred dairy herds free-graze on Waikato or Taranaki pastures along fertile river valleys or on the volcanic plains around Taranaki's snow-capped Mount Taranaki, also known as Mount Egmont. The grass is fed by a mild, wet climate (rainfall averages 1,120 mm or 44 inches in Waikato's Hamilton, and 1,565 mm or 62 inches in Taranaki's New Plymouth) and liberally applied artificial fertilisers.

The steeper land supports sheep and cattle. On the flats and rolling country, farm diversification has expanded the production of fruit and vegetables, supplying the local and export markets. The Waikato is also premium thoroughbred horse breeding country, and dairy cattle studs abound in both the Waikato and Taranaki. Although these are New Zealand's most intensively farmed regions, most of the people live in one of the many small service towns or the two major cities – Hamilton (population 106,000) and New Plymouth (population 45,000). The nation's tightest network of sealed roads link the towns, cities and farms, carrying high volumes of traffic.

A landscape flecked with blood: This peaceful, productive landscape was entirely man-made by European settlers during the 20th century. Much of the now-green pastures were the spoils of land wars between Maori and Pakeha

during the 1860s and were bloody bitter fighting.

The Waikato region was comparatively highly populated tribes and its land commu according to ancestry. It was a landscape of dense bush on the hills, peat swamp and kahikatea (white pine) forests on flat land and the low hills of the Waikato and Waipa river systems. By the 1840s and 1850s pockets of Taranaki and the Waikato were beginning to resemble a South Pacific England with their church spires, crops and villages.

The land wars disrupted it all; it took nearly 20 years for the British and colonial forces to defeat the rebellious Maori tribes who were intent on keeping what was left of their land. With the rebels either driven out or dead, and the Waikato supporters of the Maori nationalist King movement pushed south, the lands of the Waikato and Taranaki were unlocked.

What land was not confiscated by the government was effectively taken through 1862 legislation which forced the traditional Maori group ownership to be individualised. Single owners were easy prey for land agents who plied them with alcohol and money to encourage them to sell. The way was then open for the gradual development, during the 20th century, of the natural wilderness into the intensively farmed land that it is today.

It was a long, slow road for the early settler families. Years sometimes passed before they could afford to sow grass where the bush had been cleared, buy livestock and build permanent houses. Buckets and stools were carried into muddy paddocks to milk cows until primitive milking sheds were built.

One man who helped ease the transformation to the high-technology farming and processing of today was a pigtailed Chinese pedlar, Chew Chong. At first he created cash markets for butter in New Zealand; by 1884 he sent a consignment to Britain. Chew built a butter factory at Eltham, and to boost supplies of cream, he introduced sharemilking, a system whereby dairymen could run their own herds on his land for

Morokopa Falls, Waikato.

rtion of their milk payment.

y the 1900s the dairy industry was owing fast. Butter and cheese production had moved from farm to factory and farmers had formed co-operative companies – which today still govern the milk payout, and process and market dozens of dairy products worldwide. Taranaki has become the world's largest exporter of cheese, while butter and milk powder are produced in the Waikato. In both regions hundreds of stainless steel milk tankers collect the milk daily from farms.

The mountain ranges and their foothills in both regions are now mostly scenic reserves covered with native forest, crossed by rivers and streams and featuring spectacular waterfalls. A network of walkways, extended and upgraded in recent years, provides public access to these areas. Memorable public parks and gardens and thousands of private gardens are among the attractions in Hamilton and New Plymouth.

Capital of the Waikato: Hamilton is an attractive and prosperous city straddling the Waikato River, 50 km (31 miles) inland in the heart of farmland. Parkland and footpaths cover most of the city's riverbanks, popular walking and jogging routes for locals and visitors. Like the grass and crops in the surrounding countryside, Hamilton's city trees and shrubs, in public parks and private gardens, thrive in the mild climate. Much of the city's riverbanks are parkland, a restful walk for strollers and a popular route for joggers.

The 10-year-old **Waikato Museum of Art and History** is the central city's most notable riverbank amenity. Its collections include treasured Tainui (the Waikato's Maori tribe) artefacts as well as contemporary art, and New Zealand and Australian art objects. National and international touring exhibitions are a regular feature.

It was the **Waikato River** – long a vital Maori transport and trading link to the coast and the rest of the region's river network – that first brought the Europeans to the area and led to the establishment of Hamilton in the 1860s. The first businesses grew up on the riverbank and today the commercial hub of the city runs parallel to it on the west bank. River cruises offer meals and a different view of the city.

The agricultural prosperity of the region and its large population have made Hamilton New Zealand's fifth largest city. Its commerce, government offices, schools, university and industry service the region. The city has become an international centre for agricultural research, lead by the pioneering work of the Ruakura Agricultural Research Centre and the Meat Industry Research Institute. The New Zealand Dairy Board's centre for cattle semen is also based close to the city, at Newstead.

Southwest, at Templeview, is the white spire of the New Zealand headquarters for the Churh of Jesus Christ of the Latter Day Saints.

Race-horses and spas: The Waikato River is now a recreational asset for the region but of primary importance are the eight power stations which harness its waters, providing one-third of the nation's hydro-electric power. Behind

Waikato River, Hamilton.

each dam there are artificial lakes which host boating, rowing and particularly fishing enthusiasts.,

The quiet, pretty town of **Cambridge** sits on the river 24 km (15 miles) upstream from Hamilton. The town's charming Anglican church, tree-lined streets and village green – a popular summer cricket pitch – give it a very English atmosphere.

To the east of the river are the Waikato towns of Morrinsville, Te Aroha and Matamata. **Morrinsville** is itself a centre for the surrounding dairy land, with its own large processing factory (tours by arrangement) among others in the region. **Te Aroha**, on the Waihou River farther east, was once a gold town and fashionable Victorian spa sitting at the foot of 952-metre (3,123-foot) bush-clad Mount Te Aroha. The town domain has elegant bath houses and kiosks over fountains of mineral water. The world's only known hot soda-water fountain, the Mokena Geyser, is here.

Matamata is well-known for its thoroughbred racehorse stables. As with Morrinsville, the surrounding land was once part of huge holdings of land speculators. Josiah Clifton Firth took on the seemingly impossible task of clearing the Waihou River of snags to make it navigable. The three-storey blockhouse he built in 1881 stands as a reminder of the settlers' insecurity after the wars. The **Firth tower** is now part of a reserve containing a museum featuring a homestead, other buildings and collected memorabilia from the period. Several walking tracks lead into and over the nearby Kaimai-Mamaku forest park, one of them to the picturesque Wairere Falls.

From Matamata, the pine forests and farmlands of Putaruru and Tokoroa to the south are within easy reach. **Tokoroa** has only recently grown from a village to a town of about 20,000 people during the development of the huge pulp-and-paper mill at nearby Kinleith.

Maori stronghold: Down the Waikato River from Hamilton is Ngaruawahia, capital of the Maori king movement and an important Maori cultural centre. On the east riverbank in the town is the

Cattle mustering, Taranaki.

Turangawaewae Marae, its name meaning "a place to put one's feet". In the 1920s, Turangawaewae became the focal point for a revival in support for Kingitanga, inspired by Maori princess Te Puea Herangi. Her organisational abilities established a complex of buildings on 4 hectares (about 10 acres) of riverbank (this was later increased). Today the marae contains traditionally-carved meeting houses and a modern concert hall which can sleep and feed 1,200 people. The marae is not open to the public except on special occasions, but can be seen from the river bridge on the main road a little downstream.

Mount Taupiri, 6 km (4 miles) downstream, is the sacred burial ground of Waikato tribes. Near here the river's waters are used to cool a massive coal-and-gas-fired power station at **Huntly**. Its two 150-metre (492-foot) chimneys tower over the town, which stands at the centre of New Zealand's largest coalfields, opencast and underground.

Southwest of Hamilton is **Te Awamutu**, dubbed the "the rose town" for its fragrant gardens and rose shows. One of the country's oldest and finest churches, St John's Anglican Church, stands in the main street, built in 1854. Another, StPaul's, built in 1856, lies to the east of Hairini. Both are notable for their stained-glass windows. Near Hairini is **Orakau**, scene of the final battle of the Waikato land wars in 1864 when Rewi Maniapoto and 300 men, women and children fought for three days to defend a fortified pa against about 1,400 colonial soldiers.

Caves and gas: In the northern King Country, to the south, are the **Waitomo limestone caves** and glowworm grottoes. Three caves are open to the public – Waitomo, Ruakuri and Aranui. The area offers the choice of a tranquil boat ride to view the glowworms, a speleological (cave) museum, adventure caving, a model Maori village and bush walks. At **Te Kuiti**, 19 km (12 miles) further south, charismatic Maori leader Te Kooti Rikirangi took refuge and built a meeting house, later given to the local Maniapoto people as a gesture of thanks

Taranaki Mount Egmont.

for their protection. The carvings inside the house are among the finest; the structure has been restored or rebuilt five times.

The 169-km (105-mile) Te Kuiti to New Plymouth road shows the southbound traveller rugged farmed hill country, the Awakino River gorge and beautiful coast with cliffs and placid sandy bays. Tiny river-mouth settlements are popular holiday and fishing spots. After a climb up the road over Mount Messenger, **Taranaki Mount Egmont** is in full view on a clear day.

The road passes by a striking memorial to Polynesian anthropologist Sir Peter Buck just north of Urenui, his birthplace, and Motunui, a synthetic petrol plant. A visitor's centre at the main gates is open daily. Near New Plymouth, Taranaki's capital, the land flattens to fertile dairy plains encircling the dormant volcano of Mount Taranaki, a near-perfect cone 2,581 metres (8,468 feet) high.

Among the tidy green fields southwest of the city are the well-heads and processing-plant towers of the Kapuni natural gas field, and at Motonui is the world's largest gas-to-gasoline plant, using gas from the offshore Maui field.

Heritage trail: With Mount Taranaki as its backdrop, **New Plymouth** spreads down the coast. It offered a location, soils and climate immediately attractive to European settlers in the 1840s. As in the Waikato, the first missionaries and settlers found a Maori population depleted by inter-tribal wars, but nevertheless land troubles between the natives and newcomers beset the settlement from the beginning. War broke out in 1860 and eventually placed New Plymouth under virtual siege. The city has several historical buildings. St Mary's Church is the oldest stone church in New Zealand, the remains of the church vicarage, built in 1845, have been restored by the Historic Places Trust. So has Richmond Cottage, the house of three of the first settler families, and Hurworth Cottage, built in 1855 and home of four-times New Zealand premier, Sir Harry Atkinson.

But it is New Plymouth's beautiful parks which are best known. **Pukekura Park**, once wasteland, has lovely lakes, gardens, a fernery, fountains and a waterfall, lit by night. The upper lake gives a postcard-like view of Mount Egmont.

In September and November, a 360-hectare (890-acre) park, 29 km (18 miles) from New Plymouth, provides one of the world's best displays of flowering rhododendron and azalea bushes in a native bush setting. The **Pukeiti Rhododendron Trust** is also a bird sanctuary, nestling between the Kaitake and Pouakai ranges. A loop road to the park passes the Pouakai Wildlife Reserve, where native and exotic birds and animals can be seen in a bush setting.

Winter skiers and summer climbers enjoy **Egmont National Park**. There are more than 300 km (190 miles) of bush walks. Climbing to Mount Taranaki's summit is not difficult, but weather conditions change rapidly. On a clear day there are fine views across to the snow-capped peaks of the Tongariro National Park and over dairy land to the wild whitecaps of the Tasman Sea.

Sir Peter Buck's memorial, North Taranaki.

ROTORUA AND THE VOLCANIC PLATEAU

Of his visit to **Rotorua** in 1934, playwright George Bernard Shaw declared: "I was pleased to get so close to Hades and be able to return."

But Shaw was not the first to draw an analogy between Rotorua and the devil's eternal dwelling of fire and brimstone, for it was Victorian writer and war correspondent George Augustus Sala who, in 1885, christened one of the thermal areas "Hell's Gate".

To pious Anglican pioneers the region had all the hallmarks of Dante's Inferno – a barren wasteland of stunted vegetation, cratered with scalding cauldrons, bubbling mud pools and roaring geysers hurling super-heated water into a sulphur-laden atmosphere.

Today Rotorua represents pleasure and not torment, and has become one of the two jewels of New Zealand tourism (along with Queenstown in the South Island) – a place of thermal wonders, lush forests, green pastures and crystal clear lakes abounding with fighting trout. No fewer than 10 lakes are the playground of anglers, campers, swimmers, water-skiers, yachtsmen, pleasure boaters, trampers and hunters. In the mid-1990s, Rotorua became the first tourist attraction in New Zealand to host two million annual visitors from other parts of New Zealand and overseas.

The Rotorua region is situated on a volcanic rift which stretches in a 200-km (124-mile) line from White Island off the coast of the Bay of Plenty to Lake Taupo and the volcanoes of the Tongariro National Park in the Central Plateau of the North Island. More than 63,000 live in the Rotorua urban area and close-by smaller towns because tourism is not the only major industry centred there. Bordering on the city is Kaiangaroa, one of the world's largest man-made forests, and it's not the only one. Most of the exotic trees here are radiata pine, a renewable resource regularly cropped for pulp and paper, and a wide variety of timber products. The region is also prolifically farmed.

Rotorua was settled by descendants of voyagers from the legendary Maori homeland of Hawaiki, thought to be the Tahitian island group. Among the arrivals in the Te Awawa canoe around AD 1350 was the discoverer of Lake Rotorua, named in Maori tradition as Ihenga, who travelled inland from the settlement of Maketu and came across a lake he called Rotoiti, "little lake". He journeyed on to see a much larger lake which he appropriately called Rotorua, the "second lake". The city still has the greatest concentration of Maori residents of any New Zealand centre. Much of its allure to tourists is derived from the fact that it is the national "hot spot" of Maori culture.

The first European to visit "the disturbed districts", in 1830 was a Danish sailor, Captain Phillip Tapsell (a descendant of whose was appointed Speaker to the House of Representatives in 1991). On 30 October 1831, at the invitation of an Awawa tribal chief, missionaries Thomas Chapman and Henry Williams held the first Sunday service in Rotorua.

During the mid-1880s the Arawa tribe remained loyal to the British Crown and, as a result, were subjected to raids by warring Maori tribes. When the fighting ceased, the government decided to turn Rotorua into a tourist and health-spa resort. An agreement was reached in November 1880 for land on which to build a town to be leased from the Maori owners. The town was administered by The Tourist and Health Resorts Department until 1923 when Rotorua finally achieved independent status.

Liquid assets: The majority of the town's biggest hotels and a large number of motels are located on or just off Fenton Street, running north-south across the city. It is only a short drive to the popular tourist attractions but some form of transport is essential. The Government Tourist Bureau in Fenton Street will provide information on hire cars, coach excursions, trout fishing and sightseeing services.

East of the northern end of Fenton Street is a beautiful garden area dominated by the magnificent **Bath House**,

Preceding pages: Whakarewarewa. **Left,** Maori rooftop, Rotorua.

built in 1908 as a sophisticated spa centre. The Bath House now houses an interesting local museum and art gallery. The scene is more English than England when there are white-uniformed bowls and croquet players competing on the lawns in front of the Elizabethan-style building.

To the right of Bath House are the **Polynesian Pools**. Here are contained a number of thermal pools, each with its own special mineral content and varying temperatures. The Priest Pool was named after a Father Mahoney, who pitched his tent alongside a hot spring on the site in 1878 and bathed in the warm water until he reportedly obtained complete relief for his rheumatism. Other pools in the complex include the Rachel and Radium Springs.

Rotorua's world-famous thermal waters and their alleged miraculous healing properties were central to the European development of the area. In 1874, former New Zealand Premier Sir William Fox urged the government to "secure the whole of the Lake Country as a sanatorium owing to the ascertained healing properties of the water". Bubbling with optimism, Sir William enthused that the district "might be destined to be the sanatorium not only of the Australian colonies but of India and other portions of the globe".

The building of the first sanatorium began in 1880 and, although the sulphurous waters of the baths are still regarded by some as useful in the treatment of arthritis and rheumatism, most visitors and locals enjoy them as a pleasant form of relaxation – guaranteed to soothe frayed nerves, relax the body and ensure a good night's sleep. Fronting the gardens is the **Orchid Garden**, two temperature-controlled glass houses filled with exotic blooms from around the world. Wander through to the theatrette where the Southern Hemisphere's only illuminated water organ dives and dances to an ever-changing music backdrop.

Along the lakefront from the gardens is the historic Maori village of Ohinemutu, once the main settlement on the

Public gardens and the Bath House.

lake. On the site is St Faith's Church built in 1910, with its rich carvings, Maori Christ window and bust of Queen Victoria, presented to the Maori people of Rotorua as a token of their loyalty to the Crown. An adjacent 19th century meeting house took 12 years to carve and is named after the captain of the Arawa canoe, Tama Te Kapua.

Ohinemutu also has connections with Rotorua's Arawa discoverer, Ihenga. The name translates as "the place where the young woman was killed"; it is said that Ihenga's daughter Hine-te-Kakara, was murdered and her body thrown into a boiling mud pool where Ihenga set up a memorial stone, calling it Ohinemutu.

At the lakeside, float-planes, helicopters, launches and the *Lakeland Queen* paddle steamer depart on flightseeing and sightseeing trips. A popular launch excursion is to **Mokoia Island** in the middle of Lake Rotorua, where visitors stop for a dip in Hinemoa's hot pool.

The Maori have a "Romeo and Juliet" love story connected with Mokoia. A young chieftain, Tutanekai, who lived on the island, fell in love with the maiden Hinemoa, who lived in a village on the mainland. But their marriage was forbidden by family opposition. Hinemoa secretly planned to follow the sound of Tutanekai's bone flute over the water during the night and join her lover. The plot was foiled when her people beached all the heavy canoes, so Hinemoa tied gourds to her body and swam across the chilling lake, following the sounds of Tutanekai's flute. She recovered from her ordeal by warming herself in a hot pool that bears her name before being reunited with Tutanekai.

Mud and Geysers: At the southern end of Fenton Street is the **Whakarewarewa** thermal area, abbreviated to "Whaka" by the locals and a must for tourists. Unfortunately, too many visitors hurry down the main path, past a quiescent Geyser Flat and into the Maori settlement below, without savouring the attractions of the thermal area.

On Geyser Flat is **Pohutu** ("splashing"), the greatest geyser in New Zealand, thundering to a height of more

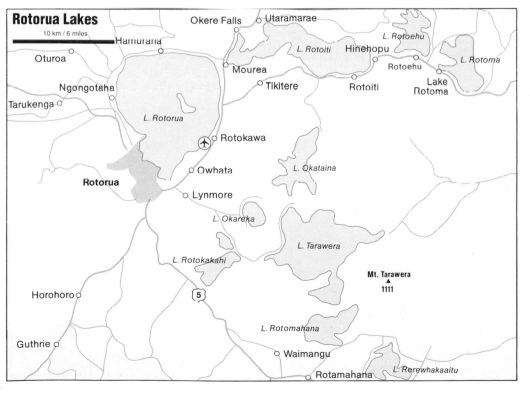

Rotorua Lakes

10 km / 6 miles

Okere Falls · Utaramarae · Hamurana · L. Rotoehu · Oturoa · L. Rotoiti · Hinehopu · L. Rotoma · Mourea · Rotoehu · Ngongotaha · Tikitere · Rotoiti · Lake Rotoma · Tarukenga · L. Rotorua · Rotokawa · L. Okataina · Rotorua · Owhata · Lynmore · L. Okareka · L. Tarawera · L. Rotokakahi · Mt. Tarawera ▲ 1111 · Horohoro · 5 · L. Rotomahana · Guthrie · Waimangu · L. Rerewhakaaitu · Rotamahana

than 30 metres (about 100 feet). The geyser is unpredictable but usually plays several times a day and sometimes almost continuously. As a warning, its eruption is often preceded by the playing of the Prince of Wales Feathers, a smaller geyser next to Pohutu. The big geyser is well worth waiting for.

At the entrance to "Whaka" is a model Maori pa incorporating a spacious meeting house, in which Maori concerts are performed in a realistic setting. Maori groups also sing and dance at Ohinemutu and in major hotels.

Close to the top entrance is the **Maori Arts and Crafts Institute** where skilled Maori carvers and flax weavers can be observed at work. The intricately carved archway to "Whaka" depicts Hinemoa and Tutanekai embracing.

The bottom path exists past the Maori settlement where tribal people have, for generations, used the thermal waters for cooking, washing and heating.

In Tryon Street, colonial-style shops in the **Little Village** sell sheepskins, furs, handicrafts and souvenirs. A greenstone carver can be watched at work. A fascinating but inexpensive item, which can be purchased from a small printery, is a reprint of the *Hot Lakes Chronicle* of 1886 containing photographs and newspaper accounts of the devastating Tarawera eruption.

Departing via Froude Street, take a look at the **Arikapakapa Golf Course**, the only one in the world which has its own boiling mud pool "traps" and hot pool "hazards".

Rainbow country: Proceeding west from Rotorua on Highway 5, just 4 km (2½ miles) from the city, is the terminus for Skyline-Skyrides. Ride their gondolas mid-way up **Mount Ngongotaha** for a breathtaking view of the city, lake and surrounding countryside. For the more adventurous, plunge downhill again in a high-speed luge cart. You can also drive to the top.

For a more relaxed stop-over, take in the fragrant delights of the neighbouring Herb Garden. Visitors will find **Rainbow** and **Fairy Springs**, containing natural pools crammed with thou-

Fire watcher at Rainbow Mountain.

sands of rainbow, brown and brook trout among 12 hectares (30 acres) of native tree ferns and natural surroundings. Huge trout can be seen through an underwater viewing window and hand-fed along with species of New Zealand deer, native birds and "Captain Cooker" wild pigs, introduced by the famous explorer himself. Live kiwis peck around in a nocturnal house. There is also a Rainbow Springs farm show.

Other trout springs are **Paradise Valley**, 11 km (7 miles) west of Rotorua, and **Hamurana Springs** located on the northern shore.

Brown trout from Britain via Tasmania were introduced to Rotorua in 1889; rainbow trout from Sonoma Creek, California, were released in 1898 and thrived.

To protect sports fisheries, it has been made illegal to buy or sell trout in New Zealand. But a trout dinner is an easy catch with fishing guides claiming a 97 percent daily "strike" rate. In fact no trip to Rotorua-Taupo is complete without a fishing expedition on the lakes. Guides supply all tackle (often including cups of "fortified" coffee) and will meet clients outside hotels, with trailer boats ready for action, or at the boat harbour.

Rainbow trout on most lakes around Rotorua and on Lake Taupo average 1.4 kg (3 pounds) but on Lake Tarawera, where they are tougher to catch, fish of 3.5 kg to 5.5 kg (8 to 12 pounds) are not uncommon. The icing on the cake after a day of fishing is having a hotel or restaurant chef prepare the catch – a service speciality which they are well used to providing.

Also west of Rotorua, through Ngongotaha, is the spacious **Agrodome** located in 142 hectares (350 acres) pasture. Three times a day 19 trained rams are put through their paces for an hour in "sheep shows" which are particularly popular with Asian tourists. Two sheep dogs, a huntaway and strong-eye, appear on stage and later give demonstrations of sheep handling in the adjacent pasture. The shearing of sheep and the hand-milking of a cow are also part of the stage show. The performance is educational and entertaining and visitors

Proud fisherman and trout at Turangi.

receive handfuls of freshly shorn wool.

Along Central Road, past Ngongotaha township, the Farm House hires out ponies and horses for riding over 600 acres of bush-edged farmland. The west-shore road continues to Okere Falls and Hinemoa Steps where, after a short walk through native forest and down a cliffside, the Kaituna River can be viewed thundering through a narrow chasm into the swirling pool below.

Proceeding north and east around Lake Rotorua, past the Ohau Channel outlet into Lake Rotoiti, an eastbound turn on to Highway 30, towards Whakatane, takes visitors to the very door of **Hell's Gate**. The Maori name, Tikitere, recalls the legend of Huritini, who threw herself into a boiling pool because her husband treated her with contempt. Tikitere is a contraction of Taku tiki i tere nei, "my daughter has floated away". The volcanic activity here covers 4 hectares (10 acres), highlighted by the Kakahi hot waterfall.

With time in hand, a drive farther down Highway 30 along the shores of Lakes Rotoiti, Rotoehu and Rotoma, with a diversion to the totally unspoiled Lake Okataina, is well worth while.

For a dip with a difference, take a side-road between Lakes Rotoehu and Rotoma to **Soda Springs**, where hot water percolates into a clear stream bed.

The eruption of Tarawera: Southeast of Rotorua, heading in the direction of the airport, is the turnoff to the forest-clad **Blue and Green Lakes**, a favourite stomping ground for joggers and a retreat for those who enjoy walking or riding the well-marked and graded trails through exotic pines and native bush. Horses and ponies are available for hire. On a fine day, Lakes Tikitapu and Rotokakahi reflect nicely contrasting blue and green colours, thus giving rise to their European names.

The road continues to Lake Tarawera via the buried village of Te Wairoa, destroyed on 10 June 1886 when an awesome eruption of Mount Tarawera blasted rock, lava and ash into the air over a 15,540-sq km (6,000-sq mile) area and buried the villages of Te Wairoa,

Silica terraces, Waiotapu.

Te Ariki and Moura, killing 147 Maori and six Europeans. The Buried Village contains items excavated from Te Wairoa including the whare (hut) of a tohunga (priest) who foretold the disaster and was unearthed alive four days after the eruption.

From Te Wairoa, before the eruption, Victorian tourists used to be rowed across Lake Tarawera to the fabulous Pink and White Terraces – two huge silica formations which rose 250 metres (820 feet) from the shores of Lake Rotomahana and were billed as one of "the eight wonders of the world" by writers of the 1800s.

Mount Tarawera ("burnt spear") looms on the eastern shores of both lakes. Flights over the crater and the thermal areas are conducted by Volcanic Wunderflites from Rotorua Airport. A thrilling landing on the mountain's slopes allows for a close inspection of the 6-km long (4-mile), 250-metre (820-ft) deep chasm caused by the volcanic explosion.

Adding to Tarawera's mysterious aura is the verified account of a ghostly war canoe full of mourning, flax-robed Maori seen by two separate boatloads of tourists on Lake Tarawera on the misty morning of 31 May 1886. Returning to Te Wairoa, the tourists found the local Maori in a state of terror for no such canoe existed in the region. Tuhuto, the tohunga, prophesied the apparition was "an omen that all this region will be overwhelmed". On a chilly, moonlit night 11 days later, Mount Tarawera fulfilled his prophecy to the letter, blasting the Pink and White Terraces off the world tourist map forever.

Twenty km (12.5 miles) south of Rotorua, on Highway 5 towards Taupo, is **Waimangu Valley**. This unspoilt thermal area contains the Waimangu Cauldron, the world's largest boiling lake.

An easy walk downhill from a tea-room leads past bubbling crater lakes, hot creeks and algae-covered silica terraces to the shores of Lake Rotomahana (a refuge of black swans), where a launch can be taken to the intensively active Steaming Cliffs and site of the lost Pink

Hopeful angler at Taupo.

and White Terraces. The valley is also the site of the extinct Waimangu ("black water") Geyser which hurled black water and mud to an incredible height of 500 metres (over 1,600 feet) between 1900 and 1904, on one occasion killing four tourists who ventured too close.

Another 10 km (6 miles) south on Highway 5 is a loop road leading to the **Waiotapu** ("sacred waters") thermal area. This contains the Lady Knox Geyser, which erupts daily at 10.15 am (with the encouragement of a little soap). Other attractions include the boiling Champagne Pool, tinted silica terraces and the Bridal Veil Falls. A free treat is a diversion off the loop road (watch for the sign) to some intriguing boiling mud pools and the Waikite Thermal Baths.

"Taupo", an abbreviation of Taupo-nui-Tia ("the great shoulder cloak of Tia"), takes its name from the Arawa canoe explorer who discovered **Lake Taupo**. The lake covers 608 sq km (235 sq miles) and was formed by volcanic explosions over thousands of years. It is now the most famous trout-fishing lake in the world, yielding in excess of 500 tonnes of rainbow trout annually to enthusiastic anglers.

The rivers flowing into the lake are equally well stocked and fishermen frequently stand shoulder-to-shoulder at the mouth of the Waitahanui River, forming what has come to be known as "the picket fence". Arrangements for boat hires can be made at the picturesque boat harbour and information centre, where a restored steamboat, *Ernest Kemp*, departs regularly on lake excursions. Or see the lake from the decks of one of a variety of other vessels.

About 40 km (25 miles) northwest of Taupo and 70 km (44 miles) south of Rotorua is the active and well-signposted **Orakei-Korako** thermal area. Maori chiefs once decorated themselves in mirror pools here, giving rise to the name which means "place of adorning".

Special features are the jet-boat journey across Lake Ohakuri, the 40-metre (130-foot) Great Golden Fleece terrace, underground hot pools in Aladdin's Cave and a huge area of silica deposits **Waimangu volcanic valley.**

which are pockmarked with hot springs.

Some 7 km (4 miles) north of Taupo, just below the junction of highways 1 and 5, is the dramatic **Wairakei Geothermal Power Station**. Super-heated water is drawn from the ground through a series of bores, enabling dry steams to be piped to electricity turbines in a nearby powerhouse. At the entrance to the field is an information office; a road to the left of the pipelines winds to a hilltop observation area.

A nearby loop road leads to the spectacular **Huka Falls** where the full force of the newly born Waikato River hurtles from a narrow gorge over a 12-metre (40-foot) ledge. Lit by bright sunshine, the ice-cold water takes on a turquoise-blue colour as it hangs in mid-air before crashing into a foaming basin. Huka means "foam"; the falls are best observed across the footbridge from the opposite side of the river.

A short distance along the loop road on the banks of the Waikato River is the famous Huka Fishing Lodge and a small replica pioneer village. Also between

Wairakei and Taupo, on a gravel road, are the **Craters of the Moon**, a wild thermal area. Visitors can gaze into a frightening abyss of furiously boiling mud and walk around a track to see steam rising from natural fumaroles in the hillside. The international golf course at Wairakei is rated among the best in New Zealand.

The Taupo Information Centre will give advice on sightseeing, attractions for children, as well as on flightseeing. Impressive scenic flights by floatplane from the lakefront, or by fixed-winged aircraft and helicopters from the airport south of Taupo, are made to snow-capped summits of the volcanoes in Tongariro National Park.

Three mountains: At the southern head of Lake Taupo is the 7,600-sq km (2,930-sq mile) **Tongariro National Park** containing the three active volcanic mountains of Tongariro (1,968 metres; 6,400 feet), Ngauruhoe (2,290 metres; 7,517 feet) and thirdly Ruapehu (2,796 metres; 9,175 feet).

The most scenic route from Taupo

leaves Highway 1 at Turangi heading for Tokaanu, not far from the Tongariro Power Station, and winds up through bush-covered mountains and around the shore of Lake Rotoaira. The alternative route is to turn off the main highway at Rangipo on to Highway 47.

A brief diversion to **Tokaanu**, 60 km (37 miles) from Taupo, reveals a small thermal area, the Domain Thermal Baths and the historic St Paul's 19th-century church. According to Maori legend the volcanic fires of the Tongariro National Park were kindled when the priest and explorer Ngatoro-i-rangi was in danger of freezing to death on the mountains. His fervent prayers for assistance were answered by the fire demons of Hawaiki, who sent fire via White Island and Rotorua to burst out through the mountaintops. To appease the gods, Ngatoro cast his female slave into the Ngauruhoe volcano – called by the girl's name, Auruhoe, by the local Maori.

Ngauruhoe with its typical volcanic cone is the most active of the three mountains and occasionally erupts in spectacular clouds of smoke and ash. A major eruption in 1954-1955 continued intermittently for nine months.

Ruapehu ("exploding hole") is a perpetually snow-capped, multiple volcano with a flattened summit stretching 3 km (1.8 miles) and incorporating an acidic, bubbling Crater Lake and six small glaciers. Ruapehu has blown out clouds of steam and ash a number of times in the past 100 years, raining dust over a 90-km (56-mile) radius in 1945.

The mountain was directly responsible for a train disaster in which 151 people died on Christmas Eve 1953. A *lahar,* or violent discharge of water from Crater Lake, roared down the Whangaehu River carrying large quantities of sand and boulders before it.

The torrent slammed into a railway bridge at Tangiwai, 35 km (23 miles) away, sweeping it into the night. Minutes later, a Wellington-Auckland express train and five carriages careened down the track, plunging to its doom in the raging river below.

Tongariro is the lowest of the three mountains with a series of small craters and the Ketetahi hot springs on the northern slopes.

The mountaintops were sacred to the Maori of the Ngati-Tuwharetoa tribe. In 1887, hereditary chief Te Heuheu Tukino made a gift of the summits to the federal government as New Zealand's first national park in order to protect them from exploitation.

For the tourist with days to spend in the park, rangers at the national park headquarters near Chateau Tongariro will give full information on walking tracks and accommodation huts. However, it is reward enough to glimpse Ngauruhoe belching its puffs of smoke on a clear day and the snow-decked Ruapehu soaring as a picture-postcard backdrop for the wild, rocky rivers on the western slopes.

Mount Ruapehu is the major ski area of the North Island. The Chateau Tongariro-Whakapapa skifield is oldest, but recently the Turoa and Tukino fields have been developed. Adventure tour operators offer white-water rafting down the Tongariro and Rangitikei rivers.

Left, raft ride at Aniwhenua Falls. Right, the distant Mount Ngauruhoe (left) and Mount Ruapehu.

POVERTY BAY AND HAWKE'S BAY

High on Kaiti Hill, overlooking the city of Gisborne and the sprawling countryside beyond, is a life-sized figure of the British explorer, Captain James Cook, looking to the mouth of the Turanganui River where he first stood on New Zealand soil. The site is historic for that reason, although the occasion – 9 October 1769 – was marred by a fracas with native Maori. The site is also noted now for the reason that Gisborne, situated on 178 degrees longitude, is the first city in the world to greet the rising sun each day. Hence, it is the Sunrise Coast.

Across the bay from Kaiti Hill is Young Nick's Head, a promontory named after 12-year-old Nicholas Young who was surgeon's boy in Cook's ship *Endeavour*. Nicholas was the first to sight land.

Silly mistake: Cook erred badly, however, in calling the region Poverty Bay because "it did not afford a single article we wanted, except a little firewood". Poverty Bay retains the name but stands for anything but poverty. It is sheep and cattle country and rich in citrus and kiwifruit orchards, vineyards, vegetable gardens and a variety of other food crops which all support a large processing industry. Its wines – particularly Chardonnay and Gewurztraminer – are among the best in the country.

As well as its fertility, Poverty Bay offers spectacular coastal vistas of white sands and sparkling blue summer waters, accompanied by the scarlet blossom of the pohutukawa, often known as the New Zealand Christmas tree because it at its best and brightest in late December. Some of this colour runs off on **Gisborne** (with an urban area population of 31,000), a city of sun and water, parks, bridges and beaches. Water sports are a recreational way of life to people whose main commercial street is only a few metres from a long, curving white sandy beach.

Gisborne lingers over its association with Cook, because for a New Zealander to walk where he walked along Kaiti and Waikanae beaches is to tread in the footsteps of history. But the area's historic wealth pre-dates his visit because the Maori inheritance is rich. Maori land-holdings – some of them leased to Europeans – are extensive; and more obviously meeting houses are numerous with carved lintels, panels and beams done in traditional style, and the unorthodox painting of patterned foliage, birds and mythical human figures. The largest is Poho-o-Rawiri (the Bosom of Rawiri), at the base of Kaiti Hill. Almost every one of the many Maori settlements along the coast has its treasured meeting house.

While Poverty Bay is tranquil today, there were many battles among the tribes in the past and during last century a prophet called Te Kooti led a prolonged rebellion against the settlers. He was exiled to the Chatham Islands, hundreds of kilometres off the east coast of the North Island, along with dozens of other Maori arrested in the 1860s. He masterminded a daring escape back to the mainland and founded a religious move-

Left, Lake Waikaremoana. **Right**, Pania, Maori maiden of Napier.

ment which still exists, called Ringatu. The government sent an army in pursuit but Te Kooti proved a formidable enemy in the wild bush of the Urewera Range, striking back with guerrilla attacks that kept him free and the government harassed. He was eventually pardoned in his old age and allowed to live with his religious followers in the King Country, far from the coastal region of Poverty Bay.

Many of Te Kooti's old haunts have been preserved in the **Urewera National Park**, 212,000 hectares (500,000 acres) of rugged mountains, forests and beautiful lakes, much of it still inaccessible to all but the toughest experienced trampers. The feature of the park is unquestionably Lake Waikaremoana ("Lake of the Rippling Waters"), rich in trout and with bush crowding to the water's edge on all but the eastern side where it is hemmed in by steep cliffs. Chalet, motel and motor camp accommodation is available at Waikaremoana, and hunting and tramping huts are available for hire throughout the park.

Quake towns: Poverty Bay runs southward to Wairoa and the Mahia Peninsula where it merges into the **Hawke's Bay** region. With similar land use to Gisborne, Hawke's Bay is centred on the twin cities of Napier and Hastings, which may be close but are strongly independent and even competitive. Napier is a seafront city with a population of 52,000, and Hastings, 20 km (12 miles) away, is an agricultural marketing centre of 55,000. The cities are bounded to the east by the Pacific Ocean (although Hastings is a little inland) and to their west plains sweep away to the Kaweka and Ruahine ranges – rugged areas for hunters and trampers.

Hawke's Bay shares with Gisborne the memory of New Zealand's worst earthquake tragedy, on 3 February 1931. Buildings crumpled under the impact of a 7.9 Richter Scale quake. What the shock did not destroy in Napier and Hastings, fire did. The death toll of 258 included a number of people killed by falling parapets. Napier was closest to the epicentre and heroic deeds were **Napier after the quake.**

performed by rescuers and by naval personnel from a sloop, *HMS Veronica*, which happened to be in harbour.

It was a time of economic depression but a sympathetic government and a sympathetic world came to Hawke's Bay's post-quake aid with funds for a massive relief and rebuilding campaign. The opportunity was taken to widen streets and a strict earthquake-proof building code was enforced. Along the seafront today is a colonnade named after the naval sloop.

It could be said that the whole of **Napier** today is a kind of memorial to the earthquake. Much of its inland sub-urban area, stretching out to the once-independent borough of Taradale in the southwest, is built on the 4,000 hectares (10,000 hectares) of former marshland the earthquake pushed up.

A more distinctive inheritance is the innercity's increasingly famous Art Deco architecture which was chosen by the architects to reflect both the era and the attitude of the new city. The collection of Art Deco buildings in the inner city, with bold lines, elaborate motifs and pretty pastel colours, is recognised internationally as extraordinary. Recognition of the quality of the architecture – and its popularity – has come only in the past few years but has come with a vengeance. Building owners are encouraged to restore and preserve the facades; and a trust has been set up to promote and protect this valued feature of the city's heritage. Civic leaders have done their bit too, developing the main street in a sympathetic fashion.

As no mention of Napier would be complete without including Art Deco, neither would it be if the city's **Marine Parade** was ignored. A collection of gardens, sculptures, fountains, earthquake memorials and varied visitor attractions, the seaside is dominated by towering rows of Norfolk pines. Marine Parade includes the statue of Pania, a maiden of local legend; and it has long boasted Marineland, New Zealand's only marine park with performing dolphins, along with an adjacent aquarium.

Hulking above the city centre is

Napier today.

Napier Hill, home to many residents. Before the earthquake it was almost an island and was the earliest developed area of the city by Europeans. Evidence of this remains in some of the fine Victorian and Edwardian homes and in the maze of twisting, narrow streets, designed before motorcars were anticipated. On the north side of the hill, next to the bustling port, is another historic area, Ahuriri, the cradle of Napier, the site of the very first European settlement in the area.

Architectural treasures from the post-earthquake period dot **Hastings**, too, in the Art Deco and Spanish Mission style. Despite their closeness, Hastings is rather a different city from Napier, laid out in a flat and formal fashion, surrounded by a rich alluvial plain which hosts a huge range of horticultural crops.

A chief attraction of Hastings is **Fantasyland**, a family-orientated fun park with such amusements as a life-sized pirate ship, a castle, a shoe in which lived the old woman with her many children, Noddy Town, and many more escapes from reality. But Hastings's main role is, as it is proudly called by locals, "The Fruit Bowl of New Zealand". A Mediterranean-type climate, pure water from an underground aquifer, and innovative growers have made this one of the most important apple-growing regions in the world; and apricots, peaches, nectarines, plums, kiwifruit, pears, berries and cherries also grow profusely here and are on offer from roadside stalls during the harvesting season, along with tomatoes, sweet corn, asparagus and peas. Most of the produce is processed for export at large food processing factories on the edge of the city.

Despite the horticultural bounty, the twin cities rely heavily on farming which has generated the region's historic wealth. Only pine forests are challenging the supremacy of sheep and cattle in the rolling hinterland. The pastoral farms are the legacy of Victorian settlers who laid claim to huge tracts of Hawke's Bay, and made their fortunes from wool and, later, sheep-meat, beef and hides. **Waipiro Bay.**

210

Hastings has a **Scenic Drive**, a signposted tour of its suburbs, parks and major visitor attractions. Among these is Oak Avenue, a magnificent 1.5 kilometre-stretch of road planted in oaks and other huge deciduous trees by a nostalgic 19th-century landowner and carefully tended by his successors.

A short distance across the plain from Hastings is "The Village", as the pretty, genteel town of **Havelock North** is known locally. It sits in the shadow of Te Mata Peak, a limestone mountain with a summit accessible by car. From the top you can enjoy the sweeping views or, if you are daring enough, you may go hang-gliding or paragliding from the steep cliff on one side.

Wine and gannets: Hastings and Napier may enjoy distinctive identities (and indulge in parochalism to go with it) but they share some significant attractions – the **Cape Kidnappers** gannet colony, for example, and the local wine industry. Cape Kidnappers is a 20- to 30-minute drive from either city, followed by a ride along the beach in one of the tractor-towed trailer vehicles to what is thought to be the largest mainland gannet colony in the world. The cape's name, incidentally, harks back to an incident involving Captain Cook and the local Maori, who attempted to abduct a Tahitian from the *Endeavour* while it lay at anchor nearby, just a week after Cook had first arrived in New Zealand and called at Poverty Bay.

About two dozen wineries are established around Napier and Hastings. Hawke's Bay is the oldest of New Zealand's wine-growing regions and sees itself as the finest. Certainly it enjoys ever-increasing recognition for the quality of its Chardonnays, Sauvignon Blancs and Cabernet Sauvignons. Most wineries are open to visitors, offering an opportunity to sample, discuss and simply enjoy the fruits of the vine.

To the south of Hastings, pastoral farming is the reason for the existence of another set of Hawke's Bay twin towns, **Waipukurau** and **Waipawa**. But near Waipukurau is a hill with one of the longest names of any place in the world: Taumatawhakatangihangakoauauo-tamateapokaiwhenuakitanatahu. The 57 letters translate into "The hill where the great husband of heaven, Tamatea, caused plaintive music from his nose flute to ascend to his beloved".

Maori have roots in Hawke's Bay marked today by the many marae (meeting grounds) in the region. And in 1872, Te Aute College was founded just south of Hastings to educate the sons of chiefs. It is still a force in Maori education.

Further south again, another culture has left its mark. Last century, hardy Norwegian and Danish settlers cleared the rain forest in southern Hawke's Bay which was so dense it had discouraged all others. They established such towns as Norsewood and Dannevirke ("Dane's Work"). **Norsewood**, although a tiny town, has a well-known woollen mill producing a range of knitted goods bearing the settlement's name. **Dannevirke**, which likes to promote its historic links with Scandinavia, is a farm service town and a convenient staging post on the busy highway between Manawatu to the south and Hawke's Bay to the north.

Gannet from Cape Kidnappers.

MANAWATU AND WANGANUI

Where does a square turn full circle? In **Palmerston North**, flourishing centre of rich agricultural Manawatu. The city's most famous feature isn't round, but nowadays it is as the city settlers wanted it. They envisaged a central public park, but instead – for three-quarters of a century – the railway ran through the middle of town. In 1962 it was shifted to the settlement's northern fringe, and the **Square** in New Zealand's second largest inland city has dramatically changed.

Named in Maori Te Marae o Hine or "Courtyard of the Daughter of Peace", the square commemorates a chieftainess named Te Rongorito who sought an end to inter-tribal warfare in the early days of European settlement. City workers enjoy their lunches on the grass here; frequent open-air displays, recitals and forums add to the informal atmosphere.

Standing in the square, you are surrounded by the city's main retail area and civic and cultural amenities. Most evident is the **Civic Centre**, extending back on to former railway land, which is also the site for an art gallery, theatre and convention centre, and a new museum and science centre. Nearby are the city's professional theatre, Centrepoint, and Square Edge, a community arts centre and shopping complex housed in the old city council building.

Over the past few years, Palmerston North has developed remarkably. New shopping centres have been built and older ones restored and refurbished. There has been a boom too in small wine bars and cafés; and a seven-cinema multiplex has been so successful that Palmerston North people are now officially the most regular cinema attenders in New Zealand. The historic Regent Theatre, formerly mainly used as a picture palace, is restored as the city's main auditorium, and the facade of a former department store has been retained for the new city library.

Education and research: Roads radiate outwards. Fitzherbert Avenue leads to

Jerusalem, Wanganui River.

the city's other major focal point, the **Manawatu River**. It is a matter of contention that the river is crossed by only one bridge, particularly one used by thousands of cars and bicycles each day en route to **Massey University** and a number of science research stations. Also over the bridge is the International Pacific College, a tertiary institution established by a Japanese company, and New Zealand's largest army base at Linton. Massey, in its beautiful garden setting, contributes greatly to economic and cultural well-being. Given the number of educational institutions in Palmerston North, it's not surprising it calls itself the Knowledge Centre of New Zealand.

On the city side of the Manawatu River, the pride of Palmerston North is **The Esplanade**, a reserve catering for light recreation, simple pleasures or peaceful contemplation, depending on one's mood. Children can enjoy the playground, and adults can join them on the miniature railway. The Lido swimming complex (including an indoor pool) adjoins the motor camp. Don't miss the Rose Garden, which has a record of developing new varieties.

A walkway girdles Palmerston North and native bush reserves are close by. The city is frequently the venue for national sports tournaments, partly because of its central location, but mostly because of its first-rate sports facilities, including a 4,000-seat stadium which is used for rock concerts and netball tests; and cricket, rugby, hockey and rugby league are all played under lights.

Exploring Manawatu: The most dramatic road and rail approach to Palmerston North and the Manawatu region is from Hawke's Bay through the rugged Manawatu Gorge. The narrow, winding road requires careful attention when driving. The growing country town of **Ashhurst** lies between the gorge and Palmerston North. Travellers can detour here to Pohangina and Totara Reserve, an area of virgin native bush favoured locally for picnics and for swimming in the Pohangina River.

Less than 30 minutes' drive south of

Dawn on the Wanganui.

Palmerston North on Highway 57 is the Tokomaru Steam Museum; visitors can picnic and swim here at Horseshoe Bend. Highway 56 heads west to beaches at Himitange and Foxton. (Not great, but well-patronised.)

Fielding is 20 minutes north on Highway 54. This large town boasts two squares, a motor-racing track and racecourse, and a stock sale on Friday mornings. The region is perhaps the best place for a stud-farm tour, certainly a worthwhile experience in Manawatu.

Historic homestead: Highway 3 proceeds northwest from Palmerston North towards Wanganui, 70 km (43 miles) away. The first point of interest along this route is **Mount Stewart**, from the summit of which there is a fine view of the rich Manawatu pastures. A memorial near the road commemorates early settlers. It's a short hop from here to the historic homestead and gardens at Mount Lees Reserve.

The largest township en route to Wanganui is **Bulls**. Further your agricultural education by branching off here toward the coast to **Flock House**, an agricultural training institute. The house was built in 1895; it was purchased in 1923 by the New Zealand Sheepgrowers, an organisation which ran a scheme to train the sons of British seamen's widows as farmers. Just north of Bulls, pleasant detours can be made to Duddings Lake Reserve (where there is boating and water-skiing) and Heaton Park (with its fine old elms and oaks). But don't trespass in Santoft Forest. You can drive quickly through Turakina but, if you have time, visit **Ratana**, a small township named after a famous Maori prophet and faith healer. A temple was built there in 1927.

River city: The river welcomes visitors on arrival at friendly **Wanganui**. It is the city's most remarkable asset and New Zealand's longest navigable river, much loved by canoeists and jet-boaters. Water trips of various kinds operate from downtown.

In the superb Wanganui Regional Museum are a store of Maori artefacts and a war canoe, Te Mata-o-Hoturoa, **Hazy, lazy...**

once used on the river. The museum also boasts a remarkable collection of Lindauer paintings.

Before further exploring Wanganui, take the lift up the Memorial Tower on **Durie Hill**. The elevator climbs 66 metres (216 feet) through the hill. But if you want to walk up, the 176 tower steps are worth the trouble on a fine day, when you will get a magnificent view of the city and river – and may even sight the South Island.

Virginia Lake is a popular stop by day and night, when a fountain plays in colour. Spend some time, too, in Sarjeant Gallery and Putiki Church. Children love the Kowhai Children's Playpark and Riverlands Family Park. For evening recreation the city has some fine restaurants. The main shopping street, lower Victoria Avenue, has been redesigned and revitalised, with arches at each end acting as gateways. Heritage buildings in the street have been restored, and the period style has been embellished by gaslights and wrought iron.

...and just biding time.

Heritage trails are a strong feature of Rangitikei, Wanganui and Palmerston North. And more and more visitors are being attracted, to Rangitikei in particular, by farm stay holidays.

Chief attractions west on Highway 3 from the city are the Bason Botanical Reserve and Bushy Park scenic reserve, both reached easily with short detours. Highway 4 north, through the Paraparas, is justly noted for its beauty. To the east of Wanganui and north of Palmerston North, the Rangitikei River – excellent in its upper reaches for white-water rafting – links with Highway 1 near Managaweka. Enquire there or in Wanganui or Palmerston North about rafting. But book well in advance, and make your journey with a member of the Professional Rafting Association.

The road to Jerusalem: One highlight of any visit to the Wanganui area is the 79-km (49-mile) **River Road**. Contact the Visitors Information Centre in Wanganui and book a seat on Don Adams's mini-bus, which leaves the city at 7am, Monday through Friday. This is your chance to sample a slice of remote New Zealand life as the driver delivers daily mail, bread and milk to the small settlements along the banks of the Wanganui River.

As you approach **Jerusalem** (Hiruharama to the Maori), you will understand why Roman Catholic missionaries established themselves at this bend in the river, and why poet James Baxter chose the serenity of this site for a commune in the early 1970s (it disintegrated after Baxter's death in 1972). It will cost you $3 to view his grave, which is now on private property.

Top of the route is **Pipiriki**, once a thriving tourist town. Pipiriki remains beautiful, however, and a base for tramping. There are many listed walks; Mangapurua, north of Pipiriki, enjoys increased fame.

The valley was settled after World War I by returning soldiers. The Depression and farming difficulties forced them out by 1942. An eerie reminder of their presence is the Bridge to Nowhere, a concrete bridge with its approaches now overgrown. You can reach the walk by jet-boat.

WELLINGTON AND THE WAIRARAPA

Tawhiri-ma-tea, the Polynesian god of wind and storm, fought many fierce battles with his earthbound brother gods in Wellington and the Wairarapa. The Cook Strait, the water separating this end of the North Island from the South Island, thus had an early start as one of the most treacherous dozen miles of open water in the world, and its citizens have a spectacular and somewhat nervy existence.

The glass capital: Early Maori saw the North Island as a great fish, rich with food for their Polynesian families. Today the mouth of the fish is as pretty a little capital city as any in the world. **Wellington's** great blue bowl of harbour is only mildly scarred by port reclamations and a clutch of high-rise offices set below green hills dotted with white wooden houses. The favourite romantic image of the locals is the best-selling print of New Zealand Company draughtsman Charles Heaphy, depicting the first sailing ships at anchor in this fledgling Victorian colony. If you are up high enough, you will see that things have not changed that much.

It is a different matter at street level. In the second half of the 1970s the city was shaken by manmade quakes, as a downtown area of quaint Victorian wedding-cake two- and three-storey premises were demolished on the grounds of earthquake risk. The replacement skyscrapers of steel and glass look equally vulnerable, so much so that locals have dubbed this "Glass City".

Wellington is often compared to San Francisco, and accurately so for it, too, has its share of painted ladies, old wooden houses done up in rainbow colours. Like San Francisco, Wellington has a cable-car zooming out of its city belly to a fine view of the harbour, beside an ivy-clad red-brick university building recently refurbished to earthquake standards. Both cities have shown off their plunging assets in cinematic car-chases, San Francisco with *Bullitt*, Wellington with one of New Zealand's most popular films, *Goodbye Pork Pie*.

After a decade of demolition, Wellington has begun to tart up the few old buildings left, like the university, the red-brick monastery on the promontory opposite, some of the downtown relics like the baroque St James Theatre and the Government Buildings, which used native woods in the masonry style of European architecture and claims the biggest wooden floor area in the world.

In-between the remnants of Wellington's Victoriana, colourful and adventurous buildings and malls and a craze for cafés selling many kinds of coffee have brightened up the city. Nowhere is this more apparent than in the generous pink and beige piazza of **Civic Square**. Centre-stage is a high-tech, exhibition-oriented Capital Discovery Place for children, tucked between the trendy steel colander of the new town hall, the trendily-painted plaster puddings of the fortress-like municipal chambers and the rectangular old town hall, the old square library refurbished as the avant-garde city gallery and the new library alongside. Within, the new library is like an industrial plant of exposed metal; outside, its gorgeous plaster curve is decorated with metal palms.

The **Old Town Hall** was saved after testimonials from visiting conductors, such as the late Leonard Bernstein, rated it one of the best symphonic halls in the world, a fitting venue for the home-base of the New Zealand Symphony Orchestra. Every second year the old and new town halls are the focus of the International Festival of the Arts, with a fringe festival all around, reinforcing Wellington's status as the capital of the performing arts in New Zealand. The nearby refurbished **State Opera House** and **St James Theatre** have been involved in hundreds of festival performances. Highlights of successive festivals have included two opera productions with international casts, with Donald McIntyre returning home to take the lead in *Die Meistersinger von Nurnberg* and Ken Russell's *Madame Butterfly*.

Nearby are the equally contrasting skew-whiff concrete, iron and wood pyramid of **Downstage**, the country's first professional theatre established in 1964, and out on the old wharf area the new building with the wedding-cake facade retained from the demolished Westport Chambers for the other professional theatre, **Circa**. While Downstage has also developed a subsidiary theatre, Taki Rua, to perform Maori and South Pacific plays, the new Circa building is a perfect example of the born-again look for the original port area.

Recent upheaval: The port operations have moved north to a new container complex. The buildings left behind are a major part of Wellington's reinvention of itself following the political restructuring of the public service under successive market-driven, privatising governments of the 1980s. Reducing public servants from 88,000 to 36,000 in five years undercut Wellington's economy and forced the city to redefine itself.

The physically-confined capital has gone about the job with typical gusto. Creative and curious arches lead from the civic centre across the main road to the old wharf area that was Welling-

ton's first development. Here a lagoon has been carved out beside the rehousing of the two traditional rowing clubs of the city, on the abandoned wharf area now undergoing similar refurbishment to London's Docklands and the old seaports of North America. The ambitious plan centres on a new $280 million **Museum of New Zealand** on the upper waterfront and restaurant and accommodation conversion of old wharf offices and warehouses. Over the last decade a waterfront saloon car race and a dragon boat race have become established holiday attractions. More recently the wharves have hosted the annual New Zealand Food and Wine Festival. The latest introduction is a week-long Scottish Festival with Highland dancing over crossed swords where once bonded goods were stored.

Despite the move of its operations a mile or so to the north, Wellington continues to rate as the busiest of the country's 13 main ports. This is largely due to the all-weather sailing of the Cook Strait rail ferries and foreign fishing

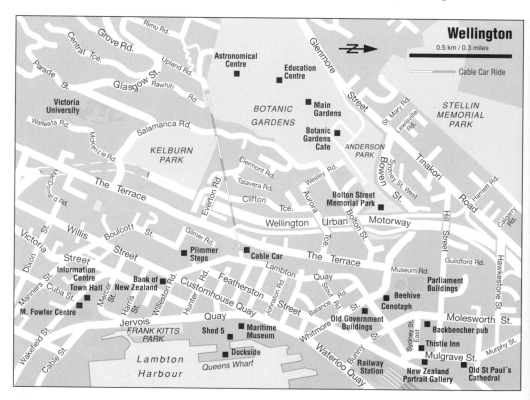

vessels calling here for registration and provisioning. The movement across this wild strait is increasing as the government-encouraged winds of competition see faster ferries enter the field. The established ferries are part of the privatised NZ Rail, owned by an American company. The government department employed 20,000; the privatised rail is a quarter of that size. Surplus rail land on the waterfront is to host a new $72 million sports stadium. The stadium and the museum are the biggest developments in the improving economic fortunes of the region.

Buzzing around the Beehive: Politicians and top public officials and business folk buzz around the capital's unique circular Cabinet offices, known as **The Beehive**. Much of the administrative and financial clout of the country is at work within these few hundred acres of largely reclaimed land.

Built in the late 1970s, the copper-domed Beehive is a soft contrast with the square marble angles of the adjacent **Parliament Buildings** (1922) and the Gothic turrets of the **General Assembly Library** (1897). The parliamentary chambers have recently had a face-lift, but without any change to the Westminster model. On the flat below the drive are the **Government Buildings** (1876) on Lambton Quay, which was where the 1840 tides lapped, with brass plaques set into the footpath at intervals along the "Golden Mile" of downtown shops, banks and insurance companies.

To one side of the Beehive is the historic red-brick Turnbull House, tucked below the pristine skyscraper Number One The Terrace, office for the Treasury, with the Reserve Bank across the road. On the other side of the Beehive and Parliament is the new **St Paul's Cathedral** and the new **National Library**, within which is the Alexander Turnbull Library with its remarkable collection of New Zealand and Pacific history. One street behind that is the **National Archives**, beside the mellow pohutukawa trees that surround **Old St Paul's** (1866), an impressive little colonial Gothic former cathedral made en-

tirely of wood, even unto the nails. This is the jewel in a city of 30 churches, many of them built in the same wooden adaptation of the soaring stone Gothic style that is a unique colonial feature.

New homelands: After work most government officials travel a few miles into the foothills or along the harbour motorway directly on the earthquake fault line to the Hutt Valley and the Eastern Bays. The Bays' bus company quite reasonably claims the finest marine drive in the world.

The Maori found these areas uninhabitable because thick native forests plunged to the water's edge and the Hutt Valley was largely a kahikatea swamp. The great earthquakes of 1848 and 1855 raised the land about five feet, enough to persuade the Pakeha it was safer to build in wood – especially after a proprietor was killed in his collapsed hotel. Reclamation of the sea was the answer to the space problem. Over the last 150 years more than 120 hectares (600 acres) have been reclaimed, half as much again as the original plan for the colony.

The Maori preferred for safety reasons to live on an island that was linked by a subsequent earthquake to the rest of Wellington. Today this suburban peninsula is called **Miramar**, Spanish for "behold the sea", and the sandy strip linking it to the city is the airport.

Hundreds of years before Cook, the great Polynesian explorer Kupe landed on Miramar and cultivated crops there, and that is where the tribe of his son Tara settled. There were enough fish and birds and sunny north-facing slopes to cultivate the delicate kumara or sweet potato, such that Tara's tribe was willing to share the area with migrating groups. Occasional marauders were repelled by fortifications developed around the headlands. For more than 600 years there was a relatively peaceful occupation of Te Whanganui a Tara, the Great Harbour of Tara.

The Pakeha musket ended that. In 1819 Te Rauparaha and other warrior chiefs led a savage assault on the local tribes, wiping out people who stood there unable to comprehend why they

Auckland express leaving Thorndon station, 1914.

were falling. The victory cannibal feast lasted weeks. The new occupiers had enemies on all sides and thus welcomed the arrival of the white tribe in 1839.

The white tribe brought with them the potato, which was easier than the kumara to cultivate. The Hutt Valley was particularly fertile – Charles Heaphy measuring 2½ meters (8 ft) in compost. The Maori gardeners of the Hutt Valley arguably kept the settlers alive in the first few years with two potato crops a year from the productive soil. The settlers were often contemptuous of the Maori and indifferent to requests that cultivation, living and burial grounds be protected. This is still apparent in the viewing platform on **Mount Victoria** overlooking the harbour, built on top of an ancient burial ground. The summit is 196 metres (643 ft), up a good road. Another viewpoint is at **Kelburn**, above the magnificent Botanical Gardens, reached by cable-car 120 metres (400 ft) from Lambton Quay.

Wakefield's settlement: The citizens of Wellington have also shown scant respect for their Pakeha founding father Edward Gibbon Wakefield. The title "Father of Wellington" was been conferred on one of the early merchant settlers John Plimmer, who complained that a place represented to him as "a veritable Eden" had proved "a wild and stern reality". Wellington is both, depending on the changeable weather. Plimmer had little cause for complaint, converting a shipwreck, the fallout from a bad day, into a flourishing trading enterprise on the beach. Like many of his fellow entrepreneurs, he added his own wharf. He ended up one of the solid citizens of the town, and his wreck ended up as the boardroom chair in the country's leading trading bank, the Bank of New Zealand.

There is no memorial to Wakefield in Wellington other than his gravesite, due in part to lingering disapproval that he served a prison term for allegedly abducting an heiress; she was willing, but her father was not, and he brought a successful court case against the young Wakefield. It was in Newgate Prison that Wakefield saw first-hand the miserable lot of England's poor and devised his scheme to attract investment from the well-off in projects that offered a chance to those with nothing. John Stuart Mill, the great libertarian thinker, was among admirers of the plan.

The practice was a mess. Idealists were thin on the ground, speculators as thick as shovels in a gold rush. Wakefield's brother, William, was in charge of acquiring land for the new emigrants, but he had to do so in four months. His quick deals with the Maori included buying Wellington for 100 muskets, 100 blankets, 60 red nightcaps, a dozen umbrellas and other goods such as nails and axes.

Wakefield claimed to have bought for £9,000 the "head of the fish and much of its body", a total of about 8 million hectares (20 million acres). He failed to understand the Maori concept of communal ownership, whereby all shared the land but the Maori reserved the areas they lived in, cultivated and used for burial. Some of the misunderstandings may have come about from the pidgin

Kelburn cable-car.

Maori and pidgin English of translator Dicky Barrett, a rotund and cheery whaler who had married into a Maori tribe and set up the first pub in Wellington, later hiring it out for government offices. Several hotels called Barretts have been erected on different downtown sites, the current one at the other end of the Golden Mile from where the original stands near Parliament.

The early settlers had little to thank Wakefield for when they were dumped on a beach at the swampy bottom of the Hutt Valley. After their tents flooded, the settlement moved to the narrow but dry site of the present city. The abandoned area is called **Petone**, meaning the End of the Sand, which eventually developed into a vigorous working-class town of heavy and light industry, dominated by the Gear Meat Company. Now the Gear has gone, the flat shoreline is becoming a popular recreational area, the workers' cottages are being gentrified and the **Settlers' Museum** commemorates the early struggles.

The enforced shift across the harbour to the narrow Wellington foreshore ensured a continuous struggle to turn back the tide. **Lambton Quay** was the beachfront where Plimmer and fellow traders set up shops, the narrowness prompting reclamations ever since. The result today is that Lambton Quay has moved several blocks from the harbour.

The first generation of wooden houses along the Golden Mile went up in smoke. The second generation of wedding-cake shops were tumbled in the 1970s in a building boom the country had not seen the like of before or since, with $200 million a year spent on the steel and glass high-rise replacements.

Wellington's wharves: The streets between the skyscrapers are narrow and windswept with few parks, but Wellingtonians have the advantage of being never more than a stone's throw from the Botanic Gardens or the wharves. The **wharves** are among the few in the world open to the public, and politicians and civil servants are among the lunchtime joggers past the puzzled Russian and Korean fishing crews. As well as

Lambton Quay in 1903.

haute fish cuisine in the new restaurants in converted stores, many office workers eat sandwiches on wharf ends. Some fish for tiddlers, others stroll into the **Marine Museum** or the nearby building with the hole in its middle selling nautical ephemera, formerly the ferry ticket office. The wharf park is popular with the lunchtime and weekend crowds, the kids careering down the Disneyesque lighthouse slide.

At the southern end, the **Overseas Passenger Terminal** occasionally hosts cruise ships, but is in constant use for conferences and exhibitions, and there is a popular restaurant. Part of the new development on the city side is a marina, matching the established one the other side, the graceful Royal Port Nicholson Yacht Club with its popular clubrooms. Beside that is the Freyberg indoor swimming pool on the edge of the city beach of **Oriental Bay**, created by the dumping of sand ballast from ships. A line of mature Norfolk pines makes this an attractive promenade with several restaurants and luxury apart-

ments, leading up to medium-rise flats and old wooden houses peppered over the steep slopes up to Mount Victoria. This suburb that faces the setting sun is often called a mini-Riviera. Where Maori once cultivated kumara, Pakeha now cultivate suntans.

Across the bay in the shadow of the hill is the country's oldest suburb of **Thorndon**, where the little wooden workers' and soldiers' cottages have been gentrified into painted ladies just like a slice of old San Francisco. The area has become New Zealand's first historic zone.

Historic walks head from here and downtown up into the luxuriant **Botanic Gardens** and the formal glory of the Lady Norwood Rose Garden and tearooms beside a park popular with lunchtime athletes. A motorway has bifurcated this old suburb and ripped out the heart of the settlers' cemetery before coming to a full-stop in the middle of town, against a brick wall of environmental opposition and denial of further government funding.

The harbour today.

From the late 1960s the citizens of gentrified Thorndon cut their conservation teeth on opposition to the motorway and saved some of the threatened old suburb. Even more successful were the residents on the other side of the city, the raffish community of the **Aro Valley** below the university, students and old-timers who repelled council plans to demolish their wooden cottages in favour of concrete.

Over the hill the stern grey **National Museum and Art Gallery** retain Maori artefacts and relics of Captain Cook, colonial life and geological and botanical specimens, awaiting the shift to new premises. Beside them the **Basin Reserve**, a lake before the earthquake drained it, is also living on borrowed time as the home of New Zealand cricket.

Behind the basin is the enclosed suburb of **Newtown**, its narrow streets teeming with new migrants from the Pacific, Asia and Europe. You can hear 20 different languages spoken at the local school, while the shops that look like the clapboard facades of a Hollywood Wild West set sell exotic foods from a dozen lands. Another valley over is **Island Bay**, which is losing the Italian fishermen from Stromboli and Sorrento who gave it its nickname of Little Italy, when there were 50 fishing craft in the bay. Now there are about 10, some still with names like *Michelangelo* and *San Marino*. A few rugged bays around this southern coast, on foot or by four-wheel-drive, you come to the famous **Red Rocks**, supposedly stained by the blood from Kupe's cut hand or his grieving grandchildren, and the seal colony.

The Italians of Island Bay have been joined by settlers from Gujurat province around Bombay, and many of the small shops are Indian-owned. In these inner suburbs you can find a Presbyterian church holding services in Niuean, a magnificent Greek Orthodox temple, Serbian Orthodox wooden church and chapel and Polish clubrooms, all evidence of Wellington's days as the first port of call for migrants.

Valley of the Hutt: In the last half-century it has been traditional for fami-

On their way home.

226

lies to follow the New Zealand trend to move from city to suburbs, the new settlements principally in the Hutt Valley and over the hills in the Porirua basin. At weekends many still go well beyond, northwest to cottages or baches (holiday homes) on the Kapiti coast, or to Paremata for underwater and on-water sports in rather less blustery conditions than the capital's harbour.

Further up the Gold Coast, as this warmer clime is known, it is possible to arrange trips out to the unspoiled native bird sanctuary of Kapiti Island, which was the capital of the warrior chief Te Rauparaha who ruled the Wellington region when the Pakeha arrived. A few miles up the Gold Coast you can enjoy the locally-made gourmet cheeses, the sheep shearing and milking of cows at Lindale and visit the vintage car collection in the Southward Car Museum.

This blander environment is also shared by the long valleys of Lower Hutt and Upper Hutt cities and satellite suburbs, where people still grow great vegetables. On the flat lands near the

flood-prone Hutt River are television and film studio facilities. Most of the time the river is peaceful enough for enjoying trout fishing, kayaking and jet-boating. Horserides and mountain biking are other attractions. Further up the valley at Silverstream is a steam train excursion along the hillside.

The other side from the city is steep, with small communities tucked into the eastern bays. A hill road away is another valley city, **Wainuiomata**, famous for its rugby league club, gateway into the serious tramping over the Rimutaka Forest Park. At the Hutt base of the hill is the collection of government science research institutes and the petrol storage wharf complex, leading into the succession of exclusive bushy bays. The final settled bay is Eastbourne, where house prices are always high, and where the image of Katherine Mansfield gentility lingers on.

It is an easy hike around this coast to view the country's first lighthouse at Pencarrow. Once the rugged coastline beyond was the preferred pathway for

Serenading on the wharf.

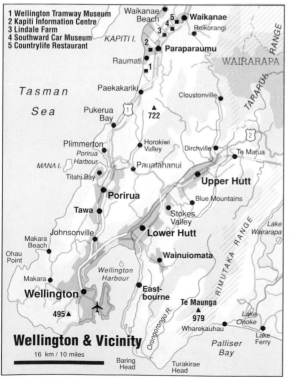

sheep herders who set up the country's first sheep stations on the Wairarapa acres. The Maori canoed the settlers across the lake and sold them the land.

Productive hinterland: Wellington's central position ensures it continues to handle almost a third of the country's 60 million annual gross tonnage. Almost half of this is produced in the adjacent farming lands of the **Wairarapa**, hundreds of thousands of acres which Wellingtonians regard as a sleepy hollow. It requires an hour or so driving over the 305 metres (1,000 ft) of the **Rimutakas**, a mountain chain cars sometimes need their own chains to negotiate in winter, while at any time of year the wind gust warnings should be taken seriously. Once a fell engine hauled people and goods up the mountain's almost vertical incline, and the relic of this is unique in the world.

The vast plain north of Lake Wairarapa was until recent times a great place to snap up an elegant old sofa or an unmodified kauri house for a song. The small towns were in decline. **Greytown** is associated with a former Governor, **Featherston** with a former prisoner-of-war camp for Japanese, who threatened a break-out and were massacred by nervous guards. Now these are places to buy adzed as well as second-hand furniture, while **Martinborough** is suddenly on the map as a producer of boutique white wines as good as anything Marlborough produces across the strait.

The large town of **Masterton** at the northern end still caters for the traditional sheep image of the area with the hosting of the Golden Shears competition every year. At just over the required 20,000 for city status, its population has shown a slight increase in recent years. However, the other towns measure only a few thousands and overall the area is still losing people, almost 10 percent in the last census figures, proving the truth of one local history describing the area's exports as primary produce and young people.

The skinniest local population is in the south, but in the duck shooting season this rises as dramatically as the lake **Farming lands of the Wairarapa.**

228

level after heavy rain. The hills and the rivers around are popular with trampers, canoeists, rafters, botanists, conservationists, hunters, and those who just like to get away from the almost 400,000 crowded into the much smaller space the other side of the Rimutakas.

Renaissance: Last century the Pakeha assumed the Maori were a dying race. At the end of this century the Maori are in a period of renaissance, with meeting houses in Wellington, Porirua and the Hutt Valley the focal point of re-learning and re-establishing their crafts and language. Marae welcomes, performances and traditional hangi food are available to visitors interested in the ways of the people of the land, the tangata whenua. The Maori concern for the environment, particularly traditional shellfish gathering areas, has been consistent. Now they are joined by environmentalists also protesting at water pollution and objecting to a scheme to drain one-fifth of mighty Lake Wairarapa, bigger than Wellington harbour.

The Pakeha have started to develop a taste for colonial museums, not just in Wellington, but in declining Wairarapa settlements such as Carterton. Here is proudly displayed the mythical canoe from which Maui fished up the North Island. The Brancepeth Homestead in the Wairarapa is prominently featured in the definitive Historic Buildings of New Zealand.

The growing awareness of the recreational and tourist value of unspoiled nature may yet save the eye of the fish, the place the Maori call "glistening waters", and also that lumpy forest nose that separates the eye from the mouth.

The marvellous thing about the mouth – Wellington – is that the crude human cosmetics applied to its cheeks have done little to dull the beauty Lieutenant Colonel Mundy described in 1848 as a "crystal bay in its bronze frame of rugged hills". Dodgy flights into Wellington and violent storms remind the local people that beauty has its price, that Tawhiri-ma-tea has not yet made his peace with fellow gods around the head of the fish.

Wellington's suburbia.

NELSON AND MARLBOROUGH

Nelson and Marlborough see themselves as a glittering sun-belt round the midriff of a country which boasts about its climate from top to toe. This metaphoric belt is elastic to cope with the great summer influx to the popular beaches and bays of the two provinces.

Nelson City's usual 36,000 population is said to double during the Christmas and New Year holiday period, and at popular beach resorts like Kaiteriteri, numbers jump from a few handfuls to thousands. They pour into hotels, motels and motor camps in cars full of children, towing caravans or boats or with tents strapped to roof-racks. Travellers, often from overseas, bring backpacks to add to the summer scene.

The approach to Nelson and Marlborough can be by road from the south, by scheduled air services from Air New Zealand Link or Ansett into Nelson or Blenheim airports or, perhaps most dramatically, by the ferry services across Cook Strait from Wellington.

Straight through the Strait: Cook Strait is a natural wind funnel for the Roaring Forties and can be one of the most unpleasant short stretches of water on earth on a bad day. But the moment you enter the **Marlborough Sounds** through the narrow entrance of Tory Channel you enter a different world, a world of myriad inlets and bays with steep hills plunging so steeply into the sea that in most places you could anchor an ocean liner within spitting distance of the shore.

There used to be a whaling station at the entrance to **Tory Channel**, the last in New Zealand when it closed in 1964, ending more than 50 years of pursuit of the migratory humpback whale by the Perano family. The channel has been the sole highway for the Peranos, and for most owners of the many holiday homes and farm properties of the Marlborough Sounds, for the better part of a century. Launch, speedboat or tug have been the means of conveyance; only a few enjoy the luxury of road

Preceding pages: the Southern Alps; Marlborough vineyards. Below, by ferry from Picton.

access, if indeed luxury is the right word for the few narrow, tortuous and dusty (or muddy) tracks that serve as roads in this part of the country. Boats are everything here – the main means of recreation and (telephones and the occasional helicopter excepted) almost the only means of communication. The doctor does his rounds by launch; the mail is delivered by launch.

The hour-long journey down Tory Channel and **Queen Charlotte Sound** aboard the big rail ferries gives only a glimpse of it all. The shores are dotted with isolated houses, many offering holiday facilities. A full exploration of the various sounds would take months.

The most famous of all Pacific explorers, Captain James Cook, visited New Zealand three times, during which he visited the Marlborough Sounds five times, spending something like 100 days in and around **Ship Cove**. He first hoisted the British flag in New Zealand there on 15 January 1770, and on a subsequent visit beached his ship *Resolution* there for some weeks. A monument has been erected at Ship Cove, near the entrance to Queen Charlotte Sound, to commemorate Cook's visits.

The commercial centre for almost all activity in the Sounds is the bustling little town of **Picton** in one of the bays near the head of Queen Charlotte Sound. Picton is the start (or finish) of the South Island section of Highway 1 and of the main trunk railway. It is the terminal for the Cook Strait ferries and the base for the assorted launches, water taxis and charter boats on which locals and visitors rely for transport. There is also a float plane providing scenic flights, as well as a short-cut to guest houses or accommodation in adjacent Kenepuru Sound. It is a mere 10 minutes' journey by float plane against a minimum of two hours by car and two days by boat.

An old trading scow, the *Echo*, is drawn up on to the beach on one side of Picton Bay, where it acts as a clubhouse for the local yacht club. It was one of the last of New Zealand's old trading scows to remain in service, though ironically these flat-bottomed sailing craft were designed for shallow river harbours rather than the deep waters of the sounds.

A shipping relic of far greater antiquity lies across the bay. The teak-hulled *Edwin Fox*, much vandalised and only just recognisable as a ship, is the only remaining East Indiaman – or ship of the British East India Company – in the world. The *Edwin Fox* came to New Zealand as a 19th-century immigrant ship and ended its working life as a storage hulk for meat-freezing works, which operated at Picton until killing was moved in 1983 closer to the centre of pastoral farming in Marlborough.

Wine and whales: Thirty km (19 miles) south of Picton, **Blenheim** is the administrative centre of sparsely populated Marlborough. Sitting squarely on the Wairau Plain, it is a pleasant if unspectacular farm service town which, since the establishment of the Montana vineyards close by, in the late 1960s, has become one of New Zealand's most important wine-producing areas. Many wineries have opened retail and food outlets here, and vineyard tours and an annual wine and food festival have

Mail by boat in the Marlborough Sounds.

become important tourist attractions.

Grapes, apples, cherries, sheep – all take advantage of the Marlborough sunshine to grow and grow fat. But nothing needs the province's hot dry days of summer more than the salt works at Lake Grassmere, where sea water is ponded in shallow lagoons and allowed to evaporate until nothing is left but blinding white salt crystals.

The coastline in the southern part of the province, in marked contrast to the sounds, is exposed, rocky and generally inhospitable. Near Kaikoura the sea and the mountains meet head-on, leaving merely a narrow beach past which the road and railway must squeeze.

The town of **Kaikoura** nestles at the base of a small peninsula which provides at least limited shelter for the fishing boats based here. The crayfish or rock lobster which they pursue on this rocky coast is sold fresh from numerous roadside stalls. Even more important now to Kaikoura's economy are the visitors who come to see the whales which congregate close to the shore.

Inland from Kaikoura, two parallel mountain ranges thrust impressively skywards, reaching their acme in the peak of Tapuaenuku, 2,885 metres (9,465 feet) above sea level. Beyond that again is the Awatere Valley and Molesworth, New Zealand's largest sheep and cattle station. The Wairau and Awatere valleys have been described as "the cradle of South Island pastoralism". They were also places where some of the most destructive overgrazing of the country's erosion-prone high country took place, until a derelict Molesworth was taken over by the government in the 1930s. Much of its 182,000 hectares (450,000 acres) has been painfully rehabilitated and the station now runs 10,000 head of cattle. Safari tours by four-wheel-drive vehicle through Molesworth to the North Canterbury resort of Hanmer Springs can be taken from Nelson.

Mussels and gold: The road from Blenheim to Nelson takes you down the attractive Kaituna Valley to **Havelock**, a fishing and holiday settlement at the

Vines near Blenheim.

head of Pelorus Sound. Havelock is like a smaller Picton, without the bustle of the inter-island ferries, but with the same feeling that all the important business of the town is waterborne. Pelorus and Kenepuru sounds are key to New Zealand's expanding aquaculture industry, their uncrowded and sheltered waters being used for growing salmon in sea cages and green-lipped mussels on buoyed rope lines. Scallops and Pacific oysters are also grown.

Just beyond Havelock is **Canvastown**, named after the tent town which popped up mushroom-like when gold was discovered on the Wakamarina River in the 1860s. It was a short-lived rush with most of the diggers going on to Otago. Canvastown remembers its brief heyday with a memorial of old mining tools and equipment set in concrete. Visitors can hire pans and still get a "show" of gold on the Wakamarina

Rai Valley is now little more than a rest stop for buses travelling the 115 km (72 miles) between Blenheim and Nelson, though once it boasted a cheese factory of high repute and a bakery which achieved national fame for the length of its loaves. A road turning off here leads to **French Pass** at the outermost edge of the sounds. This is a narrow, reef-strewn waterway between the mainland and D'Urville Island, named after 19th-century French explorer Dumont d'Urville who discovered the pass in 1827 and piloted through in an extraordinary feat of seamanship.

A city apart: With its busy fishing port sheltered behind a 10-km (6-mile) long boulder bank, **Nelson** is a city apart from the rest of New Zealand. It has never been linked with the country's railway network, and this has tended to breed a feeling of isolation which air services to Wellington have failed to alleviate. Even the acquisition of the city status (by royal charter in 1858 as the seat of an Anglican bishop), 16 years after the New Zealand Company landed the district's first settlers, sets Nelson apart from new and bigger cities. The New Zealand requirement for city status is a population of 20,000, a

Graham Valley, Nelson.

bureaucratically magical figure not achieved in Nelson until the 1950s.

The city owes more than city status to its bishop. Andrew Suter, Bishop of Nelson from 1867 to 1891, bequeathed what is considered to be the country's finest collection of early colonial watercolours to the people of Nelson. The **Suter Gallery** in which they are housed is one of the centres of cultural life in the city along with the **School of Music** and the **Theatre Royal**, the oldest theatre building in the country.

Churches (of all denominations) also contribute to the architectural atmosphere of a district which retains much from colonial days, including the pioneer homestead, **Broadgreen**. The city's churches are presided over by the Anglican cathedral on Church Hill, while a view from the Grampians Hill shows the Roman Catholic, Presbyterian, Methodist and Baptist churches all in line a little to one side, for all the world like a row of communicants.

Some of the prettiest churches, though, are in the settlements of the **Waimea Plain** – at Richmond, Waimea West and Wakefield, where the parish church of St John's was built in 1846, making it New Zealand's second oldest church and the oldest in the South Island.

Nelson's image has been built on its sandy beaches and extensive apple orchards. It also contributes a large part of the nation's production of nashi, kiwifruit and berryfruit and the whole of the national crop of hops. Vineyards are not so numerous as in Marlborough but are increasing in number, particularly in Waimea and the Moutere Hills.

Forestry and fishing are other big local industries. The handicraft revival of the 1960s saw Nelson develop as an important pottery centre, largely because of the good local clay. These days, with some impetus from the polytechnic school of design, the district's reputation as a craft centre is more widely based. Potteries still abound but weaving, silver working, glass blowing and other crafts are also well represented. The Nelson Visitor Centre organises both vineyard and crafts tours.

Colonial lounge, Broadgreen.

Golden Bay alternatives: The availability of relatively cheap small holdings and seasonal work has made Nelson province, like Coromandel, something of a magnet for people seeking alternative lifestyle communes. House trucks abound and the valleys of the Motueka River basin and **Golden Bay** have attracted many people putting into practice their theories on holistic living.

If Nelson feels isolated from the rest of New Zealand, Golden Bay is isolated even from Nelson. A single bitumen road over the steep marble and limestone Takaka Hill is the only way in for anything but birds, fish, or people with stout boots. All people and produce go this way, whether it be heavy trucks or holiday traffic heading for Pohara Beach or the **Abel Tasman National Park**.

A memorial to Abel Tasman, the 17th-century Dutchman who discovered this island for Europe, stands at Tarakohe on the road to the park which bears his name. It was here that the first rather inauspicious encounter between Europeans and the Maori took place in December 1642, when Tasman anchored his ships *Heemskerck* and *Zeehaen* only to have one of his longboats attacked. He lost four of his men, named the area "Murderers' Bay" and made no further attempt to land in New Zealand, thereby leaving the Maori in ignorance of the questionable delights of European civilisation for another 130 years.

The modern name of Golden Bay derives from the beautiful colour of the sand along the granite-edged coastline. This coast is enjoyed especially by the many people who walk the coastal track from Totaranui to Marahau or visit the Tonga Marine Reserve. The full walk takes three or four days but the less energetic can take coastal launch services from Kaiteriteri or Tarakohe to several bays along the way

Farewell Spit, at the western tip of Golden Bay, is a naturalist's delight. The 25-km (15-mile) long spit of sand curves round the bay like a scimitar, growing each year as millions of cubic metres of new sand are added by the current, which sweeps up the West Coast

and then dumps its load upon meeting the conflicting tides of Cook Strait.

More than 90 species of birds have been identified on Farewell Spit. They fly by the tens of thousands from the Siberian tundra. The spit is classed as a wetland of international importance and is managed by the government with strict limits on access. However, you can take a sightseeing trip by four-wheel-drive vehicle from Collingwood out to the lighthouse near the spit's end. Departure time depends on the tide.

Deer, trout and trampers: South of Golden Bay, even four-wheel drive-vehicles are of no use. This is the area set aside for **Kahurangi National Park**, the country's second largest national park, which includes a trackless wilderness where not even helicopters or low-flying aicraft overhead are allowed to disturb trampers.

However helicopters are used by some local fishing guides to fly anglers in to mountain rivers. They are also used occasionally (though cheaper services are available) to drop off or pick up

trampers on the popular **Heaphy Track**. This is a tramp of two to four days which starts a little way south of Collingwood and heads through the mountains, then down the West Coast to Karamea. Overnight accommodation along the way is available, for a small charge, in Department of Conservation huts but, like most parts of Nelson and Golden Bay away from the coastal plain, this is backpack country, where what you sleep in and what you eat are what you carry.

The limestone hills around Golden Bay contain some of the most extensive cave systems in the Southern Hemisphere and often attract expeditions of pot-holers from the other side of the world. **Harwood's Hole** on Takaka Hill is more than 200 metres (650 feet) deep and was regarded for many years as the deepest cave in New Zealand, until the exploration of the Nettlebed cave system under Mount Arthur.

Although Nelson itself enjoys a generally dry climate, vast deluges quite often occur in the western ranges of Golden Bay, the water seeping through the soft limestone to create the underground network of caves and rivers. A walk of 400 metres from the end of a road up the Riwaka Valley, on the Nelson side of Takaka Hill, will take you to the visible source of the **Riwaka River** where it emerges in full spate from its invisible source inside the hill.

There are other oases, too, for people of softer feet and softer muscles. A restored 1920s fishing lodge on the shores of Lake Rotorua, 90 km (56 miles) south of the city in the Nelson Lakes National Park, boasts "blue-chip" fishing water within a short walk of the front door, and 26 top-class fishing rivers within an hour's drive. St Arnaud village on the shores of Lake Rotoiti, the other glacial lake which gives the Nelson Lakes park its name, also offers comfortable accommodation and (for winter visitors) two ski fields nearby.

It also offers another route down the Wairau Valley and back to Blenheim (if you do not want to go on through the mountains to Christchurch or the West Coast) and away from the slightly dilatory life that Nelson seems to enjoy.

Left and **right**, different perspectives on the mountains at Kaikoura.

CHRISTCHURCH

Christchurch likes to boast its traditional pleasures – punting on the Avon River, riding a tram through the inner-city streets, taking coffee al fresco in the old university precinct. Such pastimes say much about the way Christchurch loves to see itself, as peculiarly English.

Yet of all New Zealand's main centres, Christchurch was the first and the most furious to adopt some rather more aggressive tactics to entice tourists. So now it's possible to take an aerial gondola up the Port Hills, the volcanic outcrop that gives the city its backdrop. Or shop in one of the many multi-lingual souvenir shops that dot the inner city. Or ride a hot-air balloon over the city and plains at dawn, ending in a champagne breakfast. Or jump on a helicopter to fly to the French charms on Akaroa, out on Banks Peninsula.

But first, the city itself. You can start at the centre, and it is easy to find – Cathedral Square is smack in the middle. There, a lofty neo-Gothic Church of England cathedral presides, as if placed in its rightful position by a divine hand that also laid out a city at the foot of the cathedral. A grid of streets spreads across the plains. The central streets assume the names of English bishoprics – minor ones, unfortunately, because by the time the city was planned in the early 1950s, the best names had already been taken for other communities of the Canterbury province.

At the limits of the city centre run four broad avenues. They enclose a square mile that echoes the "City of London". Within their bounds are tidy, tree-lined parks with names such as Cranmer and Latimer, and woe betide any city planner who even thinks about roading that may encroach on these precious parks, as past administrators have learnt.

Winding serpentine through the city is the **Avon River**. Locals like to believe the stream got its name from the river that runs through Shakespeare's Stratford. In fact, the tag came from a tiny Scottish stream that burbled past the home of one of the city's pioneering families. Along with the Port Hills to the southeast, the Avon is the city's greatest natural asset. It relieves the rectangles. Its grassy banks are wide and well-planted in trees. In a recent break with tradition, city horticulturalists have allowed the return of native grasses. The willows along one stretch allegedly grew from slips brought from Napoleon's grave on St Helena, but Christchurch is full of stories like that.

Precision planning: To the west of the Four Avenues is the massive **Hagley Park**. The planners set it aside as a barrier between city and farm. It is filled with playing fields, botanic gardens and broad open spaces modelled, Christchurch boasts, on the classic style of English landscape gardening.

Christchurch did not happen by accident. A city does not become more English than England without putting its mind to it. It was a planned Anglican settlement, masterminded largely by a young English Tory with the delightfully apt name of John Robert Godley.

Repelled by 19th-century egalitarianism and industrialisation, Godley aspired to a medieval notion of a harmoniously blended church and state, presided over by a benevolent gentry. He put together the Canterbury Association, with no fewer than two archbishops, seven bishops, 14 peers, four baronets and 16 Members of Parliament as backers. The idea was to drum up money and find settlers for the new little perfect corner of England in the South Pacific.

Only the best sort of migrant needed apply. They were to represent "all the elements, including the very highest, of a good and right state of society". To qualify for an assisted passage to the other side of the world, a migrant had to furnish a certificate from his vicar vouching that "the applicant is sober, industrious and honest", and that "he and all his family are amongst the most respectable in the parish".

From such ideals came the Canterbury Pilgrims. Their first four ships – Christchurch's *Mayflower* – berthed at the neighbouring Port of Lyttelton in 1850. By 1855, a total of 3,549 migrants had made the journey, and the city on the plains was growing.

Unfortunately and inevitably, things went wrong. Dreams of an ecclesiastical utopia crumbled under the harsh realities of colonial life. The Canterbury Association foundered. It was as difficult to revitalise Anglicanism in the New World as it was anywhere else. Christchurch's growth from the mid-1850s became less ordered, less ideal.

Yet dreams endure. To be of First Four Ships stock still brings some cachet. You can find the names of those first official migrants engraved on plaques in a corner of Cathedral Square.

A city of Godley-ness: By city planning statute, no high-rise building can go higher than the Anglican cathedral's spire. Godley-ness reigns. Any scheme to tamper with even a tiny chunk of Hagley Park meets determined opposition. Christchurch holds its traditions dear. It has also recognised that its charms have more tangible values: Japanese newlyweds come to Christchurch

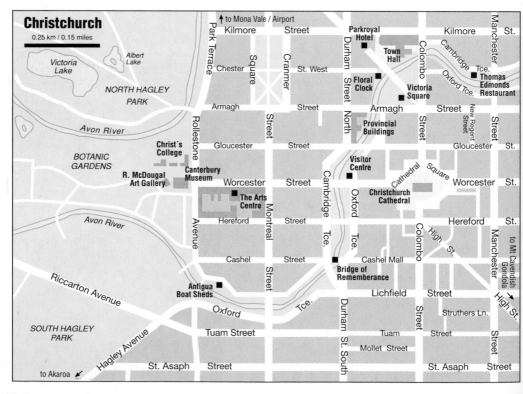

to have their marriage vows blessed in the cute Gothic charm of churches such as St Barnabas in the leafy, blue-chip real-estate suburb of Fendalton.

And there are gardens – acres and acres of them – both public and private. Somebody at one time called Christchurch the "Garden City" and the citizens have been living up to it ever since. Gardening is the biggest leisure time activity, and makes for some extremely pleasant drives and walks. Come to Christchurch – especially in late summer – and you will truly see a city that knows how to garden.

You will also find a city whose interests go deeper than pretty park-like surroundings. Christchurch is not without its share of interesting characters. Can that be a hangover of the utopian origins? Utopias generate a good number of mildly cranky individuals. Whatever the reason, take a city the size of Christchuch – only about 330,000 – where everybody who is anybody knows everybody who is anybody, put it well-away from the sea-lanes of world travel

and the result is an individualistic brew.

So Christchurch abounds in interesting stories. An instance: in the 1950s the city was rocked by a scandal that became known as the Parker-Hulme murder. Two teenage girls of good standing successfully plotted to murder the mother of one of the girls. The case shocked the city to its respectable foundations and for a generation it was spoken of in tones of hushed distaste. Recently, it has been revived in a stage-play and an award-winning film, *Heavenly Creatures*. You can visit the environs where the deed was done, Victoria Park, in the high-toned suburb of Cashmere on the slopes of the Port Hills, but as yet no enterprising entrepreneur has erected plaques to guide you to the spot. You'll have to ask locals. But be wary. The response could still be frosty.

A stroll through town: Take a walk round the city centre and you will see a few of the city's interesting sites and characters. Start, naturally, from **Cathedral Square**. It was paved as a pedestrian precinct for the 1974 Commonwealth

Punting through the centre.

Games, when the city embarked on a beautification programme. Now it is the subject of a new remodelling programme. The square is officially countenanced, Hyde Park-style, as a public speaking area.

Lunchtime on a sunny weekday is best. Star performer is the Wizard. An immigrant from Australia in the early 1970s, he has been haranguing bemused crowds ever since. Dressed in black robes or sackcloth, he delivers an impassioned line on everything from Queen and Country through feminism to his view of the causes of global warming. Be warned; his views may not coincide with those of the meteorologists. No one quite knows whether to take The Wizard seriously. Is he giving Christchurch and its Anglican antecedents what they want? Or is he being ironic? Nowadays, he has more or less official status as the city's mascot, a weird personification of the province's slogan, "Of Course You Canterbury".

During summer, the square is alive with festivals of fun and food. There are stalls selling art and crafts and ethnic foods. Lunchtime concerts run through December and January. Sadly it takes on a more sinister tone after dark, when it is not advisable to walk there alone.

The **Cathedral** itself is worth a visit. Construction began in 1864 and it is one of the Southern Hemisphere's finest neo-Gothic churches. Climb the steps up the tower past the belfry for a breathless view of the city.

Directly behind it are the offices of *The Press*, the newspaper of record for the Canterbury establishment. South down Colombo Street you will find **Ballantynes**, on the corner of the City Mall, a pedestrian precinct. Ballantynes is the establishment department store, Christchurch's Harrods or Marshall Field's. Farmers from the hinterland of the Canterbury Plains give the store their custom. The assistants dress in black and are notoriously helpful. Very other-worldly.

A walk down the **City Mall** towards the Avon River and the Bridge of Remembrance takes in some of the city's **Council Chambers.**

248

best shopping territory. Across the bridge and north along Cambridge Terrace is the city's old library, a small architectural gem. Like many others, the building has been carefully restored and now houses offices and a bank.

Along the river: Walking north along the Avon, you will come to the recently renamed **Worcester Boulevard**, route of the freshly restored traditional trams that ply the inner city. Turn left down the boulevard and you will come to the **Christchurch Arts Centre**. A mass of dreaming spires, turrets and cloisters, it once housed the University of Canterbury. When the university moved out to more spacious grounds in the suburbs, the site was dedicated to arts and crafts studios, theatres, restaurants and apartments, all nestled within the granite Gothic shells. The centre is home to the Court Theatre, a professional theatre company that has been long established as one of New Zealand's best.

The arts centre has transformed this region of the city into something of an upmarket bohemian quarter. Where once student flats ruled, pretty courtyard gardens and cappuccino machines are now *de rigueur*.

This is the heart of old Christchurch. Directly over Rolleston Avenue is **Canterbury Museum**. The building is almost as noteworthy as the exhibits. If you show a lot of interest the enthusiastic staff will reveal some of the goodies they don't have room to display. Behind the museum, all but hidden, is the municipal art gallery. The **McDougall Gallery** offers a collection of early and contemporary New Zealand art, with a staff trying hard, despite the formal architecture, to be unstuffy.

Beyond, the **Botanic Gardens** are a truly splendid celebration of the city's gardening heritage, from English herbaceous borders to native sections and glasshouses of sub-tropical and desert specimens. The gardens are enclosed within a loop of the Avon River, as it winds through Hagley Park.

Immediately north along Rolleston Avenue is **Christ's College**, very Anglican, very English public-school, still

Dean's cottage.

very proper for boys from Christchurch and all over New Zealand who intend to go places in life. The buildings, both old and new, are marvellous. The straw boater hats have been dropped in favour of more utilitarian cycling helmets for the boys who bike to school.

Centres of civic pride: Head back to town down Armagh Street and you'll pass **Cranmer Square**. On the far side is the old Christchurch Normal School. Like half of Christchurch's notable buildings, it is mock Gothic and was long ago deserted by educationalists; vandals and squatters had their way with the old folly for years. But a developer took over the buildings and transformed them into luxury apartments. The buildings also house one the city's best restaurants.

Further down Armagh Street are the old Provincial Council buildings, once the home of local government, fine examples of more modest architecture than some of the city's landmarks.

Beyond is the recently remodelled **Victoria Square**. Last century it was

the city's marketplace. Now it is a wonderful expanse of green anchored on the **Town Hall**. The hall was opened in 1972 after the city had dithered for 122 years about a civic centre, and it remains the pride of modern Christchurch. It is still one of the architectural triumphs of its time, and has been echoed around the country. Designed by local architects Warren and Mahoney, it is restrained and elegant, with an auditorium, concert chamber, conference rooms, banquet hall and restaurant overlooking the Avon and square.

The hall has been linked recently to one of the city's new architectural features, the Parkroyal Hotel. A odd ziggurat of a building, it nevertheless somehow works, flanking the northwest corner of Victoria Square. Its atrium-enclosed dining area is one of the city's smarter places to meet.

Catholic style: If you're interested in ecclesiastical architecture, seek out the city's other cathedral. The **Roman Catholic Cathedral** of the Blessed Sacrament is a High Renaissance Romanesque basilica, built early this century, in a somewhat tacky part of town. George Bernard Shaw visited the city soon after it opened and praised Christchurch's "splendid cathedral". The pride of local Anglicans turned to chagrin when they realised he was in fact talking about the Catholic basilica.

In the same territory of the city, the old railway station has been converted into a hands-on science centre, attached to a multiplex cinema centre.

Hagley Park is the best jogging circuit enjoyed by hundreds of officer workers every lunchtime. Then there is cycling, the perfect mode of transport for flat Christchurch. Hordes of school pupils and workers take to the streets on two wheels. Visitors can hire bikes, but beware of motorists. If bashful, stick to Hagley Park or streets with cycle-lanes. For a less strenuous way of getting about you can boat on the Avon, and catch an altogether new perspective on the city.

The suburbs: Out of the city centre you can tour countless streets of fine homes – if you head in the right direction. That's northwest towards Fendalton and **Victoria Square.**

Merivale, or south up to the Port Hills.

Christchurch's real estate is fiercely class-conscious, along lines that are somewhat inexplicable. **Fendalton** and **Merivale** are easily recognised, with their fine trees and secluded gardens, as havens of the wealthy. Yet cross the wrong street and values plummet. Merivale's mall is one of the city's best shopping regions, with stores and restaurants that rival the inner city.

New Brighton, by the beach, should be classy but definitely isn't. "Are you married or do you come from New Brighton?" is one of the epithets, possibly apocryphal, that attached itself to the suburb early on, denoting the loose morals that the city's "better" citizens associated with the territory.

The **Port Hills** are the only area with a clear geographical advantage over the rest of the city. Their elevation lifts them above the winter smog. The Summit Road, along the tops of the hills, gives spectacular views of the city, the plains and the Southern Alps and, on the other side, the port of Lyttelton and the hills of Banks Peninsula. There are extensive walking tracks over the Port Hills and peninsula beyond. They range from one-or two-hour strolls to ambitious hikes, with shelters to rest in. Ask at an information centre for details. The hills can be tackled by a high-tech gondola that has become one of the city's big attractions. A restaurant, bar and souvenir shops have been installed for diversion after the ride. The hardier can hire mountain bikes at the summit for an alternative route down, or an exploration of the hills.

There are many gardens up here. One of the most notable and unusual is the Garden of Gethsemane, a private garden-cum-commercial nursery that has many unusual specimens. Its little avenues and tiny trellised chapel are worth a visit. Many visitors are so captured by the setting, they get married there.

It is worth taking a drive or bus to **Lyttelton**, the sleepy-looking port over the hill from Christchurch, with its stack of charming cottages that cling to the slopes. You can return through a road

Roman Catholic Cathedral.

tunnel or drive over the hill to the seaside suburbs of Ferrymead, Redcliffs and Sumner. The transport museum at Ferrymead is a big attraction for train buffs, colonial enthusiasts and the like. Sumner has the air of an artists' retreat, an atmosphere which is now being assiduously recultivated.

On the other side of the city, the airport has an interesting **Antarctic Centre** which celebrates Christchurch's history as the stepping-off point for expeditions to the ice, both historic and more contemporary. It is well worth a visit. Nearby is **Orana Park**, a safari-style zoo with an ever-increasing range of animals roaming about on "African plains" and created islands. Cars can enter the lion enclosure, a popular feature during feeding times.

If talk of Antarctic expedition and wild animals seems a bit rugged, the rest of the family can take more refined pleasures at the many wineries that have dotted the rural outskirts of Christchurch, since Canterbury became one of New Zealand's boutique wine-growing regions. Many wineries have restaurants for a snack or lunch.

To the northeast is **Queen Elizabeth II Park**. Its stadium and swimming sports complex was built for the 1974 Commonwealth Games. City ratepayers didn't want to be landed with a white elephant, so now it has been turned into an all-round family attraction. There are water slides, a maze, go-karts and sundry other diversions.

Peninsula excursion: If you have time before you head south to the mountains and lakes, you'll want to get right out of town. **Banks Peninsula**, over the Port Hills, is the best destination for a short trip from town.

It is the scene of one of just two blunders made by Captain James Cook when he circumnavigated New Zealand in the 18th century. He mapped the peninsula as an island. He would have been right if he had come several millennia earlier. The extinct volcanoes which formed the peninsula were once separated from the mainland. (Cook's other gaffe was Stewart Island, at the

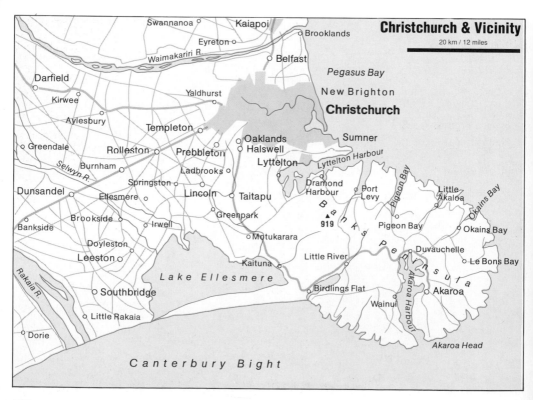

Christchurch & Vicinity
20 km / 12 miles

southern tip of the South Island, which he linked to the mainland.)

The hills of Banks Peninsula were once bush-covered, but they were long ago logged for timber. There are pocket remnants of bush, and plenty of delightful valleys and bays. Sheltered microclimates support many horticultural products and plants that cannot be cultivated anywhere else this far south, including kiwifruit. You'll also find some keen growers of exotic nuts and herbs.

Seek out Diamond Harbour, Okains Bay, Okuti Valley and Port Levy. They are fertile, inviting and unspoiled. In many other parts of the world they would be bristling with condominiums.

French settlement: But the real gem of the peninsula is **Akaroa**, about 80 km (50 miles) from Christchurch. This little settlement began its European life in 1838 when a French whaler landed. For a short while it flourished as a French settlement, and 63 migrants set out from France on the Comte de Paris to create a South Seas outpost. But they arrived in 1840 to find the Union Jack flying.

Piqued and pipped at the colonial post, the French nevertheless stayed. They planted poplars from Normandy, named streets and grew grapes, but they were outnumbered by the English.

The dream lingers though, and of late it has been brushed up for visitors. Little streets wind up the hill from the harbour front, with names such as Rue Lavaud and Rue Jolie. A charming colonial style predominates, and has been protected by town planning rules. Of most note is the **Langlois-Eteveneaux House**, now fitted out as a display with an attached colonial museum.

Many Christchurch people own holiday houses, or baches, in Akaroa or nearby. The town can become crowded in January and February. There are many bars, restaurants and cafés. Because of the isolation, restaurants tend to be pricey. Fresh catches of fish can be bought from the wharf.

Akaroa Harbour, on the south coast of Banks Peninsula, is on the doorstep of the habitat of the rare hector's dolphin. There are regular sea cruises to

Lyttelton Harbour.

catch glimpses of the dolphin and other features of the region.

Churches are among Akaroa's notable features. The Roman Catholic church of **St Patrick** is the oldest in anything like original form. It was built in 1864 and was in fact the third in town to serve Akaroa's French and Irish – hence the name – Catholics. It is a cute and cluttered little building with a Bavarian window on the east wall.

St Peter's Anglican church was built in 1863, and generously enlarged about 15 years later. It is a more austere building in the Protestant style. Most distinctive of all is the tiny **Kaik**, a Maori church some 6 km (4 miles) south of the township along the foreshore. It is a remnant of a once strong Maori presence around Akaroa Harbour, in a haunting and evocative setting.

In town, a climb through the domain, called the Garden of Tane is worthwhile on its own count, and will take you to the spectacularly-sited graveyard. Its graves must have the best views in the country and they make up a rich record of the region's history. The Old French Cemetery, on the other side of town, is a disappointment. It was the resting place of Akaroa's earliest Europeans and after a hot slog up the hill it affords a good view of the harbour. But a benevolent government tidied the place up in 1925, destroying most of the headstones for a mediocre memorial.

Further afield: Turning inland from the peninsula, Christchurch has a huge hinterland. Its province, Canterbury, runs from the Southern Alps to the sea, and stretches hundreds of miles from north to south. A popular traditional day trip is **Hanmer Springs** to the north, with its spa, horse riding and mountain walks. Hanmer is home to the old Queen Mary Hospital, built as a convalescence centre for returning war veterans and subsequently a rehabilitation centre for recovering alcoholics. Its setting, hidden in a valley off the beaten track, gave rise to an unofficial slogan: "1,200 feet above worry level." It is still there, somewhat reduced, but the visitors taking the waters arc likely to be tourists or Cantabrians visiting their holiday homes.

A comfortable and nostalgic way to see both the Canterbury Plains and the Southern Alps is the popular **TransAlpine Express**. The train pulls out of Christchurch, heads across the plains and up into the mountains at Arthur's Pass, an especially appealing trip in winter when the mountains are covered in snow. The return ride takes a day. It's popular, so book ahead.

The plains you will pass over are New Zealand's biggest, richest cropping area, though they are prone to summer droughts. For that reason, local farmers have battled for years for legal rights to take irrigation water from local rivers such as the Rakaia. Visitors here are more likely to be interested in the rivers' salmon and trout content than their irrigation water.

On the outskirts of Christchurch is **Lincoln University**, about 20km (12 miles) south of the city. It is at the centre of an agricultural campus that is at the forefront of New Zealand's farming practices. A telephone call beforehand can arrange a guided tour.

Left, museum in Langlois-Eteveneaux House. **Right**, wildlife, Akaroa Harbour.

CANTERBURY'S HIGH COUNTRY

Canterbury is a marriage of mountain and sea, bound together by snow-fed rivers that cut braided courses across the plain. The Southern Alps, the Pacific Ocean and two rivers (the Conway in the north and the Waitaki in the south) form the boundaries of this province.

The popular view of Canterbury is a patchwork plain where lambs frolic under a nor'west sky. This Canterbury exists. The plain, 180 km (110 miles) long and an average of 40 km (25 miles) wide, is the largest area of flat land in New Zealand. Canterbury lamb, bred for both meat and wool, is regarded as New Zealand's best. The Canterbury nor'wester is a notorious wind, a true *föhn* with its warm, dry, blustery weather whipping up dust from riverbeds and furrowed farmlands and receiving the blame for the moodiness of Cantabrians.

Yet Canterbury is much more. The province also encompasses New Zealand's highest mountains and widest rivers – not to overlook its pastoral and forested hills, fine beaches, and extinct volcanos and sheltered bays of Banks Peninsula. Settlement is also diverse: one of New Zealand's four main centres, two fine ports, a secondary city, many small towns and large high-country sheep stations where genteel English traditions are vigorously upheld.

Plain fascination: The Canterbury plains are merely the corridor to the province's special characteristic – sky, earth and sea, yet conveniently close to civilisation. From any point in the province one is never more than a couple of hours from mountains, lakes, beaches, plains, rivers, cities and airports.

The openness of the landscape and the ever-changing climate inspire an awareness of the environment. The traveller soon learns that southerly wind invariably brings rain and a quick drop in temperature; a nor'wester dry heat and rising rivers from its high-country rainstorms; an easterly, a chill breeze to Christchurch and along the coast.

One and a half centuries of European settlement have tamed the flat land. The treeless landscape that appeared so desolate to Canterbury's pilgrims is today a pastoral scene like no other: a patchwork of cropped fields dotted with sheep, divided by shelter belts of pines and macrocarpas, and sewn through with long straight roads that would have gladdened the hearts of the Romans.

From the air the view has a fascination. Patterned on the multi-coloured quilt of crops and pastures are vein-like shadows of ancient streams while the existing rivers gleam silver as they flow. Towns, small and large, sprawl in elegantly along the roads like aphids clinging to sap-rich stems.

From the ground the plains are less imposing. Travelling lengthwise in Canterbury is a monotonous journey, especially on the main highway between Christchurch and the province's second city, Timaru. Canterbury's finest scenery is inland, along the foothills and valleys of the Southern Alps.

Three main roads provide easy access to passes to the mountains beyond which lies Westland. Northernmost is the Lewis Pass, and its rewarding short detour to the tiny spa resort of Hanmer Springs; central is Arthur's Pass and surrounding national park of the same name; southernmost is Burke's Pass, which leads to the Mackenzie Country and the magnificent panorama of glacial lakes and alps of the Mount Cook region.

Getting healthy at Hanmer: Bypassed by conventional tourist traffic, **Hanmer Springs** survives as one of New Zealand's quietest resorts. This little village, an easy 136-km (84-mile) drive north of Christchurch, nestles in a sheltered, forested valley. Its hot mineral pools are set in a garden of giant conifers. Few experiences are more pleasurable than relaxing in these open-air pools on a winter's night, watching snowflakes dissolve silently in the steam.

A European settler stumbled upon the springs in 1859; they were harnessed by the government in 1883. Since then their recuperative powers have been used to help rehabilitate wounded soldiers, the pyschiatrically disturbed and, in more recent years, alcoholics. Origi-

Preceding pages: Church of the Good Shepherd, Lake Tekapo. Left, Arthur's Pass, Mount Rolleston.

nally maintained by the Queen Mary Hospital, the recently modernised pool complex is now controlled by the district council. The landscaped rock gardens include several plunge pools, communal pools of varying (indicated) temperatures, a fresh-water swimming pool, children's pool and a warm running stream. Several easy, well-defined paths meander through more species of exotic trees than any other plantation in New Zealand. This was the first exotic forest established by the government in the South Island; some of it was planted more than 90 years ago.

More demanding walks to the summits of Conical Hill and Mount Isobel provide magnificent panoramas. The Mount Isobel track, which passes 200 different kinds of sub-alpine flowering plants and ferns, is a naturalist's delight.

Hanmer's 18-hole golf course is one of the highest in New Zealand, while fishing, hunting, jet-boating, skiing and horse-trekking are also available.

Although Hanmer provides accommodation in the form of a licensed hotel and a good selction of motels, guest houses, holiday homes and camping grounds, the main street has retained the low-key, subdued atmosphere of a typical rural township.

Rugged beauty: From Hanmer, the road over Jack's Pass to the isolated **Clarence Valley** is worth exploring for its rugged tussocked beauty, especially upstream. A word of warning, though: the road – originally built to install and maintain the high-voltage transmission lines from the hydro schemes of Otago to Blenheim, Nelson and beyond – is an unsealed, often steep track, suitable only in good weather. It is not a through road and has locked gates at the Acheron River bridge (downstream from Jack's Pass) and at the Rainbow Station over the Main Divide. Hanmer, therefore, remains very much a "dead-end" town. Travellers have little choice but to backtrack 13 km (8 miles) to the Waipara-Reefton road (Highway 7).

Westwards this climbs up the Waisu Valley to **Lewis Pass**. This all-weather route (opened in 1939) offers a comparatively gentle, picturesque crossing

at an altitude of 865 metres (2,838 ft) through beech-covered mountains. The highway descends to Maruia Springs and then on to the Rahu Saddle, Reefton and Greymouth.

Southwards from the "Hanmer turn-off", as it is locally known, Highway 7 runs through the rolling hills of North Canterbury to its junction with Highway 1 at Waipara, passing along the way the small rural settlements of Culverden, Hurunui and Waikari. An historic pub is now Hurunui's chief claim to fame, thankfully saved from demolition and operated by local farmers. The road then passes through Waikari's limestone landscape in which the keen-eyed detect naturally-sculpted animal forms.

A touch of Switzerland: The quickest route between Christchurch and Westland is the West Coast Road (Highway 73) through **Arthur's Pass**. This, the South Island's most central pass, boasts New Zealand's version of a Swiss village. Although Arthur's Pass township, nestling in the heart of the Southern Alps 154 km (96 miles) west of

Oahu B power station.

Christchurch, lacks green pastures and tinkling cowbells, it does have a chalet-style restaurant and, in keeping with any self-respecting village in Switzerland, a railway station.

Arthur's Pass marks the eastern portal of the **Otira Tunnel**, the only rail link through the mountains. The 8½-km (5 mile) tunnel, completed in 1923 after 15 years of construction, was the first electrified stretch of line in what was then the British Empire – a necessary advance to save passengers from being choked to death by the steam locomotive's sulphurous smoke. Today the rail link between the West Coast and Canterbury remains a vital one. As an extra bonus, it is the most scenic in New Zealand; one that is covered daily between Christchurch and Greymouth by the Trans-Alpine Express.

Arthur's Pass is also the headquarters of the **national park** of the same name. Its close proximity to Christchurch and its many comparatively civilised tracks make the 100,000-hectare (247,000-acre) park one of the best utilised in the country. Mount Rolleston, 2,271 metres (7,451 ft), dominates the region in which there are 30 peaks over 1,800 metres (about 6,000 ft). Motels and a youth hostel provide accommodation.

The 924-metre (3,032-ft) pass is named after Arthur Dudley Dobson, who rediscovered the former Maori route in 1864. It marks the boundary between Canterbury and Westland, a boundary which is often reinforced by distinctive weather patterns. During a nor'wester the traveller leaves a dry and warm day on the Canterbury side of the pass and descends into heavy rain in the West Coast's Otira Gorge. Conversely, during a southerly or easterly, West Coast-bound travellers leave the rain and cold behind in Canterbury for a landscape bathed in sunshine.

Storms are often as intense as they are sudden, dropping as much as 250 mm (10 inches) of rain in 24 hours. The annual rainfall here is 3,000 mm (about 120 inches). Bad weather frequently forces the closure of the highway, which in the Otira Gorge is very steep with a

Rakaia River.

series of hairpin bends requiring special care in wet weather and in winter. The road is not suitable for caravans. (Indeed, in bad weather, the Automobile Association often advises travellers to take the longer, but easier and safer, Lewis Pass route to Westland.)

A common sight in this vicinity is the kea, the native parrot. This mountain species has criminal tendencies that surpass those of any thieving magpie, as the pioneer explorer Julius von Haast discovered when a vandalistic kea tumbled his valuable collection of native plants down a ravine, and as careless visitors discover today if they leave food or shiny belongings unattended.

Arthur's Pass, however, is not the highest point on the West Coast road. That distinction belongs to **Porter's Pass**, 88 km (55 miles) west of Christchurch, which traverses the foothills at 945 metres (3,100 ft). Porter's Pass is a popular winter destination for day-trippers from Christchurch who enjoy tobogganing and ice-skating at Lake Lyndon and skiing on the many skifields in the vicinity such as the commercial field at Porter Heights and the club fields at Craigieburn, Broken River and Mount Cheesman.

Canterbury's most popular and best developed skifield is **Mount Hutt**, 100 km (62 miles) west of Christchurch. This commercial field is serviced by the small town of Methven, 11 km (7 miles) away, which provides accommodation to suit all budgets.

Rooftop of New Zealand: The monarch of New Zealand's national park is the **Mount Cook National Park**, where the highest peaks in the land soar above the crest of the Southern Alps. Supreme is Mount Cook itself, which until 1991 was 3,764 metres (12,349 ft). However, the mountain lost almost 10 metres (about 34 ft) from its summit that year in a massive landslide. The re-surveyed official height is now 3,755½ metres (12,315 ft) which, in spite of its diminished stature, retains its standing as New Zealand's highest.

The Mount Cook alpine region was the training ground for Sir Edmund

Staying close to the herd.

Hillary, the first person to scale Mount Everest. The narrow park extends only 80 km (50 miles) along the alpine spine, yet it contains 140 peaks over 2,134 metres (7,000 ft) as well as five of New Zealand's largest glaciers.

The Mount Cook Line, which installed and operates the airport in the valley floor at the base of Mount Cook, runs daily air services to the park, only 35 minutes' flying time from either Christchurch or Queenstown. If the weather at the Mount Cook airstrip is too bad, the airline uses the Pukaki airstrip near Twizel, and then carries its passengers by road.

Paradoxically, although Mount Cook is almost due west of Christchurch, the journey by road is a circuitous distance of 330 km (205 miles). Getting there, however, is half the fun.

The main route follows Highway 1 south for 121 km (75 miles), marching easily across plain and river alike, casually belying the mighty challenges this journey once posed for Maori and pioneer. The wide rivers proved major ob-

Beware the thieving kea.

stacles to travel and settlement in the 1850s and difficult river crossings caused numerous drownings in Canterbury. Throughout New Zealand 1,115 people lost their lives in river accidents between 1840 and 1870 and it was suggested in Parliament that drowning be classified a natural death! Nowadays motorists speed over the Rakaia, Ashburton and Rangitata rivers without a thought for the hazards that once confronted travellers.

Immediately past the Rangitata River the road to the Mackenzie Country (Highway 79) branches westwards from the main highway. It leads to the foothills and the tiny town of Geraldine which snuggles into them, offering detours to an historic pioneer homestead in the Orari Gorge and excellent picnic and fishing spots in the nearby Waihi and Te Moana gorges.

Mackenzie Country: The road to **Fairlie**, a country town with a historical museum, passes a Clydesdale stud farm and the only elderberry wine cellars in New Zealand. The gentle, green countryside is left behind at Fairlie as the road, now Highway 8, rises with deceptive ease to **Burke's Pass**. At this gap through the foothills a different world stretches beyond – the great tussocked basin known as the Mackenzie Country, named after a Scottish shepherd who in 1855 tried to hide stolen sheep in this isolated high-country area.

Winding across the stark-bronzed landscape the road reaches **Lake Tekapo**, a lovely turquoise glacial lake reflecting the surrounding mountains. By the lake's edge the simple stone Church of the Good Shepherd stands in harmony with its surroundings. Nearby the high-country sheepdog which has played an essential role in building New Zealand's prosperity is commemorated in a bronze statue erected by runholders from Mackenzie Country.

Tekapo is also the base for a major aerial sight-seeing and air charter company, Air Safaris and Services, which operates scenic alpine helicopter and fixed wing flights. From the lakeside town of Tekapo the road south continues across the tussocked quilt of the

Mackenzie Basin – in summer, shimmering brown and parched in the wind-swept heat; in winter, barren and bleak with its frozen mantle of white. Winter sports are popular here, with skiing at Round Hill and ice-skating on the lake.

The road passes Irishman Creek, the sheep station where Sir William Hamilton developed and perfected the propeller-less jet boat to travel up, as well as down, the shallow rivers of the lonely back-country. Nearby, too, is the Mount John Observatory, previously used to help track United States satellites. The observatory is well-sited to take advantage of the pristine Mackenzie Country atmosphere and may be visited.

The road, for much of the way, follows the course of the man-made canal that drains Tekapo's turquoise waters to the first of the Waitaki hydro-electric scheme's powerhouses on the northern shore of **Lake Pukaki**.

Lake Pukaki today is twice the size it was in 1979 when its waters were allowed to flow unimpeded to Lake Benmore. Concrete dams now hold

Pukaki in check, forcing it to rise to a new level for controlled use in hydro-electric generation. The dams have flooded forever the once convoluted maze of streams of the broad river that flows into it from the Tasman and Hooker glaciers.

Travellers on the new highway that skirts the southern slopes of the Pukaki valley to the **Mount Cook village** might catch glimpses of the old road undulating above and disappearing into the surface of the lake far below. But that road's death by drowning drew little sympathy from those who knew it well, the travellers who rode its unsealed corrugations and choked in its dust. The new highway, sealed with an easy gradient has halved the driving time to the Tourist Hotel Corporation' "hermit's abode" – **The Hermitage**.

The village lies within the Mount Cook National Park and the development of accommodation, therefore, has been limited. Nevertheless, in addition to The Hermitage hotel, there are also self-contained A-frame chalets, the **Glencoe Lodge**, a camping ground and well-equiped youth hostel.

Well-defined tracks lead from the village up the surrounding valleys. These eventually become "climbs" that are not for novices and should only be tackled with the right equipment, and these only after consultation with the Park Board rangers.

Easier ways up the mountains are provided by ski-equipped scenic aircraft which land on the high snowfields. Skiing is available most of the year, the most exciting run being the descent of the 29-km (18-mile) Tasman Glacier.

The spectacular views of **Mount Cook**, especially when the last rays of the midsummer sun strike its blushing peak in late twilight, form the highlight of many traveller's exploration of Canterbury. The mountain, named Aorangi (Cloud Piercer) by the Maori, frequently hides shyly in a cloak of cloud, depriving sightseers of its face. But come rain or shine, this alpine region is ever-masterful, ever dramatic and a corner of Canterbury where people are dwarfed into insignificance.

Left, the Mackenzie Highland Show. **Right**, Tasman Glacier, Mount Cook.

265

THE WEST COAST: A HERITAGE OF GOLD

Hollywood has immortalised the Wild West of North America's heritage but no such fame has attached itself to the equally deserving Wild West Coast of New Zealand's South Island, where the coast and its coasters have a past as rip-roaring as that of the American West.

Today there are only shadows of former glory – of the gold rush days of the 1860s when dozens of towns with populations of thousands mushroomed around the promise of buried riches.

The hard-drinking, hard-fighting and hard-working men and women of those bygone days have left behind little more than a legend. The entire population of the 500-km (310-mile) coast is now less than it was in 1867 when it peaked at 40,000 – 13 percent of New Zealand's total population. Today West Coasters number 30,000 – less than one percent of the country's 3.3 million people – and the land itself relentlessly reclaims sites where towns such as Charleston (with 12,000 souls and 80 grog shops) once boomed.

Nowadays, a few small claims, an old dredge and a Shantytown recreated for tourists, constitute scant evidence of the robust pioneering days when fighting in the streets was a traditional Saturday night pastime. It was a young, head-strong society with money to burn and an unqualified interest in booze. Men sometimes lit their cigars with £5 notes, but women who threw gin at each other were fined for wasteful behaviour.

An independent character: Coasters are few in number, yet they have a strong identity. Officially, there is no such place as "the West Coast". The maps refer, authoritatively, to Westland; and they place the northern areas of Inangahua and Buller in the province of Nelson. Yet New Zealanders habitually refer to "the West Coast" in the understanding that the term embraces the strip of land west of the Southern Alps.

The Coasters have a reputation for being down-to-earth, genuine, rugged, independent, aggressive and hospita-ble. On the West Coast, liquor licensing laws have been flouted with impunity for years. But the West Coasters' chief "enemy" nowadays is not central government, but a conservation lobby that wants to preserve intact the native forests and birdlife. The locals, struggling to scratch a living from timber-milling and coal-mining, angrily oppose the conservationist concerns of those who live elsewhere.

The West Coast has never seduced its inhabitants with an easy life. And if it has proved wild and rough, it never promised to be otherwise. It was settled late by the Maori, from about AD 1400, but even then only sparsely. Their main interest was in the much-coveted greenstone at Arahura, carried out with difficulty first though a route north to Nelson and later across alpine passes in the Main Divide to Canterbury.

Early explorers: Neither of the two great discoverers, Abel Tasman and James Cook, were enamoured when sailing past the West Coast in 1642 and 1769, respectively. "An inhospitable

Preceding pages: in the Sullivan Coal Mine. Below, Fox Glacier.

shore" was Captain Cook's description. "One long solitude with a forbidding sky and impenetrable forest" was the view, about 50 years afterwards, of an officer in a French expedition.

So forbidding was the West Coast that European exploration did not begin in earnest until 1846. And the opinion of one of those first explorers, Thomas Brunner ("The very worst country I have seen in New Zealand") served to discourage others. His distaste resulted from the great hardships suffered on his 550-day journey through the region.

It was only in 1860 that the authorities responded positively to reports of glaciers in the south and of routes through the Alps to Canterbury: the central government bought the entire West Coast from the Maori for 300 gold sovereigns. Appropriately, European settlers then made determined attempts to find gold. By 1865 the rush was in full swing and took another five years to reach its peak.

Glaciers and rain: To the modern visitor, the West Coast appears more inviting than forbidding. It is a long narrow strip of vigorous beauty, bounded on the east by the Alps and pounded on the west by the restless Tasman Sea. Glaciers, the largest anywhere in the temperate zones, grind their way down canyon-like valleys from about 3,000 metres (10,000 ft) to a mere 300 metres (1,000 ft) above sea level. Placid, fern-fringed lakes mirror the mighty mountains and dense natural forests. Rivers cascade through a boulder-strewn valley to the Tasman. Rain falls frequently: to travel in a typical West Coast downpour is to see the virgin forest in its full glory. Waterfalls burst in great torrents; fern fronds bow graciously under the weight of raindrops; life is drenched, quenched, renewed. And when the rain is exhausted and the cloud rolls back from the mountaintops, the bush becomes a sauna alive with birdsong and – the sole flaw in this Eden – sandflies with their itch for human blood.

This is the wettest inhabited (albeit thinly) area in New Zealand: Hokitika, for instance, averages almost 3,000 mm (118 inches) annually with rain falling

West Coast fury on the rocks.

on average on 144 days of each year.

A raw savagery pervades the West Coast today. Days of hardship and disappointment are given mute testimony in the tumbledown weatherboard farmhouses and moss-covered fences. Tiny wooden churches, perched forlornly on hillsides, are now deserted outposts. Everywhere the sense of decline, not seedy but sad, is tangible. New Zealand's past is frozen here in a land without a warped infatuation with the fashionable. A time-trip back to the 1950s and beyond is an unheralded bonus for travellers in this naturally primeval and emotionally raw retreat.

Travelling up the Coast: Four routes link the region with the rest of the South Island. The opening in 1965 of the most southerly, the **Haast Pass**, has enabled travellers to trace almost the entire length of the coast as part of a round-trip through the South Island. This pass, linking Westland with the Southern Lakes of Central Otago, is also the most dramatic, providing a sudden contrast between the dry tussocked Otago land-scape and the lush vegetation to the west. Irrespective of one's point of entry – south, north or east (via either trans-alpine pass from Canterbury) – Highway 6 offers a journey of spectacular scenery from Haast down in the south to Murchison up in the north.

Most famous of the West Coast's attractions are the world-renowned **Fox** and **Franz Josef Glaciers**, about 120 km (75 miles) north of Haast. After receding steadily up the valley for four decades, both glaciers began a spectacular advance in 1982 which has since gained momentum.

Pushed by the weight of an accumulation of heavy snowfalls and ice on its main plateau, the terminal face of the Franz Josef Glacier had by late 1994 advanced one mile and was still pushing forward at the rate of about 6 meters (17 ft) a week.

Such has been the glacier's progress that its sparkling white ice can be seen again for the first time in 40 years from the altar window of **St James Anglican Church**, which sits hidden in a superb

The Old West at Glenmore Station...

setting of native bush near the centre of Franz Josef township.

The Fox Glacier's advance has been less spectacular: it has pushed forward down the valley by 600 metres (1,969 ft) over the past 12 years.

Both glaciers are located, about 25 km (15 miles) apart, in the Westland National Park, which boasts about 88,000 hectares (217,000 acres) of alpine peaks, snowfields, forests, lakes and rivers. The main highway which traverses the park's western edge passes close to both glaciers.

Narrow bush-clad roads provide easy access to good vantage points for visitors who want to view both the southernmost Fox Glacier and the more picturesque Franz Josef Glacier which is 13 km (8 miles) long. Helicopter and ski-plane flights over both glaciers provide remarkable views of the greenish-blue tints and the infinite crevasses. Guided walks are available.

Two small townships, each with a variety of accommodation, cater competitively for the needs of visitors to the glaciers. Department of Conservation offices in both towns also provide detailed information about the many walks available. These include the difficult, but rewarding, climb over the Copland Pass in the Main Divide to the Hermitage at Mount Cook. In fact, the park provides some 110 km (78 miles) of walking tracks through a sanctuary of varied native forest and birdlife, all dominated by the high peaks of Cook, Tasman and La Perouse. This trio is beautifully mirrored in **Lake Mathieson**, one of the park's three calm lakes formed by the glacial dramas of 10,000 years ago.

Whitebait and white herons: The region south of the national park has a stunning coastline. Far to the south of Haast township is an especially lonely terrain, crossed by a secondary road leading to the fishing village of Jackson Bay, where it comes to an abrupt end. This small community is swelled during the spring when keen whitebaiters descend en masse to the nearby river mouth, an annual occurrence repeated beside swift-flowing rivers all along the coast.

...and down Shantytown, Westland.

Fishing is a major preoccupation in this southern part of Westland. Haast in particular offers good surf and river fishing while, 45 km (28 miles) north at the quiet holiday spot of **Lake Pargina**, anglers are enticed by the prospect of brown trout and quinnat salmon.

A short detour west of Fox Glacier township is **Gillespie's Beach**, noted for its miners' cemetery and seal colony. Some 60 km (37 miles) further north on the main road, another detour leads to **Okarito Lagoon**, famous as the only breeding ground of the rare white heron. Okarito once boomed with 31 hotels; now only a few holiday cottages remain along with a monument commemorating the 1642 landfall of Abel Tasman.

Northwards, the main highway to **Ross** passes the idyllic Lake Ianthe. Ross was once a flourishing goldfield, producing the largest nugget (2,970 grammes/104 ounces) recorded on the coast. Nowadays, the town is a shadow, relics of its once proud history stored for posterity in a small museum.

Hokitika, formerly the "Wonder City of the Southern Hemisphere" with "streets of gold" and a thriving seaport with 100 grog shops, is 30 km (19 miles) north of Ross. It goes without saying that Hokitika is now a quiet town. However, it is served by the West Coast's main airfield and its tourist attractions include a historical museum, greenstone factories, a gold mine, gold panning and a glow-worm dell. From nearby Lake Kaniere and the Hokitika Gorge, mountaineering routes lead to Canterbury over the Browning and Whitcombe passes.

Twenty-three kilometres (14 miles) north of the town, at Kumara Junction, the highway is intersected by the Arthur's Pass Highway which links Westland and Canterbury. A few kilometres east of the junction this intersecting road enters the old gold-mining town of **Kumara**, from where a scenic detour of Lake Brunner, the largest lake on the West Coast, winds its way through dense native forest.

Gold and pancakes: Towards Greymouth, about 10 km (6 miles) north of Kumara Junction, is **Shantytown**, a re-

Pancake Rocks, Punakaiki.

production of an early gold town offering sluicing and railway ride to old Chinese workings.

At **Greymouth**, the other trans-alpine route from Canterbury connects with Highway 6. The largest town to the coast (population 3,000), Greymouth owes its commanding position to its seaport and its proximity to timber mills and coal mines.

Beyond Greymouth, the Coast Road to Westport hugs the coastline which, 43 km (27 miles) north at Punakaiki, takes on the extraordinary appearance of a pile of petrified pancakes. The **Pancake Rocks** and their blowholes consist of eroded limestone. Reached by a short and easy walk from the main road, they are best visited when there is an incoming tide and the brisk westerly causes the tempestuous sea to surge explosively through the chasms.

Thirty-two km (20 miles) north is **Charleston**, site of the once-booming centre of the Buller district, with old gold workings nearby. At a junction 21 km (13 miles) farther to the north, the coastal road becomes Highway 67, leading to the nearby town of Westport and beyond to the West Coast's northernmost town of **Karamea**, 88 km (55 miles) away. The road also provides access to two acclaimed walks – the **Wangapeka Track**, which traces the Little Wanganui River, and the 70-km (43-mile) **Heaphy Track**, a four-to-six-day tramp linking Karamea and Golden Bay.

Five km (3 miles) south of Westport, Highway 6 turns inland to follow one of the South Island's most beautiful rivers, the Buller, through its lower and upper gorges for 84 km (52 miles) to Murchison. At this point the West Coast is left behind and the road continues to Nelson and Blenheim.

Branching south: The West Coast section of this road, however, extends two branches southward, Highways 69 and 65, to connect with the Lewis Pass Highway. Highway 69, which turns off at the Inangahua Junction halfway between Westport and Murchison, traverses one of the most mineralised districts of New Zealand. Thirty-four km (21 miles) south, it enters **Reefton**, a historic town named for its famous quartz reefs. This region was abundant in gold and coal, and the story of their extraction is unfolded in the township's School of Mines and the Black's Point Museum. Other old buildings of interest are the courthouse and churches.

The other route (Highway 65) to the Lewis Pass from Murchison is mostly unsealed. It joins up with the main Lewis Pass Highway at Springs Junction, 72 km (45 miles) south.

To travel well on the West Coast the visitor needs insect repellent, no-nonsense weather-proof gear, and a taste for a strong New Zealand brew – be it beer or tea. Otherwise, however, extravagances (in clothing or conversation) are best avoided, more than a little absurd in the coast's raw surroundings. A sensitive exploration here will almost assuredly yield a sense of well-being.

The West Coast might be subject to cataclysmic earthquakes and floods, but will never be subjugated by people. It will always be more than a touch wild.

Denniston Incline, Westport.

QUEENSTOWN AND CENTRAL OTAGO

Queenstown, popularly known as the jewel in New Zealand's tourism crown, it the hub of Central Otago. It has become such a popular destination for overseas visitors that New Zealanders have cause to complain that they can't get a look in. For in less than 30 years, Queenstown has grown from a sleepy lakeside town into a sophisticated all-year tourist resort, a sort of Antipodean Saint Moritz.

Today shops are staffed by Japanese-speaking employees, hotels have Asian receptionists, and much of the town's prime lakefront land is owned by foreign investors.

But Queenstown has been nurtured on tourism and while other towns have struggled to survive in a sluggish economy, Queenstown has flourished and will continue to do so for as long as cash-rich visitors continue to flock here.

Within a radius of only a few kilometres, the ingenuity and mechanical wizardry of New Zealanders have combined with the stunning landscape to provide an unrivalled range of adventure activities.

Landscape burnished in gold: Central Otago possesses a regional personality quite distinct from other parts of the country. Some of the Southern Alps, most impressive peaks dominate its western flank, towering over deep glacier-gouged lakes. Yet its enduring impact lies with more subtlety in the strange landscape chiselled and shaved from Central Otago's plateau of mica schist rock. The rounded ranges of scorched-brown tussock resemble a blanket draped over the raised limbs of a reclining giant. Jagged outcrops of schist pierce the tussock near Central's core but elsewhere the slopes appear soft and pliant, as if a sky-jumper alighting on them would cause them to collapse in slow motion into a hollow which would gently envelope the intruder.

Such fancies come easily among Central's hills, as the day's ever-changing light casts new shadows and sculptures from the bronze forms. In the dry continental climate of the inland plateau, the pure atmosphere aids the play of light, evoking nuances few other landscapes permit. The overwhelming impression is of a stark, simple landscape burnished in glowing browns tinged with white, gold, ochre and sienna. The effect has attracted generations of landscape painters to the area.

Once seen, the subtlety of those colour variations remains in the memory forever. Never seen, they cannot be imagined. The staff of an Auckland-based national magazine discovered this when publishing a colour shot of a Central Otago scene. The lithographer, dismayed at the absence of green in the rolling hills, employed his technological skills and dye to "remedy" the brown image. His conscientious efforts roused a negative reaction, however, from the magazine's editor – a former Southlander to whom the neighbouring hills of Central Otago were familiar and dear. The blunder was fortunately rectified before the magazine went to print.

Preceding pages: on the road to Queenstown. **Left,** jet-boating on the Shotover, Central Otago.

Otago High Lakes

25 km / 16 miles

Mt. Aspiring ▲ 3027

Makarora

Matukituki R.

Lake Wanaka

Lake Hawea

Maungawera

Hawea Flat

Wanaka

Albert Town

Luggate

Motatapu R.

Harris Mts.

Richardson Mts.

Shotover R.

Cardrona R.

Pisa Range

Queensberry

Glenorchy

Kinloch

Cardrona

89

Tarras

Bendigo

Mt. Pisa

Dunstan Mts.

Arrowtown

Lowburn

Frankton

Queenstown

6

Gibbston

Cromwell

8

Chatto Creek

Lake Wakatipu

The Remarkables

Bannockburn

Von R.

Clyde

Galloway

Lochy R.

Earnscleugh

Alexandra

Kingston

6

Fruitlands

Yet idle fancies are not enough to lure people into staking out a patch of earth in arid, inhospitable country. Over nine centuries of sketchy habitation, Central Otago's bait has been successively moa, jade, grazing land, gold, hydro-electric power and now tourism.

Hunters of moa and greenstone: The first humans to set foot in the region were Maori moa-hunters who pushed inland about the 12th century AD. Central Otago could not offer lasting refuge to the magnificent endangered moa. As fire ravaged native bush and forest, the moa and other birds disappeared forever. Some of New Zealand's best moa remains have been found in the banks of the Clutha River as it winds through the plateau on its 322-km (200-mile) journey to the Pacific.

Towards the end of the 15th century, the moa-hunters were conquered by the now mysterious Ngati-Mamoe tribe moving down from the north. This group, defeated in turn two centuries later by another invading Maori tribe, supposedly fled into the forest of Fiordland and thereafter they disappeared into the mists of legend.

The victors, the Ngati-Tahu, took control of the supply of the Maori's most precious metal – the New Zealand jade known variously as pounamu, nephrite or greenstone. Hard, durable and workable, it was in demand among the Stone Age natives for adzes, chisels and weapons. So desirable was the jade, in fact, that the Maori made epic expeditions through Central Otago and the alpine divide to bring it out from the West Coast, the only place it was found, via the head of Lake Wakatipu to the east coast. It was then "processed" and exported to northern tribes.

Today, the same jade that gave the Maori as good a cutting edge as any known to Stone Age culture is a major feature in New Zealand's jewellery and souvenir industries.

Despite the lucrative trade route, the Maori population of Central was never large. The extremes of temperature (the severest in New Zealand) were too harsh for the descendants of Polynesian voy-

Queenstown.

278

agers from the tropical Pacific. In 1836, the last few remaining Maori settlements disappeared entirely when a war party from the North Island attacked on its way south.

Gold in Gabriel's Gully: For about 10 years trespassing man was absent and Central Otago slept in supreme silence, as if gathering strength for the sudden stampede of people and merino that would soon disturb the deep peace.

The European era began in 1847 when a surveyor blazed a trail for pioneers in quest of country where they could establish large sheep runs. By 1861 these new settlers were squatting on most of the potential grazing land, willingly exiling themselves to a Siberia of their own choosing. In the face of the land's indifference the run-holders persevered against the ravages wrought by winter snows, spring floods, summer droughts, fires, wild dogs, rats, rabbits and keas; they took in their stride obstacles such as dangerous river crossings, lack of roads, scarcity of food and supplies, and inadequate shelter; and all the while they toiled from dawn to dark, day in, year out. Release most often took the form of violent death.

These new settlers, predominantly of Scottish origin, had no sooner begun their self-imposed sentences than gold fever flared through Central Otago. In 1861 the first major discovery of gold "shining like the stars in Orion on a dark frosty night" was made in a gully along the Tuapeka River by Gabriel Read, a prospector with experience of the California gold rush of 1849.

Central Otago's gold boom had begun. In just four months, 3,000 men were swarming over the 5-km (3-mile) valley, probing and sifting each centimetre for glowing alluvial gold. A year on, the population of the Tuapeka goldfield was 11,500, double that of the fast-emptying provisional capital, Dunedin. Otago's income trebled in 12 months, while the number of ship arrivals quadrupled, many of the 200 vessels bringing miners from Australia's gold fields in Victoria.

In Gabriel's Gully, all miners, regardless of social rank, wore identical blue shirts and moleskin trousers. The sentiment was reflected in a song:

On the diggings we're all on a level
*   you know*
The poor out here ain't oppressed
*   by the rich*
But dressed in blue shirts,
You can't tell which is which.

This feeling of egalitarianism was echoed by a newspaper's praise of "the free and careless bluffness which is a great relief from the reserve and formality that prevail among all classes in the Old Country (England)".

Richest river in the world: The search for gold soon spread beyond Gabriel's Gully and as prospectors move inland to the then inhospitable hinterland of Central, new fields were discovered in quick succession in other valleys – the Clutha at the foot of the Dunstan Range, the Cardrona, Shotover, Arrow and Kawarau. In 1862 the Shotover, then yielding as much as 155 grammes (5½ onces) of gold by the shovelful, was known as the richest river in the world. In one afternoon two Maori men going to the rescue

The *Earnslaw* on Lake Wakatipu.

of their near-drowned dog recovered no less than 11 kg (308 ounces) of gold.

But if gold was plentiful, "tucker" was scarce. Flour and tea, augmented perhaps by poached sheep, kept many a miner barely alive. Several starved to death, especially those without the boldness of one ravenous miner, who, caught red-handed in the act of skinning a sheep, said in a defiant Irish brogue: "I'd kill any bloody sheep that bites me!" The joke went down well with the run-holder, who rode away laughing.

Arrowtown, 20 km (12 miles) from Queenstown, is now the most picturesque and best preserved gold-mining settlement in Central and arguably the prettiest small town in New Zealand. Its lead and stone beauty has endured as if to compensate for the comparatively scant evidence of the estimated 80 goldfields that mushroomed, then wilted, in Central over one hectic decade.

Barmaid bride: Ghost towns are scattered throughout the region, shadows of the calico, sod and corrugated-iron settlements that seemed "ugly" to visiting English novelist Anthony Trollope in 1872. To his eyes, though, the towns all shared one redeeming feature – libraries stocked with "strongly bound and well-thumbed" books.

Two ghost towns, Macetown and Carrona, haunt the hills above Arrowtown. **Bendigo**, near the Clutha River 25 km (15 miles) north of Cromwell (off Highway 8), is a dream ghost town, especially when the wind whistles through the tumbledown stone cottages at the bleak crossroads. A concentrated effort is required to visualise Bendigo's saloon on a Saturday night during the 1860s when "a hideous maniacal yelling... entirely overpowered and drowned every sound within a radius of a mile or so."

Behind the imagined bar, picture Mary Ann, probably the most successful novice barmaid in New Zealand's history. After being jilted on her wedding day, she fled Cromwell, the scene of her humiliation, to begin work the same day at the Bendigo saloon. In just two hours flat, the bar was drunk dry by miners

Masonic Hall, Arrowtown.

eager to see the bartender bride in all her nuptial finery.

Several tiny gold-rush towns, with substance was well as atmosphere, have refused to die so easily. The original settlement – then Tuapeka, now **Lawrence** – still survives with a strongly Victorian flavour, a nearby monument in Gabriel's Gully marking the site of Gabriel Read's discovery. Pockets of old gold towns are stitched into the ranges, gullies, gorges and valleys elsewhere in Central. Some of them, particularly in Queenstown's rugged hinterland, attract specialised four-wheel-drive tours.

Today the river valleys are clear of the calico cities that sprouted during the rush of 1860s and the dredges that savagely exhausted leftover traces of gold during the early 1900s. Few prospectors remain. Gold-fossicking is almost solely the preserve of tourists for whom it is a popular, but not (at least admittedly) very profitable, pastime.

White-water adventures: Swift-flowing rivers near Queenstown also set the scene for white-water rafting and jet-boating adventures. The latter is New Zealand's home-grown style of running rivers, upstream as well as down. Propeller-less power boats speed over rapid shallows barely ankle-deep.

These nifty craft are thrust along by their jet stream as water, drawn in through an intake in the bottom of the hull, is pumped out at high pressure through a nozzle at the rear. The typical river boat is powered by a standard automobile engine, handles seven tonnes of water a minute, can skim over shallows no more than 10 cm (4 inches) deep, and can execute sudden 180-degree turns within a single boat length.

The best-known of the dozen or so commercial options, Shotover Jet, takes passengers on a thrilling ride, swerving up and down the **Shotover River** a hair's breadth from jagged cliffs. It is without a doubt the world's most exciting jet-boat ride. Another, the Heli-Jet, offers a triple-thrill ride in helicopter, jet-boat and white-water raft.

Other commercial water adventures on Queenstown's lakes and rivers include canoeing, yachting, windsurfing, parasailing, water-skiing and hobbie-cat sailing, as well as hydrofoil and jet-bike rides. Bungee jumping from an old bridge in the Kawarau Gorge has also become a popular activity.

But traditional and sedate activities are available – trout fishing in lonely rivers and streams, for instance, or an excursion in the ageing steamship *Earnslaw*, a grand old lady of the Lake that has graced the waters of Lake Wakatipu since 1912.

Hollow of the giant: Perhaps the most haunting of Central Otago's lakes, **Lake Wakatipu** has captured man's imagination with its strange serpentine shape, rhythmic "breathing" and constant coldness. According to Maori legend, the lake is the "Hollow of the Giant" (Whakatipua), formed when an evil sleeping giant was set on fire by a brave youth, thus melting the snow and ice of the surrounding mountains to fill the 80-km (50-mile) long, double-dog-legged hollow.

In fact, the major lakes of Wakatipu,

Panning for gold.

Wanaka and Hawea were all gouged by glaciers; and the peculiar rise and fall of Wakatipu every five minutes is not the effect of a giant's heartbeat, as legend dictates, but of a perfectly natural oscillation caused by variations in atmospheric pressure.

But regardless of the origin of all three lakes, their appearance is indisputably handsome. "I do not know that lake scenery can be finer than this," enthused Trollope in 1872. "The whole district is, or rather will be in the days to come, a country known for its magnificent scenery."

Indeed, Wakatipu's beauty is so overwhelmingly apparent that New Zealanders, with their fondness for understatement, tend to downplay it in much the same way as a beautiful woman many be too determined to prove she is "not just a pretty face".

By foot, water or air: A thorough exploration of this magnificent region of snow-peaked mountains, virgin forest, uninhabited valleys and moody lakes is possible only for the traveller who takes to the air, the water, the open road and the narrow walking track.

Of all the many tracks in the Wakatipu Basin, the most rewarding is certainly the **Routeburn Track**. Trailing through splendidly isolated country at the head of Lake Wakatipu to the Upper Hollyford Valley, this 4-day trek is one of New Zealand's best, but requires a greater degree of experience and fitness than does the famed Milford Track in neighbouring Fiordland. Passenger launches ply Lake Wakatipu to otherwise inaccessible sheep stations that give tourists a taste of high-country farm life and food, pioneering days, trout fishing and seclusion. During the fishing season (1 October–31 July) charters and safaris by way of jet-boat, helicopter or four-wheel-drive vehicle are available to remote pristine waters.

Some of the finest scenic flights anywhere in the world operate from Queenstown over lakes, alps and fiords. Subject to demand and weather, a number of flightseeing and charter flights are flown daily by tour airlines, **Lake Hayes.**

including the Mount Cook Line, the company which pioneered easy tourist access to Central Otago and the Mount Cook region. Helicopter flights are operated by the Helicopter Line.

The Mount Cook Group also controls three of the largest skifields in the South Island. **Coronet Peak**, only 18 km (11 miles) by sealed road from Queenstown, has a ski season that extends from July to September. During the summer, sightseers can take chairlifts to the summit (1,645 metres/5,499 ft) for a spectacular view, while thrill-seekers can enjoy a rapid descent in a Cresta Run toboggan. The company's second major ski field is **The Remarkables**, the rugged range that forms the famous spectacular backdrop to Queenstown. (The Mount Hutt field, in Canterbury, is also now owned by the company.) Other skiing opportunities exist in the Queenstown district, with cross country and downhill trips available at Browns Basin, Mount Cardrona and Mount Pisa.

Queenstown has a wide variety of accommodation, restaurants, après-ski entertainment and shops displaying quality handcrafted New Zealand articles such as suede and leather goods, sheepskin and woollen products, local pottery, woodcarving and attractive greenstone jewellery.

Motoring the back-country: Central Otago's network of roads is among the most interesting and challenging in New Zealand. Most roads are sealed, but extra skill and caution are needed on narrower roads, particularly during the often hazardous conditions of winter. Rental-car companies advise their customers that if they drive on certain specified roads – through Skippers Canyon, for instance – they do so at their own risk without the benefit of the company's insurance cover.

An especially attractive circuit is the 50-km (31-mile) round-trip between Queenstown and Arrowtown, taking the "back" road past Coronet Peak and returning via mirror-like Lake Hayes. Besides the pastoral charm of the countryside, one can also appreciate the recent emergence of New Zealand's own

Otago landshapes.

distinctive style of architecture in the thoughtfully designed farmlet dwellings where skilled craftspeople, artists, commuters and retired folk enjoy a gentle way of life once not possible on the same land.

New Zealand's Matterhorn: Northeast of Queenstown, Highway 6 follows the upper Clutha River to its source at Wanaka, a more modest resort gaining new importance (with two ski fields and a natural ice-skating rink) since the opening of the Haast Pass in 1965. This trans-alpine route, the lowest over the Main Divide, links Central Otago with the glacier-renowned region of the West Coast. It also runs through the **Mount Aspiring National Park**, which is a 161-km (100-mile) long alpine reserve dominated by New Zealand's Matterhorn, Mount Aspiring (3,036 metres/ 9,961 ft). The park, together with the lonely valleys extending into Lake Wanaka, presents unrivalled opportunities for hiking, tramping and fishing in unspoilt wilderness.

An alternative shortcut between Queenstown and Wanaka is the Crown Range road through the Cardrona Valley. This highest in New Zealand, this route is not suitable for caravans; it is closed in winter, and even in good weather, it merely reduces the distance to be covered, not the travelling time.

Directly south of Queenstown, Highway 6 skirts Lake Wakatipu to Kingston – base for a vintage steam train, the *Kingston Flyer* – and continues south to Invercargill and the south coast. Midway, before Lumsden, it is intersected by Highway 94, a well-trodden and rewarding scenic route which branches west out of Central Otago to Southland's Lake Te Anau, and the Eglinton Valley and Milford Sound.

One of New Zealand's best-kept secrets, however, is the **Lindis Pass** (Highway 8) which links northern Central Otago with Mount Cook and the Mackenzie Country. This inland route winds through some of the loveliest and most evocative hill country in New Zealand.

Worthwhile routes: The main artery to the heart of Central Otago is the south-

Central Otago has excellent skiing.

ern extension of Highway 8 as it runs parallel with the Clutha River, past the former gold towns of Roxburgh, Alexandra, Clyde and Cromwell. These prospering towns are still vital today through their connection with Otago's lifeblood: that same mighty Clutha. The river that once surrendered gold has since, through irrigation, transformed parched land into fertile country famous for its stoned fruit.

Now, with several hydro-powered projects, it is a major generator for electricity. A dam at Roxburgh, built in 1956, has formed a 32-km (20-mile) long lake between the town and Alexandra. In 1993 a bigger dam was built close to where the Clutha River leaves the Cromwell Gorge near Clyde. The water behind has expanded through the gorge to a massive lake beyond, drowning the old town of Cromwell and much of the lower Clutha Valley.

Arrowtown holds an annual festival and Alexandra distinguishes itself by its colourful, blossom-parade tribute to spring. During the winter the townsfolk revive the good old-fashioned sports of ice-skating and curling on natural ice on the Manorburn Dam.

Gold town side trip: North of Alexandra, Highway 85 takes an easterly course through the Manuherikia Valley to the Otago coast. This road offers two worthwhile side trips, the first St Bathans, an old gold town, and the second to Naseby, a quaint atmospheric hamlet on a hillside at an altitude of 600 metres (about 2,000 ft).

Another little-publicised, good-weather road which is also worth travelling for its aura of solitude climbs Dansey's Pass to the North Otago town of Duntroon and the Waitaki River flats.

Central Otago is an intense experience whatever the time of year. In autumn, poplars planted by the settlers glow gold; in winter, nature adorns the work of people, transforming power lines into glistening lace-like threads of white across a frosty fairyland; in summer, the bronzed limbs of the hills sear the imagination. Central Otago is a land for all seasons.

DUNEDIN: OTAGO'S CONFIDENT CAPITAL

Dunedin reclines, all-embracing, at the head of a bay, a green-belted city of slate and tin-roofed houses, of spires, chimneys and churches, of glorious Victorian and Edwardian buildings, of culture, of learning. In the opinion of its 100,000 friendly citizens this is as it should be, for here is a way of life, a peace and a tranquillity that few cities can match. Growth is slowly on the move again, with the city secure in its present, sanguine about its future.

The best first view is that of the first European settlers of 1848, from the haven of **Otago Harbour**, the 20-km (12-mile) long, shallow-bottomed fiord where container ships and coastal traders now ply in place of Maori war canoes, whaling ships and three-masters.

Around the road-fringed harbourside sprout green hills; among them are the 300-metre (1,000-foot) dead volcano of Harbour Cone on the steep and skinny Otago Peninsula and the curiously cloud-carpeted cap of 676-metre (2,218-foot) Mount Cargill. Wood and brick houses, permanent and holiday (known as cribs here, and as baches in the north), beribbon the harbour perimeter, some with sections of bush and trees, others the more basic homes of fishermen, wharf workers and commuters.

Regular ferries once steamed this picturesque waterway. Sadly, there are none today, though plenty of small craft. Short of borrowing a rowboat, the traveller can hardly put to test the words of early Dunedin poet Thomas Bracken (who also composed the national anthem, *God Defend New Zealand*):

> *Go, trav'ler, unto others boast of*
> *Venice and of Rome,*
> *Of saintly Mark's majestic pile, and*
> *Peter's lofty dome;*
> *Of Naples and her trellised bowers,*
> *of Rhineland far away*
> *These may be grand, but give to me*
> *Dunedin from the Bay.*

A peninsula drive: The next-best thing to a Bracken's-eye view of Dunedin is

Preceding pages: sun hits the Matukituku River. **Below**, Dunedin from Mount Cargill.

to see it from the peninsula. Take the "low road" and return via the "high". The 64-km (40-mile) round trip can take anything from 90 minutes to a full day. Much of Dunedin's history is illustrated here. The narrow, winding road calls for careful driving, built as part of it was by convict labour for horse and buggy traffic. (The prisoners were housed in an old hulk that was dragged slowly along the seafront.)

Soon you will see **Glenfalloch**, 11 lovely hectares (27 acres) of woodland gardens; an ideal refreshment stop. At **Portobello**, visit the local museum (open Sunday 1.30pm–4.30pm or by arrangement, call 4780-255), then left to the wonderful Portobello Marine laboratory. In aquariums and "touch" tanks you will see – and fondle – everything marine from a 6-metre (20-foot) shark to a one-inch shrimp, as well as sea horses, octopi and penguins.

Further on, at **Otakou**, the Maori church and meeting house appear carved, but actually are cast in concrete. In the cemetery behind are buried three great Maori chiefs of last century – the warlike Taiaroa, Ngatata (a northern chief said to have "welcomed the Pakeha to Cook Strait") and Karetai, induced by the missionaries to abandon cannibalism and take up the Bible. The marae here is sacred to local Maori and is still the most historic Maori site in Otago. The name "Otago", in fact, is a European corruption of "Otakou". There's a Maori museum here, but to assure that it is open you must be sure to call in advance (4780-352).

Just north lie remains of the whaling industry founded in Otago Harbour in 1831, 17 years before European settlement. The try works – bricks and ashes from the fires still there, together with stanchions used to tie the whales during flensing – are clearly visible and marked by a plaque. Another across the road commemorates the first Christian service held in Otago Harbour, by Bishop Pompalier, in 1840.

Albatrosses and a castle: As you crest the hill past Otakou and look towards lofty **Taiaroa Head**, the tip of the peninsula, glance up. Those huge sea birds resting lazily on the wind like children's kites, are the world's largest birds of flight, rare Royal Albatrosses. Incredibly graceful, they swoop, turn and soar with barely a flick of their 3-metre wings. Up to 20 pairs circle the globe (at speeds of up to 110 km/70 mph) to roost here, pair mating for life and producing a chick every two years. One of these creatures, "Grandma", banded in 1947 as a breeding female, returned every second or third year to breed until 1990. Recognised then as the oldest wild bird in the world, "Grandma" has not been seen since.

The **Trust Bank Royal Albatross Centre**, opened in 1989 by Princess Anne, has viewing galleries and display areas. Escorted groups observe most of the spring-summer breeding cycle and the pre-flight peregrinations of the fledglings. To visit, contact the Centre or the Dunedin Visitor Centre (Tel: 7473-300). Take in (for free) the antics of a southern fur seal colony at Pilot Beach, below the big birds.

Tour groups at Taiaroa Head also

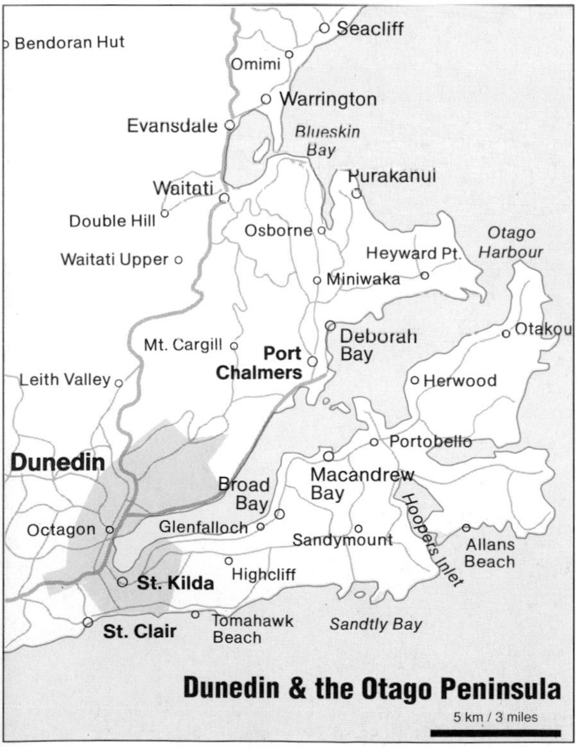

Dunedin & the Otago Peninsula

5 km / 3 miles

Map labels: Bendoran Hut, Seacliff, Omimi, Warrington, Evansdale, Blueskin Bay, Waitati, Purakanui, Double Hill, Osborne, Otago Harbour, Waitati Upper, Heyward Pt., Miniwaka, Mt. Cargill, Deborah Bay, Otakou, Port Chalmers, Leith Valley, Herwood, Dunedin, Portobello, Broad Bay, Macandrew Bay, Octagon, Glenfalloch, Sandymount, Allans Beach, St. Kilda, Highcliff, Hoopers Inlet, St. Clair, Tomahawk Beach, Sandfly Bay

visit the unusual Armstrong Disappearing Gun, built in 1886 at the height of a "Russian scare". The 15-cm (6-inch) cannon is hidden in the bowels of the earth, rising to fire (which it has done in anger but once and then only at a recalcitrant fishing boat during World War II); then sinking again for reloading.

A mile to the east, along a farm road, is **Penguin Bay**. Here, rare Chaplinesque yellow-eyed penguins strut in the surf. Contact the Dunedin Visitor Centre for viewing instructions and guided tours.

One has to return along the Taiaroa Head access road to Portobello to gain the "high road" back to the city. Up there is **Larnach Castle**, a century-old baronial manor that is New Zealand's only castle. It took 14 years to build (from 1871) as the home of the Hon. William J.M. Larnach, financier and later Minister of the Crown, who had married the daughter of a French duke and apparently thought it necessary to house his bride (and 44 servants) in the grand manner. An English workman spent 12 years carving the ceilings, along with two Italian craftsmen. The materials were imported from Europe.

The castle fell into disrepair after Larnach's bizarre suicide in Wellington's Parliament Buildings. It has now been fully restored and most of its 43 rooms, including accommodation, are open to the public. Perhaps not a grand castle on the European circuit, nevertheless Larnach has a curious fascination in such a young country.

The "high road" that leads back to suburbia has commanding views right down and up the harbour. On a fine day – and there are many of them here – you can see forever.

A seal's eye view of the Otago Peninsula and its attractions can be enjoyed most of the year from the *MV Monarch* which provides a regular tourist service from the inner harbour basin at Dunedin down the harbour to Taiaroa Head. *Southern Spirit*, a large and handsome ocean-going yacht, also takes tourists and fishermen on tours inside and outside the harbour.

In recent years the introduction of salmon smolt to Otago Harbour has resulted in a salmon fishing bonanza, most years, from November to April. Fishermen come from all over to crowd local wharves and small boats.

A proud history: Even on this Otago Peninsula drive, the traveller has never left Dunedin city. It is the largest in area of any city in New Zealand, much to the chagrin of its more voluble northern counterparts. Once, it was New Zealand's most populous, too, and the proudest and richest in all New Zealand.

In the 1860s, with the discovery of gold in the Otago hinterland and a rush that rivalled California's, Dunedin rapidly became the financial centre of the country. Immigrants flocked from around the world, head offices of national companies sprung up, industry and civic enterprise flourished. Here was the country's first university, medical school, finest educational institutions, first electric trams, then the first cable-car system in the world outside the United States, the country's first woollen mills, and daily newspaper.

Even centuries before that, the coast

Larnach Castle.

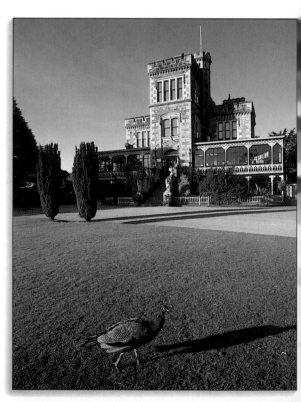

of Otago was more densely settled than any part of the North Island. The moa-hunters lived here, groups of often nomadic Maori who thrived on fish, waterfowl and the moa, the giant flightless bird that resembled a huge emu and was easy prey. At the height of the moa-hunter occupation, probably the 11th and 12th centuries, there may have been up to 8,000 Maori living in the estuaries and river mouths of Otago. As the moa retreated, the Maori followed them inland. Their fires destroyed much of the thick native bush, leaving behind the bare tussock country which today covers most of the inland hills from behind Dunedin almost to the foothills of the Southern Alps.

When Captain Cook sailed past Otago in 1770, he missed the harbour entrance, although noting the long white beaches now called St. Kilda and St Clair. "A land green and woody but without any sign of inhabitants," he logged. There were Maori there, of course, but in small numbers in nomadic communities.

Fewer than 30 years later, sealers and whalers were in the Otago region. Soon, Europeans were quite familiar with the coastline, if not always popular with the locals. In 1813, four sailors were killed and eaten by Maori; in 1817, at what is still called Murdering Beach, just north of the harbour entrance, three sealers offended natives and were killed. In retribution, their captain, James Kelly, led a massacre of what some reports say was as many as 70 Maori.

Religious fervour on the other side of the world led to the European colonisation of Dunedin. Disruption in the Presbyterian Church of Scotland gave birth to the idea of a new settlement in the colony of New Zealand where "piety, rectitude and industry" could flourish. Free Kirk advocates Captain William Cargill, a veteran of the Peninsula War, and the Rev. Thomas Burns, nephew of poet Robbie, were the leaders. The ships *John Wickliffe* and *Philip Laing* landed 300 hopeful Scottish settlers in March and April 1848 to a site already chosen by the London-based New Zealand Company and purchased – for £2,400 –

Otago University.

from the local Maori. Its first name was New Edinburgh; soon it became Dunedin (Edin on the Hill).

The settlement had been laid out from 19,000 km (12,000 miles) away, along the lines of Edinburgh, with a Princes and George streets, an Octagon and Moray Place; but with no regard for the contours of the land. This was to lead to tremendous physical problems. But the settlers, joined by later arrivals, stuck to their task nevertheless and hewed their township out of the invariably thick and often precipitous bush.

A taste of the Wild West: Once gold was discovered inland, there was no holding Dunedin back. In two years, the population of Otago rose from 12,000 to 60,000 – 35,000 of them immigrant gold-seekers. Dunedin was the arrival point for the miners, the service centre for the goldfields and the bank for the gold. With its new prosperity came the trappings of a Wild West town – saloons, gambling dens, brothels, dubious dance halls. One local bishop set tongues wagging when it was learned that a building he owned was used by a bevy of irreverent young ladies. It was eventually accepted that no fault lay with the man of the cloth. Pubs there were aplenty, breweries too, and Dunedin to this day has retained a high reputation for its well-patronised licensed premises.

Reputations: For a quarter of a century, Dunedin boomed. And where Dunedin went, the rest of New Zealand followed, until the gold ran out. Gradually, commercial and climatic attractions in the north led to the decline of the southern cities and provinces. For the last few decades, Dunedin has fought the inevitable drift north, especially through development of tertiary education facilities. Its greatly expanded university – now with 14,000 students and a reputation as the friendliest and most social in the country – the College of Education for training schoolteachers and the Otago Polytechnic together pour 20,000 youngsters into the Dunedin community, consolidating Dunedin's place as the leading city of learning in New Zealand.

Dunedin is known both as New Zealand's Scottish city and its Victorian city. The giant statue of Robbie Burns the poet, sits in the town centre, the Octagon, fittingly with the bard's back to the Anglican St Paul's Cathedral and facing what was once a corner pub. Here, too, are the country's only kilt manufacturer, its sole whisky distillery, lots of highland pipe bands and regularly celebrated Burns' Nights.

But Dunedin folk are a little weary of continual references to the "Edinburgh of the South" and "Victorian City"; there are equally fine examples of Edwardian and later-style buildings that qualify the city as the most interesting and diverse architecturally in the country. The range is delightful, from full-fashioned ornate Victoriana through Edwardian splendour to impressive Art Deco and modern concrete-and-glass structures that have won national awards.

Start in the easily locatable **Octagon**, which links Princes and George streets in the city centre. Tall, leafy trees, grass plots and comfortable benches make this a popular lunchtime gathering place.

Albatross from the colony at Taiaroa Head.

292

To the west is St Paul's, with Gothic pillars rising 40 metres (130 feet) and supporting the only stone-vaulted nave roof in New Zealand. The four-manual organ has 3,500 pipes. The "new" sanctuary and chancel, consecrated in 1971, won a national design award.

Next door are the century-old **Municipal Chambers**, designed by the noted colonial architect, R.W. Lawson, and behind it the 2,280-seat Town Hall, until recently the largest in the country. The **Municipal Chambers** have been replaced by the adjacent **Civic Centre** as local government offices, although the modern, stepped design of the Centre has drawn criticism for its contrast with the Victorian Chambers.

The city's **Visitor Centre**, as well as conference facilities, are housed in the Municipal Chambers, whose imposing clock tower and spire were re-erected in 1989 amid an overall greening and spring-cleaning of the city centre.

Moving east, down Lower Stuart Street, are classic old buildings such as the Allied Press newspaper offices, the Law Courts and the Police Station, excellent examples of art in stone. Then comes the **Dunedin Railway Station**, perhaps the finest stone structure in the country. It earned the designer, George Troup, a knighthood and the nickname "Gingerbread George". Of Flemish Renaissance style, it features a 37-metre (120-foot) high square tower, three huge clock faces, and a covered carriageway projecting from the arched colonnade.

In the main foyer is a majolica mosaic-tiled floor with nine central panels showing a small English "Puffing Billy". The original floor consisted of 725,760 half-inch Royal Doulton porcelain squares. Other ornamentation is in original Doulton china and church-like stained glass. Only two passenger trains a day now use this gingerbread house.

On the right track: Actually, Dunedin has a fascination with trains. *Josephine*, one of the country's first steam engines (a double-boiler, double-bogey, double-facing Fairlie) is in a glass case on public display beside the **Otago Early Settlers Museum**, together with

The Otago Early Settlers Museum.

JA1274, the last Dunedin-made steam locomotive to haul the main trunk-line trains. A train enthusiasts' group operates all manner of machines along a private line between St Clair and St Kilda beaches. And the Otago Excursion Train Trust has renovated vintage carriages and rolling stock and operates New Zealand's only private-hire train.

Special excursion trains run north and sometimes south on the main trunk line. Tourist trains enter Otago's hinterland through the rugged and spectacularly-bridged Taieri Gorge. Coach connections from the terminus at Middlemarch in Central Otago take onward tourists straight to Queenstown.

The country's first skyscraper is near the station – the seven-storey **Mutual Funds Building** (1910). It lies close to the original centre of Dunedin, the Stock Exchange area, where the first settlers stepped ashore in 1848. Land reclamation has since pushed back the harbour edge with a proliferation of fine old office buildings, but movement of the city centre north has forced many into use as storage areas and some into demolition. A gargoyled "bride's-cake" monument in the Stock Exchange area pays homage to founder Captain Cargill. It once sat atop men's underground toilets until public opprobrium led to the conveniences being closed.

First Church, in Moray Place, was the founders' tribute to their Father in 1867. Its spire soars 55 metres (180 feet) heavenwards. The church, another R.A. Lawson design, is arguably the most historical building in the city.

Some of the banks and other churches in the central city area inspire praise, as does the Lawson-designed Otago Boys High School tower block, dominant above the city. It is situated just below the **Town Belt**, a 200-hectare (500-acre), 8-km (5-mile) long green swath that separates city from suburbs.

A walk or drive through the Town Belt offers some of the best views of a city and harbour in New Zealand. Hear the tui and the bellbird; observe, too, the many wooded reserves and sports fields, fine golf courses, cotula-turfed bowling greens, huge heated swimming pools and fine swimming and surfing beaches. Outdoor sports live large here.

Olveston, "the jewel in Dunedin's crown", lies within the Town Belt. A Jacobean-style manor of double brick and oak, it was built in 1904 to the design of celebrated English architect Sir Ernest George for a local businessman, David Theomin. It was bequeathed to the city in 1966. The 35-room house and its furnishings and paintings, drawing thousands of visitors, is rated the best example in New Zealand of the grand style of Edwardian living. (Call 773-320 for guided tours.)

To the northern end of Dunedin are the (almost) combined campuses of the University of Otago, Otago Polytechnic and Dunedin College of Education and some 20,000 students. Dominating the Gothic rockpiles of the university is the main clock-tower building beside the grass-banked water of the Leith.

Venture beyond: Dunedin visitors should not restrict themselves to the city. On and beyond the outskirts lie fascinating sights of natural and historic beauty. Eighty km (50 miles) north are the queer **Moeraki Boulders**, huge round stones that lie "like devil's marbles" on the seashore.

The food baskets of a wrecked canoe in Maori legend, they are septarian concretions that formed on the seashore 60 million years ago by the gradual accumulation of lime salts around a small centre. Several tons in weight and up to 4.3 metres (14 feet) in circumference, they gradually appear from the bank behind the beach as the soft mudstone is weathered by the sea.

Not many kilometres to the west of Dunedin, in the Taieri River Gorge, jet-boat and white-water raft tours tumble more adventurous tourists between virgin bush-edged cliffs. For the less energetically inclined, there are plenty of trout to catch.

Both north and south of Dunedin are coastlines of immense natural beauty and quality of lifestyle, peopled by relatively few and still to be visited by the tourist hordes.

Inland, to Central Otago, lies another world again.

Moeraki Boulders.

SOUTHLAND AND REMOTE FIORDLAND

Speak to the historical purist and you will learn that Southland is a contradiction. Officially, there is no such province. Question him further and you will find contradiction in his answers.

When Southland's early European settlers demanded provincial government in 1861, they forgot the canny nature of their Scottish background and in nine heady years developed town, country, rail, road and other signs of civilisation to such an extent that the provincial government was declared bankrupt. As a result, their province was legally and administratively fixed to their neighbour, Otago, in 1870.

Yet despite this, the future of the province was assured because the 103,000 people who call themselves Southlanders today have scant regard for the historical purist's arguments about their legitimacy. They live in New Zealand's southernmost land district – Murihiku, the last joint of the tail, as the Maori called it. Their "province" takes in about 32,000 sq km (some 20,000 sq miles); its boundary starts just above Milford Sound on the West Coast, skirts the southern shores of Lake Wakatipu bordering Central Otago, and meanders its way through some of the lushest, most productive land in New Zealand to join the southeast coast near an unspoiled area called Chaslands.

Southland is a province of contrast. Signs of Maori settlement go back as far as the 12th century around the southern coast and, since those days of rapid development in the 1860s, its people have developed a land of unlimited potential for agricultural purposes and regained the conservative reputation for which their largely Scottish forebears were known. Yet there is a grittiness in the Southland character. It manifests itself in an agrarian excellence that would not have otherwise been achieved had conservatism dominated.

Contrast continues in the land itself. On the West Coast, deep fiords lap towering mountains and snow-capped peaks reach skywards amidst a myriad of vast bush-clad valleys in an area called, not surprisingly, Fiordland. Inland stretch the two massive plains on which the province's prosperity has grown to depend, surrounding the commercial heart the city of Invercargill, and eventually reaching the southern and southeastern coasts.

Tuataras and aluminium: The 57,000 people who live in **Invercargill** reside close to an estuary once plied by steamers and sailing ships. The city's Scottish heritage is well-reflected in street names; its original town planners were generous in the amount of space devoted to main thoroughfares and parks. Today, Queens Park provides a wide range of both passive and active recreational pursuits, from sunken rose gardens and statuary by Sir Charles Wheeler to a golf course and swimming pool.

The southernmost city in the Commonwealth, and the eleventh largest in New Zealand, Invercargill was the first to have within its pyramid-shaped **museum** a "tuatarium" where lizards

Preceding pages: ancient forest of Fiordland. **Below**, **Oyster fleet at Bluff**.

(tuatara) whose forebears survived the Stone Age can be viewed in a large, natural habitat.

Invercargill is also the stepping off point for Southland. Twenty-seven km (17 miles) south is **Bluff** and the journey to this port town emphasises Southland's agricultural development. A massive fertiliser works, processing phosphate rock imported from various foreign lands, underpins the fact that Southland's soils need constant nourishment. Deer farms along both sides of the road are evidence of fast-developing new pastoral industry. Thirty years ago, deer were found only in the bush; today they are raised on farms by the thousands; their velvet, in particular, is keenly sought.

There is no mistaking Bluff as a port town. The air is dashed with salt; large vessels tie up at a massive man-made island within the inland harbour (cleverly created so that tidal flows were not disturbed); and workers toil around the clock. Aluminium-clad, snake-like machines, their tails buried in a large building and their heads in ships' holds, dis-

gorge hundreds of thousands of carcases of frozen lamb and mutton for worldwide markets.

Across the harbour, three buildings 600 metres (2,000 feet) long, surrounded by other massive structures and dominated by a chimney stack 137 metres (449 feet) high, make up the Tiwai Point aluminium smelter, which produces 244,000 tonnes of aluminium a year. Tucked away on the lonely Tiwai peninsula, where almost non-stop winds disperse effluent, the smelter, which underwent a $400 million upgrade in the mid-1990s, is the major industrial employer in the south with 1,100 working directly for the company and perhaps twice that number indirectly.

Yet Bluff is famous also for something that just lies there, waiting to be picked up. Beneath the Foveaux Strait, a 35-km (22-mile) stretch of water that separates Stewart Island from the mainland, lie beds of oysters. In recent years these beds have been stricken by disease but steps have been taken to help them recover, and it is hoped the 23-

Bluff smelter.

boat oyster fleet from Bluff will be able soon to start normal dredging again. Tales have it that many visiting football teams in Southland have been taken to Bluff before their match and have left the province beaten but craving for more of the delicious soft-bellied molluscs. Despite a ban on export, the reputation of Foveaux Strait oysters is worldwide.

For New Zealand, Bluff is the end of the road. From Bluff, the visitor gazes out to sea, taking in Dog Island and its lighthouse, Stewart Island, then the great emptiness of the Great South Basin, beyond which lie only a few sub-Antarctic islands and the vast white expanse of Antarctica. A signpost and restaurant have been erected at Stirling Point, not far from the port, stating the distance to London, New York and other faraway places. This is as close as many will ever get to the bottom of the world.

Fish and fiords: Southeast of Invercargill lies the small fishing port of **Waikawa**, reached by comfortable road through rolling countryside which not long ago was scrub- and bush-covered.

Vast areas of bush remain in Southland, well-managed and controlled. At the end of the road, 5 km (3 miles) from Waikawa, is the remains of a petrified forest buried millions of years ago at a place called **Curio Bay**. This freeze-frame of time has caught every grain of timber in the fossilised stumps; boulders which have broken open through some unknown force show patterns of leaves and twigs. Waikawa is on the Southern Scenic Route, a major tourism highlight in the south which stretches from Balclutha in South Otago, along the southern coast, past Waikawa, and eventually ends in Te Anau.

No dedicated angler could make the journey southeast without stopping at an unremarkable bridge. It crosses the Mataura River and it is among the very best brown trout fisheries anywhere. Nearly 500 km (300 miles) of fishing waters stretch along Southland's three main fishing rivers – the Mataura, the Oreti and the Aparima – which cut the province in three.

In addition, there are at least eight

One of New Zealand's rarest birds: the takahe.

smaller rivers (the Wyndham, Mimihau, Hedgehope, Makarewa, Lora, Otapiri, Dunsdale and Waimatuku) and numerous streams well-stocked with brown trout. The angler who goes home empty-handed has been holding his rod at the wrong end.

Flat as it is, there are few days in Invercargill when residents cannot raise their eye to the mountains, tens of kilometres away bordering **Fiordland**. For those in a hurry, this vast natural area can be reached in less than two hours across the central Southland plains via Winton and Dipton, over the Josephville Hill, through Lumsden, until rolling tussock country indicates land of an altogether tougher nature.

This journey through prime country bearing several million head of stock, aptly shows how Southland has grown on agricultural production, the most significant change recently being a conversion of many sheep farms to dairy units. This has manifested itself in the building of a huge $50 million milk powder plant at Edendale in Eastern Southland, with promise of further expansion to come.

The historic town of **Riverton** nestles by the sea, 38 km (24 miles) from Invercargill. Sealers and whalers made Riverton their home in 1836 and Southland's first European settlement still bears signs of those times. Preservation is a way of life here; recently, the New Zealand Historic Place Trust offered a whaler's cottage for sale for the sum of just $1, so long as the owner preserved it to the trust's specifications.

Ten km (6 miles) farther is **Colac Bay**, another historic area. Scrub-covered hills to the west once boasted a town of 6,000 people during the gold-rush days of the 1890s. Nearby is the town of **Orepuki**, where history merges with the present: what once was a court-house is now a sheep-shearing shed.

Thundering surf follows the traveller between Orepuki and Tuatapere along a fine ocean view. Looming darkly across Te Wae Wae Bay are bush-clad mountains, the first signs of what is to come. From the timber town of **Tuatapere**,

Local deer sale.

where fishing and deer-hunting stories are as common as logs from the town's mills, the road heads north, close to the recreational mecca of Lake Monowai and from there proceeds to Lake Manapouri. Standing majestically ahead is Fiordland.

A lost tribe: With an area of 1,209,485 hectares (nearly 3 million acres), Fiordland is New Zealand's largest national park and a World Heritage Park. That first glimpse across Lake Manapouri, to sheer mountains and remote deep valleys on the other side of the lake, gives the observer some understanding of why some Maori legends – such as that of the mythical lost tribe of Te Anau – never lose their romantic hold in this wild region.

Fiordland is a land of firsts. Captain James Cook discovered **Dusky Sound**, largest of the fiords, in 1770. He returned three years later and established, among other things, New Zealand's first brewery. Of course, he also established other important things while refitting his ship, such as a workshop and a smithy. In 1792, New Zealand's first residential home was built in the Sound for whalers and the following year the New Zealand shipbuilding industry was born in Dusky Sound when a 65-tonne vessel was floated.

Today, fishermen still manoeuvre small boats along the jagged coast where once sealers and whalers eked out an existence. Most of these isolated sounds can be reached only by sea or air, or by the hardiest of trampers.

But there are two glorious opportunities of experiencing the mountains, the sea and the bush together. One is by taking a launch across **Lake Manapouri** to its West Arm. Ponder man's folly, for once planning to raise this lake by 27 metres (90 feet) for hydro-electric purposes. Conservation eventually prevailed, although a massive power station, 200 metres (650 feet) under the mountains at West Arm, was built to supply power for the Tiwai Point aluminium smelter; and the lake level can now be controlled. But a necessary part of the construction was the building of

Takitimu Mountains.

a road from West Arm across the Wilmot Pass, through rainforest, to the Hall Arm of Doubtful Sound in an area known as Deep Cove. Here water from Lake Manapouri is discharged into the sea by a 10-km (6-mile) tailrace tunnel under the mountains. In spite of this development, it remains virgin country.

Headquarters of this vast wilderness is the developing tourist town of **Te Anau**, where hotels, motels and lodges mingle alongside Lake Te Anau with the homes of its 3,000 residents. The valley floors behind the town are the scene of perhaps the biggest land projects in New Zealand, with scores of new farms being developed. A highlight is the **glow-worm caves** on Lake Te Anau which, although believed to have been known to early Maori explorers, were only rediscovered in 1948.

Eighth Wonder: The second way to the sea through Fiordland is via road to **Milford Sound**, world-renowned and described by Rudyard Kipling as "the eighth wonder of the world". Authors and artists have struggled to describe the beauty that unfolds as the road follows Lake Te Anau for 30 km (19 miles), enters dense forests, and passes through such features as the "Avenue of the Disappearing Mountain" where the eyes are not to be believed. Forests, river flats and small lakes pass by as the journey through the mountains progresses, until the road drops toward the forested upper Hollyford Valley at Marian Camp.

From there, the road splits in two directions. One arm ventures into the no-exit Hollyford with its Murray Gunn Camp, a haunt for hundreds with one of the Fiordland's true characters. The main highway proceeds west, steeply up the mountain to the eastern portal of the **Homer Tunnel**. Named after the man who discovered the Homer Saddle between the Hollyford and Cleddau valleys in 1899, this 1-km tunnel was completed in 1940 after five years. It was not until 1953, however, that it was widened sufficiently for road traffic. Avalanches claimed the lives of three men; and in 1983, a road overseer was killed

Sterling Falls, Milford Sound.

near the area. Homer can be Fiordland at its roughest.

From the Milford side, the road drops 690 metres (2,264 feet) in 10 km (6 miles) between sheer mountain faces to emerge into the Cleddau Valley with its awe-inspiring chasm. Eventually it reaches the head of Milford Sound, where fine accommodation awaits to remind the traveller of life's contrasts. Boat trips regularly carry visitors 16 km (10 miles) to the open sea. The sound is dominated by unforgettable **Mitre Peak** – a 1,836-metre (6,024-foot) pinnacle of rock – and several landmarks, notably the Bowen Falls (162 metres or 531 feet). Milford tends to buzz with daytrippers, but remains remarkably empty at either end of the day.

Footing it: There is another way to get to Milford Sound – by launch and on foot. A launch takes walkers from Te Anau to Glade House at the head of the lake. From there, through some of the most majestic scenery nature can devise, walkers take three days to reach the Sound via the **Milford Track**. They carry their own gear, but meals and sleeping accommodation are provided at huts along the way.

It is a journey for the reasonably fit, with such obstacles as the 1,122-metre (3,681-foot) McKinnon Pass, but the track is not difficult. Mountain and forest scenery, including the well-protected flora and fauna for which the region is famed; scores of waterfalls, including the spectacular 571-metre (1,873-foot) Sutherland Falls; lakes and spilling mountainside rivers can be viewed at close quarters. At night, a friendly international camaraderie exists at the Pompolona and Quintin huts. The track is open from November until April.

Fiordland also boasts other world-renowned treks as well, including the **Routeburn Track** and the spectacular **Kepler Track** which meanders along mountain tops and through valleys across the lake from Te Anau. Red deer shooting is encouraged in specified areas. The park's native bird life – including the takahe flightless bird, thought extinct until rediscovered in 1948 – is strictly protected. From park headquarters in Te Anau, numerous delightful bush walks can be recommended; similar hikes for the less energetic crisscross the Manapouri area. Launch trips and scenic flights give the traveller a new perspective.

Fiordland is to Southland, and to New Zealand, what the *Mona Lisa* is to the Louvre – an incomparable highlight. Those departing Southland travel north towards Queenstown via **Kingston**, where a vintage steam train, the *Kingston Flyer*, recreates a transport mode of the last century between Fairlight and Kingston. Alternatively, motorists proceed northeast toward Dunedin via the Mataura Valley; Southland's second largest town, Gore; and the rich countryside of Eastern Southland.

In the background stand the Hokonui Hills, which divide the two main plains of the province. In those hills, illicit whisky stills once produced a potent brew. Watch closely as you leave, and you may see a wisp of smoke, for there are those who claim the long arm of the law has not reached all the moonshiners.

Left, Reflection at Mirror Lakes. Right, Milford Track.

STEWART ISLAND

A beautiful, peaceful island on the southern fringe of the world lies across Foveaux Strait, 20 minutes by air from Invercargill and 45 minutes by catamaran from Bluff. **Stewart Island**, lapped by both the Pacific and Antarctic, rests easily as New Zealand's anchor.

Its early settlers left a wealth of history now gone – sawmills, whaling stations and tin mines included. Today, most of the 450 Stewart Islanders depend upon the industry of their forebears. Their small fishing boats venture into often-stormy waters around the rocky coast for the blue cod, the more lucrative crayfish (rock lobsters) and other marine species. Their main base, Oban and Halfmoon Bay, is on the north end of this triangular, 172,000-hectare (425,000-acre) island, but the land itself extends about 65 km (40 miles) north to south and 40 km (25 miles) east to west.

Many newcomers arrive on this island seeking tranquillity. On smaller isles around Stewart, meanwhile, Maori families still capture succulent young muttonbirds (sooty shearwaters), as did their ancestors. Maori have been granted exclusive rights to the isles where the muttonbirds breed after a round-the-world migration.

Harsh contentment: Stewart Island's harsh life is dominated by the weather and the sea. Those who choose to live here must be determined; all too often they know premature loss and sorrow. But they live on a bush-clad island whose beauty breeds contentment. It was little wonder the Maori called it Rakiura, "heavenly glow".

The first impression is one of peace. Here, road vehicles are subservient to pedestrians. There is no chance of life in the fast lane. Roads total a mere 20 km (12 miles). Both the island's airstrip and its port are close to **Oban**, where most residents live. Comfortable accommodation retains an individualistic approach to tourism. It's the island's way. The small museum has the island's history.

Preceding pages: on the South Island's wild coast. Left, Paterson Inlet, Stewart Island.

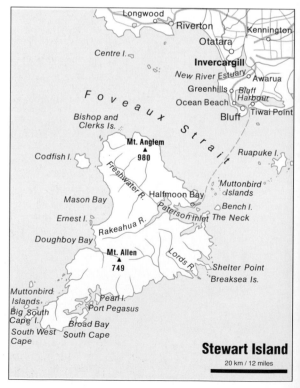

The South Seas Hotel, a 30-bed establishment in the centre of Oban, is the main community focus, but there are also a more up-market lodge, motels and backpacker accommodation catering for the island's growing tourist needs. The island now boasts its own electricity scheme but its way of life remains laidback and easy-going. For tourists seeking something different, a visit is a must. But even for those who feel like conserving their energy, the easy walks within reach of Oban deserve attention.

Native bush and fern, and moss-carpeted glades, team with native bird life according to the season. In spring, tui and bellbirds call out through the forest. In summer, the curious weka and the tomtit are present, while in winter, the fantail hovers about. Always, there is the swish of the wood pigeon as it flies from tree to tree. The island is a birdwatcher's paradise.

Over the hill from Halfmoon Bay is the large **Paterson Inlet**, which juts deep into the island's hinterland. Tracks and small roads take the walker to many of its beauty spots; launch trips are also available. A highlight is a trip to Ulva Island in the inlet's centre. Farther inside are the remains of an old sawmill and whaling station. In Big Glory Bay a salmon farm has been established.

For the fitter visitor, longer and popular tracks meander around much of the island. They take in such exotically named haunts as Port William, Christmas Village and Yankee River. Off Stewart Island's western coast is **Codfish Island**, once a European settlement whose harshness of life eventually proved overwhelming; today it is a protected sanctuary for birds. Sea-fishing trips can be made, and most parts of Stewart Island are a deer hunter's dream. The white-tailed deer in particular is highly sought.

With daylight savings time in summer it is often light on Stewart Island until 10pm. At that time, on a clear night, it is worth standing on Observation Rock above Paterson Inlet to see why the Maori name for Stewart Island is so apt.

Stewart islander.

CHATHAM ISLANDS: WHERE DAY BEGINS

Flung in icy seas to the east and south of New Zealand are many tiny islands, all under New Zealand's sovereignty. The Auckland Islands, Campbell Islands, Antipodes Islands and the Chatham Islands are among the world's loneliest places, where few mainland New Zealanders have ever ventured.

Scientists and meteorologists are the only regular visitors to most of them. They contain unique birdlife and they are early warning stations for the winds, storms and frigid airflows that can sweep up to New Zealand from the Antarctic.

Home of the Morioris: One group, the **Chathams**, has a resident population of about 780. About 800 km (500 miles) east of Christchurch, the Chathams are world leaders in at least one respect – the three main islands in the groups are inched just inside the International Dateline. As a result Chatham Islanders are among the first in the world to see the new morning. The Chathams are where time begins.

The Chathams were settled about AD 1200 by Polynesian mariners from the eastern Pacific. Once on the islands, these settlers – known as Morioris – became stranded. The windy islands had no trees big enough to build canoes to sail onwards. So they remained and developed a culture of their own.

The first European to sight the islands was Lieutenant William Broughton, in 1791. Other Europeans came to settle in 1840, five years after a party of New Zealand Maori arrived to conquer and enslave the native Chatham Islanders. The history of relations between the Moriori and Maori is the subject of fierce academic debate, of claim and counterclaim. From an estimated peak of more than 1,000, the Moriori population dwindled to only 12 by 1900, wiped out by disease, massacre and desolation. It is believed there are no pure-blooded Moriori people alive today.

If you're looking for a geographic parallel to the Chathams, think of the

The last Moriori family, circa 1910.

Falkland Islands in the South Atlantic. The weather is wild, and communication with the rest of New Zealand is difficult – and ambiguous. The islands have a half-hour time difference with the rest of New Zealand, and it is symbolic of a wider gulf.

Islanders talk about "going to New Zealand" when they venture to the mainland, but they rely on support from central government to keep their tiny economy going. They resent intrusion and have tried to make their much-loved home more self-sufficient. Successive governments in Wellington have looked for new ways to deal with the Chathams, with limited success. When a recent government working party included among its recommendations the possibility that subsidies to the islands be cut, the bureaucrat who made the suggestion found himself on the end of "hang 'em high" recriminations on the Chathams. But the islanders are vexed by paternalism from "New Zealand".

The latest "solution" to the Chatham Islands problem came in 1990 with the establishment of the Chatham Islands Enterprise Trust, seeded with NZ$8 million to look at ways of fostering sheep-farming and fishing, the island's two biggest activities, and develop transport, social networks and new ventures such as tourism.

If Chatham Islanders don't look to their land for support, through sheep, chances are they are crayfishermen, exporting to mainland New Zealand, Australia and the United States. Among the current hopes for the future is honey, bringing new jobs. Another new venture is to tap a truly abundant resource – wind. Wind farming could at least to make the Chathams more self-sufficient.

Since 1913, the Chathams have had a radio station, whose main job was to broadcast daily weather forecasts. It has picked up calls from vessels in trouble all around New Zealand and during World War II it took calls from stricken vessels throughout the South Pacific.

A world of its own: The islands suffered a crisis when the shipping service supplied by the rusty old *Holmdale* freighter was withdrawn. Central government came to the islanders' aid with a subsidised tug and barge service for a while, but now a containerised ship from the Cook Islands line, in the South Pacific, runs a regular service to bring supplies of groceries, petrol, machinery and much else, including videotapes.

There are scheduled air links as well, with up to five flights a week from Napier, Christchurch and Wellington. There are two places to say – a homely traditional hotel "downtown" in the main settlement of **Waitangi** and a lodge a couple of miles upcountry. Many families are happy to take lodgers. Walking, hunting and birdwatching are among the attractions, along with the unique experience of one of the world's truly isolated places. Expect real hospitality.

To love the Chathams, you've got to be able to get along with a small group of people in confined circumstances. While there's a round of make-shift concerts and parties, some can't stand the isolation, and are back on the next sailing. You have to be a special breed to live on the edge of the world.

Albatrosses are common on the islands.

THE COOK ISLANDS AND THE PACIFIC

Captain James Cook opened up the South Pacific to the world during his three journeys of discovery in the 1760s and 1770s and, during the 19th century, New Zealand developed a very strong relationship with many of the small island nations he placed with such great accuracy on the map of the world.

Although there has been no direct political association with Western Samoa since soon after the end of World War II, Samoans make up the largest single ethnic group of New Zealanders, after Pakeha and Maori; and the social ties continue to be strong.

Among the many discoveries Cook made were some of the atolls that make up his namesake nation, the **Cook Islands**, and the 60-metre (197-ft) high limestone rock called **Niue**. These, once administered by New Zealand, now have almost total independence – but their inhabitants are New Zealand citizens.

The first Polynesian settlement of the Cook Islands occurred about AD 700, probably by immigrants from the Society Islands. The first Europeans to see the northern islands were Spanish. Mendana passed Pukapuka in 1595, Quiros saw Rakahanga in 1606. However, it was not until Captain Cook visited the sizeable southern islands of Mangaia and Atiu in 1777 that knowledge of the group became substantial. Cook named the archipelago the Hervey Islands, but they were later renamed in his honour. Captain William Bligh of *HMS Bounty* discovered Aitutaki in 1789, and then his mutineers, under Fletcher Christian, visited Rarotonga seeking an isle refuge.

A special relationship between New Zealand and the Cooks negotiated in 1965 gives the Cooks self-government but provides for the exercise by New Zealand of some responsibilites for defence and foreign affairs. Those responsibilities do not take away any rights of control from the Cook government. The same sort of relationship was negotiated with Niue in 1974.

There are 15 islands in the Cook group spread across 2.2 million kilometres (1.3 million miles) of the Pacific Ocean – nine of them in a southern group and six in an even more dispersed northern group. The population is 18,000. Some of the islands are uninhabited and most people live on **Rarotonga** (about 12,000), the capital, 1,630 nautical miles northeast of Auckland. The island is on latitude 23 degrees south, just east of the International Date Line; so when it is noon on Monday in Auckland, it is 1.30 on Sunday afternoon in Rarotonga. Tourism – mainly focused on Rarotonga – is the backbone of the Cooks' economy, supplemented by tropical fruit and vegetables and some economic aid from New Zealand.

High, volcanic island: Rarotonga attracts 58,000 visitors a year, about 30 percent each from New Zealand and UK/Europe, 25 percent from the United States and 8 percent from Australia. The administrative and industrial centre are on the Avarua side of the island, and an airport was opened as long ago as 1972.

Preceding pages: idyllic islands. **Left,** three boys of Rarotonga at the starting point of early migrations. **Right,** floral welcome.

Rarotonga is a high volcanic island, oval in shape and about 32 km (20 miles) in circumference, with a narrow coastal plain skirting the high mountains. It is encircled by a lagoon enclosed by an offshore reef. To the north and west, the lagoon is broken and narrow; this is where **Avarua** and Avatiu Harbour are located. On the southern side of the island, the lagoon is broad and provides the best swimming. There are some channels to the open sea.

If you decide to take the coastal road – Ara Tapu, "The Sacred Way" – you can drive around the island in about two hours, or you can take two days if you choose to dawdle and take in the sights. A short distance inland is the Ara Metua, a narrow, largely unsealed road which parallels the coast road but is broken into sections. The well-sealed Ara Tapu has many spokes leading to this inner road, from which several no-exit jeep tracks and footpaths head into the mountain valleys. A cross-island hike past the 412-metre (1,351-ft) needle of Te Rua Manga offers some fine scenery.

Cars, mopeds and bicycles are available for hire in Avarua, and tourists may enjoy horse rides, fishing trips, small-boat sailing and other recreations.

Nineteenth-century architecture is one of Rarotonga's charms. The most impressive buildings are the Cook Islands Christian Church in Avarua and an old church at Titikaveka village on the southern coast. Opposite the entrance to the Avarua church are the ruins of the palace of Queen Makea Nui Ariki; they are tapu (forbidden) and should not be approached. In the church cemetery is the tomb of Robert Dean Frisbie, the Cook Islands' most famous literary figure, author of *The Book of Pukapuka*.

Departure for New Zealand: Just west of Avarua is the man-made harbour of **Avatiu**, where inter-island motor vessels, a fishing fleet and visiting yachts find haven. Offshore sits the wreck of the *SS Maitat*. At Muri, there are offshore islands and the headquarters of the Rarotonga Sailing Club. Beyond Muri on the east coast is Ngatangiia Harbour, a beautiful place with a wide

Left, tropical boating.

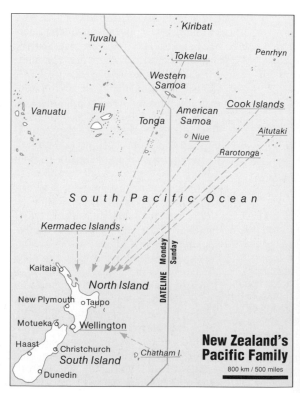

New Zealand's Pacific Family

800 km / 500 miles

channel to the sea. Legend says it was from here that great Polynesia voyaging canoes set out for New Zealand and other Pacific destinations.

The Rarotongan Resort Hotel is first-class, and the Pacific Resort provides luxury accommodation used by many overseas visitors. The largest is the Edgewater. There are a number of motels with good accommodation. Rarotonga is a very relaxed resort, ideal for switching off, South-Pacific style. Air New Zealand and Polynesian Airlines provide regular services.

For most of the year, the climate in Rarotonga and Aitutaki is balmy, with cooling southeast tradewinds, warm sunshine and occasional showers. In summer, from December to March, days can be cloudy and the weather sometimes oppressively hot. The months from April to June are most comfortable. From June to October, days and nights can be cool by island standards.

Rarotonga, with the airport of Avarua on the coast.

From Rarotonga, you can visit all the other islands in the Cook group. Nearby **Aitutaki**, with a population of 2,000,

has also developed tourist trade, while Atiu, Mangaia, Mauke and Mitiaro offer some accommodation. Along with the other primitive southern islands of Manuae, Palmerston and Takutea, these are uplifted coral atolls with reefs formed close against high coastal cliffs. All of the southern islands are very fertile. Adequate rainfall and sufficient soils allow the cultivation of many tropical fruits and vegetables, including oranges and other citrus fruits, bananas, tomatoes, pineapples and kumara.

The northern Cook Islands, which are made up of the six atolls of Manihiki, Rakahanga, Penryhn, Pukapuka, Nassau and Suwarrow, are lonely, desolate and remote.

Niue Island: About 2,000 Niueans make their home on the 258-sq km (100-sq mile) island, plus several dozen Europeans. More than 1,000 people live at the administrative centre of **Alofi**.

Niue was first colonised from Samoa, about 560 km (350 miles) to the northwest, in ancient times. Tongans also came to the island. The Polynesian dia-

lect of Niue has affinities with Samoan, and Samoan radio broadcasts, newspapers and travel maintain links between the two places. Local time is 50 minutes behind Rarotonga, or 23 hours and 20 minutes behind New Zealand.

There are no harbours on Niue. High coastal sea cliffs loom over close coral reefs. A canoe passage and lighter landing at Alofi allows the servicing of cargo and passenger ships that anchor offshore. To the south of Alofi is a good airstrip capable of taking intermediate jet aircraft. The internal road system consists of a 64-km (40-mile) road, which more or less follows the coast, and two cross-island roads.

Tourism is still at an early stage of development. The Niue Hotel – first on the island – has a limited number of rooms to go with its bar, swimming pool and magnificent view. Outdoor activities offered on the island include swimming, snorkelling, fishing, reef walking and cave exploration,

Niue was discovered by Captain Cook in 1774. The London Missionary Society established teachers on the island from the mid-1840s onward. Today about three-quarters of the small population belong to the Ekalesia Niue (Niuean Church) which was set up by the missionaries.

The Tokelau atolls: One of the most remote island groups in the world, Tokelau is, however, part of New Zealand. It consists of three atolls: Nukunonu, Fakaofo and Atafu. All are formed by islets set about reefs which together form expansive inner lagoons. Sitting between 8 and 10 degrees south and about 480 km (300 miles) north of Western Samoa, its time is 23 hours behind Auckland.

The growth of the atoll population to about 1,700 in the post-World War II period has been too much for the limited resources of the prevailing coconuts-and-fish economy. The New Zealand government has more than once stepped in with resettlement programmes that have brought hundreds of Tokelauans to live in New Zealand, mostly around the areas of Taupo and Rotorua.

Island couple.

There are no ports, and visits by small cargo vessels are infrequent. The lagoons can receive amphibious aircraft from Samoa.

Not surprisingly, there are few tourist facilities. Those who undertake a journey to Tokelau should plan well in advance, making inquiries about entry, transportation, and what supplies of food and equipment should be taken.

Visitors should be sensitive to local cultural mores. The islanders refer to themselves as Maori – a word meaning "natural to the place". There are New Zealand Maori, Cook Islands Maori, Niue Maori and so on. They possess a certain innocence, but are none the less keenly aware of the attitudes exhibited by visitors. You should smile, give the friendly greeting of "kia orana", and shake a few hands.

Polynesians detest a sour face; they stay cheerful despite the hardships of their own lives. They don't like to haggle over a deal; outside hotels, most are embarrassed by tips. Small gifts are appreciated, but this does oblige the recipient to give something in return.

In spite of their happy-go-lucky nature, islanders take their Christian faith seriously. Protestantism was widely accepted early in the 19th century. Catholics, Mormons and other denominations then followed. Attending an island church service is a delightful thing to do. Neat and clean dress is generally expected, with hats for ladies and ties for gentlemen.

Formal occasions call for formal attire. Bikinis should be worn with discretion. These island communities are still, to some extent, in the Victorian age.

A visit to the South Pacific means a lot of time will be spent in the water. Swimmers should get local recommendations about safe bathing areas as reef currents can be dangerous. Those who walk on reefs should wear canvas shoes, as cuts or grazes from live coral are notorious for turning septic. Never put your hands in holes or niches in the reef: moray eels have sharp teeth, cone shells have lethal stingers, and other sea creatures lurk in unseen corners.

Touring.

INSIGHT GUIDES
Travel Tips

FOR THOSE
WITH MORE THAN
A PASSING INTEREST
IN TIME...

Before you put your name down for a Patek Philippe watch *fig. 1*, there are a few basic things you might like to know, without knowing exactly whom to ask. In addressing such issues as accuracy, reliability and value for money, we would like to demonstrate why the watch we will make for you will be quite unlike any other watch currently produced.

"Punctuality", Louis XVIII was fond of saying, "is the politeness of kings."

We believe that in the matter of punctuality, we can rise to the occasion by making you a mechanical timepiece that will keep its rendezvous with the Gregorian calendar at the end of every century, omitting the leap-years in 2100, 2200 and 2300 and recording them in 2000 and 2400 *fig. 2*. Nevertheless, such a watch does need the occasional adjustment. Every 3333 years and 122 days you should remember to set it forward one day to the true time of the celestial clock. We suspect, however, that you are simply content to observe the politeness of kings. Be assured, therefore, that when you order your watch, we will be exploring for you the physical—if not the metaphysical—limits of precision.

Does everything have to depend on how much?

Consider, if you will, the motives of collectors who set record prices at auction to acquire a Patek Philippe. They may be paying for rarity, for looks or for micromechanical ingenuity. But we believe that behind each $500,000-plus

bid is the conviction that a Patek Philippe, even if 50 years old or older, can be expected to work perfectly for future generations.

In case your ambitions to own a Patek Philippe are somewhat discouraged by the scale of the sacrifice involved, may we hasten to point out that the watch we will make for you today will certainly be a technical improvement on the Pateks bought at auction? In keeping with our tradition of inventing new mechanical solutions for greater reliability and better time-keeping, we will bring to your watch innovations *fig. 3* inconceivable to our watchmakers who created the supreme wristwatches of 50 years ago *fig. 4*. At the same time, we will of course do our utmost to avoid placing undue strain on your financial resources.

Can it really be mine?

May we turn your thoughts to the day you take delivery of your watch? Sealed within its case is your watchmaker's tribute to the mysterious process of time. He has decorated each wheel with a chamfer carved into its hub and polished into a shining circle. Delicate ribbing flows over the plates and bridges of gold and rare alloys. Millimetric surfaces are bevelled and burnished to exactitudes measured in microns. Rubies are transformed into jewels that triumph over friction. And after many months—or even years—of work, your watchmaker stamps a small badge into the mainbridge of your watch. The Geneva Seal—the highest possible attestation of fine watchmaking *fig. 5*.

Looks that speak of inner grace *fig. 6*.

When you order your watch, you will no doubt like its outward appearance to reflect the harmony and elegance of the movement within. You may therefore find it helpful to know that we are uniquely able to cater for any special decorative needs you might like to express. For example, our engravers will delight in conjuring a subtle play of light and shadow on the gold case-back of one of our rare pocket-watches *fig. 7*. If you bring us your favourite picture, our enamellers will reproduce it in a brilliant miniature of hair-breadth detail *fig. 8*. The perfect execution of a double hob-nail pattern on the bezel of a wristwatch is the pride of our casemakers and the satisfaction of our designers, while our chainsmiths will weave for you a rich brocade in gold *figs. 9 & 10*. May we also recommend the artistry of our goldsmiths and the experience of our lapidaries in the selection and setting of the finest gemstones? *figs. 11 & 12*.

How to enjoy your watch before you own it.

As you will appreciate, the very nature of our watches imposes a limit on the number we can make available. (The four Calibre 89 time-pieces we are now making will take up to nine years to complete). We cannot therefore promise instant gratification, but while you look forward to the day on which you take delivery of your Patek Philippe *fig. 13*, you will have the pleasure of reflecting that time is a universal and everlasting commodity, freely available to be enjoyed by all.

Should you require information on any particular Patek Philippe watch, or even on watchmaking in general, we would be delighted to reply to your letter of enquiry. And if you send us

fig. 1: The classic face of Patek Philippe.

fig. 4: Complicated wristwatches circa 1930 (left) and 1990. The golden age of watchmaking will always be with us.

fig. 6: Your pleasure in owning a Patek Philippe is the purpose of those who made it for you.

fig. 9: Harmony of design is executed in a work of simplicity and perfection in a lady's Calatrava wristwatch.

fig. 10: The chainsmith's hands impart strength and delicacy to a tracery of gold.

fig. 5: The Geneva Seal is awarded only to watches which achieve the standards of horological purity laid down in the laws of Geneva. These rules define the supreme quality of watchmaking.

fig. 7: Arabesques come to life on a gold case-back.

fig. 2: One of the 33 complications of the Calibre 89 astronomical clock-watch is a satellite wheel that completes one revolution every 400 years.

fig. 11: Circles in gold: symbols of perfection in the making.

fig. 3: Recognized as the most advanced mechanical regulating device to date, Patek Philippe's Gyromax balance wheel demonstrates the equivalence of simplicity and precision.

fig. 8: An artist working six hours a day takes about four months to complete a miniature in enamel on the case of a pocket-watch.

fig. 12: The test of a master lapidary is his ability to express the splendour of precious gemstones.

PATEK PHILIPPE
GENEVE
fig. 13: The discreet sign of those who value their time.

So, you're getting away from it all.

Just make sure you can get back.

AT&T Access Numbers
Dial the number of the country you're in to reach AT&T.

AMERICAN SAMOA	633 2-USA	**INDIA**◆	**000-117**	NEW ZEALAND	000-911
AUSTRALIA	**1800-881-011**	**INDONESIA**◆	**001-801-10**	*PHILIPPINES	105-11
CHINA, PRC◆◆◆	**10811**	*JAPAN	0039-111	**SAIPAN**¹	**235-2872**
COOK ISLANDS	09-111	**KOREA**	**009-11**	SINGAPORE	800-0111-111
FIJI	004-890-1001	**KOREA**◇◇	**11**✱	SRI LANKA	430-430
GUAM	**018-872**	MACAO	0800-111	*TAIWAN	0080-10288-0
HONG KONG	**800-1111**	*MALAYSIA◆	800-0011	THAILAND◆	0019-991-1111

Countries in bold face permit country-to-country calling in addition to calls to the U.S. **World Connect**℠ prices consist of **USADirect**® rates plus an additional charge based on the country you are calling. Collect calling available to the U.S. only. *Public phones require deposit of coin or phone card. ◇◇From public phones only, push the red button, wait for dial tone and then dial. ¹May not be available from every phone. ◆Not available from public phones. ◆◆◆Not yet available from all areas. © 1994 AT&T.

Here's a travel tip that will make it easy to call back to the States. Dial the access number for the country you're in to get English-speaking AT&T operators or voice prompts. Minimize hotel telephone surcharges too.

If all the countries you're visiting aren't listed above, call **1 800 241-5555** for a free wallet card with all AT&T access numbers. Easy international calling from AT&T. **TrueWorld Connections.**

Getting Acquainted

Time Zones 322
Climate 322
Government 322

Planning The Trip

What to Bring/Wear 322
Health 322
Currency 322
Public Holidays 323
Getting There 323

Practical Tips

Emergencies.................... 323
Business Hours 323
Tipping 323
Media 323

Getting Around

Domestic Travel.............. 324

Where To Stay

Hotels and Motels 324
Motor Camps 329
Farm and Homestay 329

Eating Out

What To Eat 330
Where To Eat 330

Attractions

Culture 331
Shopping 333

Further Reading

Collections &
Anthologies..................... 334
Other Insight Guides 335

Art/Photo Credits 336
Index 337

Getting Acquainted

There is only one time zone throughout the country – 12 hours in advance of Greenwich Mean Time (GMT).

From early October until late March, time is advanced by one hour to give extended daytime throughout the summer.

(Time in the remote Chatham Islands 800 km [500 miles] east of Christchurch, is 45 minutes ahead of New Zealand Standard Time). Travellers from the Western Hemisphere, moving west into New Zealand lose a full day crossing the International Dateline, and regain a full day returning eastwards from New Zealand. Because the country is so advanced in time, being close to the International Dateline, it is one of the very first nations to welcome each day (preceded only by Fiji and some other small Pacific Islands).

During Standard Time periods, when it is noon (Monday) in New Zealand it is:

12am in London (Monday)
1am in Bonn, Madrid, Paris and Rome (Monday)
3am in Athens (Monday)
4am in Moscow (Monday)
5.30am in Bombay (Monday)
7am in Bangkok (Monday)
8am in Singapore and Hong Kong (Monday)
9am in Tokyo (Monday)
10am in Sydney (Monday)
2pm in Honolulu (Sunday)
4pm in Los Angeles (Sunday)
7pm in New York and Montreal (Sunday)
9pm in Rio de Janeiro (Sunday)

Climate

New Zealand has three main islands – the North Island, the South Island and Stewart Island – running roughly from north to south over 1,600 kilometres (994 miles), between 34 and 47 degrees south.

The climate is generally temperate with rainfall spread fairly evenly throughout the year. The summer and autumn seasons from December through May are the most settled and the best for holidaying. New Zealanders traditionally take their main family holiday break at Christmas through January; so visitors are advised to make sure of advance bookings for accommodation and domestic transport over this period because of the pressure on facilities.

Winds can be strong at any time on the Cook Strait, between the two main islands, but summer days are generally warm and pleasant in most regions.

Winters can be cold in the central and southern North Island and coastal districts of the South Island, but can be severe in central regions of the South Island.

Government

New Zealand has a centralised democracy with a Western-style economy. As the result of a referendum at the last general election, the first past the post system will be replaced by a form of proportional representation.

Planning The Trip

What To Bring/Wear

For summer visits, you are advised to bring sweaters or wind-breakers for the cooler evenings or brisk days, specially for those regions south of the top half of the North Island.

Medium thick clothing with a raincoat or umbrella is adequate for most regions most of the year, but in midwinter in the tourist areas of Rotorua, Taupo and Queenstown, winter clothing and shoes are essential.

New Zealand is noted for the brilliance of its light. This can lead to severe sunburn on days when the temperature may be deceptively low. It is important to wear sunscreen lotions.

Health

All persons entering New Zealand are required to complete passenger declarations on arrival and departure.

Limited medical treatment is available free to visitors but health insurance is recommended.

The following classes of people are prohibited by law from entering regardless of their country of origin, either as tourists or immigrants:

● Those suffering from tuberculosis, syphilis, leprosy, or any mental disorders.

● Those convicted of an offence which drew a sentence of imprisonment for more than one year.

● Those who have previously been deported from New Zealand.

Agricultural Regulations

Because New Zealand relies heavily on agricultural and horticultural trade with the rest of the world, it has stringent regulations governing the import of animals, and the import of vegetable and animal matter. Visitors planning to bring in any material of this sort should make detailed inquiries at the New Zealand Government offices overseas before proceeding.

Currency

There is no restriction on the amount of domestic or foreign currency (or traveller's cheques expressed in New Zealand currency) a visitor may bring into New Zealand.

A visitor may also take out without limitation any unused funds from those brought in. Currency conversion facilities are available at Auckland, Wellington, and Christchurch International Airports.

The New Zealand Dollar, divided into 100 cents, is the unit of currency. The country adopted decimal currency in 1967 after having previously followed the British system of pounds, shillings and pence. The value of the New Zealand Dollar, in relation to overseas currencies, varies.

American Express offers Travelers Cheques built for two.

Cheques *for Two*℠ from American Express are the Travelers Cheques that allow either of you to use them because both of you have signed them. And only one of you needs to be present to purchase them.

Cheques *for Two* are accepted anywhere regular American Express Travelers Cheques are, which is just about everywhere. So stop by your bank, AAA* or any American Express Travel Service Office and ask for Cheques *for Two*.

Travelers Cheques

Don't be overcharged for overseas calls.

Save up to 70% on calls back to the U.S. with WorldPhone.®*

While traveling abroad, the last thing you need to worry about is being overcharged for international phone calls. Plan ahead and look into WorldPhone – the easy and affordable way for you to call the U.S. and country to country from a growing list of international locations.

Just dial 1-800-955-0925 to receive your free, handy, wallet-size WorldPhone Access Guide – your guide to saving as much as 70% on phone calls home.

When calling internationally, your WorldPhone Access Guide will allow you to:
- Avoid hotel surcharges and currency confusion
- Choose from four convenient billing options
- Talk with operators who speak your language
- Call from more than 90 countries
- Just dial and save – regardless of your long distance carrier back home

WorldPhone is easy. And there's nothing to join. So avoid overcharges when you're traveling overseas. Call for your free WorldPhone Access Guide today – before you travel.

Call 1-800-955-0925.

THE TOP 25 WORLDPHONE COUNTRY CODES.		
COUNTRY / WORLDPHONE TOLL-FREE ACCESS #	**COUNTRY** / WORLDPHONE TOLL-FREE ACCESS #	
Australia (CC)◆	**Japan** (cont'd.)	
To call using OPTUS ■ 008-5511-11	To call anywhere other than the U.S. 0055	
To call using TELSTRA ■ 1-800-881-100	**Korea** (CC)	
Belgium (CC)◆ 0800-10012	To call using KT ■ 009-14	
China (CC) 108-12	To call using DACOM ■ 0039-12	
(Available from most major cities)	Phone Booths + Red button 03, then press *	
For a Mandarin-speaking Operator 108-17	Military Bases 550-2255	
Dominican Republic 1-800-751-6624	**Mexico** ▲ 95-800-674-7000	
El Salvador ◆ 195	**Netherlands** (CC)◆ 06-022-91-22	
France (CC)◆ 19▼-00-19	**Panama** 108	
Germany (CC) 0130-0012	Military Bases 2810-108	
(Limited availability in eastern Germany.)	**Philippines** (CC)◆	
Greece (CC)◆ 00-800-1211	To call using PLDT ■ 105-14	
Guatemala ◆ 189	To call PHILCOM ■ 1026-12	
Haiti (CC)+ 001-800-444-1234	For a Tagalog-speaking Operator 108-15	
Hong Kong (CC) 800-1121	**Saudi Arabia** (CC)+ 1-800-11	
India (CC) 000-127	**Singapore** 8000-112-112	
(Available from most major cities)	**Spain** (CC) 900-99-0014	
Israel (CC) 177-150-2727	**Switzerland** (CC)◆ 155-0222	
Italy (CC)◆ 172-1022	**United Kingdom** (CC)	
Japan ◆	To call using BT ■ 0800-89-0222	
To call to the U.S. using KDD ■ 0039-121	To call using MERCURY ■ 0500-89-0222	
To call to the U.S. using IDC ■ 0066-55-121		

(CC) Country-to-country calling available. May not be available to/from all international locations. Certain restrictions apply.
+ Limited availability.
▼ Wait for second dial tone.
▲ Rate depends on call origin in Mexico.
■ International communications carrier.
◆ Public phones may require deposit of coin or phone card for dial tone.

WorldPhone℠
From MCI
Let it take you around the world.

* Savings are based on typical hotel charges for calls back to the U.S. Your savings may vary depending upon originating country and hotel, time of day and length of call. All rates effective 7/94.

Public Holidays

National public holidays are:

New Year's Day, January 1
New Year's statutory holiday, the first working day following New Year's Day
Waitangi Day, February 6
Good Friday/Easter Monday
Anzac Day, April 25
Queen's Birthday, generally the first Monday in June
Labour Day, generally the last Monday in October
Christmas Day, December 25
Boxing Day, December 26
Christmas statutory holiday, the first working day following Boxing Day

In addition each provincial region has a holiday to celebrate the provincial anniversary. The dates are:

Wellington, January 22
Northland and Auckland, January 29
Nelson, February 1
Otago and Southland, March 23
Taranaki, March 31
Hawke's Bay, October 20
Marlborough, November 1
Canterbury, December 1
Westland, December 1

If the day falls on a Saturday or Sunday then the following Monday is taken.

Getting There

By Air

New Zealand – as an island nation and one of the most isolated countries in the world – is now almost entirely dependent on air travel. Of the over 1 million tourists who visit each year, more than 99 percent arrive on services provided by international airlines. The remainder arrive by cruise ships which occasionally call at either the Bay of Islands, Auckland Tauranga or Wellington.

The main gateway is the Auckland International Airport at Mangere, 24 km (15 miles) south of the city's downtown area. Bus and taxi transfers are available.

There is a fine international airport at Harewood, quite close to Christchurch, the main South Island city, and recently more and more airlines are scheduling flights here, as tourism arrivals into both New Zealand and the South Island steadily increase.

The airport at Wellington, the capital city, has restricted access for most wide-bodied aircraft types because of runway length.

New Zealand has direct air links with the Pacific Islands, the major Australian cities, and through many Southeast Asian destinations and North America to Europe. Again because of the isolation, flights linking New Zealand with countries other than Australia and the Pacific Islands tend to be long-haul and passengers arriving are advised to allow themselves time to rest during the first day or two of their stay.

By Sea

Most of the shipping lines which operate cruises in the South Pacific originate their services from Sydney and fly passengers to and from New Zealand, but P&O Line, Sitmar, Royal Viking, and an increasing number of cruise lines make calls on New Zealand during the year, mostly during the November through April period. Some cargo vessels also take small groups of passengers.

Practical Tips

Emergencies

In an emergency dial 111 for ambulance, police or fire. Call boxes mostly operate with telephone cards, however there are some coin and credit card public telephones. Telephone cards can be bought at most convenience stores and petrol stations.

Business Hours

Shops are generally open for business from 8.30am to 5.30pm Monday through Friday and from 9am through early afternoon on Saturday. Main cities and the larger tourist areas have many shops which are open seven days a week. Trading banks are open during normal working hours Monday to Friday.

Tipping

Tipping is not expected or obligatory in New Zealand though it is acceptable to tip for courteous and efficient service in restaurants and hotels.

Media

There is a high level of literacy in New Zealand with English being the main language and Maori the indigenous language. Most communities have a library, and sales of books, magazines and newspapers on a per capita basis are unparalleled anywhere in the world. The *New Zealand Herald*, the Auckland morning daily, sells better than one copy for every four people in Greater Auckland, a figure that is regarded as well past saturation for any other city in the world. Almost every large town has its newspaper and community newspapers abound in towns, provincial cities and in the suburbs of major cities.

The high level of book sales has seen all the major British publishing houses set up distribution organisations in New Zealand. The industry is supported by fine book shops and excellent libraries.

There are two television channels which are administered by a nominally independent government corporation in addition to a third, privately owned channel. There is also a private subscription television corporation offering three further channels, including CNN.

Getting Around

Domestic Travel

By Air

Air New Zealand and Ansett New Zealand are the two main domestic carriers. Air New Zealand uses Boeing 737 jets and F27 turbo-prop aircraft while Ansett New Zealand uses BAE 146 jets. There are also a number of smaller regional carriers. Helicopters are readily available in main cities and in tourist resort areas.

By Sea

Several passenger and vehicular ferries link the North and South Islands, between and Wellington. There are frequent daily crossings in both directions though it is important to booking vehicle space in advance during summer holiday periods. The journey time varies from 90 minutes (catamaran) to 3 hours.

By Rail

Comfortable passenger train services are available on the main trunk lines between Auckland and Wellington on the North Island and between Christchurch and Invercargill on the South Island. There are a number of other daily trains following tourist routes which have limited service.

Meals and refreshments are available on inter-city services and trains on tourist routes. A commentary is given on some services.

Commuter and/or train services are available in each of the four main centres, but in Wellington, the train service to northern suburbs and satellite cities reaches reasonable levels of regularity and frequency.

By Road

There is an excellent scheduled coach network throughout the country using modern and comfortable coaches, some with toilets. Again it is wise to reserve seats in advance, especially during the summer months.

All towns and cities have 24-hour taxicab services. Chauffeur-driven cars are also readily available as are hire cars offering a wide range of vehicle types. Driving is on the left side of the road. Main road surfaces are good and conditions are usually comfortable, the main problem being wet road surfaces after heavy showers. Roads are well signposted by the Automobile Association.

Hirers of cars must be 21 years old, must hold a current New Zealand or International driver's licence, or one issued in any of the 1949 convention countries (128 members) or the German Federal Republic or Switzerland. Third party insurance is compulsory.

There are excellent camping grounds in all towns and cities throughout the country and caravans and trailers may be hired. Many camping grounds have excellent cabins as well as camp sites (see under accommodation).

Compressed natural gas and liquid petroleum gas are cheaper than standard petrol and many vehicles are now fitted for these alternative fuels.

A comprehensive range of services for motorists is available from the Automobile Association, and reciprocal membership arrangements may be available for those holding membership of foreign motoring organisations.

Where To Stay

Hotels & Motels

Hotels of an international standard are available in most cities, in many provincial cities, and in all resort areas frequented by international tourists. In smaller cities and towns, more modest accommodation in hotels is often relaxed and enjoyable for visitors on holiday.

Small motels have proliferated throughout the country and are almost always clean and comfortable with facilities ideal for family holidays.

There is currently no national system of grading hotels and motels and standards do vary, but the location of the accommodation and the tariff will give a reliable indication. Travel agents are good sources of information and will be able to give details of concessions generally available for children. (A guide is: children under two years of age, free; two to four, quarter of tariff; five to nine, half tariff; ten years and over, full tariff).

Some popular hotels and motels in the four main cities and in some of the many popular resort areas are listed below. Goods and Services Tax (GST) of 12 percent is added to most bikes. All prices in this list (brought to the nearest dollar) include GST unless otherwise indicated.

Auckland

(TELEPHONE CODE: 09)
Aberdeen Motel, 76 Great South Road, Remuera; tel: 524 5381; fax: 523 3581. 18 rooms (max occ. 4–5). Double from $67.50, each additional person $13.50.
Auckland Airport Travelodge, Corner Ascot & Kirkbride Roads; tel: 275 1059; fax: 275 7884. 243 rooms (max occ. 3). Single/twin $202.50. 5 km to airport and 17 km to city. Sauna, gymnasium, outdoor swimming pool, children's play area.
Auckland Gateway Airport Lodge, 206 Kirkbride Road, Mangere; tel: 275 4079; fax: 275 3232. 51 rooms (max occ. 4). Doubles $79, each additional person $11.25, no charge for children under 2 years. 3 km to airport. Near town centre and winery. Conference facilities.
Barrycourt Motor Inn and Convention Centre, 10–20 Gladstone Road, Parnell; tel: 303 3789; fax: 377 3309. 102 rooms (max occ. 5). Standard $99, each additional person $18. 2 km to city, 1 km to beach. Licenced restaurant, bar and spa.
Best Western International Motel, 6 Sarsfield Street, Herne Bay; tel: 535 5213; fax: 537 4437. 10 rooms (max occ. 4). Double/chalets $81, water-

A Wise Man Never Thinks How Far He's Come. He Thinks How Far He Can Still Travel.

FINE CHAMPAGNE COGNAC
REMY MARTIN
XO
SPECIAL

REMY XO BECAUSE LIFE IS WHAT YOU MAKE IT

Swatch. The others just watch.

seahorse/fall winter 94-95

shockproof
splashproof
priceproof
boreproof
swiss made

swatch ✚
SCUBA 200

front units $87.75, each additional person $9. Handy to Marina. Close to bowling, golf and tennis clubs and restaurants.

Domain Lodge, 155 Park Road, Grafton; tel: 303 2509; fax: 303 1376. 28 rooms (max occ. 5). Twin/Double $95.65, each additional person $11. 20 m to shopping centre. Adjacent to park and children's playground.

Garden Inn, 10 Tidal Road, Mangere; tel: 275 0194. 62 rooms (max occ. 5). Single/Double $80. Each additional person $15. Near airport. Close to Budget and Thrifty car rentals.

Grafton Oaks Hotel, 121 Grafton Road, Grafton; tel: 309 0167; fax: 377 5962. 44 rooms (max occ. 4). $135, each additional person $12. 1 km to city centre, 3 km to beach.

Hyatt Auckland Hotel, corner Waterloo Quadrant and Princes Street; tel: 366 1234; fax: 303 2932. 275 rooms (max occ. 3). Single/Twin/Double $185, each additional person $40. 200 m to city. 24 hour room service, convention facilities, business centre, restaurants and ballroom.

Mon Desir Hotel, 144 Hurstmere Road, Takapuna; tel: 489 5139; fax: 489 8809. 37 rooms (max occ. 4). Single $100, twin $115. On Takapuna Beach. Restaurant, pool and sauna.

Mount Albert Lodge, 201 Carrington Road, Mount Albert; tel: 846 2199; fax: 846 2127. 25 rooms (max occ. 5). Twin $70, each additional person $10. 100 m to shops and restaurants. Handy to golf and racecourse.

Oakwood Manor, 610–612 Massey Road, Mangere; tel: 275 0539; fax: 275 0534. 54 rooms (max occ. 6). Studio suites with kitchen $105, economy suites $95. Group discounts available. Courtesy transport to and from airport 24 hours a day.

Pan Pacific Auckland Hotel, corner Vincent Street and Mayoral Drive; tel: 366 3000; fax: 366 0121. 286 rooms (max occ. 3). Twin deluxe $360, free for children under 17 sharing with their parents. 1 km to waterfront. 24 hour room service, hotel shops, currency exchange, doctor.

Park Towers Hotel, 3 Scotia Place; tel: 309 2800; fax: 302 1964. 103 rooms (max occ. 3). Single/Double from $90, free for children under 12 sharing with their parents. Central city location. Restaurant, house bar.

Poenamo Motor Inn, corner Northcote & Sunnybrae Roads, Northcote; tel: 480 6109; fax: 418 0365. 24 rooms (max occ. 3). Twin/Double $77, each additional person $13.50. Adjacent to golf course, 4 km to beach.

Quality Hotel Airport, corner Kirkbride and Ascot Roads, Mangere; tel: 275 1059; fax: 275 3322. 160 rooms (max occ. 3). Single/Double $180, suites available. 3 km to airport, 17 km to city. Gymnasium, heated swimming pool, restaurant, bar, 24 hour room service, parking, car rental. Close to golf course.

Quality Hotel Anzac Avenue, 150 Anzac Avenue; tel 379 8509. 110 rooms (max occ. 3). Single/Double $184. Central location, good harbour views. Restaurant, bar and sauna.

Quality Hotel Logan Park, 187 Campbell Road, Greenlane; tel: 634 1269; fax: 636 8115. 222 rooms (max occ. 3). Single/Double $141.75, each additional person $16.87. Situated in parklike setting. Conference facilities, spas and swimming pools.

Quality Hotel Rosepark, 100 Gladstone Road, Parnell, tel: 377 3619. 117 rooms (max occ. 5). Single/Double $171. Distance to city: 1.5 km. Spas and video available.

Ranfurly Evergreen Motor Inn, 285 Manukua Road, Epsom; tel: 638 9059; fax: 630 8374. 12 rooms (max occ. 5). Single/Double $78.75, each additional person $12. 500 m to restaurants, 1 km to racecourse and showgrounds. On airport bus route.

Regent of Auckland, Albert Street; tel: 309 8888; fax: 379 6445. 332 rooms (max occ. 3). Twin $355. Centrally located luxury hotel. Large ballroom. Japanese restaurant, pastry shop. Fitness centre and swimming pool.

Royal Park Lodge, 161 Great South Road, Green Lane; tel: 524 7988; fax: 524 9262. 20 rooms (max occ. 2). Single/Double $101. 3 minutes to racecourse, park, and showgrounds.

Sheraton Hotel, 83 Symonds Street; tel: 379 5132; fax: 377 9367. 407 rooms (max occ. 3). Single/Double $229, each additional person $50. Downtown. Excellent city views. Indoor swimming pool, spa, restaurants and bars.

Whitaker Lodge Motel, 21 Whitaker Place; tel 377 3623; fax: 377 3621. 21 rooms (max occ. 5). Single $84, Double $94, each additional person

$17. Located on fringe of business district. Quiet and peaceful.

White Heron Hotel, St Stephens Avenue, Parnell; tel: 379 6860; fax: 309 1540. 72 rooms (max occ. 4). Single/Double $165, each additional person $16.88. Close to major attractions.

Christchurch

(TELEPHONE CODE: 03)

Admiral Motel, 168 Bealey Avenue; tel: 379 3554; fax: 379 3272. 9 units (max occ. 6). Single $76.50, Double $85.50 each additional person $13.50. Near Cathedral Square and town hall.

Airport Gateway Motor Lodge, 45 Roydvale Avenue, Burnside; tel: 358 7093; fax: 358 3654. 30 motel suites (max occ. 6). Single/Double $85, each additional person $16.80. 2 km to airport.

Airport Lodge Motel, 105 Roydvale Road, Burnside; tel: 358 5119; fax: 358 7164. 24 rooms (max occ. 7). Single/Double $78, each additional person $15.75. 8 km to city centre, 2.5 km to airport.

Ashleigh Court Motel, 47 Matai Street West, Lower Riccarton; tel: 348 1888; fax: 348 2973. 10 rooms (max occ. 6). Single/Double $80, each additional person $13.50.

Autolodge Motor Inn, 72 Papanui Road, St Albins; tel: 355 6109; fax: 355 3543. 74 rooms (max occ. 3). Single/Double $97, each additional person $11.

Belmont Motel, 170 Bealey Avenue; tel: 379 4037; fax: 366 9194. 18 rooms (max occ. 6). Single/Double $98, each additional person $15.

Carlton Hotel, corner Papanui Road and Bealey Avenue; tel: 355 6159. 10 rooms (max occ. 2). Single $35, Double $50. 1.5 km to city centre. Close to town hall.

Colonial Inn, 43 Papanui Road, Merivale; tel: 355 9139; fax: 355 5457. 27 rooms (max occ. 6). Single/Double $74, each additional person $15.

Cotswold Motor Inn, 88 Papanui Road; tel: 355 3535; fax: 355 6695. 71 rooms (max occ. 6). Single/Double $90, each additional person $15. 2 km to city centre. Authentic period furnishings and decor.

Diplomat Motel, 127 Papanui Road, Merivale; tel: 355 6009; fax: 355

6007. 16 rooms (max occ. 6). Single/Double $92.20, each additional person $11.

Gothic Heights Motel, 430 Hagley Avenue; tel: 366 0838; fax: 366 0188. 15 rooms (max occ. 5). Single/Double $91, each additional person $14.

Latimer Lodge, 30 Latimer Square; tel: 379 6760; fax: 366 0133. 53 rooms (max occ. 4). Single/Double $99, each additional person $11.25. 500 m to city centre.

Noah's Hotel, Corner Worcester Street and Oxford Terrace; tel: 379 4700; fax: 379 5357. 208 rooms (max occ. 3). Single/Double $264.

Pacific Park Christchurch, 263 Bealey Avenue; tel: 379 8660; fax: 366 9973. 66 rooms (max occ. 2). Single/Double $100.15. Private sheltered location.

Parkroyal Christchurch, corner Kilmore and Durham Streets; tel: 365 7799; fax: 365 0082. 297 rooms (max occ. 4). Single/Double $337.50. Connected to town hall and convention centre.

Quality Hotel Durham Street, Corner Kilmore and Durham Streets; tel: 365 4699; fax: 366 6302. 160 rooms (max occ. 3). Single/Double $168. Close to town hall, and convention centre.

Quality Hotel Central, 766 Colombo Street; tel: 379 5880. 90 rooms (max occ. 3). Single/Double $156.25. Parking. Close to city centre.

Russley Hotel, Roydvale Avenue, Burnside; tel: 358 8289; fax: 358 3953. 68 rooms (max occ. 3). Single $79, Double $90. 2 km to airport, 8 km to city centre.

Southern Comfort Motel, 53 Bealey Avenue; tel: 366 0383; fax: 366 0382. 10 rooms (max occ. 4). Single/Double $82, each additional person $12. Restaurant and parks in immediate vicinity.

The George, 50 Park Terrace; tel: 379 4560; fax: 366 6747. 53 rooms (max occ. 4). Single/Double $164.55.

The Towers, Corner Deans Avenue and Kilmarnock Street; tel: 348 0613. 34 rooms (max occ. 4). Single/Double $80, each additional person $15. 3 km to city centre.

Windsor Court Motel, 136 New Brighton Road, Shirley; tel: 385 8032; fax: 385 7544. 7 rooms (max occ. 8). Single/Double $70.20, each

additional person $12.50. Quiet, well off the road. 10 minute drive to 7 golf courses.

Dunedin

(TELEPHONE CODE: 03)

Abbey Motor Lodge, 900 Cumberland Street and 680 Castle Street; tel: 477 5380; fax: 477 8715. 55 units (max occ. 5). Single/Double $123, each additional person $21.50. Indoor heated pool, sauna and spa.

Adrian Motel, 101 Queens Drive, St Kilda; tel: 455 2009; fax: 455 6222. 17 rooms (max occ. 7). Single/Double $75, each additional person $14. 3 km to city centre. Near beach.

Cargill's Motor Inn, 678 George Street; tel: 477 7983; fax: 477 8098. 51 rooms (max occ. 3). Single $92.50, Double $112.50. 1.5 km to city centre.

Leisure Lodge Motor Inn, Duke Street, Dunedin North; tel: 477 5360; fax: 477 5460. 81 rooms (max occ. 4). Single/Double $110, each additional person $15. 200 m to shopping centre. Adjacent to the Botanical Gardens.

Pacific Park, 22 Wallace Street, Roslyn; tel: 477 3374; fax: 4771434. 59 rooms (max occ. 5). Single/Double $100. 400 m from Moana Pool.

Quality Hotel Dunedin, Upper Mornay Place; tel: 477 6784; fax: 474 0115. 54 rooms (max occ. 4). Single/Double $135. 300 m to city centre.

Shoreline Hotel, 47 Timaru Street; tel: 455 5196; fax: 455 5193. 36 rooms (max occ. 3). Single/Double $90. Close to harbour.

Southern Cross Hotel, 118 High Street; tel: 477 0752; fax: 477 5776. 110 rooms (max occ. 3). Single/Double $159, each additional person $20. Centrally located. 1 km from Moana Pool.

Fox Glacier

(TELEPHONE CODE: 03)

A1 Motel, Fox Glacier; tel: 751 0804. 10 rooms (max occ. 5). Single/Double $75, each additional person $12. 1.6 km from Post Office and restaurant. 20 km from beach.

Fox Glacier Hotel, Fox Glacier; tel: 751 0839; fax: 751 0868. 52 rooms (max occ. 4). Single/Double $95, each additional person $15. Restaurant.

Golden Glacier Motor Inn, Fox Glacier; tel: 751 0847; fax: 751 0822. 51 rooms (max occ. 4). Single/Double $90, each additional person $15. Restaurant.

Franz Josef Glacier

(TELEPHONE CODE: 03)

Franz Josef Hotel, Main Road; tel: 752 0719; fax: 752 0709. 47 rooms. Single/Double $157.50, each additional person $20.25.

Glacier Gateway Motor Lodge, Main Road; tel: 752 0776; fax: 752 0732. 25 rooms (max occ. 5). Single/Double $85, each additional person $13. 500 m to restaurants and shops, glacier access road.

Glacier View Motel, Franz Josef Glacier; tel: 752 0705; fax: 752 0761. 13 units (max occ. 6). Single/Double $75, each additional person $12. 2.5 km to airport, 1.5 km to restaurant. Spectacular mountain and glacier views.

Rata Grove Motel, 6 Cron Street; tel: 752 0741. 10 units (max occ. 6). Single/Double $79, each additional person $13.50. 50 m to the local shops, restaurant and Post Office, 6 km from Franz Josef Glacier.

Westland Motor Inn, Franz Josef; tel: 752 0728; fax: 752 0709. 100 rooms (max occ. 3). Single/Double $112.50, each additional person $20.25. One minute to Post Office, shops, restaurant and bar. 6 km to Glacier.

Hanmer Springs

(TELEPHONE CODE: 03)

Alpine Spa Lodge, corner Amuri Drive and Harrogate Streets; tel: 315 7311. 35 rooms (max occ. 8). Single/Double $66, each additional person $15. 50 m to shops and pool complex.

Hanmer Resort Motel, 7 Cheltenham Street; tel: 315 7362. 15 rooms (max occ. 6). Single/Double $75, each additional person $13. Adjacent to hot mineral pools.

The Chalets, Jacks Pass Road; tel: 315 7097. 9 rooms (max occ. 8). Single/Double $70, each additional person $12. 1 km to restaurant and shopping centre.

Greenacres Motel, Conical Hill Road; tel: 315 7125. 13 units (max occ. 6). Single/Double $75, each additional person $12. 500 m from Hanmer

THOMAS COOK
MASTERCARD
TRAVELLERS CHEQUES...

...HOLIDAY ESSENTIALS

Travel money from the travel experts

THOMAS COOK MASTERCARD TRAVELLERS CHEQUES ARE
WIDELY AVAILABLE THROUGHOUT THE WORLD.

Pack your trunks for a holiday that's smooth as silk.

Few countries can provide such a choice of exotic holiday experiences as Thailand.

Elephants still roam wild in Thai forests and have played an important cultural and working role since the early days of the Kingdom.

Today, you can enjoy the unforgettable thrill of a trek atop your own private elephant, on trails that lead through lush northern forests.

If riding a two-ton elephant isn't the holiday you had in mind, how about sailing aboard a traditional seventeen metre junk in the Andaman Sea?

Or relaxing in a luxury hotel and swimming in crystal blue waters at one of Thailand's famous beach resorts?

ROYAL ORCHID

Holidays

Then there's the shopping - but that's another story.

The first thing you need is our Royal Orchid Holidays brochure. In it you'll find every holiday imaginable in this exotic and mystical land.

Pick up a free copy from your travel agent or nearest Thai office and discover the treasures of the Kingdom.

And, of course, the best way to fly to Thailand is on Thai International, where you'll enjoy our world renowned Royal Orchid Service while you fly there smooth as silk.

INSIGHT GUIDES

COLORSET NUMBERS

North America
160 Alaska
173 American Southwest
184I Atlanta
227 Boston
275 California
180 California, Northern
161 California, Southern
237 Canada
184C Chicago
184 Crossing America
243 Florida
240 Hawaii
275A Los Angeles
243A Miami
237B Montreal
184G National Parks of America: East
184H National Parks of America: West
269 Native America
100 New England
184E New Orleans
184F New York City
133 New York State
147 Pacific Northwest
184B Philadelphia
172 Rockies
275B San Francisco
184D Seattle
Southern States of America
186 Texas
237A Vancouver
184C Washington DC

Latin America and The Caribbean
150 Amazon Wildlife
260 Argentina
188 Bahamas
292 Barbados
251 Belize
217 Bermuda
127 Brazil
260A Buenos Aires
162 Caribbean
151 Chile
281 Costa Rica
282 Cuba
118 Ecuador
213 Jamaica
285 Mexico
285A Mexico City
249 Peru
156 Puerto Rico
127A Rio de Janeiro
116 South America
139 Trinidad & Tobago
198 Venezuela

Europe
155 Alsace
158A Amsterdam
167A Athens
263 Austria
107 Baltic States

219B Barcelona
1187 Bay of Naples
109 Belgium
135A Berlin
178 Brittany
109A Brussels
144A Budapest
213 Burgundy
122 Catalonia
141 Channel Islands
135E Cologne
119 Continental Europe
189 Corsica
291 Côte d'Azur
165 Crete
226 Cyprus
114 Czech/Slovak Reps
238 Denmark
135B Dresden
142B Dublin
135F Düsseldorf
149 Eastern Europe
148A Edinburgh
123 Finland
209B Florence
154 France
135C Frankfurt
135 Germany
148B Glasgow
279 Gran Canaria
124 Great Britain
167 Greece
166 Greek Islands
135G Hamburg
144 Hungary
256 Iceland
142 Ireland
209 Italy
202A Lisbon
258 Loire Valley
124A London
201 Madeira
219A Madrid
157 Mallorca & Ibiza
117 Malta
101A Moscow
135D Munich
158 Netherlands
111 Normandy
120 Norway
124B Oxford
154A Paris
115 Poland
202 Portugal
114A Prague
153 Provence
177 Rhine
209A Rome
101 Russia
130 Sardinia
148 Scotland
261 Sicily
264 South Tyrol
219 Spain
220 Spain, Southern
101B St. Petersburg
170 Sweden
232 Switzerland

112 Tenerife
210 Tuscany
174 Umbria
209C Venice
263A Vienna
267 Wales
183 Waterways of Europe

Middle East and Africa
268A Cairo
204 East African Wildlife
268 Egypt
208 Gambia & Senegal
252 Israel
236A Istanbul
252A Jerusalem-Tel Aviv
214 Jordan
270 Kenya
235 Morocco
259 Namibia
265 Nile, The
257 South Africa
113 Tunisia
236 Turkey
171 Turkish Coast
215 Yemen

Asia/Pacific
287 Asia, East
207 Asia, South
262 Asia, South East
194 Asian Wildlife, Southeast
272 Australia
206 Bali Baru
246A Bangkok
234A Beijing
247B Calcutta
234 China
247A Delhi, Jaipur, Agra
169 Great Barrier Reef
196 Hong Kong
247 India
212 India, South
128 Indian Wildlife
143 Indonesia
278 Japan
266 Java
203A Kathmandu
300 Korea
145 Malaysia
218 Marine Life in the South China Sea
272B Melbourne
211 Myanmar
203 Nepal
293 New Zealand
205 Pakistan
222 Philippines
250 Rajasthan
159 Singapore
105 Sri Lanka
272 Sydney
175 Taiwan
246 Thailand
278A Tokyo
255 Vietnam
193 Western Himalaya

Township, 800 m from thermal pools.
Larchwood Motels, 12 Bath Street; tel: 315 7281. 16 rooms (max occ. 6). Single/Double $80, each additional person $20. Handy to squash courts, hot pools and forest walks.

Marlborough Sounds

(TELEPHONE CODE: 03)
Gem Resort, Bay of Many Caves; tel: 579 9771. 11 rooms (max occ. 10). Single/Double $65, each additional person $15. In the heart of Marlborough Sounds. Lovely holiday retreat.
Punga Cove Tourist Resort, Endeavour Inlet; tel: 579 8561. 9 rooms (max occ. 8). Single/Double $70, each additional person $40. Own private beach. Good swimming and excellent fishing.
Raetihi Lodge, Kenepuru Sound; tel: 573 4300. 18 rooms (max occ. 2). Single $75, Double $130 includes all meals. Games room and outdoor activities.
The Portage Hotel, Kenepuru Sound; tel: 573 4309. 42 rooms (max occ. 4). Single/Double $89, each additional person $25.

Methven

(TELEPHONE CODE: 03)
Canterbury Hotel, tel: 302 8045. 11 rooms. Single $30.
Mount Hutt Motel, State Highway 77; tel: 302 8382; fax: 302 8616. 10 units (max occ. 6). Single/Double $92.20, each additional person $18.

Mount Cook

(TELEPHONE CODE: 03)
Mount Cook Chalets, Mount Cook; tel: 435 1809. 18 rooms (max occ. 6). Single/Double/Quad $106.88.
Mount Cook Travelodge, Mount Cook; tel: 435 1809. 57 rooms (max occ. 4). Single/Double $185.65, each additional person $20. 1 km to the Hermitage Hotel.
The Hermitage Hotel, Mount Cook; tel: 435 1809; fax: 435 1879. 104 rooms (max occ. 3). Single/Double $220, each additional person $22.50. 50 km from Twizel. Excellent views.

Paihia

(TELEPHONE CODE: 09)
Aarangi-Tui Motel, Williams Road; tel: 402 7496. 7 units (max occ. 6). Single/Double $56, each additional person $12.50. Centrally situated. 500 m to Post Office, beach, shopping centre and restaurant.
Abel Tasman Lodge, Waterfront, Marsden Road; tel: 402 7521; fax: 402 7576. 25 units (max occ. 5). Single/Double $70. On beach front. 50 m to restaurant, 100 m from Post Office and shopping centre.
Aloha Motel, Seaview; tel: 402 7540. 15 units (max occ. 9). Single/Double $79, each additional person $13.50. 500 m to shopping centre.
Autolodge, Marsden Road; tel: 402 7416; fax: 402 8348. 76 rooms (max occ. 3). Single/Double $110, each additional person $8. 25 km to airport, 20 m to beach. Conference facilities 100 people.
Beachcomber Resort, 1 Seaview Road; tel: 402 7434; fax: 402 8202. 46 rooms (max occ. 5). Single/Double $88. Near Post Office, town centre and restaurants. Own private beach with safe swimming. Sea view from every room.
Casabella Motel, McMurray Road; tel: 402 7387; fax: 402 7166. 21 rooms (max occ. 4). Single/Double $79, each additional person $10. 50 m to shopping centre, 80 m to beach. Adjacent to restaurant.
Cook's Lookout Motel, Causeway Road (off York Road), Haruru Falls; tel: 402 7409. 12 rooms (max occ. 6). Single/Double $50, each additional person $10. 3 km to town centre and shopping centre. Garden surroundings.
Marlin Court Hotel, corner Seaview and McMurray Roads; tel: 402 7693; fax: 402 7910. 12 rooms (max occ. 6). Double $85, each additional person $12. 1 km to ferries and historical sites. Close to city centre.
Quality Resort Waitangi, Waitangi; tel: 402 7411; fax: 402 8500. 145 rooms (max occ. 3). Single/Double $130, each additional person $16.50. On historic reserve. Restaurant, bar, swimming pool and conference rooms.

Queenstown

(TELEPHONE CODE: 03)
Alpine Sun Motel, 14 Hallenstein Street; tel: 442 8482; fax: 442 6432. 10 units (max occ. 5). Single/Double $65, each additional person $12. Located in central business district.
Ambassador Motel, 2 Man Street; tel: 442 8593; fax: 442 8797. 16 units (max occ. 6). Single/Double $93, each additional person $16. 75 m to town centre, 10 km to airport.
Bellevue Court, 39 Shotover Street; tel: 442 7562; fax: 442 7560. 5 rooms (max occ. 5). Single/Double $85, each additional person $12. Each unit has private patio/deck. Ski hire on premises.
Blue Peaks Lodge, Corner Stanley and Sydney Streets; tel 442 9224; fax: 442 6847. 60 units (max occ. 6). Single/Double $85, each additional person $14. 6 km to airport.
Earnslaw Motor Lodge, 53 Frankton Road; tel: 442 8728; fax: 442 7376. 25 rooms (max occ. 5). Single/Double $90, each additional person $12. In lakeside location on main road into town.
Holiday Inn, Sainsbury Road, Fernhill; tel: 0800 655 557; fax: 442 7354. 150 rooms (max occ. 4). Single/Double $180, each additional person $31.50. 1.5 km to town. Restaurant and bar.
Lake Hayes Motel, Lake Hayes Road; tel 442 1705. 7 units (max occ. 6). Single/Double $70, each additional person $12. Overlooking Lake Hayes, 8 km to Queenstown.
Nugget Point Resort, Arthurs Point; tel 442 7273; fax: 442 7308. 35 rooms (max occ. 6). Single/Double $245. 15 km to airport, 7 km to town.
Quality Hotel Terraces Queenstown, 48 Frankton Road; tel: 442 7950; fax: 442 8066. 85 rooms (max occ. 5). Single/Double $184. Restaurant and Bar.
Queenstown Parkroyal, Beach Street; tel: 442 7800; fax: 442 8895. 139 rooms (max occ. 4). Single/Double $180. Situated on lake front. Restaurant and bar.
The Lodges, 8 Lake Esplanade; tel: 442 7552; fax: 442 6493. 15 rooms (max occ. 7). Single/Double $140, each additional person $12. 2 blocks to town centre. Situated on lake front.

Turner Heights Townhouses, top of Turner Street; tel: 442 8383; fax: 442 9494. 13 rooms (max occ. 6). Single/Double $101.25 each additional person $16.87.

Rotorua

(TELEPHONE CODE: 07)

Acapulco Motel, corner Malfroy Road and Eason Street; tel: 347 0452; fax: 347 9568. 15 rooms (max occ. 5). Single/Double $70, each additional person $13. Quiet location near city centre. 500 m from restaurant and shops.

Devonwood Manor, 312 Fenton Street; tel: 348 1999; fax: 346 2855. 35 rooms (max occ. 6). Single/Double $80, each additional person $12. 1 km to city centre. Built in English Manor style.

Gibson Court Motel, Gibson Street; tel: 346 2822; fax: 348 9481. 10 rooms (max occ. 4). Single/Double $88, each additional person $11. 1 km to thermal reserve. A short drive to local racecourse.

The Grand Hotel, Corner Hinemoa and Fenton Streets; tel: 348 2089; fax: 346 3219. 40 rooms (max occ. 2). Single/Double $70, each additional person $12. Located in city. Restaurant and bars.

Quality Resort Rotorua, Eruera Street; tel: 347 1234; fax: 348 1234. 227 rooms (max occ. 2). Single/Double $180. Adjacent to Polynesian Pools. Full fitness centre. 100 m to city centre, 500 m from lake.

Lakewood Manor, corner Lake and Bennetts Roads; tel: 346 2110; fax: 346 3985. 37 rooms (max occ. 3). Single/Double $99, each additional person $12. 10 minutes to city centre, 5 minutes to Aquatic swimming centre.

Lake Plaza Rotorua Hotel, Lake end of Eruera Street; tel: 348 1174; fax: 346 0238. 200 rooms (max occ. 4). Single/Double $135, each additional person $16.90. Opposite Polynesian Pools. 500 m to city centre.

Manary Motor Lodge, 77 Robinson Avenue; tel: 345 6792; fax: 345 9339. 27 rooms (max occ. 4). Single/Double $70, each additional person $14. Situated on lake front. Private hot pools.

Maple Grove Motel, 4 Meade Street; tel: 348 1139. 10 rooms (max occ. 8). Single/Double $60, each additional person $12. 3 km to city centre, 500 m to thermal reserve.

Motel Monterey, 50 Whakaue Street; tel: 348 1044; fax: 346 2264. 15 rooms (max occ. 6). Single/Double $65, each additional person $10. 200 m to city centre. Quiet but handy to shops, restaurant and lakefront.

Muriaroha Lodge, 411 Old Taupo Road; tel: 346 1220; fax: 346 1338. 6 rooms (max occ. 4). Single/Double $280. Luxury accommodation. 3 km to city.

Okawa Bay Resort, Mourea, Lake Rotoiti; tel: 362 4599; fax: 362 4594. 42 rooms (max occ. 3). Single/Double $150, each additional person $15. On the shores of Lake Rotoiti, trout fishing, water skiing. Conference facilities.

Princes Gate, 1 Arawa Street; tel: 348 1179; fax: 348 6215. 27 rooms (max occ. 4). Single/Double $120, each additional person $10. Near city centre, restaurants, shops.

Puhi Nui Motor Lodge, 16 Sala Street; tel: 348 4182; fax: 347 6595. 40 units (max occ. 5). Single/Double $95. Heated outdoor pool and spa. 2 km from city centre.

Quality Hotel Rotorua, Fenton Street; tel: 348 0199; fax: 346 1973. 136 rooms (max occ. 3). Single/Double $134. Adjacent to racecourse, sportsground and golf courses.

Regent Motels, 39 Pukaki Street; tel: 348 4079. 15 rooms (max occ. 7). Single/Double $70, each additional person $12. Centrally located, close to restaurants.

Sheraton Rotorua, Fenton Street; tel: 348 7139; fax: 348 8378. 130 rooms (max occ. 4). Single/Double $230. Restaurant and bars.

Solitaire Lodge, Road 5, Lake Tarawera; tel 362 8208; fax: 362 8445. 10 rooms (max occ. 4). Single/Double $450/$620 including all meals. Stunning lake edge location. Luxury accommodation.

THC Rotorua, Whakarewarewa; tel: 348 1189; fax: 347 1620. 124 rooms (max occ. 3). Single/Double $157.50, each additional person $22.50. Hangi and Maori concert every night. Located in heart of thermal area.

Tiki Lodge, 69 Lake Road; tel 348 3913. 6 units (max occ. 7). Single/Double $55, each additional person $10. 2 km to Rainbow Springs, herb gardens. Adjacent to Kuirau Park.

Utuhina Hot Springs Lodge, Lake Road; tel: 348 5785. 10 units (max occ. 13). Single/Double $70, each additional person $9.

Willow Lodge Motel, 156 Fairy Springs Road; tel: 348 7335. 8 rooms (max occ. 7). Single/Double $75, each additional person $12. Adjacent to Rainbow/Fairy Springs. 4 km to city centre.

Wylie Court Motor Lodge, 345 Fenton Street; tel: 347 7879; fax: 346 1494. 28 rooms (max occ. 6). Single/Double $100, each additional person $14.50.

Russell

(TELEPHONE CODE: 09)

Duke of Marlborough Hotel, The Strand; tel: 403 7829; fax: 403 7828. 29 rooms (max occ. 3). Single/Double $70, each additional person $13. Situated on waterfront adjacent to ferry terminal.

Dukes Lodge, Russell; tel: 403 7899; fax: 403 7289. 12 rooms (max occ. 6). Single/Double $100, each additional person $11. Situated on waterfront.

Flagstaff Homestead, Queen Street; tel: 403 7862. 4 rooms (max occ. 6). Single/Double $70, each additional person $10. 200 m to Post Office, shopping centre, restaurant, 100 m to waterfront.

Hananui Lodge Motel; tel: 403 7875. 14 rooms (max occ. 6). Single/Double $70, each additional person $10. Opposite beachfront. Handy to museum and historic buildings.

Mako Hotel, Wellington Street; tel: 403 7770. 7 rooms (max occ. 5). Single/Double $100, each additional person $15. 200 m to waterfront.

Motel Russell, Matauwhi Road; tel: 403 7854. 13 rooms (max occ. 7). Single/Double $60, each additional person $13.50.

Te Maiki Villas, Flagstaff Road; tel: 403 7046; fax: 403 7106. 9 villas (max occ. 6). Single/Double $150, each additional person $22.50. Quality accommodation close to the beach. All villas self contained.

Te Anau

(TELEPHONE CODE: 03)

Aden Motel, 59 Quintin Drive; Tel: 249 7748; fax: 249 7434. 12 units (max occ. 7). Single/Double $75, each additional person $13. Close to lake and shops.

Explorer Motel, 6 Cleddau Street; tel: 249 7156; fax: 249 7149. 11 rooms (max occ. 6). Single/Double $90, each additional person $15. 500 m to town centre.

Laskeside Motel, Lake Point Drive; tel: 249 7435; fax: 249 7529. 13 units (max occ. 8). Single/Double $80, each additional person $15. Centrally located. 100 m to restaurant.

Luxmore Resort Hotel, Main Street; tel: 249 7335; fax: 249 7272. 105 rooms (max occ. 4). Single/Double $120, each additional person $16. Within 300 m from all services and attractions. 100 m from lakefront.

Matai Lodge, 42 Mokonui Street; tel: 249 7349. 7 rooms (max occ. 3). Single/Double $70.

Quality Hotel Te Anau, Lakefront; tel: 249 7421; fax: 249 8037. 105 rooms (max occ. 3). Single/Double $135. Lakefront garden setting. Restaurant and bar.

Te Anau Downs Motor Inn, Milford Highway; tel: 249 7811; fax: 249 7753. 68 rooms (max occ.6). Single/Double $90, each additional person $17. Situated on the highway to Milford Sound. Quiet. Licensed restaurant.

Te Anau Travelodge, Te Anau Terrace; tel: 249 7411; fax: 249 7947. 112 rooms (max occ. 3). Single/Double $112.50. Restaurant and bar.

Wairakei

(TELEPHONE CODE: 07)
Wairakei Resort, Wairakei; tel: 374 8021; fax: 374 8485. 130 rooms (max occ. 3). Single/Double $110, each additional person $16.90. Situated in thermal area, adjacent to quality golf course.

Waitomo Caves

(TELEPHONE CODE: 07)
THC Waitomo, tel: 878 8227; fax: 878 8858. 37 rooms (max occ. 3). Single/Double $130, each additional person $16.90. Close to limestone caves. 19 km from Te Kuiti.

Wellington

(TELEPHONE CODE: 04)
Academy Motor Lodge, 327 Adelaide Road; tel: 389 6166; fax: 389 1761.

16 rooms (max occ. 6). Single/Double $87, each additional person $14. 400 m to shopping centre and restaurant. 4 km to city centre.

Airport Hotel, 16 Kemp Street, Evans Bay; tel: 387 2189; fax: 387 2787. 120 rooms (max occ. 4). Single/Double $109. Near aquatic centre and shops.

Apollo Lodge Motel, 49 Majoribanks Street; tel: 385 1849; fax: 385 1849. 34 units (max occ. 5). Single/Double $100, each additional person $15. Close to zoo, 300 m to shopping centre.

Bay Plaza Hotel, 40 Oriental Parade; tel: 385 7799; fax: 385 2936. 78 rooms (max occ. 4). Single/Double $112, each additional person $11.

Halswell Lodge, 21 Kent Terrace; tel: 385 0196; fax: 385 0503. 19 units (max occ. 3). Single/Double $80. Located in the centre of entertainment and restaurant facilities.

Harbour City Motor Inn, 92 Webb Street; tel: 384 9809; fax: 384 9806. 25 units (max occ. 5). Single/Double $135, each additional person $13.50.

Jade Court, 44 Huanui Street, Porirua East; tel: 237 5255; fax: 237 5254. 10 units (max occ. 6). Single/Double $80, each additional person $12. Within walking distance to shops.

James Cook Centre, The Terrace; tel: 499 9500; fax: 499 9800. 260 rooms (max occ. 3). Single/Double $255, each additional person $22.50. Mid city, 750 m from railway station.

Parkroyal Wellington, Corner Grey and Featherton Streets; tel: 472 2722; fax: 472 4724. 230 rooms (max occ. 4). Single/Double $315. 5 star central city Hotel.

Plaza International Hotel, 148 Wakefield Street; tel: 473 3900; fax: 473 3929. 200 rooms (max occ. 4). Single/Double $260, each additional person $28. Restaurant and bar.

Portland Towers Hotel, 24 Hawkestone Street; tel: 473 2208; fax: 473 3892. 114 rooms (max occ. 3). Single/Double $125, each additional person $13.50. 2 mins to parliament centre.

Quality Hotel Plimmer Towers, Corner Boulcott Street and Gilmer Terrace; tel: 473 3750; fax: 473 6329. 94 rooms (max occ. 4). Single/Double $200. Centrally situated, near ferry terminal, cable car and railway station.

Quality Hotel Oriental Parade, 73 Roxburgh Street, Mt Victoria; tel: 385 0279; fax: 384 5324. 117 rooms (max occ. 3). Single/Double $175. Close to city centre.

St George Hotel, Corner Willis and Boulcott Streets; tel: 473 9139. 90 rooms (max occ. 6). Single/Double $80, each additional person $13.50. Centrally located.

The Tas Hotel, Corner Willis and Dixon Streets; tel: 385 2153; fax: 385 1311. 37 rooms (max occ. 4). Single/Double $120, each additional person $11. Mid city.

Willis Lodge, 318 Willis Street; tel: 384 5955; fax: 384 5697. 23 units (max occ. 3). Single/Double $105. 1 km to city centre. Close to tennis centre and museum.

Motor Camps

Beside the hotels, motor inns, and motels listed, there are numerous small motels dotted around the country. Many offer kitchen facilities and often full kitchens and dining tables to make it possible for families to have meals in the units. At some motels a cooked breakfast is available, and the units are serviced daily.

Most "Motor Camps", as they are called offer communal washing, cooking and toilet facilities. The camper is required to supply his own trailer or tent, but camps in larger towns and in the cities have cabins available.

Motor Camps are licensed under the Camping Ground Regulation (1936) and they are all graded by the Automobile Association. It is important to check on the standards with the Automobile Association and to check camp site availability and, if necessary, make bookings over the summer months because New Zealanders are inveterate campers.

Farm and Homestay

Accommodation is available now on farms throughout the country. Visitors may share the homestead with the farmer and his family, or, in many cases may have the use of a cottage on the farm. This is one of the fastest growing forms of holiday in New Zealand over the past decade and it is an excellent way for visitors to see the real New Zealand which has been dependent on pastoral farming for its economic well-being since the earliest colonial days. Farming families are usually excellent hosts at the friendliest personal level.

Many New Zealand families, both on farms and in the towns, will be pleased to host both local and overseas visitors. These hospitable places may be contacted through the following organisations:

Homestay Ltd, P.O. Box 25, 115 Auckland; tel: 09 575 5980; fax: 09 575 9977.

Hospitality Plus, Hunters Road, Taupaki, Auckland; tel: 09 810 9175; fax: 09 810 9448.

New Zealand Farm Holidays, P.O. Box 256 Silverdale, Auckland; tel: 09 425 5430; fax: 09 426 8474.

New Zealand Home Hospitality, P.O. Box 309 Nelson; tel: 03 548 2424; fax: 03 546 9519.

New Zealand Travel Hosts, 279 William Street, Kaiapoi; tel/fax: 03 327 6340.

Rural Holidays New Zealand, P.O. Box 2155 Christchurch; tel: 03 366 1919; fax: 03 379 3087.

Rural Tours "The Country Experience" NZ, 92 Victoria Street, Cambridge; tel: 07 827 8055; fax: 07 827 7154.

Sam Horrocks and Co, Rd 2 Ngaruawahia; tel: 07 825 4864; fax: 07 825 4887.

The Youth Hostel Association offers an extensive chain of hostels to members throughout New Zealand. Details of their location and membership of the organisation can be obtained from: Youth Hostel Association of New Zealand, P.O. Box 436 Christchurch, New Zealand.

Eating Out

What to Eat

The abundance, variety and quality of fresh meat and garden produce fill the New Zealand larder with riches on which an authentic cuisine has been built, New Zealand's market gardens are perhaps only equalled by those of California. The surrounding seas are the source of at least 50 commercially viable varieties of fish and shellfish.

The proliferation of imaginative restaurants and the multitude of excellent home cooks has only come about in the last 20 years. During this time cuisine went from the monotonous roast meat and boiled vegetable followed by stodgy puddings, to the gastronomic delights evolved by following and adapting cuisine of other countries.

New Zealand cuisine has created dishes using foods readily available locally. In the past it was thought that the only style of food was the cooking of the country's English forefathers and the French cooking taught to budding professional chefs. Where once no leeway was allowed, chefs have now shrugged off these shackles and realise that cooking is imagination and flair, not just rigid adherence to the basics. With many New Zealanders travelling extensively overseas, insular attitudes towards food have long disappeared.

So what are the riches of New Zealand's food? Vegetables such as asparagus, globe artichokes and avacados – luxuries in some countries – are abundant. Silver beef, or Swiss chard, which is treasured elsewhere, is virtually taken for granted in New Zealand. Kumara is the waxiest and most succulent of the world's sweet potatoes, and pumpkin, put to good use in the country's cooking, is often shunned by other countries. New Zealand's kiwifruit, apples, tamarillos, passion-fruit, boysenberries, strawberries, and pears are among fruit shipped all over the globe. Other fruit include pepinos, babacos and prince melons.

New Zealand lamb is perfection; a crown roast lamb or lamb spare ribs are well worth a try, as is the beef. Fish is abundant and of superior quality as well as the shellfish – crayfish, lobster, paua (abalone), tua tua and toheroa. Game is also plentiful.

Wine has vastly improved. Until 30 years ago only hybrid grapes were grown to produce sherries, ports, and mediocre table wines. It is now generally accepted that the country produces some of the best white wines. New Zealand's cool maritime climate and its summer rains produce light, elegant fruity wines. More attention is being given to the production of red wines which have begun to emerge in the past few years.

While tacos, pizzas and kebabs are happily offered alongside the more traditional meat pies and fish and chips, so too is wine, by the glass or carafe, served alongside the traditional glass or jug of beer. New Zealanders, with Australians, are among the biggest beer drinkers in the world. It has been claimed that many of New Zealand's beers, also available locally, rank equal with the great beers of Denmark and Germany. Beer has regained respectability as the drink to have with meals.

Where To Eat

There are hundreds of good restaurants in Auckland, Wellington, Christchurch and Dunedin, and many places in between.

All the resort towns have good quality restaurants and the increasing number of them specialise in ethnic meals, most notably Chinese, Indian, Italian and Thai. Some of the better-known and well-established restaurants are listed below. BYO, of course, means "Bring Your Own" and indicates a restaurant licensed for the consumption, though not the sale, of alcohol.

Auckland

Antoines, 333 Parnell Road; tel: 379 8756.
Ariake, Quay Towers; tel: 379 2377.
Fisherman's Wharf, Northcote Point; tel: 418 3955.

Flutes, 407 Mt Eden Road; tel: 630 1143.
Green Elephant Cafe, 27 Rutland Street; tel: 379 7084.
Harbourside, 1st Floor, Ferry Building, Quay Street; tel: 307 0556.
Java Jive, Ponsonby Road; tel: 376 5870.
Le Brie, St. Patricks Square; tel: 373 3955.
Marina, Half Moon Bay; tel: 537 0905.
New Orient, Strand Arcade, Queen Street; tel: 379 7793.
Porterhouse Blue, 58 Calliope Road, Devonport; tel: 445 0309.
Prego, 226 Ponsonby Road; tel: 376 3095.
Rick's Cafe Americain, Victoria Park Market; tel: 309 9074.
Rosinis, 20 High Street; tel: 307 0225.
Tony's The Original One, Wellesly Street; tel: 373 4196.
Tony's Lorne Street; tel: 373 2138.
Tony's Mission Bay Restaurant, 71 Tamaki Drive; tel: 528 5419.
Wheeler's, 43 Ponsonby Road, tel: 376 3185.

Christchurch

Bahn Thai, 319 Stanmore Road, Richmond; tel: 381 1611.
Chung Wah II, 61 Worcester Street; tel: 379 3894.
Grimsby's, Corner Kilmore and Montreal Streets; tel: 379 9040.
Henry Africa's, 325 Stanmore Road; tel: 389 3619.
Il Felice, 150 Armagh Street; tel: 366 7535.
Kanniga's Thai, Carlton Courts, Papanui Road, (BYO); tel: 355 6228.
Kurashiki, MFL building, 749 Colombo Street; tel 366 7092.
Scarborough Fare, Scarborough Road, Sumner; tel: 326 6987.
Shangri-la, 321 Durham Street; tel: 379 5720.
Tiffany's, Corner of Durham and Lichfield Streets; tel: 379 1350.

Dunedin

Blades, 450 George Street; tel: 477 6548.
95 Filleul, 95 Filleul Street; tel: 477 7233.
Thyme Out, 5 Stafford Street; tel: 474 0467.

Wellington

Angkor Cambodian Restaurant, 43 Dixon Street; tel: 384 9423.
Armidillo Café, 129 Willis Street; tel: 384 1444.
Brer Fox, 10 Murphy Street, (BYO); tel: 471 2477.
Genghis Khan Mongolian BBQ, 25 Majoribanks Street; tel: 384 3592.
The Grain of Salt, 232 Oriental Parade; tel: 384 8642.
Il Casino, 108 Tory Street; tel: 385 7496.
La Spaghettata, 15 Edward Street; tel: 384 2812.
Marbles, 89 Upland Road, (BYO); tel: 475 8490.
Pierres, 342 Tinakori Road, (BYO); tel: 472 6238.
Shorebird Seafood Restaurant, 301 Evans Bay Road; tel: 386 2017.
Wellington Settlement, 155 Willis Street, (BYO); tel: 385 8920.

Attractions
Culture

New Zealand has a relatively short recorded history but all the main centres, most of the provincial cities and many quite small towns have museums. There has also been an explosion of interest in the visual arts since World War II and art galleries with fine collections have been established.

Museums

National Museum of New Zealand, Buckle Street, Wellington. This fine 50-year old building, features displays of Maori traditional art and culture including wood carvings and decorated houses, canoes, weapons and other artifacts. The displays amount to one of the best collections of Polynesian art and artifacts in the world, and there are also Micronesian and Melanesian collections and many exhibits from South East Asia. Other exhibits are: European discovery and settlement from New Zealand, geological history of the region; collections of flora and fauna, including the remains of the large flightless bird which once inhabited New Zealand, the Moa. Open daily 10am to 4.45pm (the National Art Gallery is in the same building.)

Far North Regional Museum, Centennial Buildings, South Road, Kaitaia. Collections include a "colonial" room, Maori artifacts, and a reconstructed Moa display, also a large room that houses the de Surville anchor and associated display, and the Northwood photographic collection. Open 10am to 5pm (Monday to Friday), 1pm to 5pm (Saturday and Sunday), and 10am to 7pm, Christmas to February (daily).

Captain Cook Memorial Museum, York Street, Russell. Named after Captain James Cook, the museum houses mainly local relics of early European settlement. These include specimens of Maori culture, war exhibits, whaling gear, and relics of the early traders and missionaries. Open 10am to 4pm (Monday to Saturday), 2pm to 4pm (Sunday), 8am to 5pm daily during school holidays.

Auckland Institute and Museum, Auckland Domain. Set in beautiful parklands in Auckland's best known park, the War Memorial Museum's exhibitions include a wonderful selection of Maori and Pacific artefacts and carvings. Other sections include material devoted to: New Zealand natural history; Asian, and other applied arts; maritime and war history; the history of Auckland; and a planetarium. The Institute administers the Institute Library, Auckland Astronomical Society, an anthropology and Maori Studies, a conchology section, and the Ornithological Society of New Zealand. Open: daily 10am to 5pm.

The Bath House – Rotorua's Art and History Museum. The gallery houses a number of collections tracing the development of painting and print making in New Zealand. Included are major works by Christopher Perkins, Rita Angus, Colin McCahon, Toss Woollaston, WG Baker and a host of other contemporary New Zealand painters. Also an impressive collection of images of the Maori in paintings and portraits. The museum boasts a collection of 6,000 prints of the volcanic plateau area, and a colonial cottage reflecting the period 1870 – 1900 when Rotorua was settled by Europeans. There is a Kauri gum collection and a widlife display which relates to the timber industry which dominates the region. A new wing has also been dedicated to the local Te Arawa Maori people and portrays a wide variety of their artifacts.

Canterbury Museum, Rolleston Avenue, Christchurch. Opened in 1870, the museum is the world's largest display hall on Antarctica. Exhibits include and 87 foot (27 metre) skeleton of an Antarctic blue whale and equipment used in various expeditions. There is an associated reference library and theatre where films are shown. Other features include a hall of oriental art, an ornithological display, a costume gallery, a street of shops, and a Maori cultural section including artifacts from the moa-hunting era. Open daily 10am to 4.30pm.

Lakes District Museum, Buckingham Street, Arrowtown. The collection is housed in a two-storey, renovated, former bank building built in 1875 and contains mining and geological items such as gold and mineral specimens, gold-miner's tools, and relics of the Chinese miners. Domestic and agricultural items, old implements and machinery, and a collection of horse-drawn vehicles are also on display. A collection of 3,000 early photographs, books and documents, relates to local history from 1862 to the 1920s. Open: daily 9am to 5pm.

Otago Museum, Great King Street, Dunedin. It houses excellent collections and displays including Pacific collections, halls of Melanesia and Polynesia, a Maori hall, halls of maritime history and marine life, ceramics including Greek pottery and sculpture, New Zealand birdlife and an Otago historical collection. Open: 10am to 5pm (weekdays), 1pm to 5pm (weekdays).

Otago Early Settlers Museum, 220 Cumberland Street, Dunedin. First opened in 1908, collections include records and documents of emigration and early settlement in the Otago area. A wide range of pioneer relics, including folk crafts, costumes, whaling relics, gold relics and household devices. Paintings and photographs depicting early settlers and settlements can also be seen. Open: 8.30am to 4.30pm (Monday to Friday), 10.30am to 4.30pm (Saturday), 1.30pm to 4.30pm (Sunday).

Museum of Transport and Technology (Motat), Great North Road, Western Springs, 5 km from downtown Auckland. Displays include aircraft, a working tramway and railway, vintage cars, carriages, the development of printing and photography, calculating machines from the abacus to the computer, and a colonial village where buildings are preserved and stored. Among the many exciting exhibits are the remains of Richard Pearse's aircraft which twice flew successfully in March 1903, three months after the Wright Brothers, and "Meg Merrilees," an F class saddle-tank locomotive built by the Yorkshire Engine Co. of Leeds, England, in 1874. Open: 9am to 5pm (weekdays), 10am to 5pm (weekends and public holidays).

The Steam Traction Society Museum, Lethbridge Road, 4 km north of Fielding. Unique in New Zealand in that it specialises in British traction engines, steamrollers, and portable engines. Twenty exhibits, in various states from running, being restored, to awaiting restoration, can be seen. Open: Sunday afternoons, the third Sunday of each month being a Steam Day. Also open at any time by arrangement with the Secretary.

The Ferrymead Trust, situated on a 40-hectare site alongside the Heathcote River, Christchurch. The trust's historic park includes many historical exhibits; vintage machinery, cars, bicycles, gigs, fire engines, tramcars, railway engines, aeroplanes, home appliances, and agricultural and printing equipment. Special features include rides on a 1.5 km tramway and a 1 km railway. The last Kitson steam tram locomotive with trailers built in Leeds, England, in 1881 may be seen. Open: daily 10am to 4.30pm.

Queenstown Motor Museum, Brecon Street, Queenstown. This museum complex contains more than 60 exhibits which, though they periodically change, always include veteran and vintage cars and motor cycles, as well as post vintage and post World War II models and aero engines. Some of the many makes on display are Bentley, Rolls-Royce, Aston Martin, Maserati, Mercedes, and many other European specialist cars. Included is a range of American cars including Model T Fords. Open: daily 9am to 5.30pm.

Army Memorial Museum, State Highway No. 1, south of Waiouru. The museum houses many artefacts from New Zealand's military history including weapons, uniforms, photographs, paintings, medals, equipment, diaries, personal effects, and other memorabilia from the Maori Wars to the present day. Open: daily 9am to 4.30pm.

Waikato Museum of Art and History, corner of Victoria and Grantham Streets, Hamilton. This handsome, five-level building takes full advantage of its riverbank location. The restored Maori war canoe, Te Winika, and contemporary Tainui carving and tukutuku weaving are on permanent display. A changing programme of exhibitions draws on the museum's large collection of New Zealand fine art, Tainui and Waikato history. National and international touring exhibitions also feature regularly.

Art Galleries

New Zealand has 21 public art galleries. The largest ones are listed below.

The Auckland City Art Gallery, Wellesley/Kitchener Street, Auckland. First opened in 1888 its collection includes New Zealand paintings, sculpture, drawings, prints, and photographs from the 1800s to the present day. Also an extensive Frances Hodgkins collection. There are European Old Master paintings and drawings, a small Gothic collection, and a collection of 19th and 20th-century Japanese prints. Also international sculptures and prints. Open: daily 10am to 4.30pm. Free guided tours at 12pm (Monday to Friday), 2pm (Sunday).

Govett-Brewster Art Gallery, Queen Street, New Plymouth. This is one of the best collections of contemporary art in New Zealand. Most New Zealand artists of note are represented, with works by Patrick Hanly, Michael Illingworth, Colin McCahon and Brent Wong. Also an important collection of Len Lye kinetic sculptures, painting and film. Open: 10.30am to 5pm (Monday to Friday), 1pm to 5pm (Saturday to Sunday).

Sargeant Gallery, Queen's Park, Wanganui. This has a permanently exhibited New Zealand collection, which includes oils, watercolours, and prints from the 19th and 20th centuries. Also included is 19th and 20th-century Western art, with British oils, watercolours, and prints, as well as European works including drawings by Poccetti, The Denton Collection of 19th and 20th-century photography, and an exhibition of World War I posters and cartoons. Open: 10.30am to 4pm (Monday to Friday), 10.30am to 12pm (Saturday), 1.30pm to 4pm (Sunday).

Manawatu Art Gallery, 398 Main Street, Palmerston North. The gallery collection concentrates on New Zealand works, from as early as 1880 and also including works by all major contemporary painters. It houses two large collections of drawings by James Cook, and oils, watercolours and drawings by H. Linley Richardson. Open: 10am to 4.30pm (Tuesday to Friday), 1pm to 5pm (Saturday, Sunday and public holidays).

Dowse Art Gallery, Civic Centre, Lower Hutt. This gallery concentrates on New Zealand art, mainly contemporary, with some earlier works. Open: 10am to 4pm (Monday to Friday), 1pm to 5pm (Saturday to Sunday).

National Art Gallery, Buckle Street, Wellington. The National Gallery's collections include New Zealand, Australian, British and foreign 19th and 20th century paintings, drawings, graphic art and sculpture. Accent is on New Zealand art from 1840, with a wide selection of early watercolours, oil paintings and drawings. Also a wide range of etchings and engravings of old and modern Masters. Open: daily 10am to 4.45pm.

Wellington City Art Gallery, 50 Victoria Street. This gallery concentrates less on collecting work than on mounting temporary New Zealand art and design shows. Open: daily 10am to 6pm, and 10am to 8pm Wednesday.

Bishop Suter Art Gallery, Bridge Street, Nelson. The main collections are watercolours which include works by John Gully, J.C. Richmond, C.Y. Fell, Frances Hodgkins and James Nairn. Open: 10am to 4pm (Tuesday to Sunday).

Robert McDougall Art Gallery, Botanic Gardens, Rolleston Avenue, Christchurch. The Robert McDougall Art Gallery houses representative works of Dutch, French, Italian, and especially Bristish painting, drawing, printmaking and sculpture as European art forms. The New Zealand collection is one of the most comprehensive in the region especially of the Canterbury works. Open: daily 10am to 4.30pm.

Dunedin Public Art Gallery, Logan Park, Dunedin. First established in the 1880s, it houses a large collection of 18th and 19th-century English watercolours, as well as major oil portrait and landscape artists from between the 16th and 19th centuries. The New Zealand collection ranges from the mid-19th century, and includes a retrospective collection of Frances Hodgkins. Open: 10am to 4.30pm (Monday to Friday), 2pm to 5pm (Saturday, Sunday and public holidays).

Other provincial public art galleries are:

Forum North Arts Centre, Whangarei.
Waikato Art Museum, Hamilton.
Hawke's Bay Exhibition Centre, Hastings.
Aigantighe Art Gallery, Timaru.
Forrester Art Gallery, Oamaru.
Hocken Library, University of Otago, Dunedin.

Shopping

What To Buy

SHEEPSKIN
With more than 50 million sheep in New Zealand, it comes as no surprise that one of the country's major shopping attractions are its sheepskin and woollen products. You are unlikely to find cheaper sheepskin clothing anywhere in the world and the colour and variety of sheepskins and sheepskin products make an ideal gift or souvenir. Many shops stock a huge range of coats and jackets made from sheepskin, slinkskin, possum, deerskin, leather and suede. Car seat covers are popular as are sheepskin floor rugs. The bigger retailers pack and post any items overseas.

WOODCARVINGS
Maori woodcarvings are widely available. The most traditional Maori area of New Zealand is the East Cape and you should use your initiative and hunt in this area if you are looking for something authentic.

GREENSTONE
New Zealand jade, more commonly referred to as greenstone, cannot match the quality of Chinese or Burmese jade but nevertheless is a distinctive Kiwi product. Widely available, the jade is worked into jewellery, figurines, ornaments, and Maori tikis. The West Coast (South Island) is the major area where greenstone continues to be mined. Factories in the West Coast towns of Greymouth and Hokitika allow visitors to see the jade being worked.

HANDICRAFTS
There has been an explosion of handicrafts in recent years, the products of which are sold by local craftsmen and craftswomen in situ and by local shops catering specifically to tourists. Pottery is perhaps the most widely available craft product, though patchwork, quilting, padded boxes, canework, handspun knitwear and weaving, woodcarving, Kauri woodware, wooden toys, bark pictures, paintings, glassware and leatherware are among the enormous range of crafts.

Where to Buy

Most shopping centre needs can be catered for in Auckland, Wellington and Christchurch. Auckland's Queen Street is an obvious place in which to part with one's money; while Karangahape Road, one of Auckland's busiest and oldest established commercial streets, offers a wealth of interesting shopping. Located at the top, of Queen Street, "Karangahape" translates as "winding ridge of human activity" and aptly describes the bustle. It is the variety of stores, together with an ethnic cross-section comprising Auckland's Polynesian and European community that gives the street its character. Small second-hand clothing and furniture shops compete for business with spacious department stores. Another centre for shopping in Auckland is the harbourside Downtown complex. A glass-walled walkway connects with the Downtown Airline (Bus) Terminal, itself a shopping centre, making it an excellent location for tourists wanting a last-minute browse.

In Wellington the main shopping streets are in Willis Street and Customhouse Quay; while in Christchurch, the Cathedral Square vicinity offers the best bargains. Anybody intending to pass through Queenstown can rest assured that the streets bristle with souvenir shops. Prices are usually fixed but bartering is becoming common. Queenstown is the exception to normal retail hours, with most shops open seven days a week for extended hours.

Further Reading

Bearing in mind that New Zealand boasts the highest per capita readership of books and periodicals anywhere in the world, it is well worth paying a visit to some of New Zealand's fine bookshops. Whitcoull's is the country's major bookstore (and stationer) and offers a good selection of quality titles. There is a wealth of reading related to New Zealand.

Collections & Anthologies

A Book of New Zealand, ed. by J.C. Reid and Peter Cape, Collins, 1979. An anthology of New Zealand writing, embracing fiction and non-fiction. Most of the passages included are brief excerpts from well-known works.
Anthology of Twentieth Century New Zealand Poetry, selected with an introduction by Vincent O'Sullivan. Oxford University Press, 1976.
Automobile Association Road Atlas of New Zealand, Hamlyn, 1978.
Automobile Association Road Atlas of New Zealand Countryside, Hamlyn, 1978.
Automobile Association Book of New Zealand Walkways, Landsdowne Press, 1982.
Encyclopaedia of New Zealand, ed. by A.H. McLintock, 3 vols. NZ Government Printer, 1966. A complete and detailed reference work on New Zealand.
Heinemann New Zealand Dictionary, ed. by H.W. Orsman, Heinemann Educational, 1979.
Into the World of Light: An Anthology of Maori Writing, ed. by Witi Ihimaera and D.S. Long. Heinemann, 1982.
New Zealand Atlas, ed. by Ian Wards, Government Printer, 1976.
New Zealand Encyclopaedia, ed. by Gordon McLauchlan, David Bateman Ltd., 1984. A one volume, family A-to-Z covering all aspects of New Zealand

life.
New Zealand in Maps, ed. by A.G. Anderson, Hodder and Stoughton (London), 1977.
New Zealand Love Poems, chosen by James Bertram, McIndoe, 1977.
New Zealand Short Stories, chosen by Lydia Wevers, Oxford University Press, 1984.
Oxford Book of Contemporary New Zealand Poetry, chosen by Fleur Adcock, Oxford University Press, in association with Auckland University Press, 1982.
Penguin Book of New Zealand Verse, ed. by Allan Curnow, Penguin, 1966.
Wise's New Zealand Guide, a gazetteer of New Zealand, Wise Publications, 1979 (7th Edition).

General

Alexander, L., *Adventure Holidays in New Zealand*, Independent Newspapers Ltd., 1982.
Archey, Sir Gilbert, *Maori Art and its Artists*, Collins, 1977.
Braithwaite, Erroll, *New Zealand and its People*, Government Printer, 1974.
Blumhardt, D., *The Coming of the Maori*, Whitcombe and Tombs, 1974. An account of the migration to New Zealand by the first Polynesians, written by a distinguished Maori and Pacific scholar.
Buller, Sir W.L., *Birds of New Zealand* (new edition ed. by E.G. Turbott). Whitcombe and Tombs, 1967.
Burnett, A.A. and R., *The Australia and New Zealand Nexus*, Australian Institute of International Affairs, Canberra, 1978.
Burton, D., *Two Hundred Years of New Zealand Food and Cookery*, Reed, 1982.
Cameron, Don. *Memorable Moments in New Zealand Sport*, Moa Publications 1979.
Cobb, L., and Duncan, J., **New Zealand's National Parks**, Hamlyn, 1980.
Cross, Ian, *The God Boy*, Whitcombe and Tombs, 1972. One of the most successful novels published since World War II by a New Zealand writer.
Docking, G.C., *Two Hundred Years of New Zealand Painting*, A.H. and A.W. Reed, 1971.
Dollimore, H.N., *The Parliament of New Zealand and Parliament House*, Goverment Printer, 1973.
Downes, P.E., *Shadows on the Stage:*

The first Seventy Years on Theatre in New Zealand, McIndoe, 1975.
Easton, B., *Social Policy and the Welfare State in New Zealand*, Allen and Unwin, 1980.
Fleming, Sir C.A., *The Geological History of New Zealand and its Life*, Auckland University Press, 1979.
Forster, R.R., and L.M., *Small Land Animals of New Zealand*, McIndoe, 1970.
Forrester, Rex, and Illingworth, N., *Hunting in New Zealand*, A.H. and A.W. Reed, 1979.
Frame, Janet, *Owls Do Cry*, W.H. Allen, 1961; *A State of Seige*, Pegasus Press, 1967; *Living in Maniototo*, Braziller (New York), 1979. A selection of three novels by New Zealand's best known living writer of fiction.
Franklin, S.H., *Trade Growth and Anxiety – New Zealand Beyond the Welfare State*, Methuen, 1978. An account of social and political developments in New Zealand since World War II.
Gee, Maurice, *Plumb*, Faber and Faber (London), 1979; *Meg*, Faber and Faber (London), 1981; *Sole Survivor*, Faber and Faber (London), 1983. *Plumb* is one of the best known and critically praised novels of recent years in New Zealand. *Meg* and *Sole Survivor* are the later works in this trilogy.
Grimshaw, P., *Women's Suffrage in New Zealand*, Oxford University Press, 1972.
Guthrie-Smith, W.H., *Tutira: The Story of a New Zealand Station*, A.H. and A.W. Reed, 1969. (4th Edition). This is a New Zealand classic, the work of a sheep farmer and amateur naturalist in the late 19th and early 20th centuries.
Henderson, J. Jackson, K. and Kennaway, R., *Beyond New Zealand, the Foreign Policy of a Small State*, Methuen, 1980.
Hilliard, Noel, *Maori Girl*, Heinemann (London) 1971. This novel is one of the biggest sellers written by a New Zealander in the past 25 years.
Houghton, B.F., *Geyserland: a Guide to Volcanoes and Geothermal Areas of Rotorua*, The Geological Society of New Zealand.
Hunt, Sam, *Collected Poems*, Penguin Books, 1980. A collection of the work of a contemporary folk poet.
Hyde, Robin, *The Godwits Fly*, Hurst and Blackett (London), 1938. The best known novel by a New Zealand woman.

Ihimaera, Witi, **Tangi**, Heinemann, 1974; **Whanau**, Heinemann, 1974; **The New Net Goes Fishing**, 1977. Three works by the best known Maori fiction writer.

King, Michael, and Barriball, Martin, **New Zealand in Colour**, A.H. and A.W. Reed, 1982.

Laing, R.M. and Blackwell, E.W., **Plants of New Zealand**, Whitcombe and Tombs, 1964.

Lousley, D.P., **Guide to the Ski Fields of the South Island**, McIndoe, 1976.

McCormick, E.H., **New Zealand Literature**; **A Survey**, Oxford University Press (London), 1959; **Portrait of Frances Hodgkins**, Oxford University Press, in association with Auckland University Press, 1981, **Omai, Pacific Envoy**, Auckland University Press, 1977.

McDowall, R.M., **New Zealand Freshwater Fishes: A Guide and Natural History**, Heinemann Educational, 1978.

McLean M.E., and Orbell, M., **Traditional Songs of the Maori**, Oxford University Press and Auckland University Press, 1979.

Metge, J., **The Maoris of New Zealand**, Routledge (London), 1976. A full account of Maori life before and after European settlement. The best introductory book on the subject.

Mitcalfe, B., **Maori Poetry: The singing Word**, Price Milburn, 1974.

Moore, L.B., and Irwin, J.B., **The Oxford Book of New Zealand Plants**, Oxford University Press, 1978.

Morrieson, Ronald Hugh, **Scarecrow**, Angus and Robertson (Sydney), 1963; **Came a Hot Friday**, Angus and Robertson (Sydney), 1964. Two of four black comedy novels written by a small town New Zealander unknown in his lifetime, which have become remarkably successful since the end of the 1970s, and have been re-issued by Heinemann, Dunmore Press, and Penguin several times.

Morton, J.E., and Miller, M., **The New Zealand Sea Shore**, Collins, (London) 1973.

Salmon, J.T., **The Native Trees of New Zealand**, Reed, 1980.

Sargeson, Frank, **Collected Stories**, Penguin, 1982. A full collection of the stories of a man who for many years was the best known short story writer in the country.

Simmons, D.R., **The Great New Zealnd Myth; A study of the Discovery and**

Origin Traditions of the Maori, A.H. and A.W. Reed, 1976. A recent commentary by an ethnologist on the meanings of the Maori traditions relating to the discovery of New Zealand by Polynesian seafarers.

Simpson, Keith, **History of New Zealand**, Allen Lane (London), 1980 (also available in paperback by Penguin). This is the most popular history of the country ever published, written by the professor of History at the University of Auckland. It is a standard work.

Stirling, E., Eruera, **The Teaching of a Maori Elder**, Oxford University Press, 1980.

Thompson, K.W., **Art Galleries and Museums of New Zealand**, A.H. and A.W. Reed, 1981.

Tuwhare, Hone, **No Ordinary Sun**, McIndoe, 1977. A best-selling collection of the work of New Zealand's leading Maori poet.

Yerex, David, **The Farming of Deer, World Trends and Modern Techniques**. Agricultural Promotion Associates, 1982. A world authority writes on New Zealand's development of the unique pastoral farming of deer.

Other Insight Guides

The *Insight Guides* series includes almost 200 titles covering every continent. Books which highlight destinations in this region include *Australia*, *Sydney*, *Melbourne*, and the *Great Barrier Reef*.

Insight Pocket Guides

There is also a complementary series of more than 100 *Insight Pocket Guides* providing timed itineraries designed for the reader with limited time. Titles which cover this region include *New Zealand* and *Fiji*.

Photography by
John G. Anderson 196
Air New Zealand 315, 316L, 318
Auckland Institute and Museum 35, 41,
44/45, 49, 51, 52, 53, 54, 59, 136, 157, 224
Auckland Public Library Photograph
Collection 48, 222
Marcus Brooke cover, 16/17, 72/73,
168/169, 194, 202, 247, 274/275
Marcus Brooke/APA Photo Agency 148
Craig Darling 218, 255
Andrew Eames 159, 232/233
Manfred Gottschalk 203, 234
Dallas & John Heaton 283
Peter Hutton Collection 30/31, 32, 34, 40, 42
Dawn Kendall 29, 108
J Kugler/APA Photo Agency 82
Landsdown-Rigby 12/13, 78, 81, 83, 84R,
155, 175, 182
Dennis Lane 211
Max Lawrence 10/11, 25, 69, 74/75, 76, 85,
86, 87, 88, 89, 90/91, 93, 98, 100/101,
107, 110/111, 112, 114, 116/117, 118, 119,
120, 122/123, 125, 129, 130, 132, 133,
144/145, 146/147, 152/153, 162, 163, 164,
166, 167, 170, 171, 172, 174, 176, 178/179,
180, 181, 183, 184, 185, 186, 188, 189, 190,
191, 192/193, 198, 199, 200, 201, 205, 207,
209, 210, 212, 213, 214/215, 216/217, 225,
229, 230/231, 235, 236, 237, 238, 239, 240,
242/243, 244, 245, 248, 249, 251, 253, 254,
256/257, 258, 260, 261, 262, 263, 264, 265,
266/267, 268, 269, 270, 271, 272, 273, 276,
278, 279, 280, 281, 282, 286/287, 288, 290,
291, 292, 293, 295, 296/297, 298, 299, 300,
301, 302, 303, 304, 305, 308
Ian Lloyd 309
Lodestone Press 55, 57, 60
Claire McKay 312/313, 319
Mourie and Dingle Adventures 204
New Zealand Tourist Board 9, 68, 71, 121,
126, 127, 128, 221R, 228, 250
Otago Daily Times 28
Photobank 62, 66, 67, 103, 106, 139, 142/
143, 221L, 223, 284/285, 311
Fritz Prenzel 24, 115, 165
S Pumati/APA Photo Agency 227R
G.R. Roberts 26, 27
Paul Van Reil 162, 206
Allan Seiden 140/141, 306/307
Dr David Skinner 134/135, 137, 138, 226
The Auckland City Art Gallery 104, 109
The New Zealand Herald & Weekly News 64,
65, 105R, 105L, 208
Terence Barrow Collection 33, 36, 37, 38, 43,
70, 80, 92, 94R, 94L, 96, 97R, 97L, 314, 317
Topham Picturepoint 1, 154
Tony Stone Worldwide 14, 99
Adina Tovy/APA Photo Agency 84L
Alexander Turnbull Library 18, 46, 50, 58,
61, 63, 102, 310

Maps Berndtson & Berndtson

Visual Consultant V. Barl

A

Abel Tasman National Park 239
Adare, Cape 137
Agrodome 199
Aitutaki, Cook Islands 317
Akaroa 52, 245, 253–54
Albatross Centre, Trust Bank
  Royal 289
Alexandra 285
Alofi, Niue Island 317
Amundsen, Roald 137
Antarctica 23, 24, 25, 26, 27, 42,
  136–38
Antipodes Islands 310
Aparima, River 300
Arahura 268
Arrowtown 280, 285
Arthur's Pass 254, 260
Arthur's Pass National Park 261
arts and crafts 103–109
Ashhurst 213
Asians 82
Aspiring, Mount 284
Atkinson, Sir Harry 58, 191
Auckland 77, 109, 125, 127, 155–67
  Aotea Centre 161
  history 156
  Museum of Transport
    and Technology 159
  National Maritime Museum 159
  Old Customhouse
  suburbs 163
  shopping 158
  restaurants 162
  zoo 165
Auckland Harbour Bridge 165
Auckland Domain 164
Auckland Islands 310
Aupori Peninsula 176
Avarua, Cook Islands 316
Avatiu, Cook Islands 316
Avon, River 245
Awakino Gorge 191

B

Balclutha 300
Ballance, John 58
Ballantyne, David 69
Banks, Joseph 41
Banks Peninsula 41, 245, 251,
  252, 259
Barrett, Dicky 224
Barrett, Richard 51
Baxter, James K. 105, 215
Bay of Islands 47, 48, 171–73

Bay of Plenty 183-85
Beaglehole, Dr J.C. 39
Bellinghausen, von 137
Bendigo 280
Bledisoe, Lord 173
Blenheim 235
Bligh, Captain William 315
Blue and Green Lakes 200
Bluff 299-300
Bolger, Jim 67
Bombay Hills 155, 167
Bracken, Thomas 288
Brett, Cape 175
Broadgreen 238
Broughton, Lieutenant William 310
Brown, William 164
Brunner, Lake 272
Brunner, Thomas 269
Buck, Sir Peter 94, 191
Buffalo Beach 182
Bulls 214
bungee-jumping 114
Burke's Pass 263
Burns, Thomas 291
Busby, James 51, 173
Butler, John 48
Butler, Samuel 120
Byrd, Admiral 137

C

Cable Bay 177
Cambridge 189
Campbell, Sir John Logan 164
Campbell Islands 24, 310
camping 115
Campion, Jane 105, 107
Canterbury 119, 254, 259–64
Canvastown 237
Cape Kidnappers 211
Cardrona Valley 284
Cargill, Captain William 291, 294
Carrona 280
Carterton 229
Castle, Len 108
Central Otago 277–85
Chapman, Thomas 195
Charleston 268, 273
Chaslands 298
Chatham Islands 24, 207, 310–11
Chew Chong 187
Christchurch 136, 245–54, 259
Christian, Fletcher 315
Clarence Valley 260
Clutha, River 278, 280, 283, 285
Clyde 285
Cobham, Lord 185
Codfish Island 309
Colac Bay 301
Colenso, William 49, 172
Collingwood 240
Colville, Cape 182
Colville 182
Conway, River 259
Cook, Captain James 39, 40–43, 48,
  93, 136–37, 161, 171, 175, 177,
  180, 182, 183, 207, 235, 252,
  268–69, 291, 302, 315, 317

Cook, Mount 113, 262–63, 264, 271
Cook Islands 79, 80–81, 315-19
Cook Strait 219, 234
Cooks Bay 182
Coopers Beach 177
Coroglen 182
Coromandel 181
Coromandel Peninsula 108, 180–84
Coronet Peak 283
Craters of the Moon 203
Cromwell 280, 285
Crown Mountains 284
Curio Bay 300

D

d'Urville, Dumont 237
D'Urville Island 237
dairy farming 187-91
Dalmatians 84
Danes 83
Dannevirke 83, 211
Dargaville 177
Darwin, Charles 49
Devonport 166
Diemen, Anthony van 39
Dog Island 300
Doubtless Bay 177
Drury 158, 167
Dunedin 125, 279, 288–94
Duntroon 285
Dusky Sound 42, 302
Dutch 84

E

Eden, George, Earl of Auckland 161
Eden, Mount 157, 161, 164
Edendale 301
Eglington Valley 284
Egmont, Mount 187, 191
Egmont National Park 191
Eltham 187
Erebus, Mount 138

F

Fairlie 263
Farewell Spit 239–40
farming 119–21
fauna 25, 26, 28, 29
Featherston 228
Fendalton 251
Ferrymead 252
Fielding 214
Fijians 81
Fiordland 298, 301–304
Firth, Josiah Clifton 189
fishing 114, 173–74, 199, 202, 272
Fletcher Bay 182
flora 29
Fomison, Tony 104
Foveaux Strait 299
Fox, Sir William 196
Fox Glacier 270, 271
Foxton 214
Frame, Janet 105
Franz Josef 271

Franz Josef Glacier 270
Freemans Bay, Auckland 157
Fresne, Marion du 175
Freyburg, Bernard 70
Frisbie, Robert Dean 316
Fuchs, Sir Vyvian 138

G

Gabriel's Gully 279, 281
geology 23–29
George III, King 182
Germans 84
Gillespie's Beach 272
Gisborne 207
Glenbrook Vintage Steam Railway 167
Glenfalloch 289
Godley, John Robert 245–46
gold 279
Golden Bay 239–40
Gondwana 23–29
Gore 304
Grace, Patricia 103, 105
Great Barrier Island 167
Grey, Sir George 55, 167
Grey, Zane 173, 175
Grey Lynn, Auckland 79
Greymouth 260, 261, 273
Greytown 228

H

Haast Pass 270
Hairini 190
Hall, Roger 107
Hamilton, Sir William 264
Hamilton 187, 188
Hamurana Springs 199
Hanmer Springs 254, 259
Harvey, Les 163
Harwood's Hole 240
Hastings 208, 210-11
Hauraki Gulf 114, 155, 156, 157, 159,
    167, 180
Havelock 236–37
Havelock North 211
Hawaiki 185
Hawea, Lake 282
Hawke's Bay 41, 119, 208–11
Hayes, Lake 283
Heaphy, Charles 219, 223
Heaphy Track 240, 273
Helensville 158, 165
Hell's Gate 200
Henderson 165, 176
Hillary, Sir Edmund 113, 137–38,
    262–63
Himitange 214
    Boyd massacre 47
    history 23–71
    geological origins 23–29
    Maori beginnings 33–37
    missionaries 49
    Treaty of Waitangi 54
    New Zealand Wars 56
    voyages of discovery 39–43
    World War I 59
    World War II 60

Hobson, Lieutenant-Governor William
    54, 55, 157, 161–62, 172
Hobson, Mount 162
Hobson Bay 162
Hobsonville 162
Hodges, William 161
Hodgkins, Frances 103
Hokianga Harbour 177
Hokitika 269, 272
Hokonui Hills 304
Holyoake, Keith 65
Homer Tunnel 303
Hone Heke 55, 174–75, 177
Hongi Hika 175, 176
horse racing 131–33
Hot Water Beach 182-83
Howick 158, 164
Huapai 165
Huka Falls 203
Hulme, Keri 103, 105
Huntly 190
Hutt, Mount 262
Hutt Valley 227, 229

I

Ianthe, Lake 272
Ihimaera, Witi 103, 105
immigration 77, 79–85
International Date Line 310, 315
Invercargill 298
Irish 82
Island Bay, Wellington 226
Italians 84

J

Jackson Bay 271
Jerusalem 105, 215
jet-boating 114, 281
Jews 83
Jones, John 52

K

Kahurangi National Park 240
Kaiangaroa 195
Kaikohe 177
Kaikoura 236
Kaimai-Mamaku forest park 189
Kaitai 171
Kaitaia 177
Kaiteriteri 234, 239
Kaituna, River 200
Kapiti 227
Kapuni 191
Karamea 240, 273
Karangahake Gorge 183
Katikati 184
Kauaeranga Valley 181
Kawakawa 171, 174
Kawarau Gorge 281
Kawau Island 167
Kawerau 185
Kaweka Mountains 208
Kawiti 174, 175
Kendall, Thomas 49
Kennedy Bay 182

Kepler Track 304
Kereopa 185
Kerikeri 171, 175
Kidnappers, Cape 211
Kingston 284, 304
Kinleith 189
Kipling, Rudyard 149, 303
Kirk, Norman 65
kiwifruit 121, 183, 184
Kiwifruit Country 183
Kohimarama Bay, Auckland 164
Kokorareka 43, 47, 55
Kuaotuna Beach 182
Kumara 272
Kumeu 165
Kupe 171, 177, 182, 222

L

Lange, David 66
Larnach, William J.M. 290
Larnach Castle 290
Lawrence 281
Lewis Pass 260
Lincoln University 254
Lindale 227
Lindis Pass 284
Lye, Len 104
Lyndon, Lake 262
Lyttelton 251

M

Macetown 280
Mackenzie Country 263
MacLoughlin, Jim 184
Mahia Peninsula 208
Managaweka 215
Manapouri, Lake 302
Manawatu, River 213
Manawatu 119, 211, 212–14
Mangamuka Scenic Reserve 177
Mangapurua 215
Maning, Frederick 52
Manorburn Dam 285
Mansfield, Katherine 103, 227
Manuherikia Valley 285
Manukau 158
Manukau Harbour, Auckland 155
Maori 33-37, 79, 87–89
Maori art 37, 93-99
Maori culture 79, 164, 189–90, 195,
    198, 229, 289
Maori legends 19, 176, 177, 197, 200,
    204, 281
Maori tribes 35, 157, 187, 278
Maori Waitangi Treaty 173, 174
Marahau 239
Marlborough 119, 234–37
Marlborough Sounds 234, 235
Marsden, Samuel 48, 157, 175
Martin, Sir William 54
Martinborough 228
Mason, Bruce 106
Masterton 228
Matamata 189
Mataura, River 300
Mathieson, Lake 271

Mawson, Sir Douglas 137
McCahon, Colin 103
McIntyre, Peter 104
McMurdo Sound 136, 138
Mercury Bay 41, 182
Merivale 251
Messenger, Mount 191
Methven 262
Michener, James A. 70, 149
Milford Sound 284, 303
Milford Track 149, 282, 304
Mission Bay, Auckaland 164
Mitre Peak 304
Moehau Range 182
Moeraki Boulders 294
Mokena Geyser 189
Mokoia 157
Mokoia Island 197
Molesworth 236
Monowai, Lake 302
Moore, Mike 66, 67
Morioris 310
Morrinsville 189
Motonui 191
Motuihe Island 167
Motunui 191
Motutapu Island 156, 167
Mount Aspiring National Park 284
Mount Cook National Park 262, 264
Mount Cook village 264
mountaineering 113
Moura 200
Moutere Hills 238
Moutueka, River 239
Muldoon, Sir Robert 66
Munday, Lieutenant Colonel 229
Murchison 273
Murihiku 298
Myers, Arthur 161

N

Napier 208, 209–10
Naseby 285
Nelson 108, 234, 239–40
Nelson City 234, 237–8
Nelson Lakes National Park 240
New Brighton 251
New Caledonia 24, 28
New Plymouth 187, 188, 191
Newmarket 161, 163
Newstead 188
Newtown, Wellington 79, 226
Ngaruawahia 189
Ngata, Sir Apirana 88
Ngauruhoe, Mount 203, 204
Ngawha Hot Mineral Springs 177
Ngongotaha, Mount 198
Ngongotaha 200
Ninety Mile Beach 176, 177
Niue Island 79, 315, 317–8
Norsewood 83, 211
North Cape 171
North Head 166
North Island 149, 155–229
North Shore, Auckland 161, 165
Northland 161, 171–77
Norwegians 83

O

Oban, Stewart Island 308
Ohakuri, Lake 202
Ohinemutu 196–97
Ohope Beach 185
Okahu Bay, Auckland 163, 164
Okarito Lagoon 272
Okere Falls 200
Olveston 294
One Tree Hill, Auckland 164
Opononi 177
Opotiki 185
Opua 174
Orakau 190
Orakei-Korako 202
Orepuki 301
Oreti, River 300
Orewa 166
Otago 51, 270, 277–85, 288, 289
Otago Harbour 288
Otakou 289
Otehei Bay 173, 175
Otira Tunnel 261

P–Q

Paihia 171, 172, 174, 175, 176
Pakatoa Island 167
Paku, Mount 183
Palmer, Geoffrey 67
Palmerston North 212, 215
Pancake Rocks 273
Panmure, Auckland 157, 158
Papakura 158
Paradise Valley 199
Parahaki, Mount 177
Parakai 165
Paremata 227
Pargina, Lake 272
Parnell, Auckland 157, 163
Paterson Inlet, Stewart Island 309
Pauanui 183
Pencarrow 227
Penguin Bay 290
Picton 235
Piercy Island 175
Piha 165
Pipiriki 215
Plimmer, John 223
Pohangina, River 213
Pohangina and Totara Reserve 213
Pohutu Geyser 197
Poles 85
Polynesians 29, 33–34, 79, 162
Porirua 229
Port Charles 182
Port Hills 251
Port Jackson 182
Porter's Pass 262
Portobello 289
Pouakai Wildlife Reserve 191
Poverty Bay 41, 119, 207–208
Puhoi pub 166
Pukaki, Lake 264
Punakaiki 273
Putararu 189
Queenstown 114, 277, 282

R

Rai Valley 237
Rakino Island 167
Rangipo 204
Rangitaiki Plains 185
Rangitata, River 263
Rangitikei, River 204, 215
Rangitikei 215
Rangitoto Island 156, 167
Rarotonga, Cook Islands 315
Ratana 214
Read, Gabriel 279, 281
Reefton 273
Reeves, William Pember 58
Reinga, Cape 96, 171, 176, 177
Remarkables Mountains 283
Rimutaka Forest Park 227
Rimutaka mountains 228
Ring, Charles 181
River Road, Wanganui 215
Riverton 301
Riwaka, River 240
Rolleston, Mount 261
Ross, James Clark 137
Ross 272
Ross Island 136
Rotoaira, Lake 204
Rotoehu, Lake 200
Rotoiti, Lake 200, 240
Rotokakahi, Lake 200
Rotoma, Lake 200
Rotomahana, Lake 149, 201
Rotorua, Lake 196, 197, 240
Rotorua 87, 195–98
Routeburn Track 282, 304
Roxburgh 285
Ruahine mountains 208
Ruapehu, Mount 203, 204
Runaway, Cape 185
Russell 43, 47, 55, 161, 177, 174, 175

S

Sala, George Augustus 195
Samoans 80
Sandspit 167
Scott, Robert Falcon 137
Seddon, Richard John 58, 159
Selwyn, Bishop George Augustus 176
Shackleton, Ernest 137
Shantytown 268, 272–73
Shaw, George Bernard 195, 250
Shoe Island 183
shopping 158, 162
Shotover, River 279, 281
Sinclair, Keith 69
skiing 204, 283
Slipper Island 183
Soda Springs 200
Solander, Daniel 41
South Island 234–304
Southern Alps 254, 259, 277
Southern Lakes 149
Southland 119, 298–304
Spirits Bay 177
sports 125–133, 155
St Bathans 285

St Heliers Bay, Auckland 155, 163, 164
Stevenson, Robert Louis 149
Stewart, Mount 214
Stewart Island 41, 252, 299, 300, 308–9
Stony Bay 182
Sumner 252
Suter, Andrew 238
Swanson 165

T

Taiaroa Head 289
Tairua 183
Tamaki (Auckland) 156
Tangiwai 204
Tapsel, Philip 52
Tapsell, Captain Phillip 52, 195
Tapu 181
Tapuaenuku, Mount 236
Tarakohe 239
Taranaki, Mount 187, 191
Taranaki 187-91
Tarawera, Lake 199, 200, 201
Tarawera, Mount 200–201
Tarlton, Kelly 172
Tasman, Abel 39, 40, 136, 177, 239, 268
Taupiri, Mount 190
Taupo, Lake 114, 195, 199, 202, 203
Taupo 203
Tauranga 184
Tawawera, Mount 149
Te Anau, Lake 284, 303
Te Anau 300, 303, 304
Te Ariki 200
Te Aroha, Mount 189
Te Aroha 189
Te Awamutu 190
Te Kaha 185
Te Kanawa, Kiri 103
Te Kao 176, 177
Te Kooti 207–8
Te Kuiti 190
Te Mata Peak 211
Te Puke 183, 184–85
Te Wairoa 200
Tekapo 263
Templeview 188
Thames 180
Thierry, Baron de 52
Thorndon, Wellington 225
Three Kings Islands 177
Tikitapu, Lake 200
Timaru 259
Titirangi 165
Toi 171, 185
Tokaanu 204
Tokelau atolls 318–9
Tokelaus 79, 81
Tokomaru Steam Museum 214
Tokoroa 189
Tonga 79, 80–81
Tonga Marine Reserve 239
Tongans 81
Tongariro, Mount 203, 204
Tongariro, River 204

Tongariro National Park 191, 195, 203
Torbay 158
Totaranui 239
tramping 113
Trollope, Anthony 149, 280, 282
Tuapeka 279, 281
Tuatapere 301
Tunzelmann, Alexander von 137
Turanganui, River 207
Turangi 203
Turehu 182

U–V

Upham, Charles 70
Urenui 191
Urewera National Park 208
Urupukapuka Island 173
Victoria, Mount (Auckland) 166
Victoria, Mount (Wellington) 223
Victoria, Queen 173
Visscher, Frans 39
Vogel, Sir Julius 58
Volkner, Rev. Carl 185

W–Z

Waihau Bay 185
Waiheke Island 167
Waihi 180, 183, 184
Waihou River 181, 189
Waikaremoana, Lake 149, 208
Waikari 260
Waikato, River 187, 188, 203
Waikato 119, 161, 187–91
Waikawa 300
Waikino 183
Waimangu Valley 201
Waimate North 176
Waimauku 165
Waimea Plain 238
Wainuiomata 227
Waiotapu 202
Waipa, River 187
Waipara 260
Waipawa 211
Waipoua Kauri 177
Waipukurau 211
Wairakei Geothermal Power Station 203
Wairarapa 219, 228–9
Wairau Valley 240
Wairere Falls 189
Wairoa 208
Waitahanui, River 202
Waitakere Ranges 165
Waitaki, River 259
Waitangi, Chatham Islands 311
Waitangi, Treaty of 54, 68
Waitangi 172–73, 174
Waitangi Treaty House 172–73
Waitemata Harbour 155
Waitomo caves 190
Waiwera 158, 166
Wakamarina, River 237
Wakatipu, Lake 278, 281–82
Wakefield, Arthur 54

Wakefield, Edward Gibbon 50, 52, 56, 223
Wakefield, William 54, 223
Walters, Gordon 103
Wanaka, Lake 282, 284
Wanaka 284
Wanganui, River 215
Wanganui 214–15
Wangapeka Track 273
Warkworth 167, 171
Webber, John 161
Weller, Edward 51
Weller, George 51
Weller, Joseph 51
Wellington 85, 109, 161, 219–228
The Beehive 221
  Botanic Gardens 225
  Civic Square 219
  Museum of New Zealand 220
  Mount Victoria 223
  National Museum and Art Gallery 226
  St Pauls Cathedral 221
wharves 224
Wellsford 171
Wendt, Albert 103, 105
West Coast (South Island) 82, 268–73
Western Springs, Auckland 165
Westland 268
Westland National Park 271
Westport 273
Whakatane, River 185
Whakatane 185, 200
Whangaehu, River 204
Whangamata Beach 182
Whangaparaoa 158
Whangapoua 182
Whangarei 171, 177
Whangaroa Harbour 176
White Island 185, 195
Whitianga 182
Williams, Henry 172, 195
wineries 211, 235
zoo 165